THE
SPHINX

THE
SPHINX

---

*Franklin Roosevelt, the Isolationists,
and the Road to World War II*

NICHOLAS WAPSHOTT

W. W. NORTON & COMPANY

New York · London

For information about permission to reproduce selections from this book,
write to Permissions, W. W. Norton & Company, Inc.,
500 Fifth Avenue, New York, NY 10110

For information about special discounts for bulk purchases, please contact
W. W. Norton Special Sales at specialsales@wwnorton.com or 800-233-4830

Manufacturing by Courier Westford
Book design by Charlotte Staub
Production manager: Louise Parasmo

Library of Congress Cataloging-in-Publication Data

Wapshott, Nicholas.
The sphinx : Franklin Roosevelt, the isolationists, and the road to World War II /
Nicholas Wapshott. — First edition.
    pages cm
Includes bibliographical references and index.
ISBN 978-0-393-08888-5 (hardcover)
1. World War, 1939-1945—Diplomatic history. 2. United States—Foreign
relations—1933-1945. 3. Roosevelt, Franklin D. (Franklin Delano), 1882-1945—
Political and social views. 4. Kennedy, Joseph P. (Joseph Patrick), 1888-1969—Political
and social views. 5. Lindbergh, Charles A. (Charles Augustus), 1902-1974—Political
and social views. 6. Isolationism—United States—History—20th century. I. Title.
D753.W27 2014
940.53′112—dc23
                    2014031388

W. W. Norton & Company, Inc.
500 Fifth Avenue, New York, N.Y. 10110
www.wwnorton.com

W. W. Norton & Company Ltd.
Castle House, 75/76 Wells Street, London W1T 3QT

1 2 3 4 5 6 7 8 9 0

To
William
and Oliver

CONTENTS

THE SPHINX

*How Franklin Roosevelt's cryptic character
led him to be dubbed the Sphinx.*

IF YOU TRAVEL NORTH from New York City along the east bank of the
Hudson River, you will before long come to Hyde Park House, Franklin Roosevelt's country home, preserved more or less as he left it on
his death in 1945. Among the exhibits displayed in a glass case in his
presidential library is an eight-foot-tall papier-mâché sculpture of a
sphinx. The mythical Egyptian creature with a lion's body, the wings
of a bird, and a human head whose cryptic smile defied translation
bears Roosevelt's face, complete with pince-nez spectacles—a nod to
his fifth cousin Theodore, the Republican president—his trademark
cigarette holder and smoldering cigarette, and his narrowed, smiling eyes above a broad grin.

The statue was commissioned as a joke by the Gridiron Club's
White House correspondents as a satirical centerpiece for their
annual dinner in December 1939, attended by the president as
principal honored guest.[1] The purpose of portraying Roosevelt as
a sphinx was to let it be known to the president that the press were
flummoxed by his persistent reluctance to make clear whether he
would run for reelection in the contest of November 1940. Roosevelt's ambiguity on the subject had become almost as much a story
as whether he would run. Roosevelt so enjoyed the sphinx joke that
he immediately acquired the sculpture and had it shipped to Hyde
Park to adorn the nascent library that would mark his presidency.

For years, the president had dodged and weaved on the question
of whether he would run. He had told some friends he was ready to

retire to become a gentleman farmer at Hyde Park. To muddy the waters, he had encouraged many unsuitable and unelectable Democrats to throw their hats in the ring to succeed him. He had told others that he had simply not made up his mind. No one, not even his wife, Eleanor, nor his mother, Sara, knew which way he would jump. The sphinx in the White House was unfathomable. And the longer he wavered, the less chance there was that any rival could raise the funds to challenge him.

Roosevelt's sphinx-like inscrutability was typical of him. Throughout his life, he had adopted a studied ambiguity about almost every aspect of his life, both political and personal. Born into wealth and living in a grand house surrounded by a large country estate, he was in most respects a conventional New York aristocrat. He was educated at Groton School, the Episcopalian boarding school for the sons of the well-to-do considered the most exclusive school in the whole of the United States, then Harvard University, making him a standard product of America's white Anglo-Saxon Protestant governing elite. He was an athletic man of action. His boundless energy and personal confidence, underpinned by an annual trust fund income of $120,000 ($1.6 million in 2014 terms), lifted him above the less driven bluebloods with whom he shared his privileged background.[2]

Yet his political views were far from usual for a young man of his elevated social status. While his dashing distant older relation Theodore had been a Republican president, albeit of a progressive sort, and had encouraged his young protégé to enter politics, Franklin followed his father into the Democratic Party. His early steps on the political ladder in New York meant having to overcome the natural conservatism and innate Republicanism of the country people in Dutchess County and persuade them that, despite his Democratic leanings, he would look after them as any good patrician would.

He smothered the traditional upstate voters' suspicion of his upper-class manners and upper-class demeanor by exercising the quality that would eventually lead him to inhabit the White House: an effortless and irresistible personal charm. In addition, he was physically attractive and approached those less fortunate than himself with an easy, agreeable manner. His biographer Conrad Black described Roosevelt at this time as "slender, clean-shaven, mellifluous, and prone to make his points with a debonair wave of his cigarette-holder."

Upon this secure social foundation Roosevelt established an unlikely political career, which, by the time of World War One, saw him as assistant secretary of the navy in Woodrow Wilson's administration. Alongside him was Theodore Roosevelt's niece Eleanor. When Theodore had given her away at their wedding ceremony, on St. Patrick's Day, March 17, 1905, he had cracked, "There's nothing like keeping the name in the family."[3] But, as with everything else about him, Franklin Roosevelt's marriage and his romantic and sexual life was a study in equivocation. There was little doubt he loved Eleanor as a wife. They had six children together, and to all outward views it was a perfect marriage.

Yet Franklin's eye wandered, often little further than toward distant members of the Roosevelt family who were recruited ostensibly to help him run his private office, and it wandered repeatedly. His sexual drive was so insistent that not even the polio he contracted at age thirty-nine, while summering at the family's vacation home on the Canadian island of Campobello in 1921, brought his womanizing to a halt. Paralyzed from the waist down, in permanent discomfort, unable to walk unless his legs were reinforced with iron calipers, and largely confined to a wheelchair, he still found a way to both woo women and commit adultery with them.

Roosevelt's philandering took place with the tacit consent, if not approval, of Eleanor. In September 1917, while unpacking her husband's suitcase, she stumbled upon love letters from Lucy Page Mercer, her social secretary, and the marriage was thrown into disarray. Betrayed and bruised, the strong-willed Eleanor made her husband an uncompromising and nonnegotiable offer: he must abandon his mistress forthwith and appear a devoted husband or face divorce. The loving marriage was irrevocably broken, but Eleanor was prepared to allow it to seem intact for the sake of her five children. Rather than abandon his soaring political career, Franklin accepted Eleanor's conditions. To please his long-suffering wife, he agreed to allow her to follow an independent course and establish a public career of her own.

It was a bargain Roosevelt was in no position to refuse if he was to pursue his ambition: to follow Theodore Roosevelt into the White House. A sex scandal and a conspicuous divorce would have stopped Franklin in his tracks. His affair with Mercer turned out to be a turning point in a marital arrangement that was always as much dynastic as a love match.[4] What became one of the most powerful marriages in American history was forged in the heat of adultery into a formidable personal and political alliance.

The ambiguity at the core of his marriage was echoed through his politics. While his views were liberal, to maximize his appeal he liked to appear a political chameleon, blending in with whomever he needed to please in order to move on to the next stage in his ambitions. His country neighbor and eventual close government colleague Henry Morgenthau had learned that when Roosevelt said he was "100 percent" behind an idea, it meant nothing. The differences between what Roosevelt thought, what he said, and what he did were quite distinct.

So long as Theodore Roosevelt was alive, Franklin was under his sway. After Wilson took the United States into World War One on the Allied side—after a German U-boat torpedoed an American passenger ship, the *Housatonic*, off the Isles of Scilly—Theodore, much to Eleanor's fury, tried to persuade Franklin to resign his post and "get into uniform at once."[5] A similar stunt leading the all-volunteer Rough Riders in the Spanish–American War of 1898 had transformed Theodore into a nationally known, swashbuckling war hero, and he felt Franklin should follow suit.

In January 1919, with the war won, Franklin and Eleanor embarked on a hastily arranged tour of Europe, ostensibly to "wind up naval affairs in Europe, dispose of what could be sold and ship home what could be used."[6] The real purpose, however, was a voyage of reconciliation to save their sputtering marriage. The couple had only been at sea for a few days when, on January 6, 1919, news came by ship's telegraph of Theodore Roosevelt's death by heart attack in his sleep.[7] The sudden demise of his maverick mentor marked a profound change in the young assistant secretary of the navy's thinking. Over the course of the trip, the influence of the opportunistic Theodore Roosevelt slowly gave ground in Franklin's mind to the loftier sentiments of Woodrow Wilson.

An epiphany took place when the Roosevelts traveled home from

Paris with the president's party the following month. They were shown the first copy of the League of Nations charter by a *New York Times* reporter when they boarded the *George Washington* at Brest and Eleanor recalled "how eagerly we read it through!"[8] Over luncheon, Wilson took Franklin and Eleanor into his confidence and explained why he thought it essential that the isolationist Republicans who were determined not to ratify the Treaty of Versailles should be defeated and that America should be allowed to join and lead the League. "The United States must go in or it will break the heart of the world, for she is the only nation that all feel is disinterested and all trust," Wilson told them.[9]

The Treaty of Versailles became the first treaty in America's history that the Senate did not ratify. Without American participation, the League soon showed its impotence in the face of territorial aggression by Japan and Italy and fell into abeyance. Wilson's successor, Warren G. Harding,[10] declared that "the issue of the League of Nations is as dead as slavery."[11] America returned to its happy isolation, protected on the east and west by vast oceans and on the north and south by the Monroe Doctrine, which declared the western hemisphere to be under the undisputed influence of the United States. Wilson's failure to take into account the strong isolationist feeling in the Senate and his inability to forge a compromise had led inexorably to America's failure to join the League. But it was not just hostility in the Senate that Wilson underestimated. As Franklin Roosevelt's son Elliott observed, "[Wilson] made costly mistakes, the greatest of which was a failure to recognize the intrinsic isolationism of the American people."[12]

The reasons for the president's defeat were not lost on Roosevelt, whose political good fortune continued. In the 1920 election, he was the Democratic vice presidential candidate on the ticket of James M. Cox, the governor of Ohio, whose principal plank was ratification of the Versailles Treaty and America's membership of the League of Nations.[13] Roosevelt remained fully in favor of the League but was aware it would be a hard sell. "The League will not die," he declared in his speech at the 1920 San Francisco convention accepting the number two position on the ballot. "Today we are offered a seat at the table of the family of nations to the end that smaller peoples may be truly safe to work out their own destiny. . . . We shall take that place. I say so because I have faith—faith that this nation has no selfish destiny."[14]

It was wishful thinking. As Roosevelt biographer Ted Morgan observed, "After the wartime years of sacrifice and rationing, and the thousands of families who had lost a son or a brother, the American people did not want high-minded thoughts about international cooperation but a chance to improve their lives."[15]

The League proved an idea before its time. In November 1920, it was, as a correspondent wrote to Roosevelt, "about the most effective millstone that any party, bent on suicide, has tied about its neck."[16] Nonetheless, spurred by the thought that at just thirty-eight he had beaten TR to the vice presidential nomination by four years, in late September Franklin set off on his first national campaign. Ferried around in his own private railroad carriage, the *Westboro*, he visited twenty states in eighteen days, giving seven speeches a day. By election day he had visited thirty-two states and spent sixty sleepless nights in a sleeping car.

Eleanor joined him briefly, to boost her husband's support among women who were voting for the first time since winning suffrage, but she soon returned home, unable to adjust to the gossip, politicking, card-playing, and cigar-smoking of a campaign train. Roosevelt, however, found he was in his element, getting to know the whole country "as only a candidate for office or a traveling salesman can,"[17] and freely trading on his link to TR. Such audacity attracted not only the disdain of the isolationist McCormick family's *Chicago Tribune*, which reported that "Franklin is as much like Theodore as a clam is like a bear-cat,"[18] but the disavowal of TR's eldest son, Theodore Roosevelt Jr.,[19] fresh from fighting on the Western Front, who told a group of cattle-raising Rough Rider veterans in Wyoming, "He does not have the brand of our family."[20]

On November 2, 1920, Cox and Roosevelt were routed by Warren Harding and Calvin Coolidge, who won 61 percent of the popular vote and carried the electoral college by 404 votes to 127. To Roosevelt's embarrassment, even New York state went Republican. One of his mother's gardeners, of German descent, told Franklin that he had voted Republican because a relative had written from the old country complaining of food shortages, which he blamed on Wilson and the Versailles Treaty. When Franklin asked him, "Are you not an American citizen?" he replied, "Yes, but if America joins with England and France against Germany, I am a German."[21] It was a remark that would echo in Roosevelt's mind in the years ahead.

After serving four years as governor of New York state, Roosevelt became the Democratic presidential candidate and was elected to the White House in 1932 at a time of dire national emergency. The stock market crash of 1929 took place on President Herbert Hoover's watch, throwing the national economy into disarray and spurring a General Depression that threw millions out of work. The 1932 election turned on which candidate Americans believed would prise them from the mire. Foreign affairs were barely mentioned.

After his victory, Roosevelt spent his first two terms attempting, through the New Deal and other ingenious devices that employed state agencies, to reduce the misery of mass unemployment stemming from a collapse in business activity. But the 1930s were also a time of rising dictatorships in Europe and a growing threat to democracy everywhere. It was in these circumstances, with a second world war on the horizon, that Roosevelt had to decide whether to allow his name to be placed on the 1940 presidential ballot.

As time passed, he had come to fear that the rise of Fascism in Italy, Nazism in Germany, and an increasingly bellicose military in Japan would lead to a war in Europe and the Far East that the United States could not avoid. He concluded privately that only he would be able to check the predominantly isolationist sentiments of the American people and prepare them for the prospect of war. But if he were to pull off the unprecedented feat of winning the presidency for a third term, it would take all his ambiguous wiles and ingenuity at equivocation. Hence his vagueness when answering questions from the press and his own party leaders about his intentions.

Ranged against him were a number of strong characters determined to keep America from intervening to protect the democracies which, as the Thirties progressed, were threatened by Japanese, Italian, and German invasion. Among those who campaigned against American involvement in what Thomas Jefferson had called in his inaugural address "entangling alliances"[22] were some of the most influential in the land. There were the Old Contemptibles (Woodrow Wilson's implacable opponents in the battle over the ratification of the Versailles Treaty by the Senate) and their descendants in Congress, who maintained a close watch on the executive branch nudging the nation toward war. They were joined by a number of very rich men: newspaper owners such as William Randolph Hearst and Colonel Robert McCormick;[23] popular public figures such as the motor manufacturer Henry Ford, the transAtlantic flier Charles Lindbergh Jr., and the movie mogul Walt Disney; and financiers such as Joseph P. Kennedy, who harbored political ambitions that included the presidency.

There were well-defined differences between those who fought to keep America out of conflict. Some were isolationists pure and simple, who wished the nation to retreat behind its borders and even limit its trade with the outside world. Some were internationalist isolationists, who felt that America's ability to sustain itself economically allowed it to strictly limit its contacts with foreign nations except for trade. And some were noninterventionists, who believed that America could continue trading without taking sides in foreign disputes. But such differences in definition were of little importance to Roosevelt.

To him, these groups soon combined into a single phalanx of opponents, ready to hinder at every turn his attempts to persuade the American people that the United States, by now the largest economy in the world, could no longer remain aloof from the existential threat posed by the dictators who were expanding their borders through force of arms and putting democracy to the sword. To win the people round, Roosevelt embarked on a tentative and delicate subterfuge, stressing the danger of America remaining isolated while declaring that he had no desire to allow the United States to take up arms against another nation. It was a tightrope walk between alarmism and complacency, for which his complex and sophisticated character was ideally suited.

And so it was that the president was portrayed in newspaper cartoons and in the Gridiron dinner sculpture as a sphinx. The British statesman Winston S. Churchill once described Russia as "a riddle wrapped in a mystery inside an enigma."[24] He might just as well have been describing Franklin D. Roosevelt, the man he would befriend and collaborate with to purge the world of Nazism.

THE
SPHINX

CHAPTER ONE

LONDON CALLING

*Kennedy asks Roosevelt a favor;
the bargain between fixing the economy
and staying out of foreign wars.*

ONE AFTERNOON IN the fall of 1937, behind the closed doors of the Oval Office, President Franklin Roosevelt asked his friend the businessman, stock trader, and movie mogul Joseph P. Kennedy, "Would you mind taking your pants down?" The request was met with a blank stare. "We couldn't believe our ears," recalled the president's son James, who had arranged the meeting. "Did you just say what I think you said?" asked Kennedy. The president replied, "Yes, indeed."

James Roosevelt recalled that "Joe Kennedy undid his suspenders and dropped his pants and stood there in his shorts, looking silly and embarrassed." The president told Kennedy, "Someone who saw you in a bathing suit once told me something I now know to be true. Joe, just look at your legs. You are just about the most bow-legged man I have ever seen."

According to the president, bandy legs were a deal-breaker in Kennedy's bid to become America's top envoy in London. "Don't you know that the ambassador to the Court of St James's has to go through an induction ceremony in which he wears knee britches and silk stockings?" asked the president. "When photos of our new ambassador appear all over the world, we'll be a laughingstock."

Kennedy dearly wanted to become the first Irish American ambassador to London and was not sure whether the president was kidding.[1] After a moment's thought, he said he could ask the Brits

1

whether tails and striped pants would be acceptable to Buckingham Palace instead of the traditional fancy dress.

Roosevelt, chuckling as Kennedy pulled up his trousers, was not sure. "You know how the British are about tradition," he said. "There's no way you are going to get permission, and I must name a new ambassador soon."[2] If the Brits were prepared to bend protocol and Kennedy could get a response within two weeks, the president suggested that perhaps Kennedy could after all go to the ball.

The Oval Office striptease was a typical Roosevelt prank to let Kennedy believe he was an intimate, one of his inner circle. But it was also a humiliating ritual that showed who was boss. After twenty years of knowing the president, the red-haired, chalk-skinned Kennedy was still unsure when the president was joking and when he was in earnest, whether he was in or out. Just six years apart in age, the two seemed close. They met several times a week to talk politics and spent weekends together in Marwood, Kennedy's mansion at Potomac, outside Washington, modeled after Château de Malmaison, the home of Josephine Bonaparte. But the two men deeply distrusted each other. Roosevelt liked to play on Kennedy's lack of social confidence, while his own embrace of the presidency was absolute. As one observer put it, he enjoyed "a love affair with power. . . . Almost alone among our presidents, [he] had no conception of the office to live up to; he was it. His image of the office was himself-in-office."[3] The ambassadorship was the latest battle in a war of attrition that had already lasted nearly a decade.

Whether Kennedy went to London was hardly the president's top priority. The nation faced three interwoven problems and Roosevelt had set himself specific goals in response. The first was to improve the depressed economy, so that the 10 million still out of work could find jobs. The second, at a time when Adolf Hitler,[4] the Nazi dictator of Germany, Benito Mussolini,[5] leader of Italy's Fascist government, and the Japanese military were stampeding the world toward war, was "to get the American people to think of conceivable consequences without scaring the American people into thinking that they are going to be dragged into war."[6]

Preparing the nation for war would require wooing Americans away from the isolationism in which they had found comfort, which in turn meant defeating, by fair means and foul, leaders of the movement who thought the troubles of the world were none of America's business. High among them was Kennedy, a Democratic presidential contender, whose Irish American roots and business sensibility persuaded him that there was nothing to be gained by siding with the democracies.

Others included "yellow press" newspaper baron William Randolph Hearst[7] and Father Charles Coughlin,[8] the anti-Semitic Roman Catholic priest who counted his weekly national radio audience in millions and urged, "Keep America safe for Americans."[9] There was the transatlantic aviator Charles Lindbergh,[10] a national hero with links to the Nazi high command, and Henry Ford,[11] the anti-Semitic industrialist whose Model T had transformed America into a car-driving democracy.

A third, related aim for the president was to rearm America as quickly as possible. And, because he felt he alone was capable of achieving all three goals, Roosevelt was slowly coming to the conclusion he would need a third presidential term. The next presidential contest would occur in November 1940. As he pondered whether to permit Kennedy to go to London, Roosevelt weighed up whether the overweening ambition of his multimillionaire rival could be put to good use in achieving one or more of his cardinal aims.

A great deal had taken place since Roosevelt had championed Wilson's League of Nations as vice presidential candidate in the election of 1920, primarily the collapse of the economy following the Wall Street crash of October 1929. In the 1932 campaign that won Roosevelt the White House, the failed economy was the voters' overriding concern and foreign affairs was hardly an issue. As the historian Selig Adler put it, "Debts, taxations, the foreclosing of mortgages, wholesale bankruptcies, bank failures, plummeting farm prices, and the fruitless hunt for jobs occupied the American mind."[12]

For most the choice was simple: between the incumbent, Herbert Hoover,[13] who had presided over the crash and America's slide into the Great Depression and appeared to have little grasp of how or even whether the federal government should play a role in helping a recovery, and Roosevelt, a fresh face who railed against Hoover's inaction and suggested, without offering many specifics about his "New Deal,"[14] that he could get the country back to work. Hoover's self-professed impotence in the face of the financial crisis gave Roosevelt the feeling that victory was his if he did not make an error. So he avoided saying anything about foreign policy.

Mindful that the mood of America was isolationist, both sides counseled caution in foreign matters. The Democratic ticket demanded the "settlement of international disputes by arbitration" and "by consultation and conference in case of violation of treaties," but was careful not to mention the League of Nations nor Wilson's defeat at the hands of the Senate. Meanwhile, Republicans rejected outright "alliances or foreign entanglements."[15] On election day, November 8, 1932, Roosevelt trounced Hoover by 23 million votes to 16 million (57 percent to 43 percent) and by 472 electoral college votes to 59. He was sworn in on Saturday, March 4, 1933.

American intervention in the Great War was still a painful memory and the desire to stay out of any war was widespread. Isolationism came in many forms. In the Midwest, in the upper Mississippi valley, living at great distances from the Atlantic and Pacific oceans, farmers of Scandinavian or German descent tended to believe the Great War had been cooked up by Wall Street and munitions peddlers. Some subscribed to a "devil theory" which held that, when it seemed German forces might take Paris, American arms dealers and financiers who were owed money by the Allies—Britain, France, and Italy—had forced Wilson into the conflict to safeguard their money.[16] Only in the rural South, settled largely by Anglo-Saxon immigrants who populated it with slaves, was isolationism largely absent.

In the cities it was a different story. Many German and Austrian Americans believed that Versailles had imposed humiliating conditions upon their home countries and were appalled by Wilson's decision to fight alongside the Allies. Some, particularly those from former British colonies, resented Britain and its imperial ways. Among the hyphenates, few were more hostile than Irish Americans, who had witnessed from afar the bloody suppression of the armed Irish rebellion of 1916. They asked, how could Wilson at Paris demand self-determination as an eternal right for every oppressed nation in the world but the Irish?[17]

"The bare fact that the [Treaty] had proved acceptable to the British Empire aroused the instant antagonism of the 'professional' Irish-Americans, the 'professional' German-Americans, the 'professional' Italian-Americans, and all those others whose political fortunes depended upon the persistence and accentuation of racial prejudices," wrote Wilson's public relations chief, George Creel.[18]

As well as those who opposed war for nationalist reasons, pacifists and liberals were appalled by the scale of the slaughter between 1914 and 1918. Senator Homer T. Bone[19] of Washington state spoke for many when he declared that "the Great War . . . was utter social insanity, and was a crazy war, and we had no business in it at all."[20] In the decade after the Armistice, popular peace groups formed, among them the National Council for Prevention of War, the Women's International League for Peace and Freedom, the American Committee for the Outlawry of War, and S.O.S. (Stop Organized Slaughter).

The most bizarre manifestation of this pacific thread of isolationism was Veterans of Future Wars. Founded in 1936 by eight Princeton undergraduates, VFW demanded, only half in jest, that the government pay every man of conscription age $1,000. Since they would not survive the next war, they argued that they deserved to be compensated in advance. VFW members paraded in military caps worn at right angles and saluted with palms outstretched, as if demanding their pay. The female equivalent of the VFW was the Future Gold Star Mothers, who demanded widows' pensions so they could visit their future husbands' graves. In a display of strength at Columbia University, one hundred and fifty Mothers clutching "war orphan" dolls marched behind a drum majorette twirling an invalid's crutch.[21]

Added to these ostensibly light-hearted isolationists were earnest liberals who, when the Great War was raging, railed at Wilson's treatment of domestic opponents of the conflict. Perhaps the most prominent victim of this crackdown was the perennial socialist presidential candidate Eugene V. Debs, dubbed a "traitor to his country" by Wilson for urging resistance to the draft, found guilty of sedition, and given a ten-year prison sentence.[22] There were also progressives who believed that the war was a distraction from necessary and urgent domestic reforms.

At the core of isolationism was a band of nationalists who coagulated around ultra-patriotic societies such as the League of Loyal Americans, out of Boston, whose motto was "One Tongue, One

Ideal and One Flag," the Sentinels of the Republic, and the American Flag Movement, whose aim was to have the Stars and Stripes
flying above every home. At the far edge of such nationalist fervor
was the Ku Klux Klan, five million strong at its most terrifying,
who led the clamor for laws to limit immigration to 150,000 white
northern Europeans or Anglo-Saxons per year. Their campaign cul-
minated in the 1924 Johnson–Reed Act, which severely restricted
immigration.

Fiscally conservative isolationists blamed the Great Depression
on America's participation in the war. It was widely believed that the
prosperity enjoyed in wartime and the boom of the Roaring Twenties
had stoked prices too high, a state of affairs that had to be corrected
by deflation in the 1930s. Never mind that this made little economic
sense. As the slump began to take hold, "We had it coming" became
a common expression. Senator George W. Norris[23] was not alone in
linking domestic economic troubles to Wilson's involvement in the
war. He read out in the Senate a plea from a bankrupt Nebraska con-
stituent, who complained, "[We] are being driven from our homes by
'Writs of Assistance' [instructions to evict] in the hands of our sher-
iffs. It is the tragic heritage that has come down to us from this so-
called 'war to end wars.'"[24] The best way to avoid a repetition of the
boom and bust that was blighting the country was to avoid involvement in future wars.[25]

Among the increasingly determined congressional isolationists,
the old battle cry "Keep out of the League" was superseded by "Keep
out of War." In a letter to Gerald P. Nye,[26] Republican senator from
North Dakota, one man explained why he favored isolation. "As a
potential soldier, I object to the prospect of becoming cannon fod-
der in the 'next war'; as a future taxpayer, I object to enriching arms
manufacturers by impoverishing my fellow Americans; and, most
important, as a Christian, I object to preparing to run a bayonet
through my brother from another country."[27]

Riding this wave of isolationism was a clutch of senators led by
"The Irreconcilables," the sixteen who had most fiercely opposed
ratification of the Versailles Treaty and had insisted that America
should stay out of the League of Nations.[28] Some were isolationists pure and simple, others were internationalists who nonetheless
thought America should avoid intervening in others' wars. Chief

among Wilson's opponents was Henry Cabot Lodge, the prickly Republican senator from Massachusetts, who believed that America should avoid commitments and in doing so remain free to counter threats to its own shores. He thought the League a well-meaning diversion but showed considerable prescience about where a threat was likely to emerge. "We would have this country strong to resist a peril from the West, as she has flung back the German menace from the East," he said. "We would not have our country's vigor exhausted, or her moral force abated, by everlasting meddling and muddling in every quarrel great and small, which afflicts the world."[29]

Lodge was rivaled in the bitterness of his opposition to interventions abroad only by Senator William Edgar Borah, the "Lion of Idaho," who in 1917, like Lodge and Theodore Roosevelt, was a leading war hawk.[30] When peace came and Wilson presented the Versailles Treaty for ratification, Borah spelled out his reservations. "It is in conflict with the right of our people to govern themselves free from all restraint, legal or moral, of foreign powers," he told the Senate.[31] Other opponents of the League, such as Senator Hiram W. Johnson, a former Democratic governor of California, had also backed American entry into the war.[32]

During the battle against the Treaty, this group of senators was funded by a pair of Pittsburgh industrialists, the banker and aluminum smelter Andrew W. Mellon[33] and the coke and steel king Henry Clay Frick.[34] They were supported by a gang of press magnates, among them Frank A. Munsey,[35] with his trio of New York papers (the *Sun*, the *Telegram*, and the *Herald*), Colonel Robert McCormick, owner of the *Chicago Tribune*, and William Rockhill Nelson,[36] proprietor of the *Kansas City Star*.

The prize, however, was William Randolph Hearst, whose personally penned front-page rants were disseminated through the largest media company in the world. Hearst boasted thirty newspapers read by more than twenty million people daily, including the *San Francisco Examiner* and the *New York Daily Mirror*, seven magazines, including *Cosmopolitan* and *Harper's Bazaar*, and news wire and syndication services.

When Roosevelt was elected, the prospect of America becoming involved in another war seemed remote. Just days before the stock market crash in September 1929, Hoover wrote to his secretary of state, Henry L. Stimson,[37] "It seems to me there is the most profound outlook for peace today that we have had any time in the last century. . . . The dangers of war during the next six or ten years for [the United States or Britain] in any direction are inconceivably less than they have been at any period since the Great War."[38]

The only cloud on the horizon had emerged the previous year in Manchuria, a Chinese province long under the influence of the Japanese, who considered it key to their prosperity. Not only were 90 percent of Japanese foreign investments in Manchuria, but it was rich in raw materials that Japan lacked, such as coal, iron, and timber, and produced a great proportion of the soybeans that were a staple of the Japanese diet. When Chinese nationalist forces under Chiang Kai-shek began to loosen Manchuria from the Japanese grip, a bellicose military clique in Tokyo overruled the civilian government and ordered a full-scale invasion.

In September 1931, 10,400 Japanese troops poured into Manchuria and fanned out across the province. The invasion provided the first major test of the Treaty of Versailles. America and the European powers declared that they would not recognize the Japanese claim to Manchuria and the Europeans considered economic sanctions. After demanding a ceasefire, the League insisted that the Japanese withdraw. Tokyo countered by bombing the British commercial redoubt of Shanghai, 700 miles south of Manchuria.

America and Europe did nothing. No one was in a mood for embarking on another war, starting with Hoover, who told his cabinet that as the Japanese actions "do not imperil the freedom of the American people . . . we shall not go along on war or any of the sanctions economic or military for those are the roads to war."[39] The *Philadelphia Record* reported, "The American people do not give a hoot in a rain barrel who controls North China."[40]

Taking offense at a mild reprimand delivered by the League, the Japanese withdrew from the world body, "taking as a souvenir the Pacific islands held under League mandate."[41] The Japanese incursion in Manchuria served notice on countries that bordered the Pacific, America included, that the regime in Tokyo was prepared to back its expansionist ambitions with force.

Just as threatening were events unfolding in Germany. By November 1932, when Roosevelt trounced Hoover at the polls, the German economy was near collapse. Industrial production had slumped by 60 percent since before the war and half the nation's adults were jobless. With extremists of left and right agitating to exploit the misery, the new Weimar Republic tottered. In 1932, the eighty-five-year-old World War One hero Field Marshal Paul von Hindenburg[42] beat Nazi party leader Adolf Hitler in a presidential election, but before long the Nazis won control of the German parliament, the Reichstag, and began disrupting ordered government. Afraid that the economic cataclysm would invite a Communist revolution, industrialists joined with the military and the aristocracy to persuade Hindenburg to ask Hitler to lead the government.

On January 30, 1933, three months after Roosevelt was elected, Hitler became chancellor of Germany, promising to overturn the Versailles Treaty, to wrest back German territory awarded to other nations, to reoccupy the demilitarized Rhineland, and to place the economy under state control in order to put the nation back to work.

Some in America thought a more immediate threat to peace was a continuation of the Great Depression that offered political extremists a rare chance to exploit the human misery that stemmed from six million being without work. At the depth of the slump, a quarter of Americans were without jobs; by the end of 1932, a million were jobless in New York City alone. Food lines at soup kitchens became a common sight in Chicago and Philadelphia, where one in four went to bed hungry. More than 11,000 of the nation's 24,000 banks had failed, taking with them the life savings of thousands of families.

The land built by immigrants became a land of emigrants as Americans fled to find work abroad. Even those with jobs found their wages cut as the prices of the goods they made spiraled downward. The collapse in prices was particularly savage in country areas, where sinking crop prices led to the eviction of thousands of farmers.

A lot was riding on the simple optimism Roosevelt's election had provided. But if he were to be awarded a second term four years later, he had to deliver stability and jobs without delay. In his inaugural address, Roosevelt compared the task the nation faced to that of waging war:

Our greatest primary task is to put people to work. If we are to go forward, we must move as a trained and loyal army. . . . I assume unhesitatingly the leadership of this great army of our people dedi-cated to a disciplined attack upon our common problems.[43]

Starting with a hectic hundred days of action, Roosevelt needed to juggle votes to pass New Deal legislation. Southern Democrats were mostly fiscally conservative and doubted the wisdom of many aspects of the New Deal's spending measures, while congressmen from the prairies were largely progressive isolationists who sup-ported federal intervention in the economy. An unstated bargain was struck whereby isolationist congressmen from the Midwest gave the president a more or less free hand to stimulate the economy so long as he did not prevent them from passing new laws to prevent America becoming involved in war. In early 1933, Roosevelt thought it a bargain worth making.

The president had an early chance to make clear that he put domestic recovery before internationalism when in June 1933 the London Economic Conference opened. The British sent a long mem-orandum saying what they expected of Roosevelt, penned by Ambas-sador Sir Ronald Lindsay,[44] who warned that the Depression was "essentially international in its character" and could not "be rem-edied by isolated action on the part of individual Governments" but only by "international action on a very broad front."[45]

Roosevelt, however, had no intention of becoming embroiled in arrangements that would prevent him introducing measures he believed essential to restore the nation to health. He had pledged at his inauguration, "The emergency at home cannot wait."[46] Before he was prepared to start negotiating trade, currency, and other issues, let alone the war debt amnesty that Britain and other European nations were demanding, he wanted to give the New Deal a chance to work.

As a first step, the Europeans proposed pegging currencies to gold, a move that would prevent Roosevelt from manipulating the value of the dollar. Since the Depression, domestic prices in America had collapsed. By adjusting the dollar price, Roosevelt hoped to end crippling deflation and raise prices so farmers and manufacturers could sell their goods at a profit.

To the dismay of the other sixty-five nations at the conference, Roosevelt, relaxing aboard the USS *Indianapolis* off Maine, sent what came to be known as his "Bombshell Message" to secretary of state Cordell Hull[47] in Paris, making clear that he intended to put American recovery first. Railing at the "old fetishes of the so-called international bankers," he said, "The sound internal economic system of a nation is a greater factor in its well-being than the price of its currency" and he ruled out fixing the dollar to gold. The Europeans were appalled that the president had dared put America first.

While Roosevelt began pushing his raft of New Deal measures through Congress, isolationists began a slow march through the House and Senate to outlaw involvement in conflicts that might arise from the growing belligerency in Europe and Asia. The first, in 1934, was the Johnson Act. The law made it illegal for Americans to lend money to foreign governments in default of their debts to American creditors. The act was a response to widespread public anger about the failure of the wartime Allies to repay $10.5 billion borrowed from Wall Street to fund World War One. In 1934, twenty years after the money had been lent, the debt remained unpaid.

The war debt issue had not long before caused the French to reinvade Germany. The Versailles Treaty demanded that the Germans and Austrians should compensate the Allies some $33 billion for destruction wrought during the war. By 1922, however, the Weimar government could no longer afford to pay and defaulted. The Allies, in turn, declared that because Germany had not paid them, they could not afford to repay their American debts. Drawing upon a nonpayment of reparations clause in the treaty, the French and Belgians invaded the Ruhr, Germany's industrial heart, to exact their pound of flesh.

German workers went on strike rather than accommodate their new French masters. Anxious that events in the Ruhr might ignite another war, President Harding's secretary of state, Charles Hughes,[48] had urged acceptance of the Dawes Plan, under which the US would lend $200 million to Germany. This merely stemmed the anguish for a while, and in 1929 a second effort was made to solve the war debt/reparations dispute: the Young Plan, which reduced the sum Germany owed from $33 to $8 billion and extended the term of repayment to fifty-nine years. It was against this background that the Johnson Act was passed. Roosevelt duly signed it into law.

In the spring of 1934, in response to a best-selling book, *Merchants of Death* by Helmuth C. Engelbrecht, which asserted that America's entry into World War One was a conspiracy of Wall Street bankers and arms manufacturers, the tenacious Republican senator from North Dakota, Gerald Nye, launched a Senate inquiry, the Munitions Investigation Committee. Roosevelt and Hull were at first anxious that the Senate inquest, packed with isolationist lawmakers from the Midwest, would limit their ability to rearm. They reluctantly offered support in the hope that the Senate would recommend federal government control over the arms industry—useful in the event of war.

The munitions makers mounted a persuasive defense of their actions, even though, as Selig Adler wrote, "the armament companies welcomed world disarmament as much as bootleggers welcomed the end of prohibition."[49] When the Nye committee offered its verdict in seven reports written over 14,000 pages, it was with some reluctance that it found the charge of criminal complicity between bankers and arms makers not proven.

At the end of June 1934, Hitler liquidated his Nazi rivals in what became known as the Night of the Long Knives, and in August, on Hindenburg's death, he combined the roles of president and chancellor, pronouncing himself Der Führer. One of his first actions was to remove Germany from the League of Nations, which brought to a premature end the stalled General Disarmament Conference in Geneva, intended to limit each nation's military spending.

Stirrings of war across the Atlantic prompted two contradictory responses in America. A growing number of realists urged rearmament, in the belief that if war broke out in Europe it would be impossible for America to remain above the fray. The isolationists, who believed that World War One had demonstrated there was nothing to be gained by becoming involved in foreign conflicts, doubled down. Roosevelt did not know what to make of what was going on in Europe. "Things are moving so fast," he said in 1935, "I feel my opinion of the situation today may be completely changed tomorrow."[50] The novelist Ernest Hemingway, who was to make his name reporting from war-torn Europe, wrote:

No European country is our friend nor has been since the last war and no country but one's own is worth fighting for. Never again should this country be put into a European war through mistaken idealism, through propaganda, through the desire to back our creditors.[51]

Roosevelt, ever wary of showing his hand, privately sided with the realists. On January 16, 1935, he sent to the Senate a proposal that had been lingering in Washington since 1929, that America join the World Court (the International Court of Justice) to put the settlement of international disputes on a legal footing. The president sent a message to the Senate stressing that the "sovereignty of the United States will in no way be diminished or jeopardized" and that binding the world together in a worldwide legal framework would allow America to "throw its weight into the scale in favor of peace."[52]

Johnson responded that it was "the worst moment" to join the Court, "for Europe sits over a volcano, and America will be dragged into war."[53] Nonetheless, the measure looked likely to be approved until senators began receiving a barrage of anti-Court propaganda inspired and orchestrated by Hearst and Coughlin. Correspondence from constituents opposing America's entry into the World Court was so heavy that it was delivered in wheelbarrows. The measure was ultimately defeated. However, the fact that the president was in favor of the Court suggested to isolationists that Roosevelt could not be trusted. As Adler explained, "While [Roosevelt] had not tried too hard to have his way, he had said enough to indicate to them that his hands needed to be tied to the isolationist steering gear."[54]

To prevent Roosevelt from backsliding, senators began to introduce neutrality measures. The first Neutrality Act, of August 31, 1935, obliged the president, in the event of an outbreak of a war abroad, to define it as such and make illegal the supply of American arms to all combatants. American ships were prevented from delivering war supplies to participants and a National Munitions Board was set up to place the armaments industry under federal control. Roosevelt signed the measure into law. Within two months, war broke out in Ethiopia and the new legislation was put to the test.[55]

Sensing the weakness of the League of Nations and eager to boost his standing at home, in October 1935 Mussolini invaded Ethiopia to capture its mineral wealth. The League responded more aggressively against Italy than it had against Japan, banning the sale to Italy of key commodities such as oil, iron, steel, coal, and coke so long as the war continued. But none of the banned goods were essential for Italy to wage war, and they were also freely available from countries that did not belong to the League.

When it transpired that two senior British politicians had attempted to mollify Mussolini by agreeing to Italy retaining the two-thirds of Ethiopia he had already overrun, it was clear that even Britain had decided not to resist the dictator's demands. The League was impotent. Appeasement was born. Fighting in Ethiopia was horribly one-sided, Mussolini's superior troops and sophisticated equipment easily overcoming the poorly armed Ethiopian forces. America's new neutrality law made little difference to the outcome. Italy did not need American arms and Ethiopia was in no position to buy them on the scale and at the speed required.

Even when the US neutrality legislation lapsed half way through the Ethiopian conflict, the return to the status quo ante made no difference. Not long after his forces had in May 1936 deposed the Emperor of Abyssinia, Haile Selassie, and marched through the streets of Addis Ababa in triumph, Mussolini withdrew Italy from the League.

The second Neutrality Act, of February 1936, extended the ban on shipping arms to combatants for a further fourteen months and added a ban on financial loans to belligerents. More troubling to Roosevelt was the obligation to declare as combatants countries who merely sided with a nation involved in a war, a provision that undermined efforts of noncombatant League members who attempted to enforce a peace.

With Britain and France reluctant to embark on a war, with the League proving itself powerless, and with America determined to stay out of war, the dictators were free to do as they wished. It did not take long before Hitler took advantage. A free pass given to Japan in Manchuria and the rout in Ethiopia suggested that there was no longer the international will to prevent landgrabs. In March 1936, Hitler marched into the demilitarized Rhineland. Again London, Paris, and Washington stood by as aggression triumphed.

Then, in July 1936, came the Spanish Civil War. When the elected Loyalist government of Spain, supported by Communists and bolstered by Stalin's Soviet regime, came under attack from conservative forces in the Spanish military, led by Francisco Franco,[56] a general serving in Spanish Morocco, the democracies again washed their hands of it. Even France, at risk of being surrounded by Fascist governments, failed to act. The Spanish conflict soon became a bloody proxy battle between the competing ideologies of communism and fascism. Spain became a testing ground for the effectiveness of Hitler's weaponry and the German high command's military strategies.

On October 25, 1936, Hitler and Mussolini signed an anti-Communist mutual defense pact, and the following month Germany and Japan combined to form an anti-Soviet pact. The following year, Italy joined them, completing the triangle of aggressors that became known as the Axis. The ominous maneuverings of the dictators only stoked the fires of isolationism in America. As Adler explained, "Isolationism always becomes virulent when armed intervention is imminent, for the policy promises a reprieve from the horrors of war."[57]

In November 1936, Roosevelt was reelected in a landslide on the boast that he had helped calm the nation's jittery nerves after the collapse of the economy and had made progress toward restoring America to economic health.[58] On the campaign trail, he continued to stress his devotion to peace. At a rally in New York he declared, "The nation knows that I hate war, and I know that the nation hates war. I submit to you a record of peace, and on that record a well-founded expectation for future peace."[59]

His grand bargain with the isolationists to accede to their demands if given a free hand to manage the economy had paid off. But it came at a price. America remained woefully ill-prepared for war. From 1935 onward, however, as the drumbeat of war began to be heard around the world, Roosevelt asked for and was granted by Congress more funds for the armed forces and, with General Douglas MacArthur[60] as army chief of staff, he began preparing for a war very different from the trench-bound stasis of World War One. The newly equipped US forces would fight in tanks and airplanes.

Roosevelt was intrigued by Hitler's solution to unemployment: public works and putting men in uniform. "When this man Hitler came into control of the German Government, Germany [was] busted . . . a complete and utter failure, a nation that owed everybody, disorganized, not worth considering as a force in the world,"[61] he said. "There is no one unemployed in Germany, they are all working in war orders." He added, "eventually they will have to pay for it."[62] Even at this early stage, it was clear to Roosevelt that war was a means for Hitler to distract attention from his domestic difficulties. "Hitler—bad shape—war as way out,"[63] he noted.

In May 1937, the third Neutrality Act made permanent the elements of the previous neutrality acts and, in light of the still unresolved Spanish Civil War,[64] gave the president the right to declare internal conflicts a state of war. There was, however, a new element. Combatants were allowed to buy war goods from America so long as they were prepared to pay cash and could haul the arms away in non-American ships. This "cash-and-carry" provision revealed a mercenary side of the isolationists, who, under the pretext that they were against war, were happy to sell arms if there was money to be made. As Borah explained, "We seek to avoid all risks, all danger, but we make certain to get all profits."[65]

The weight of opinion in favor of the new law was so overwhelming[66] that Roosevelt made no attempt to halt it. The *New York Herald Tribune* mocked the measure as it would neither keep America neutral nor prevent another world war, describing it as "an act to preserve the United States from intervention in the war of 1917-18."[67] As Adler explained, "The congressional isolationists, so anxious to keep out of the war, actually helped invite a foreign catastrophe of such immense proportions that no nation could have escaped its consequences."[68]

This was evident to Roosevelt, who, after years spent biting his tongue rather than risk the success of the New Deal, determined to take a stand. In July 1937, the Japanese and Chinese once again went to war, but this time it was to be war to the bitter end. Japan started on a campaign of territorial expansion with the whole of the western Pacific seaboard in its sights. It was the final straw for the president, who, in Chicago on October 5, abandoned gentle warnings for plain speaking. He told his audience:

the very foundations of civilization are seriously threatened. . . . Civilians, including vast numbers of women and children, are being ruthlessly murdered with bombs from the air. In times of so-called peace, ships are being attacked and sunk by submarines without cause or notice. Nations are fomenting and taking sides in civil warfare in nations that have never done them any harm.

He took aim at those hampering America's efforts to maintain the peace by passing neutrality laws:

The peace, the freedom and the security of 90 percent of the population of the world is being jeopardized by the remaining 10 percent, who are threatening a breakdown of all international order and law. . . . When an epidemic of physical disease starts to spread, the community approves and joins in a quarantine of the patients in order to protect the health of the community against the spread of the disease. . . . War is a contagion, whether it be declared or undeclared.[69]

IT WAS A FORLORN HOPE, perhaps, but the president had given public notice that he was prepared to halt the dictators if given enough support. But would it be forthcoming? He was aware that he was up "against a public psychology of long standing—a psychology which comes very close to saying, 'Peace at any price.'"[70] Sensing the mood of the audience and the nation, Roosevelt confided to his speechwriter, Samuel I. Rosenman,[71] "It's a terrible thing to look over your shoulder when you are trying to lead and find no one there."[72]

CHAPTER TWO

ONE GOOD TURN

Roosevelt in Kennedy's debt,
Hearst threatens Roosevelt's chances
for the Democratic presidential nomination,
the power of Father Charles Coughlin.

THE RELATIONSHIP BETWEEN Franklin Roosevelt and Joseph P. Kennedy had been troubled from the start. When America entered World War One, Kennedy, a married man with two children and a young wife expecting a third, had avoided the draft. Eager nonetheless to be seen to be of public service, he put aside his lucrative career in finance and volunteered to help manage Bethlehem Steel's Fore River Shipyard in Quincy, Massachusetts.

This put him in the direct line of fire of Roosevelt, the dynamic young assistant secretary of the navy, who aggressively agitated for the speedy delivery of naval vessels protecting transatlantic shipping from German submarines. As Kennedy recalled, "We never got along then. He would laugh and smile and give me the needle, but I could not help but admire the man."[1]

It was inevitable, perhaps, that the two would eventually clash. When a pair of Argentine battleships were returned to the shipyard for urgent repairs only a short time after they had been commissioned, Argentina claimed the shipyard was at fault and should bear the cost. The shipyard refused and held the ships pending final payment. Roosevelt, eager to keep Argentina sweet, pressed Kennedy to release the vessels and proposed that the State Department might guarantee payment of the outstanding amount.

Kennedy, under orders from the shipyard owners to keep the dreadnoughts until the money was in the bank, insisted upon full settlement. Roosevelt began negotiating with Kennedy, who recalled him to be "the hardest trader I ever came up against."[2] Unable to reach a deal, Roosevelt ordered marines to the shipyard to commandeer the battleships, then deliver them to the Argentines. "I was so disappointed and angry that I broke down and cried," Kennedy recalled.[3]

The next time Kennedy encountered Roosevelt was in very different circumstances, with Roosevelt in need of financial help for his 1932 presidential campaign and Kennedy eager to take a first step on his own political career. In the intervening years, Kennedy had made a vast fortune at stockbrokers Halle and Stieglitz on Wall Street and as a movie mogul in Los Angeles. Having made enough for him and his rapidly expanding family to live comfortably for the rest of their lives, Kennedy began to imagine a life in politics, though he had no intention of working his way up from the bottom. He would buy himself in at the highest level.

What the limit of his ambition was, he did not know. He insisted to anyone who asked, "There is no public office that would interest me."[4] But to his wife, Rose,[5] he was more candid. "I am a restless soul," he said. "Some would call it ambition."[6] As he watched Roosevelt from afar he slowly concluded that, with the right headwind, even the presidency might be within his reach.

Roosevelt was too canny to be caught expressing critical views of those he needed to make use of, but nearly a decade later he would let slip his true feelings about Kennedy. "Joe is and always has been a temperamental Irish boy, terrifically spoiled at an early age by huge financial success," he confided to his son-in-law John Boettiger.[7] "Thoroughly patriotic, thoroughly selfish and thoroughly obsessed with the idea that he must leave each of his nine children with a million dollars apiece when he dies (he has told me that often). . . . Sometimes I think I am 200 years older than he is."[8]

Although Kennedy "inherited a Democratic label at birth,"[9] in the early 1920s he weighed whether to join the Massachusetts Republican Party and gave a large sum of money to the presidential campaign of ex-Republican Robert M. La Follette, Sr.,[10] who was the candidate of the Progressive Party in the 1924 presidential contest.

La Follette had been against America entering World War One and vehemently opposed Wilson's efforts to join the League of Nations.

Then Kennedy appeared to turn toward the Democrats. Hearing that Kennedy was toying with backing Democratic candidate Governor Al Smith[11] of New York in the 1928 presidential election, Roosevelt, one of Smith's campaign managers, wrote a flattering note suggesting that "there are some matters upon which I would appreciate your suggestions."[12] But Roosevelt was misinformed about Kennedy's intentions. Though considering himself "a good Democrat,"[13] Kennedy threw his support behind the Republican Herbert Hoover, who in November beat Smith in a landslide.

A little over a year later, however, with Hoover floundering, the smart money on who would become president in the 1932 election shifted to Roosevelt, who had succeeded Smith as governor of New York in January 1929. A few years later, Kennedy liked to dress up his switch as a principled change of heart. "I knew that big, drastic changes had to be made in our economic system and I felt that Roosevelt was the one who could make those changes," he told a reporter. "I wanted him in the White House for my own security and for the security of our kids—and I was ready to do anything to help elect him."[14]

Roosevelt's friend and country neighbor Henry Morgenthau[15] made the initial approach to bring Kennedy and his money on board, inviting him to lunch with Roosevelt in the governor's mansion in Albany. Back home in Westchester that evening, Kennedy told Rose he believed Roosevelt was the man to save America. Two years later, in May 1932, Kennedy consummated the union, taking a trip to Warm Springs, Georgia, where the governor was undergoing water therapy to ameliorate the crippling polio he had contracted in the summer of 1921. Kennedy agreed to support Roosevelt and join him at the party convention in Chicago the following month.

Having recruited Kennedy, Roosevelt immediately put him to use. From his time as a Hollywood movie magnate, Kennedy counted as a friend William Randolph Hearst. While Hearst's wife remained in New York, he lived with his mistress, the actress Marion Davies, more than thirty years his junior, at Hearst Castle, his antique-stuffed architectural hotchpotch in San Simeon, California, surrounded by 240,000 acres of scrub populated by zebras, camels, llamas, and kangaroos. Hearst, an isolationist, often tilted at Roosevelt. For Roosevelt to stand any chance of winning the Democratic nomination, the tyrant would have to be appeased.

Hearst once craved the presidency himself, but he was hardly equipped for retail politics. A lumbering man with an elongated face and an incongruously high-pitched voice, he was a poor public speaker. Having inherited $100 million from his railroad baron father, he was used to getting his way and had little patience for the collaborative work and glad-handing expected of a political hopeful. He was highly opinionated, rarely inhibited by good taste or sound judgment, and incapable of keeping acerbic thoughts to himself.

Those very qualities, however, made him an effective populist newspaper proprietor whose editors and journalists did his bidding. According to legend, when one of his illustrators, Frederick Remington, who had been dispatched to the war in Cuba in 1897, cabled his news desk, "Everything is quiet. There is no trouble here. There will be no war," Hearst shot back, "You furnish the pictures and I'll furnish the war."[16]

At the turn of the century, Hearst forced his way into the Democratic Party leadership stakes by setting up a newspaper in Chicago to influence the 1900 convention. After failing to become the running mate of candidate William Jennings Bryan, Hearst turned his fire on the Republican ticket of President William McKinley[17] and his vice presidential candidate, Franklin Roosevelt's distant cousin Theodore. But the forthright Hearst soon overstepped the mark of good taste. In a tirade against the president, his *Evening Journal* wrote that if "bad men can be got rid of only by killing, then killing must be done."[18] When a short time later McKinley was shot dead by an assassin, the public blamed Hearst and burned him in effigy.

Undeterred, Hearst was elected to Congress in 1902 representing Midtown Manhattan, and two years later mounted a campaign for the presidency that went nowhere. In 1905 he ran for mayor of New York and lost; the following year he put himself forward for the governorship of New York and lost. In the 1912 presidential contest, in an attempt to prevent Wilson from winning the Democratic nomination, Hearst put his media properties behind the front-runner, isolationist Champ Clark.[19] When Wilson won both the nomination and the presidency with no help from Hearst, the press magnate championed opposition to America entering World War One on the Allied side, declaring, "We are simply wasting sorely needed men and supplies by sending them abroad."[20]

Ignored by the unimpeachable Wilson, Hearst next ordered his papers to oppose joining the League of Nations. Then Hearst met his political Waterloo. He again tried and failed to win the Democratic nomination for the New York governorship, eventually backing his rival, Smith, who won the subsequent election. Hearst took the defeat badly and, when Smith did not appoint Hearst's slate of friends to the state judiciary, began waging a poisonous campaign against the governor.

Though Smith had no control over the dairy market, Hearst blamed him for a sharp hike in the price of milk, which, Hearst charged, threatened children with malnutrition. Smith was appalled by the assault. When, on her deathbed, the governor's mother uttered the words, "My son did not kill the babies!" Smith became determined to confront the tyrant.

He hired Carnegie Hall in New York and challenged Hearst to a debate. The press baron ran scared. "I have no intention of meeting Governor Smith publicly or privately," he blasted. "I find no satisfaction in the company of crooked politicians, neither have I time nor inclination to debate with every public plunderer or faithless public servant whom my papers have exposed."[21] In a theatrical coup, Smith pressed on with the debate without Hearst, telling the audience, "Of course, I am alone. I know the man to whom I issued the challenge, and I know that he has not got a drop of good, clean, pure red blood in his whole body." Accusing Hearst of "the gravest abuse of the power of the press in the history of this country," Smith, quoting from Psalms, urged New Yorkers to "get rid of this pestilence that walks in the darkness."[22]

Smith lost the governorship in 1920, and two years later put himself forward for a New York Senate seat at the same time as Hearst. When Smith let it be known that he would not allow his name to go forward for the subsequent governor's race if Hearst's name appeared on the same ticket, Roosevelt intervened, telling diplomat and lawyer Joseph E. Davies,[23] "I had quite a tussle in New York to keep our friend Hearst off the ticket and to get Al Smith to run."[24] As this proved to be Hearst's last attempt to win public office, Roosevelt could claim to have snuffed out the fifty-nine-year-old press baron's political ambitions.

More than a decade later, Hearst was confronted with an invidious choice when he was obliged to take sides in the race between Smith and Roosevelt to become the 1932 Democratic presidential candidate. Hearst dismissed the two men as "Wall Street internationalists."[25] He certainly could not throw his weight behind Smith, which left him with the prospect of Smith's principal rival, Roosevelt, who had been governor of New York since 1928 and of whom he also had a low opinion.

Not only had Roosevelt abetted Smith's public humiliation of Hearst, but he held foreign policy positions that Hearst deeply disliked. Roosevelt had backed Wilson's intervention in World War One and remained committed to taking America into the League of Nations. At first, Hearst backed Roosevelt. "As Roosevelt is a probable presidential nominee and the one we are most likely to support, we should keep him and his policies before the nation," he told the editor of his *New York American*. "There has been no adequate promotion of him in our papers. We should begin now to see that there is."[26]

But as the convention in Chicago drew nearer, Hearst floated his own candidate, John N. Garner,[27] a little known Democrat from San Antonio, Texas, who was "opposed to all foreign entanglements."[28] To launch Garner's bid for the presidency, Hearst ordered his editors to forget Roosevelt and commend Garner to readers. In a nationwide radio address, Hearst blasted Roosevelt and others as "all good men in their way, but all internationalists—all, like Mr. Hoover, disciples of Woodrow Wilson, inheriting and fatuously following his visionary policies of intermeddling in European conflicts. . . . We should personally see to it that a man is elected to the Presidency this year whose guiding motto is 'America First'."[29]

Garner's belated arrival in what had been a two-horse race jeopardized Roosevelt's chances of winning outright on the first ballot in the summer convention in Chicago. As Garner was running as a "favorite son" in Texas, Roosevelt was deprived of the state's forty-two primary votes. Then, after a vigorous campaign on Garner's behalf by Hearst's West Coast media properties, Garner caused an upset in California, winning a further forty-four votes. Roosevelt still led the field, but Garner stood between him and a first ballot win. If the convention was split, it would take hard bargaining and a great deal of luck for Roosevelt to win the nomination.

All attention in the Roosevelt camp turned toward plotting how Hearst could be persuaded to ask Garner to stand aside. The stumbling block appeared to be Roosevelt's continuing support for the League. Roosevelt's people deputed Wilson's confidant, Colonel Edward M. House, to contact Hearst to assure him their candidate's views on the League had changed since 1920 and that the candidate would like privately to set Hearst's mind at rest. Hearst's robust riposte, in a signed editorial splashed across the front pages of twenty-eight papers, ridiculed Roosevelt's attempt to keep his change of mind quiet.

"If Mr. Roosevelt has any statement to make about his not now being an internationalist, he should make it to the public publicly and not to me privately," he declared. "He should make his declaration publicly that he has changed his mind and that he is now in favor of keeping the national independence which our forefathers won for us, that he is now in favor of not joining the League."[30]

Roosevelt had genuinely been having second thoughts about the wisdom of pressing on with American entry into the League. Since his journey across the Atlantic with Woodrow Wilson in 1919, he had been in favor of the principle of world government and the United States joining the League of Nations. He had watched in despair as the isolationists in the Senate had defeated the ratification of the Treaty of Versailles. He had concluded that continuing to try to sell the League would be futile.

In 1924, therefore, Roosevelt had suggested there be "a brand new permanent International organization, i.e., to kill the existing League and set up something in its place,"[31] a body that Congress could agree to join. It was with a mind to announce a change of direction, then, that Roosevelt telephoned Hearst to discuss their differences.

Two days after Hearst's front-page blast, Roosevelt issued a statement. "The League of Nations today is not the League conceived by Woodrow Wilson," he wrote. "Too often through these years its major function has been not the broad overwhelming purpose of world peace, but rather a mere meeting place for the political discussion of strictly European national difficulties. In these the United States should have no part. . . . American participation in the League would not serve the highest purpose of the prevention of war."[32] It was an embarrassing climb-down by Roosevelt and a triumph for Hearst.

Roosevelt's about-turn alarmed many of his key supporters, starting with the editorial board of the *New York Times*, who complained, "It will be generally regretted, we think, that Governor Roosevelt should have been so plainly swayed by political motives in this public recantation." After a meeting of grumbling internationalists, Roosevelt's sidekick Robert W. Woolley[33] told House, "Every man there looked as if he might be attending his own funeral. . . . I don't suppose the Governor of New York will ever realize the extent of the tragedy which he wrought in that entirely unnecessary statement. . . . Hearst's cohorts here are having the time of their lives raucously laughing at the manner in which their chief brought the Governor of New York to his knees. They boast that from now on Roosevelt is at Hearst's mercy."[34]

The ever-pragmatic Roosevelt attempted to reassure Woolley:

Can't you see that loyalty to the ideals of Woodrow Wilson is just as strong in my heart as it is in yours? But have you ever stopped to consider that there is a difference between ideals and the means of attaining them? Ideals do not change, but methods do change with every generation and world circumstance. Here is the difference between me and some of my faint-hearted friends. I am looking for the best modern vehicle to reach the goal of an ideal while they insist on a vehicle which was brand new and in good running order twelve years ago.[35]

After the Democratic primaries, Roosevelt was the clear leader in the nomination race but still about two hundred votes short of the two-thirds needed to be elected on the first ballot. Garner, with ninety pledged votes, held the balance, making Hearst the kingmaker. The newspaperman was enjoying his moment of power and let it be known that he was in no hurry to make up his mind. The continuing uncertainty was perfect for increasing sales of his newspapers, as each twist and turn in the run-up to the Democratic convention stoked the appetite of a public eager to hear what trick Hearst would pull next.

To heighten the temperature of an already torrid contest, on

April 24 Hearst wrote another front-page editorial, headed "A Plague On Both Your Houses." He revealed that despite Roosevelt's public flip-flop on the League, he was still not satisfied. "The unknown American man is not going to be benefited by Mr. Roosevelt's plan to put this country into foreign complications by the trap door of the League Court," Hearst wrote, a mischievous intervention that provoked pandemonium in the Roosevelt camp.

Aware of Kennedy's Hollywood links to Hearst, Roosevelt's team asked the Boston financier to fly to San Simeon to persuade the press baron to plump for Roosevelt. Kennedy landed at a small beachside airport beneath the architectural mishmash Hearst called "The Ranch." With little facility for small talk or interest in the fine art that surrounded him, he quickly got down to business. The upshot was that Hearst could not bring himself to back his archrival Smith, but before he released Garner's votes he needed further reassurance from Roosevelt that he would keep the US out of foreign wars.

By the time delegates began assembling at the end of June in the Chicago Stadium, a faux Greek temple larger than New York's Madison Square Garden, the convention was still wide open. For the first time in thirty years, Hearst decided not to attend in person and holed up in San Simeon, operating the votes he had bought by remote control. Before long, the telephone wires between Chicago and the Coast were melting with offers of bargains, concessions, trade-offs, and about-turns.

Roosevelt was now vulnerable to a surprise fourth candidate, who emerged in the shape of Newton D. Baker,[36] Wilson's secretary of war, from Cleveland, Ohio. His backers in Illinois, Indiana, and his home state had held back their votes in order to mount a surprise run. Kennedy was deputed to call Hearst and explain that the convention was on the edge of electing the bellicose Baker, who would certainly take America into the League. Hearst told Kennedy that he would make up his mind when he was good and ready.

After three inconclusive ballots in the middle of the night, the Roosevelt camp was in despair. The longer the process, the more likely that the convention would break the logjam by picking Baker— or some other dark horse candidate. Kennedy was again asked to call Hearst.

Arthur Krock,[37] the *New York Times* Washington correspondent, overheard Kennedy make the call. "W. R., do you want Baker?" Kennedy asked. Hearst did not. "If you don't want Baker, you'd better take Roosevelt, because if you don't take Roosevelt, you're going to have Baker." Hearst thought for a while and made it clear he was not happy to be railroaded.

He asked Kennedy whether another candidate might emerge and suggested Albert Ritchie, the four-term governor of Maryland. Kennedy held fast. "No, I don't think so," he said. "I think if Roosevelt cracks on the next ballot, it'll be Baker."[38] Hearst reluctantly directed Garner to release his delegates, in exchange for Garner taking the vice presidential slot on the Roosevelt ticket. Roosevelt won the nomination on the following ballot and flew to Chicago to announce that he was offering "a New Deal for the American people."[39] It was the first mention of what would become his trademark economic recovery legislation.

Roosevelt now owed Kennedy a huge favor. The Bostonian enjoyed one outstanding virtue: he came bearing lots of cash. He gave $25,000 ($415,000 in 2014 terms) to Roosevelt's campaign and lent the Democratic National Committee $50,000 more. Now that the candidacy was secure, Kennedy was encouraged to become a bundler—to call his rich friends and tap them for funds, starting with Hearst, who, despite his persistent misgivings, sent $25,000. Kennedy wrote Hearst, "Considering the fact that there are only two contributions equal to yours, you can well understand what a terrific sensation this check made."

Kennedy told Hearst that passing the check to the campaign through him "helps a great deal in having consideration paid to any suggestion that I might want to make." In a veiled acknowledgment that they shared a common interest in holding Roosevelt to his promise to keep America out of the League, Kennedy added, "Whenever your interests in this administration are not served well, my interest has ceased."[40]

As his granddaughter Amanda Smith reported many years later, "The financier's enthusiasm and support [for Roosevelt] would always be tempered and punctuated by critical outbursts."[41] After Kennedy visited Roy Howard,[42] chairman of the Scripps–Howard newspaper chain, Howard wrote to Newton Baker that Kennedy was "quite frank in his very low estimate of Roosevelt's ability" and held in contempt the governor's "immaturity, vacillation, and general weak-kneed character." Kennedy's aim in sticking by Roosevelt was to ensure that others did not "unmake Roosevelt's mind on some of the points on which Kennedy had made it up for Roosevelt."[43] Roosevelt was aware of Kennedy's backbiting but found him useful. His general policy was, in any case, to keep his enemies close to him.

As well as keeping Hearst sweet, Kennedy was tasked with minding Father Charles Coughlin, an opinionated, Canadian-born Roman Catholic priest based at the National Shrine of the Little Flower in the Royal Oak suburb of Michigan, who through his gift for oratory had built a weekly audience on Sunday afternoons of 30 million on thirty-five radio stations coast to coast. The Shrine, an imposing Italianate church, was constructed with hundreds of thousands of dollars donated by the priest's radio following. In 1930, as the Great Depression took hold, Coughlin had moved from discussing religion to politics, declaring himself the friend of the common man.

The priest's political statements became so partisan that CBS, anxious not to offend federal authorities that demanded impartiality on the airwaves, dropped him from its roster. When in January 1931 Coughlin wrote to Roosevelt asking for support against CBS's censorship, Roosevelt sent a noncommittal letter.

Coughlin roundly and colorfully condemned the un-American activities of socialists and Communists as well as the greed of big businessmen. He was an unashamed anti-Semite, blaming "international financiers" for the Wall Street crash and the Depression. He warned against being drawn into foreign wars. Deeply hostile to Hoover, as the 1932 presidential election approached Coughlin began preaching, "It is either Roosevelt or ruin," and, "I will never change my philosophy that the New Deal is Christ's Deal."[44]

In May 1931, Roosevelt received a letter from Eleanor's brother, G. Hall Roosevelt, the controller of Detroit, that Coughlin "would like to tender his services. He would be difficult to handle and might be full of dynamite, but I think you had better be prepared to say yes or no."[45] Coughlin's support was a mixed blessing. Despite his religious demeanor, he was a hard-drinking, free-cursing businessman in a dog collar, part Elmer Gantry, part Huey Long (the charismatic populist governor of Louisiana).

Roosevelt met Coughlin for the first time in early 1932, in Albany.

The priest came away with the impression that the two men had a pact. "He said he would rely on me, that I would be an important advisor," Coughlin recalled.[46] When Eleanor was asked what her husband thought of Coughlin, she said, "He disliked and distrusted him."[47] Still, the Democrats invited the radio priest to address the 1932 Chicago convention. When he returned to Michigan, he cabled Roosevelt, "I am with you to the end. Say the word and I will follow." A month later he wrote, "I am willing to adopt your views which I know will be just and charitable. But the main point is that we work in harmony."[48]

As Coughlin's biographer Donald Warren put it, "Roosevelt and his staff viewed the relationship with Royal Oak as an awkward, imbalanced, and even seriously unsettling threat."[49] Roosevelt complained to James Farley, his campaign manager in 1932 and 1936 and Postmaster General, "[Coughlin] should run for the Presidency himself. Who the hell does he think he is?"[50] Kennedy, the Roosevelt campaign's most prominent Catholic, was charged with keeping the priest on message and began making visits to Royal Oak. Kennedy became "fascinated by Coughlin's talent on the radio," recalled James Roosevelt. "He recognized it as demagoguery, but revelled in what the priest could accomplish."[51] Besides, his attempts to tame Coughlin meant that Roosevelt was even more in Kennedy's debt.

Invited to join the Roosevelt presidential campaign's executive committee, Kennedy declined because of personal differences with Roosevelt's close adviser and political mentor Louis Howe, but he agreed to contribute to Roosevelt's speeches on business and finance in the hope that Roosevelt would appoint him Treasury secretary. Kennedy worked up some ideas that emerged in a speech delivered by Roosevelt on August 20 in Columbus, Ohio, in which businessmen and stock traders in Hoover's America were traduced as "promoters, sloganeers, mushroom millionaires, opportunists, adventurers of all kinds."[52] To "act as a check or counterbalance" to the "ruthless manipulation of professional gamblers in the stock markets and in the corporate system,"[53] Roosevelt argued that the nation's financial industry should be reformed, regulated, and policed by a federal body, an idea that would lead to creation of the Securities and Exchange Commission.

The following month, Kennedy joined Roosevelt aboard his campaign train traveling the Pacific Coast. Riding in the carriage just ahead of the president's own, Kennedy had finally made it to the inner sanctum. If Roosevelt won, a cabinet job might be in the cards. On election night, he threw a party at the Waldorf-Astoria in New York, and when it became clear that Roosevelt had won by a landslide, taking forty-two states to Hoover's six, the band played "Happy Days Are Here Again."[54] Kennedy was encouraged in his ambition to join the administration when, to fill time between the election on November 8 and the inauguration on March 4, he was invited to join Roosevelt and many of the campaign's principal donors aboard Vincent Astor's yacht for a victory cruise up and down the Florida coast.

Soon after the election, Coughlin arrived at the president-elect's New York City home on East 65th Street bearing a wish list of Catholics whom he and his bishop, Michael Gallagher, who defended Coughlin from the Catholic hierarchy, thought suitable to be ambassadors in Latin America. Roosevelt stalled, claiming that the incoming secretary of state, Cordell Hull, had already agreed to the appointments. "I'll tell you what I can do," said Roosevelt. "You can have the Philippines if you want."[55] Coughlin named as governor-general his friend and political ally Frank Murphy, mayor of Detroit, who as a child had been one of the priest's altar boys.

Kennedy felt he had every reason to believe he would be offered a cabinet position. But weeks passed and there was no call from Roosevelt. His hopes were briefly raised when he received a telegram from Will Hays,[56] the Hollywood film censor, addressing him as "Mr. Secretary," to which he was obliged to write, "The only secretarial job that I would ever consider would be one to General Will Hays." "I have no desire for political preferment," he lied. He wrote a similar note to Hiram Brown, president of RKO: "As far as my accepting any position under [Roosevelt], I can assure you it is the farthest thing from my mind. I went into the fight for the fun it gave me, and there is no hope of an ultimate reward."[57]

Roosevelt had no intention of giving Kennedy the important job of secretary to the Treasury, and added his name to a list of candidates for the mostly ceremonial role of Treasurer of the United States, with responsibility for printing banknotes, minting coins, and writing his signature on dollar bills. But even that sinecure was put out of his reach by the intervention of his old enemy and the new president's dear friend, Louis Howe,[58] for whom the arrival in the White House of his protégé Franklin Roosevelt was the crowning moment of a long career spent in smoke-filled rooms.

When the protracted silence emanating from the president-elect's office suggested that there would be nothing for him in the new administration, Kennedy moodily retreated to his seaside estate in Palm Beach for the winter, taking with him Raymond Moley,[59] architect of the president's "Brain Trust." There, Kennedy complained about the new president to anyone who would listen. "I heard plenty of Kennedy's excoriation of Roosevelt, of his criticisms of the President-elect," recalled Moley. "There must have been hundreds of dollars in telephone calls to provide an exchange of abuse of Roosevelt between Kennedy and W. R. Hearst. The latter by this time was wondering why he had ever supported Roosevelt."[60]

In March, after a month of brooding, Kennedy sent Roosevelt a cable laced with praise about how good the new administration was looking. The president cheerily replied, "Do be sure to let us know when you are going through Washington and stop off and see us."[61] Irritated by the brush-off, Kennedy invited himself to the White House. Roosevelt welcomed him in the Oval Office with a beaming smile. "Hello, Joe," he said. "Where have you been all these months? I thought you'd got lost."[62]

CHAPTER THREE

NEW DEALERS

Kennedy joins Roosevelt's administration,
helps temper Father Coughlin's dissent, and claims
his just reward. Roosevelt starts to prepare himself for
a third term and the American people for war

AFTER THE PRESIDENT passed him over in 1932, Kennedy resumed his business life, fully exploiting his links to the Roosevelt family. In September 1933, he and Rose sailed to London, taking with him the president's son James and his wife, Betsey. While the women shopped and looked at the sights, Kennedy and the young Roosevelt set about exploiting a popular plank in Roosevelt's 1932 platform: the imminent repeal of the 1919 Eighteenth Amendment that had outlawed the sale and consumption of alcohol.

The resumption of legal drinking offered an obvious business opportunity. Using James Roosevelt as his entrée, Kennedy negotiated exclusive distribution deals with some of Britain's top purveyors of alcohol, among them Scotch whisky distillers Haig and Haig and John Dewar, and gin makers Gordon's. Kennedy also obtained federally issued permits for the sale of alcohol "for medicinal purposes" in America,[1] so by the time the final state, Utah, ratified the Twenty-First Amendment, which overturned Prohibition, his warehouses were stacked with cases of whisky and gin ready for sale.

Eventually Roosevelt did offer Kennedy a job: as New York director of the New Deal's National Recovery Administration. Thinking it of insufficient importance, Kennedy declined the offer. When ill health forced Treasury secretary William H. Woodin[2] to resign at the end of 1933, Kennedy was again passed over for the post, this time in favor of Roosevelt's neighbor and friend Henry Morgenthau Jr., who had inherited a real estate fortune and farmed Christmas trees in Dutchess County. An economic conservative, Morgenthau was malleable. Roosevelt explained, "I couldn't put Joe Kennedy in [Morgenthau's] place . . . because Joe would want to run the Treasury in his own way, contrary to my plans and views."[3]

It was not long before Kennedy's name suggested itself for a most delicate government position. After the passage of the Securities Exchange Act in 1934, a new body was established to police the financial sector, the Securities and Exchange Commission. Roosevelt asked Kennedy to become its chairman. The thought of naming a poacher turned gamekeeper appealed to Roosevelt's sense of mischief, but it was also sound politics. Routinely accused of being hostile to bankers and big business, Roosevelt thought appointing Kennedy, as one of their number, would ensure that Wall Street types cooperated fully with the new body.

In a memo to the president, Ray Moley, who had helped drive the SEC legislation through Congress, described Kennedy as "the best bet for Chairman because of executive ability, knowledge of habits and customs of business to be regulated."[4] When Kennedy was asked by Moley to consider the appointment, he demurred. "I don't think you ought to do this," he said. "It will bring down injurious criticism." "I know darned well you want this job," said Moley. "But if anything in your career in business could injure the President, this is the time to spill it." As Moley recalled, "With a burst of profanity he defied anyone to question his devotion to the public interest or to point to a single shady act in his whole life. . . . He would give his critics—and here again the profanity flowed freely—an administration of the SEC that would be a credit to the country, the President, himself, and his family—clear down to the ninth child."[5] Kennedy accepted the post.

The Kennedy appointment provoked incredulity in the press. The *New Republic*'s John T. Flynn, a sharp critic of both Wall Street and the president, cried, "I say it isn't true. It is impossible. It could not happen."[6] Within the administration, too, there was doubt that Kennedy was the right man. Secretary of the Interior Harold Ickes[7] confided to his diary:

> I am afraid I do not agree with [Roosevelt] as to the chairman he is
> going to name for the Securities Commission. He has named Joseph
> P. Kennedy for that place, a former stock market plunger. The Presi-
> dent has great confidence in him because he has made his pile, has
> invested all his money in Government securities, and knows all the
> tricks of the trade. Apparently he is going on the assumption that
> Kennedy would now like to make a name for himself for the sake of
> his family, but I have never known many of these cases to work out
> as expected.[8]

Kennedy would prove his doubters wrong. He was a tireless public servant and his energy and application ensured the SEC's success.
Kennedy reveled in the position; at last he was enjoying power and
had no one to restrain him but the president. One of the items on
his desk of which he was most proud was a white telephone with a
direct line to the White House. He used his time in Washington to
establish himself as an important figure in the administration and
to become better acquainted with the congressmen and senators he
would need if he were to make a presidential bid. And he cemented
his ambiguous friendship with Roosevelt.

While Rose and the family remained in Bronxville, Kennedy
leased Marwood, a ten-bedroom country mansion outside Potomac,
Maryland, where he lavishly entertained politicians, journalists,
film stars, and, on a regular basis, the president himself. As Eleanor toured the country promoting her own progressive agenda,
Roosevelt was often left alone in the White House, and he enjoyed
visiting Kennedy at weekends. The president relished the SEC chairman's glamorous lifestyle, the informality and privacy of Marwood
despite its grandeur, the early sight of new movies Kennedy had
shipped in from Hollywood, and the dry martinis on tap.

For the next couple of years Roosevelt and Kennedy got on
famously. Krock, the *New York Times* journalist whom Kennedy kept
on retainer as an amanuensis and shill, recorded one of the president's visits. "The party soon became very merry," he wrote. "The
President's laughter rang out over all, and was most frequent. After
a reasonable number of mint juleps, which the President said would
be 'swell', they dined in the same mood."[9] He continued, rather less
plausibly, "[The president] consults Mr. Kennedy on everything,

and when the argument is over, President and adviser relax like two school boys." [10]

Eleanor encouraged Kennedy's candor with the president, whom she knew would ignore advice he did not agree with. "I want you to go right on telling Franklin exactly what you think," she told him. [11] Kennedy reciprocated, dropping by the White House several times a week. Yet there remained a tension in the friendship, with the president relentlessly teasing Kennedy and playing practical jokes to delineate the roles of master and supplicant.

Typical of Roosevelt's taunting of Kennedy was a memo ordering that "in view of the sleepless nights and hectic days of the Chairman of the SEC, in view of his shrunken frame, sunken eyes, falling hair, and fallen arches, he is hereby directed to proceed to Palm Beach and return to Washington six hours after he gets there . . ." then, on the following page "and after ten intervening days have passed by (fooled again)." [12]

Having established the SEC and ensured its smooth running, Kennedy became impatient. One evening in May 1935, on his way to the White House to tender his resignation, Kennedy caught sight of a placard screaming that the Supreme Court had declared the National Recovery Act, a cornerstone of the New Deal, unconstitutional. Aware that this was no time to add to the president's woes, he tore up his resignation letter. By August, however, he was again determined to return to private life. He complained that working for Roosevelt was costing him $100,000 a year in lost income and that his government salary barely covered his telephone bills.

In early September he resigned, thanking Roosevelt for being "unfailingly considerate and stimulating." [13] In his letter accepting the resignation, the president warmly paid tribute to Kennedy's "skill, resourcefulness, good sense and devotion to the public interest" and promised that "in the future, as in the past, I shall freely turn to you for support and counsel." [14] Kennedy insisted that he was finished with government work. "I am leaving public life today for good," he wrote to the *New York Times* publisher, Arthur Hays Sulzberger. [15] "I am going to feel that I'm out of politics—if this is politics—for the rest of my natural life." [16]

But Roosevelt still needed Kennedy, and he was asked to try to

stem the torrent of vitriol hurled at Roosevelt each week by Coughlin. Once one of his most avid admirers, the radio priest had become
a fierce critic, peddling a populist domestic agenda and an isolationist foreign policy. In 1934, the priest founded the National Union for
Social Justice as a third political force designed to steal votes from
the president. He planned to team up with Huey Long, the former
governor of Louisiana who had taken to spouting primitive leftist
rhetoric from the Senate. A poll suggested that in the coming election, six million voters, many of them traditional Democrats, would
support Long and Coughlin.

Coughlin condemned the New Deal as "two years of surrender,
two years of matching the puerile, puny brains of idealists against
the virile viciousness of business and finance, two years of economic
failure."[17] The priest opposed Roosevelt's efforts to join the World
Court, a body proposed at Versailles in 1919 to deliver a common
world standard of justice, suggesting that membership would "lead
to the pilfering of Europe's $12 billion war debt to the United States,
participation in another war, and the destruction of the American
way of life."[18] When the president's attempt to join the World Court
was defeated, Senator William Borah, one of the most intractable
isolationists, wrote to Coughlin, "How deeply indebted we are to you
for the great victory."[19]

Coughlin was such a threat to Roosevelt that it was decided the
president should try to smother the priest with his famous charm.
In September 1935, Kennedy arranged an audience with Roosevelt at
Hyde Park. With Kennedy by his side, the president invited Coughlin by telephone. "Hiya Padre!" he said. "Where have you been all the
time? I'm lonesome. I've got a couple of days down here. Come on
down and see me."[20] When the priest hesitated, citing a funeral as an
excuse, the president insisted that he take the overnight train. Kennedy met Coughlin at Albany, where the first thing to greet the priest
on the station platform was a placard announcing that the rabble-
rousing leftist from Louisiana, Senator Huey Long, Coughlin's partner in populist radicalism, had been shot dead.

By the time the two men arrived at Springwood in Kennedy's
Rolls-Royce, the president had not yet risen, so Kennedy and Coughlin helped themselves to breakfast. As soon as Roosevelt emerged, he
got down to business. With Long dead, the time was propitious for a

deal with Coughlin. "Cards on the table, Padre, why are you cooling off to me?"[21] the president asked. As the priest fumbled for words, Roosevelt told Kennedy to "go out and look at the pigs" so he and the priest could be alone. An exchange of views took place in which Coughlin, by his account, did most of the talking.

He said that his disenchantment stemmed from information he had received suggesting that federal money was being funneled to Communists in Mexico. Roosevelt promised to look into it. (No convincing evidence was forthcoming.) When Coughlin proposed that the Treasury should inflate the economy to preserve jobs and that the Federal Reserve should be abolished, the president shrugged his shoulders. "Don't be so innocent as to think that the President of the United States can also be the Congress of the United States," he said. "I'm only the President."[22]

Roosevelt stressed to Coughlin that if he persisted in his opposition, it would invite the return of a Republican administration, which the priest would not like. When the evening drew in, Roosevelt asked Coughlin and Kennedy to stay for dinner, but they declined. To the press, Roosevelt dismissed the Coughlin summit as merely "a social visit." Asked whether Coughlin was now "back on the reservation," the president replied, "I don't know."[23] Pressed on what part Kennedy played in the encounter, Roosevelt could not resist saying, "I have no idea, except to act as a chauffeur, I guess."

Kennedy and Coughlin drove to Great Barrington, Massachusetts, in the nearby Berkshire Mountains to meet Francis Keelon, a financier and Roman Catholic whom Coughlin hoped would fund his National Union for Social Justice and a national weekly newspaper, *Social Justice*. Meanwhile, Roosevelt asked the Postmaster General and chairman of the Democratic National Committee, James Farley, to investigate Coughlin's finances and explore how the Canadian had become a US citizen.

Despite the Hyde Park powwow, Coughlin's attacks on the president and the New Deal continued. The priest began flirting with the Republicans, claiming that "a renovated Republican Party possessing a contrite heart for its former misdeeds and an honest standard-bearer in whom I could repose complete confidence are all that are necessary to convert this nation from Rooseveltism."[24] Coughlin began discreet negotiations with Hoover, whom, when president, he had castigated as "the banker's friend, the Holy Ghost of the rich, the protective angel of Wall Street," with a view to an electoral pact between the Republicans and his National Union for Social Justice.

The priest's broadcasts increasingly criticized Roosevelt himself. In one, Coughlin boasted, "As I was instrumental in removing Herbert Hoover from the White House, so help me God, I will be instrumental in taking a Communist foe [Roosevelt] from the chair once occupied by Washington."[25] One time he described the president as the "anti-God," at another, as "a liar and a betrayer." He kept up the accusation that Roosevelt was a closet Communist. "The New Deal is surrounded by atheists," he said. "Surrounded by red and pink Communists and by 'frankfurters of destruction'"[26]—a thinly veiled allusion to Roosevelt's Treasury chief, Felix Frankfurter.[27]

Roosevelt and Coughlin met again in the White House on January 8, 1936, and parted without agreement. Again Roosevelt turned to Kennedy to counter the venom emanating from the Shrine of the Little Flower and shore up the Catholic vote. Coughlin asked Kennedy to ask the president to appoint one of his protégés to a federal judgeship in Detroit. Kennedy passed on the name to James Roosevelt with a note saying that "the President will decide whether it is worthwhile to make a gesture to Father Coughlin." No gesture was forthcoming.

Coughlin went back on the attack. As the general election neared, his National Union, under the name Union Party, began nominating candidates and selected a presidential hopeful, William Lemke,[28] a Republican supporter of the New Deal who had not forgiven Roosevelt for opposing his Frazier–Lemke Farm Bankruptcy Act, which would have obliged the federal government to refinance delinquent farm mortgages.

Coughlin went on the stump and vilified the president at every turn, dubbing him "Franklin Double-Crossing Roosevelt," a "liar," and a "great betrayer." "When an upstart dictator in the United States succeeds in making this a one-party form of government, when the ballot is useless, I shall have the courage to stand up and advocate the use of bullets," he said.[29]

With the election only a month away, Kennedy decided to intervene. On October 5, 1936, on Coughlin's old network, CBS, he declared, "I resent the efforts which are now being made for low, political purposes to confuse a Christian program of social justice with a Godless program of Communism." The reference to "social justice" was not lost on the radio audience. If Roosevelt was the dictator some had suggested, Kennedy said, he would surely have closed down free speech. "We could have had a dictatorship in the twinkling of an eye—President Roosevelt's eye. . . . If there were any semblance of Communism or dictatorship or regimentation in this country, the words liar and betrayer would have been uttered only once." He ended by announcing, "I'm for Roosevelt."

Come election day, Roosevelt enjoyed the greatest landslide in America's history: 28 million votes against Republican candidate Alfred Landon's[30] 17 million, and a near-sweep of the electoral college, losing only two small states.[31] Lemke won less than 2 percent of the vote and the Union Party did not win a single seat in the House or Senate.

The day after the election, Coughlin told his supporters, "We have a one-party system now."[32] The priest promised to abandon public life, telling his listeners, "I hereby withdraw from all radio activity in the best interest of the people . . . It is better, both for you and for me, for the country I serve and the Church I love, for me to be forgotten for the moment."[33] Kennedy could claim again that his timely intervention had contributed to the president's victory and the demise of one of his principal enemies, for which he deserved to be suitably rewarded. He still had his eye on the Treasury.

After the election, Roosevelt abruptly discovered the limits of his powers. The year 1937 proved an annus horribilis, as a succession of interrelated events combined to frustrate him. He told assistant attorney general Robert H. Jackson,[34] "I'm sick of sitting here kissing people's asses to get them to do what they ought to be volunteering for the Republic."[35] The trouble stemmed from the Supreme Court striking down key parts of the New Deal legislation as unconstitutional. The president found the defiance of the justices hard to bear and determined he would punish them by curtailing their powers.

Under the guise of helping older judges cope with advancing age, Roosevelt cooked up a plan with the attorney general, Homer Cummings,[36] to have his revenge on the recalcitrant Supreme Court. He would create six new young justices to supplement those aged over seventy, leaving him free to rescind the ruling that parts of the New

Deal were unconstitutional. The president assumed, as did the press and most lawmakers, that Congress would cooperate in executing this vengeful plan.

When, the previous year, Roosevelt had floated the idea of "increasing the number of justices so as to permit the appointment of men in tune with the spirit of the age,"[37] there had been little hostility. Before long, however, Roosevelt was cast as an aspirant dictator undermining the separation of powers guaranteed in the Constitution. There was also stern opposition from the justices; James McReynolds[38] swore that he would "never resign as long as that crippled son-of-a-bitch is in the White House."[39]

Roosevelt persisted, justifying his plan by declaring that the justices were perpetuating the Depression. "The Court has been acting not as a judicial body, but as a policy-making body," he told Americans in a radio "fireside chat." But Roosevelt had not counted on the chairman of the Senate Judiciary Committee, Henry Ashurst of Arizona,[40] a colorful frontiersman whose contorted utterances in the Senate had earned him the title "Five-Syllable Henry" and the "Silver-Tongued Sunbeam of the Painted Desert." But it was his other nickname, the "Dean of Inconsistency," that pointed to the undoing of Roosevelt's plan to pack the Court. After being against it, then for it, then against it, it became clear that the wobbling Ashurst's committee would not recommend the legislation to the full Senate. The president had been defeated.

Roosevelt's attempt to curb the Court yielded some benefit for the administration, as from then on the justices trod more carefully when deeming new legislation unconstitutional. Nor was Roosevelt's popularity much affected; the issue proved too technical to capture the public imagination. But the whole affair demonstrated, for the first time, that Roosevelt was not omnipotent. Speculation over who might follow him into the White House in 1940 increased.

The second crisis of the administration in 1937 was also of Roosevelt's making and arose from his decision to wind down federal government efforts to bolster the faltering economy. When, in the spring of 1937, production, profits, and wages returned to their pre-1929 levels, and unemployment dropped to 14.3 percent from 16.9 percent the previous year, Marriner Eccles,[41] the Federal Reserve chairman, suggested to the president that the New Deal had worked and it was time to return to more orthodox ways of managing the economy. Spending cuts, tax increases, and a credit squeeze were announced as job creation schemes began to be wound up.

By the fall of 1937, however, the economy was heading back into recession and what came to be known as "the Roosevelt Recession" took hold. Industrial production slumped by a third, prices fell by 3.5 percent, and unemployment climbed to 19 percent, or 46 million Americans, through 1938.[42] One day in mid-October, stock prices suffered the worst single-day fall since 1932. Despite attempts by Roosevelt to blame the return to recession on businessmen—the attorney general, Robert H. Jackson, suggested that the New Deal had "set out a breakfast for the canary and let the cat steal it"[43]—the president had made a profound error.

Watching Roosevelt's discomfort was Joe Kennedy. The president had given no indication of his intentions about running again in 1940, but it was assumed he would abide by the convention laid down by Washington, and confirmed by Jefferson, that two presidential terms were the maximum.[44] Kennedy believed the presidency was within his grasp. "He thought he was about the most qualified individual on earth to be President," recalled his aide Harvey Klemmer.[45] "He thought his services had so impressed the country. And there was money behind [a presidential bid] for a gigantic propaganda machine."[46]

There was one significant drawback: Kennedy's Roman Catholicism. There remained widespread prejudice against Catholics, particularly among Democratic voters in the South. In his *Diplomatic Memoir*, not published until after his death, Kennedy went some way toward explaining why he was considering a presidential run. "No one can lightly turn away a serious suggestion from his friends that he is worthy of succeeding to the presidency of the United States," he wrote. "There were many reasons that militated against my candidacy for that office, including my Catholic faith, but even these might be overcome."

Central to his appeal, he felt, was his isolationism. A sincere promise to keep America out of war might, he thought, be popular enough across both parties to compensate for the prejudice against his Catholicism in the Democratic South. Kennedy was also prepared to spend a large portion of his fortune to win the White House. All would depend on whether Roosevelt decided to run.

Kennedy knew that if he were to make a run for the presidency, he needed to remain on good terms with Roosevelt. That is why, in the run-up to the 1936 election, Kennedy had used his money, influence, and personal capital to court favor with Roosevelt and help ensure the president remained in the White House. To have the support of the incumbent would be important if he mounted a presidential bid. In pursuit of that aim, Kennedy had volunteered for the campaign in order to mollify the businessmen who believed the administration was anti-business. He had said he could think "of no more definite symptom of this danger [to democracy] than the unreasoning malicious ill-will displayed by the rich and powerful against their common leader."[47]

Kennedy had asked Krock to ghost-write a pamphlet, "I Am For Roosevelt: A Business Man's Estimate of the New Deal."[48] The president pronounced it "splendid," "of real service," and "a distinct step in sane education of the country" that "will bear good fruit for many years to come."[49] To remind the president that supporting his reelection came at a high personal cost, Kennedy told him, "Some of my friends in the business and financial world have told me . . . I have had my last job from anyone in the business world once the book is published."[50] Kennedy had won praise for the tract, the New York *Daily News* declaring it "the best answer we have yet seen to those who blindly hate President Roosevelt for having saved their shirts and possibly their skins."[51]

Shortly after Roosevelt's reelection in 1936, Kennedy was offered his just reward. The president asked Kennedy to take a wholly unexpected job. Roosevelt was aware that if the increasingly bellicose behavior of the dictators in Germany and Italy led to war that threatened British shipping, America would need a large merchant fleet of its own. In 1936 he had encouraged the passing of the Merchant Marine Act, revamping the inefficient web of federal subsidies that encouraged the building of new merchant ships. Recalling Kennedy's knowledge of shipyard management, in February 1937 the president approached him to chair a new body, the Maritime Commission, to oversee the construction drive.

When the job was offered, Kennedy feigned a lack of interest, suggesting it was Roosevelt's charm, not his own ambition, that led him to accept: "I can say no to that fellow on the telephone, but face to face he gets me."[52] But there was also a selfish motive. If he were to stand for president, Kennedy would need to display more experience in government than simply the SEC chairmanship. "I felt I was through with the Government service," Kennedy wrote Roosevelt in his acceptance letter, "but if you feel that I can be of any help at all in the present situation, of course, I am delighted to serve."[53]

Kennedy negotiated a new lease on Marwood and resumed his old Washington routine. While he had acquired a reputation for competence and courage at the SEC, it soon became clear that the Maritime Commission was a cursed chalice. There was an urgent need for America to build ships fast, if the new merchant fleet was to be ready before war broke out in Europe. And the current US merchant fleet was in such bad shape that 85 percent of its ships would have to be replaced within five years.

Yet Kennedy soon discovered that the recently passed legislation was inadequate and perhaps unworkable. Both shipowners and the trade union representing merchant seamen were populated by small-minded men so caught up in their own worlds that they did not grasp the national emergency they were expected to meet. Kennedy was unhappy. For once, his dynamism was met with inertia. When an obstructionist union leader questioned his right to manage the industry, Kennedy called up Frances Perkins,[54] Roosevelt's labor secretary, and told her "not to send any more bums like that in here trying to tell me what my authority is."[55]

With Roosevelt's friend Morgenthau running the economy, the Treasury still seemed beyond Kennedy's reach, but in the fall of 1937 news arrived that the American ambassador in London, Robert Worth Bingham, was profoundly ill and likely to resign. Bingham was suffering from abdominal Hodgkin's disease, a pernicious form of lymph-node cancer. Kennedy lost little time in recruiting James Roosevelt to suggest him for the London job.

At first, Roosevelt did not take the request seriously. "When I passed [Kennedy's request] on to Father, he laughed so hard he almost toppled from his wheelchair," recalled James.[56] After sleeping on the idea, Roosevelt appeared to change his mind. First Kennedy was summoned to the Oval Office to show off his knees, then he was called back to talk with Roosevelt and the starchy secretary of state Cordell Hull, who was far from convinced that an Irish American multimillionaire known for his isolationist views was a good fit for such a sensitive job.

Roosevelt spoke to Kennedy about a recent event in the news: a new member of the Supreme Court, Hugo Black, had failed to reveal that he had been a Ku Klux Klan member. Asked about the propriety of hiding such damning information, Kennedy offered a disarming response. "If Marlene Dietrich asked you to make love to her," he said, "would you tell her you weren't much good at making love?"[57] While the president laughed out loud at Kennedy's vulgar candor, the straight-laced Hull was aghast.

After the meeting, the president had all but made up his mind that it would be good politics to send Kennedy to London when he alighted on an alternative post he thought would suit Kennedy just as well, that of commerce secretary. James put the idea to Kennedy but was told it was the ambassadorship or nothing. There was method in Kennedy's thinking.

His enormous wealth meant he could fund his own presidential bid,[58] and he believed that the combination of his service to the Democratic Party and his high-level federal government posts qualified him to succeed the president. He had spent his time in Washington cultivating congressmen and the press. Despite his public displays of loyalty to Roosevelt, he had taken the precaution of maintaining good relations with the president's enemies, such as Hearst and Coughlin, in the event that they might prove useful. Even when Coughlin had roasted the president in the summer, Kennedy had written thanking the priest "for all the kind things you are saying about me. I feel like the fellow on his vacation who sends the postal card back to his friends saying, 'Wish you were here'."[59]

Kennedy's résumé was missing foreign policy experience, which is why the London ambassadorship was so appealing. As ambassador to the Court of St. James, Kennedy could acquire foreign expertise by dealing with the world's leaders at a turning point in history. He could express his isolationist viewpoint from within the administration, which would demonstrate an independent turn of mind.

Kennedy's isolationism was more than opportunism. A businessman before all else, he believed that America should remain aloof from the world's conflicts the better to benefit from the profitable opportunities presented by war. As an Irish American, he was reluctant to bolster Britain's efforts to appease the dictators. As he explained, he "could not forgive those who had been responsible for sending the infamous Black and Tans into rebellious Ireland."[60] Above all, Kennedy was aware that the vast majority of American voters were anxious to keep out of war. Who better to represent isolationists in the administration than an arch-isolationist?

The key to Kennedy's ambition at this stage was to keep his presidential ambitions to himself. Interviewed at the time of "Why I'm for Roosevelt," he declared, "I have no political ambitions for myself or for my children."[61] Few believed him. Kennedy's coyness on the issue certainly did not fool Roosevelt, who was also obliged to disguise his own intentions about a third term lest he set off an alarm that would limit his options. He, too, obfuscated when asked whether he would run in 1940, though there was widespread speculation that he would. In September 1937, *Liberty* magazine asked commentators who the Democratic candidate in 1940 would be. Roosevelt's aide Stephen Early[62] reported to the president, "The survey shows a surprising and overwhelming belief that you will be the nominee and the first third-term President."[63]

Whether to send Kennedy to London was therefore part of a broader calculation by Roosevelt about leaving his options open for contesting the 1940 election, second only to his assessment of how soon, as seemed likely, the dictators would drag the democracies into war. The president mostly kept his own counsel. To maximize his room for maneuver, he rarely touched on fundamental political matters with anyone. But in the interstices of his private letters to his dearest friends, Roosevelt's views were becoming clear.

In a cryptic observation to Colonel House on Germany's secret rearmament program, Roosevelt wrote in June 1937, "In all foreign relations the 'prognosis' is better than a few months ago but the patient will die of the 'armament disease' in a few years unless a major operation is performed."[64]

In the "quarantine" speech in Chicago on October 5, 1937, Roosevelt tested public opinion. "The peace of the world and the welfare and security of every nation, including our own, is today being threatened," he declared.[65] While there was little opposition to his pessimistic tour d'horizon, Roosevelt played down the speech. As expected, his words were well received in London, Paris, and Moscow and greeted with disdain in Tokyo and Berlin. The response from the isolationists was as swift as it was predictable.

Reminding readers that Roosevelt was the true heir of Wilson, Hearst's *Boston Herald* trumpeted, "Americans will not be stampeded into going 3,000 miles across water to save [the democracies]. Crusade, if you must, but for the sake of several millions of American mothers, confine your crusading to the continental limits of America!"[66] Six leading pacifist groups accused the president of wanting to draw America into war.

Roosevelt expressed surprise to House, Woodrow Wilson's foreign affairs adviser, that the "quarantine" speech had not elicited more criticism. "I verily believe that as time goes by we can slowly but surely make people realize that war will be a greater danger to us if we close all the doors and windows than if we go out in the street and use our influence to curb the riot," he wrote.[67]

Another friend Roosevelt felt he could confide in was his old Groton headmaster, Endicott Peabody.[68] Roosevelt wrote:

> I am fighting against a public psychology of long standing—a psychology which comes very close to saying, "Peace at any price." I have felt, however, that there will be a growing response to the ideal that when a few nations fail to maintain certain fundamental rules of conduct, the most practical and most peaceful thing to do in the long run is to "quarantine" them. I am inclined to think that this is more Christian, as well as more practical, than that the world should go to war with them.[69]

Ambassador Bingham sailed home from Britain at the end of November for urgent surgery in New York and resigned the ambassadorship on December 8. The same day, the White House leaked the Kennedy appointment to the *New York Times*. Still, the president kept Kennedy waiting. By unhappy coincidence, Kennedy was that evening entertaining White House correspondents and their spouses to dinner. His response to their persistent enquiries was, "It sounds like just one of those things."[70] He ordered the waiters to keep everyone's glasses full, while sticking to water himself lest he become indiscreet.

But he confided to the Hollywood censor, Joseph Breen,[71] that the ambassadorship was in the bag and complained in advance that "London is cold, dreary and foggy."[72] He wrote to Woodrow Wilson's former secretary, Joseph Tumulty,[73] "Although I have not received the appointment . . . I would like to tell you that under the law of inherent probability I may."[74]

When Roosevelt finally announced the appointment, it was not universally welcomed. Senator James F. Byrnes,[75] a fellow Irish American, objected because the international situation was so delicate with "wars and rumors of wars" that "I do not believe you can promote peace on earth by sending an Irishman to London." Then Byrnes changed his mind, joking that he would send the new ambassador a copy of a book on etiquette by Emily Post "to assist him in qualifying for service at Saint James and for entrance to the sacred portals of Claridge's."[76]

Kennedy wrote to Byrnes, "I haven't any idea how well I will get along abroad, either from the point of view of doing very much for the country, or doing a job of which my friends will feel proud, but if I don't get the results that I feel are necessary I would get out at once." To maintain the fiction that the London appointment was no more than an opportunity to serve the nation, he assured Byrnes, "I have never had political ambitions and have none now. I am only vitally concerned with where we are headed."[77]

For the president, Kennedy's appointment was a canny ruse. Removing the slippery, super-rich Bostonian from the domestic scene would hamper Kennedy's plans for a presidential run, so long as he stayed put in London. Once there, he would need the president's consent to return. It was little wonder that when Dorothy Schiff,[78] owner of the liberal *New York Post*, dined privately at Hyde Park with Franklin, Eleanor, and Sara Roosevelt, the president merely shook his head when his wife referred to "that awful Joe Kennedy."[79] Exiling Kennedy to London, Roosevelt thought, was "a great joke, the greatest joke in the world."[80]

CHAPTER FOUR

CLIVEDEN AND
WINDSOR CASTLE

The Kennedys take London, Joseph Kennedy
befriends Neville Chamberlain, joins the Cliveden Set,
stays with the King at Windsor Castle, and prepares for
a presidential run. Hitler invades Austria.
Franklin Roosevelt springs his trap.

HAVING LANDED HIMSELF the London ambassadorship, Kennedy showed little appetite for taking up the post. It was a full six weeks between his appointment and his lone departure for England on February 23 aboard the *Manhattan*. Rose, admitted to the hospital with appendicitis, stayed behind with all nine Kennedy children.

Before he set out, Kennedy visited Roosevelt in Hyde Park to understand what his role in London amounted to. One concern was the division in the British government over how to deal with the dictators. Two days before, the government of prime minister Neville Chamberlain[1] had been shaken by the resignation of its young foreign secretary, Anthony Eden,[2] who opposed Chamberlain's policy of recognizing the Italian conquests in Ethiopia and was alarmed by Italian troops being sent to fight against the Republican government in Spain.

Roosevelt instructed his new ambassador to stay within the bounds of the diplomatic corps he was joining, to keep his personal views to himself, and not to jeopardize America's freedom to act. Kennedy concluded from the meeting that the president's "firm intention of keeping our country out of any and all involvements or commitments abroad"[3] meant that as ambassador he would be free to tell the British they could not expect help if they waged war.

The president's close confidant and Dutchess County gentleman farmer neighbor, Treasury secretary Henry Morgenthau Jr., wrote in his diary that Roosevelt "considered Kennedy a very dangerous man and that he was going to send him to England as Ambassador with the distinct understanding that the appointment was only good for six months and that, furthermore, by giving him this appointment, any obligation that he had to Kennedy was paid for." Morgenthau subscribed to the general assumption that Kennedy would not last long in London and that if he was to mount a presidential run he would have to return to America some time during 1939.

As with his job at the SEC and the Maritime Commission, after a year in a new post Kennedy tended to become itchy. If he was to run in the Democratic presidential primaries, he would have to return to the United States by early 1940. He was so rich that he did not need to raise money to campaign, but he needed time to buy an organization and scare off competitors. That gave him less than two years in the London post. He primed his close colleagues that he would not be away for long. "I haven't any idea how well I will get along abroad," he told his confidant Jimmy Byrnes, "but if I don't get the results that I feel are necessary I would get out at once."[4]

The ambassador conveyed the same message, posing as modesty, at the first off-the-record briefing he gave in London to American reporters. He joked that the length of his stay would depend on how they reported his progress. Stressing that he only "temporarily" enjoyed the president's confidence, he suggested that it was just a matter of time before Roosevelt called him home. "I hope all you boys will be down to see me off when I am recalled," he joked.[5]

The likely briefness of Kennedy's new appointment became a standing joke in his messages home. "Well, old boy," he wrote to James Roosevelt, "I may not last long over here, but it is going to be fast and furious."[6] Anxious about the damage Kennedy could wreak upon America's standing, Morgenthau asked Roosevelt whether it was not a risk to send a known isolationist and vocal critic of the administration to London, where his actions would be beyond control. "I have made arrangements to have Joe Kennedy watched hourly," Roosevelt replied. "The first time he opens his mouth and criticizes me, I will fire him."[7]

As Morgenthau recalled, "He said two or three times, 'Kennedy is too dangerous to have around here.'"[8] While the wily Morgenthau understood the depth of antipathy in which the president held Kennedy, for once he failed to understand the extent of the humiliation the president had in store for his would-be successor. Kennedy was keenly aware that he would be closely watched. He told the press crammed into his stateroom before setting sail for London, "I'm just a babe being thrown into . . ." to which, before he could finish, a wag added, "the lion's mouth?"[9] Kennedy beamed in agreement.

Kennedy did arrive plumb in the lion's mouth, but not quite as he imagined. Britain was in a state of high tension. The international situation was deteriorating by the day and war crept ever closer. The Spanish Civil War dragged on, Italian forces pressed their advantage in Ethiopia, Japanese troops continued to penetrate Manchuria, and Germany's Nazi government was casting envious eyes toward Austria, Czechoslovakia, and Poland. London was full of talk of war and rumor of war, just as in 1913–14, the year leading to World War One. As Margaret L. Coit, the biographer of Roosevelt's friend the independent financier and freelance statesman Bernard Baruch,[10] put it, "England was dancing, dancing in the great country houses, their doors flung open now for the last time, gardens festooned with girls who would vanish in blitz and fire."[11] The new ambassador's second son, John F. Kennedy,[12] recalled, "You had the feeling of an era ending, and everyone had a very good time at the end."[13]

On November 5, 1937, Hitler had informed a secret conference of German military and diplomatic leaders in the Reich Chancellery in Berlin of his intention to invade Austria, Czechoslovakia, Lithuania, and Poland.[14] Roosevelt's aim of keeping America out of war and Ambassador Kennedy's insistence that war was unnecessary and therefore unthinkable were about to be put to the test. It was telling that Roosevelt did not confide in Kennedy that in January 1938 he had privately proposed to prime minister Neville Chamberlain that he, the president, host a summit in Washington of world leaders, including the dictators, to draw out Hitler's and Mussolini's intentions and demonstrate America's commitment to democracy and international order. To Roosevelt's amazement, on January 14 Chamberlain declined the offer. As the prime minister had said after Roosevelt's "quarantine" speech, "It is always best and safest to count on nothing from the Americans but words."[15]

Kennedy landed in Plymouth, England, on March 1, and no sooner had he settled himself into the ambassador's residence, the sumptuous thirty-six-room former home of the banker John Pierpont Morgan at 14 Prince's Gate, Kensington, than he was summoned to 10 Downing Street to meet Chamberlain, whom he instantly found congenial company. The prime minister was a forbidding, starchy character that few even in his immediate circle found approachable. Yet Kennedy judged him to be "a strong, decisive man, evidently in full charge of the situation here." But Kennedy gave the prime minister no encouragement. He told him, "The United States must not be counted upon to back Great Britain in any scrape, right or wrong. . . . I talked to him quite plainly and he seemed to take it well."[16]

Kennedy discovered in Chamberlain a fellow trader; the prime minister was the son of the archetypal Midlands businessman Joseph Chamberlain,[17] and his views on trade and commerce were similar to Kennedy's own. The Conservative Party was largely populated at the top by landowners and aristocrats, leading Chamberlain proudly to declare that "although I cannot boast of the blueness in my veins or of the fame of my forebears, I am yet prouder of being descended from these respectable tradesmen than if my ancestors had worn shining armor and carried great swords."[18]

Kennedy recognized in Chamberlain one of his own. He understood the mercantilist approach to politics and told Cordell Hull he felt close to the prime minister because he could "talk Chamberlain's language."[19] Kennedy biographer Richard J. Whalen wrote of Chamberlain, "He plunged into foreign affairs with the boundless goodwill and ignorance of a banker who believed that two parties always could be reconciled, if only the terms of trade were made sufficiently attractive."[20] Before long, while carefully maintaining the fiction that he was close to the president, Kennedy was able to boast, "I'm just like that with Chamberlain. Why, Franklin himself isn't as confidential with me."[21] Getting on well with Chamberlain aside, Kennedy also found he liked—though he thought him a little chilly—the new foreign secretary, Lord Halifax,[22] whom Ickes described as "tall and spare with ascetic features. He gives the impression of being a zealot."[23]

Chamberlain's foreign policy was one of appeasement, though the word had not yet assumed the sense of naïve, feckless, cowardly accommodation of evil it was to acquire. As Hull explained, "The word 'appeasement' appeared frequently in dispatches from London, though it had not then begun to bear the opprobrium later given it. It still meant honest, however mistaken, efforts to reach peaceful agreements with the dictators to prevent their plunging the world into war."[24] Chamberlain, like Roosevelt, was aware that the memory of World War One persisted and that it was good politics to try to meet the dictators' demands in a way that would not draw Britain into another war. More than 900,000 Britons had been killed in the Great War and the more than two million who returned home wounded were reminders of the horrors of the conflict.[25] (American isolationist sentiment was underpinned by the memory of comparatively few: 116,515 Americans killed and 204,002 wounded.)

There was also a belief among the appeasers that Fascism was preferable to Communism and that if accommodated Hitler would destroy Bolshevism in Russia. It was believed by distinguished British public figures, such as the economist John Maynard Keynes, that Germany had been poorly treated by Versailles and that some of Hitler's complaints, particularly about German minorities caught behind border revisions, were valid. In his Commons resignation speech, Eden made clear that he remained an appeaser, though a robust one. "We cannot make progress in European appeasement . . . if we allow the impression to gain currency abroad that we yield to constant pressure," he said.[26]

As well as ingratiating himself with political leaders, Kennedy made certain to charm the London press, reminding them that "right now [the average American] is more interested in how he is going to eat and whether his insurance is good, than in foreign politics."[27] It was an early indication that Kennedy would be peddling his own isolationist line, in defiance of the president's ambiguous statements about the prospect of war.

Kennedy soon discovered that disloyalty worked both ways. At a luncheon with the socialist Harold Laski,[28] the London School of

Economics professor who taught both Kennedy's sons, Joe Jr. and John, Kennedy heard that the president, in a letter to Laski, had made unflattering remarks about him. Kennedy was hurt that Roosevelt's suspicion of him was becoming public knowledge in London. Kennedy was further reminded that some back home did not wish him well when, at a cocktail party, he heard that the president's close confidant Harry Hopkins,[29] the WPA administrator, had written in a private letter that the president believed "that Kennedy, while a great fellow, was also a sharp operator who would bear watching."[30]

After barely a week in London, Kennedy convinced himself there was no war on the horizon, despite growing evidence of German bellicosity. Hitler was pressing Austria to redraw its borders so that "German" Austrians could live in the Third Reich. But when, on March 9, in a courageous act of defiance, the Austrian Chancellor Kurt Schuschnigg[31] announced a referendum that he was confident would reject German annexation, Kennedy failed to take sides. He wrote in his diary, "No general war is visible in the immediate future."[32]

The following day, Kennedy lunched with Winston Churchill,[33] Britain's most articulate opponent of the dictators, who believed that war in Europe was both inevitable and imminent. In typically colorful language, Churchill told Kennedy that the British lion would have "its tail wrung" if it condoned Italian aggression in Ethiopia and that the smaller European nations would be placed on notice. Churchill warned Kennedy that Germany was fast rearming and that instead of appeasing Hitler, Britain needed to stand firm against his increasingly impossible demands.[34]

Still Kennedy believed war could be averted. "Nobody is going to fight a war over here unless Germany starts shooting somebody," he wrote Roosevelt on March 11.[35] "Hitler and Mussolini, having done so very well for themselves by bluffing, they are not going to stop bluffing until somebody very sharply calls their bluff."[36] The very next day, March 12, Hitler anticipated Schuschnigg's referendum and imposed the Anschluss (German for "annexation"), absorbing Austria into the Third Reich. As German troops streamed across the undefended border, Austrians cheered and festooned them with flowers.

It was with American voters in mind that Kennedy drafted an

address to the London Pilgrims Society, an Anglo-American body "to foster better Anglo-American relationships through cooperation of top banking and manufacturing institutions," that by convention was always the first audience to hear from a new American ambassador. Instead of the usual bromides, Kennedy was intent on "saying something and thereby breaking a precedent of many years' standing."[37] Although he had assured members of the American Correspondents' Association that he "had no political aspirations whatever and any reports they had seen to the contrary were unfounded," he described his Pilgrims speech as "intended primarily for home consumption,"[38] making clear to Americans reading reports of the speech that he believed it would not serve America's interests to be sucked into another European war. As was the custom, a draft was sent back to the State Department for approval.

Kennedy's speech alarmed secretary of state Cordell Hull, who thought it "too isolationist in its every implication"[39] and, in a diplomatic dispatch of March 14, declared the wording "subject to [more] possible misinterpretation than would appear advisable."[40] He demanded changes, adding, to ensure his instructions were carried out, that the president "heartily approves" of his intervention. Kennedy was told to cut the sentence, "It is only when our vital interests are definitely affected that we are moved to action," and the line, "The United States, as this now stands, has no plans to seek or offer assistance in the event that war . . . should break out in the world."[41] Despite Hull's cuts, Kennedy's isolationist message was clear: the Brits shouldn't count on America to bail them out of war. It was not what the anxious four hundred listening in the audience wanted to hear.

On March 16, Kennedy was visited by Waldorf Astor,[42] an American-born multimillionaire turned British Conservative politician and owner of the *Observer*. Astor was eager to let the ambassador know that, in light of the Austrian occupation, "some of the leading men [in Britain] believe that immediate war is a greater danger than they like to let the public know."[43] Kennedy promptly called Hull and suggested that the secretary of state put off a speech he was about to give that fired a shot across Hitler's bows. Irritated by Kennedy's presumption, Hull ignored the advice and told the National Press Club in Washington on March 17 of America's earnest intention to rearm "to work for law, order, morality, and justice throughout the world." He rejected the appeal of America as "a self-constituted hermit state." "We may seek to withdraw from participation in world affairs," Hull declared, "but we cannot thereby withdraw from the world itself. Isolation is not a means to security; it is a fruitful source of insecurity."[44]

To keep his name before American decision-makers, opinion-formers, and primary voters, on March 21 Kennedy began sending long round-robins giving his explanation of what was going on in Europe and what America's response should be. The missives, marked "private and confidential," were sometimes tailored to flatter a specific mover or shaker. Among many others on Kennedy's list were prominent isolationists such as Hearst and known isolationist lawmakers, in particular members of the House and Senate foreign relations committees; newspaper proprietors such as Roy Howard, who ran Scripps–Howard newspapers; columnist Walter Lippmann; Hearst's obedient general manager T. J. White; Arthur Krock, who, although the *New York Times*'s most prominent Washington reporter, was on Kennedy's payroll; the financier Bernard Baruch; senators Burton K. Wheeler, Pat Harrison, and Key Pittman; the president's confidant Senator James Byrnes; Supreme Court justice and New Deal opponent James McReynolds; and the president's son James.[45] The president was conspicuously not on the list.

The first thousand-word dispatch referred to "my speech before the Pilgrims. I worked very hard on it and intended it to reassure my friends and critics alike that I have not as yet been taken into the British camp. It seemed to me that it was imperative, just now, to tell our British cousins that they must not get into a mess counting on us to bail them out."[46] On reading the missive, Borah, chairman of the Senate Foreign Affairs Committee, commended the ambassador for his acuity. Kennedy immediately replied, "The more I see of things here, the more convinced I am that we must exert all of our intelligence and effort toward keeping clear of any involvement. As long as I hold my present job, I shall never lose sight of that guiding principle."[47]

Eager to continue to stress his differences over war policy with the administration, on March 28, even as Hitler began pressing for the Sudeten "Germans" living in Czechoslovakia to be consumed by the Reich, Kennedy sent out a second dispatch. Czechoslovakia was a new state created by the 1919 Treaty of Saint-Germain in the wake of World War One. The Sudetenland, the Czech region that bordered Germany, was inhabited by 3.5 million German speakers, many of whom were Nazi sympathizers.

"I can't see how anyone could (a) believe that a general war will break out during the remainder of this year or (b) could figure it would affect the United States very adversely if it did," he wrote, before predicting that "a deal will be made with Italy [allowing it to keep its Ethiopian conquests] . . . Germany will get whatever it wants in Czechoslovakia. . . . The Czechs will go, hat in hand, to Berlin and ask the Führer what he wants done and it will be done." As a former stock trader, Kennedy could not resist pointing out the chilling truth that "a few more months of depression of values will have us and the rest of the world so deeply in the doghouse that war might seem to be an attractive way out."[48]

Compared to the ominous daily news from around the globe, the arrival on the USS *Washington* on March 17 of six more members of the handsome, broadly smiling Kennedy clan—Rose, eighteen-year-old Kathleen (known as Kick), thirteen-year-old Pat, twelve-year-old Bobby, ten-year-old Jean, six-year-old Teddy, and later twenty-two-year-old Joe Jr., a Harvard senior, twenty-year-old John, a Harvard sophomore, nineteen-year-old Rosemary, and sixteen-year-old Eunice[49]—offered Londoners some much needed light relief. Primed by the ambassador's press agent, *New York Times* State Department reporter Harold Hinton, who worked under Krock, Fleet Street welcomed the Kennedys as if they were visiting Hollywood stars. It was the beginning of a Kennedy cult that was to last for the rest of the century.

Newsreel cameras filmed their antics, photographs of them graced the society pages, and their escapades at parties filled the gossip columns. "King George Asks to See Kennedy's Nine Children" and "Queen Talks Babies with Mrs. Kennedy" were typical headlines. Rose recalled that Fleet Street "seemed fascinated by the idea of a large and lively Boston Irish family descending on the London diplomatic scene."[50] Surrounded by his wife and children, a beaming Kennedy told reporters, "Now I've got everything. London will be just grand."[51]

More importantly for Kennedy's presidential ambitions, Henry Luce's[52] *Life* magazine joined in the feeding frenzy. Under the headline "The Nine Kennedy Kids Delight Great Britain," *Life* reported, "The Kennedy Kids are nine. If Father Joseph Patrick Kennedy ever gets to be President, he will owe almost as much to that fact as to the abilities which earned him $9,000,000. England has taken them all, including extremely pretty and young-looking Mrs. Kennedy, to its heart."[53] Kennedy himself could not have written it better.

The Kennedys' arrival in London coincided with a most unusual time. The complacent world of high society was still in some turmoil following the abdication a little over a year before of King Edward VIII over his love for the twice-divorced American Wallis Simpson.[54] Many of the city's most prominent hostesses found themselves on the wrong side, supporting the king against the government, and were obliged to pay a heavy price when the throne was passed to Edward's brother, George VI.[55] Suddenly they found they were no longer receiving official invitations and their influence was waning.

One who had escaped embarrassment was an energetic Virginian, Nancy Astor, who, on the ennoblement of her husband, Waldorf, in 1918, had succeeded him as a member of Parliament. She liked to bring government ministers and diplomats together at weekends at Cliveden House, the Astors' vast country home in Buckinghamshire, to the west of London.[56] Nowhere was the prospect of war more earnestly addressed than in the margins of the hospitality lavished by the Astors. Nancy liked to collect notable people and counted herself a friend of everyone from Mahatma Gandhi and Charles Chaplin to George Bernard Shaw, Rudyard Kipling, and T. E. Lawrence.

Nancy Astor took an immediate shine to Rose when they met at the American Women's Club on March 30. Rose recalled, "[Nancy] is great fun anyplace, talks about everything, anything, intelligently and with gusto and with an inexhaustible sense of humor." Within the week, the Kennedys were dining with the Astors at their palatial London residence in the corner of St. James's Square, sharing a table with Winston and Clementine Churchill and the head of the Anglican church, the Archbishop of Canterbury. Churchill, however, was an odd man out at the Astors', as he condemned appeasement at every turn.

Soon enough, the Kennedys were invited to Cliveden. On the

face of it, to be the guest of an Anglo-American aristocrat mixing with ministers and prominent members of the British ruling class was an innocent enough pastime. The Kennedys were used to being shunned by Boston WASPs because of their Irish descent, and to be treated regally by the British upper crust was a belated vindication of their social standing. What could go wrong?

At the center of those who attended Cliveden parties in 1938 were a group of friends who, having served on the staff of the High Commissioner for Southern Africa, Lord Milner,[57] had joined forces. To varying degrees, each shared Waldorf Astor's anti-Semitism and Nancy Astor's belief that war could be averted if only the democracies were to accommodate the dictators' wishes. There was Lord Lothian,[58] a friend of Astor's since undergraduate days at New College, Oxford, who had tipped off the *Washington Post* that Edward VIII was having an affair with Wallis Simpson. Sympathetic to the Germans, he thought the Versailles Treaty a travesty, and when in March 1936 Hitler ordered troops into the Rhineland he defended the action, saying, "After all, they are only going into their own back garden."[59]

There was the arch-appeaser Sir Nevile Henderson,[60] British ambassador in Berlin, whose view of German bellicosity was, "If we handle [Hitler] right, my belief is that he will become gradually more pacific. But if we treat him as a pariah or mad dog we shall turn him finally and irrevocably into one."[61] An almost permanent fixture was Geoffrey Dawson,[62] editor of Waldorf's brother Gavin's newspaper, *The Times*, the house organ of the British establishment that relentlessly promoted appeasement. He once confessed, "I do my utmost, night after night, to keep out of the paper anything that might hurt [readers'] susceptibilities."[63]

Another Cliveden fixture was Lord Halifax, an Oxford friend of Waldorf's, whose devotion to avoiding war had commended him to Chamberlain as the obvious successor to Eden in the Foreign Office. Halifax had been invited to a hunting party in Germany by the Nazi minister of aviation Hermann Göring the previous November, and in a meeting with Hitler suggested that while Chamberlain's government thought German designs upon parts of Austria, Czechoslovakia, and Poland were illegitimate, adjustments to borders might be achieved by negotiation.

Joe Kennedy's views were entirely compatible with the hard core of appeasers he met at Cliveden, but his embassy staff would have done him a favor if they had drawn his attention to what the press and many opponents of appeasement felt about the company the Astors kept and the role they played in orchestrating Chamberlain's policy. In November 1937, Claud Cockburn,[64] a former *Times* journalist and Communist, wrote in his pamphlet *The Week* that the clique around the Astors were discreetly conducting diplomatic negotiations with the Third Reich at Cliveden.[65] Few took notice of the report.

The following month, Cockburn returned to the subject under the heading "The Cliveden Set," Britain's "other Foreign Office," and the soubriquet soon captured the public imagination. As Cockburn recalled, "The thing went off like a rocket."[66] "Within a couple of weeks [the notion that Cliveden was a nest of appeasers] had been printed in dozens of leading newspapers, and within six had been used in almost every leading newspaper of the Western world. Up and down the British Isles, across and across the United States, anti-Nazi orators shouted it from hundreds of platforms. No anti-Fascist rally in Madison Square Garden or Trafalgar Square was complete without denunciation of the Cliveden Set."[67] The British liberal paper *Reynolds News* described the Cliveden Set as "Britain's Secret Rulers" and the most influential cartoonist of the day, David Low of the *Evening Standard*, dubbed the Astors and their friends the "Shiver Sisters," whose motto was "Any sort of Peace at any sort of Price." In one cartoon he portrayed Nancy Astor at the front door of Cliveden with her arm outstretched in a Hitlerian salute.[68]

Cockburn may have exaggerated the extent of influence over British foreign policy exerted by those attending Cliveden weekends, but the description stuck.[69] Before long, American papers, too, were reporting the antics of the Cliveden Set and drawing attention to the fact that Joe and Rose Kennedy were an integral part of it. Most damaging was a piece in the influential "Washington Merry-Go-Round" gossip column by Drew Pearson and Robert S. Allen,[70] syndicated by Scripps–Howard. "Latest American to be wooed by the Clivedon [sic] group is genial Joe Kennedy, new Ambassador to Britain. Reports are that Joe has been taken in just a bit by the Clivedon charm."

Kennedy was incensed and sent the pair a cable: "Your story on the Cliveden Set is complete bunk. There is not one single word of truth in it and it has done me a great deal of harm."[71] Kennedy complained to Pearson and Allen, "I have never been to Cliveden, and I have seen very little of the persons who go to make up that so-called 'set'."[72] His indignation, however, was short-lived. In a billet-doux to Nancy Astor at the beginning of May, he wrote, "You see what a terrible woman you are, and how a poor little fellow like me is being politically seduced. O weh ist mir!"[73] The damage, however, had been done. Not only had Kennedy found new friends among the principal appeasers, he was now closely associated in the public mind with Chamberlain and his submissive approach to Hitler's aggression.

This perception was reinforced by a meeting on April 24 between Chamberlain and the Nazi leader of the Sudetenland, Konrad Henlein,[74] to sound out Britain's response to his demand to redraw the map of Czechoslovakia. Instead of the prime minister and the Sudeten pretender meeting at Downing Street or the Foreign Office, the Astors hosted the meeting at Cliveden.

Kennedy's part in the Cliveden kerfuffle did not escape the White House. At the end of March, Roosevelt teased his ambassador about being seduced by the Brits. "When you feel that British accent creeping up on you and your trousers riding up to the knee, take the first steamer home," he wrote.[75] Despite Kennedy's insistence that his Irish ancestry would inoculate him from what he called "British wiles," his head was soon turned when he fell under the spell of King George and Queen Elizabeth.

"We all went to a ball last night given by Lady Astor for the King and Queen," he wrote his sister Loretta. "You would have had a lot of fun watching your little brother having the first dance with the Duchess of Kent and the second with Queen Elizabeth."[76] Within two weeks of the president's note, Kennedy and his wife were invited to spend the weekend at the royal couple's weekend retreat, Windsor Castle, where fellow guests included Chamberlain and Halifax.

Kennedy's diary betrays how impressed he was by his new friends' lifestyle. He and Rose "were shown to a beautiful sitting room" hung with "gorgeous paintings" before changing into black tie for a sumptuous dinner. "I sat on the Queen's right," he boasted to his diary. "She was dressed in pearls and on her left sat the Prime Minister. On my right sat Lady Halifax, Lady-in-Waiting to the Queen." Rose sat on the right of the king and made small talk about her children.

Late that night, Rose wrote in her diary, "I must be dreaming that I, Rose Kennedy, a simple young matron from Boston, am really here at Windsor Castle, the guest of the queen and two little princesses."[77] To her daughter Pat, she wrote, "We have just spent a most delightful day here after a very brilliant dinner party last night. I sat on the right of the King, and I was so thrilled," adding in a PS, "Please keep this note, dear."[78] While dressing in black tie for dinner in their regal suite at the castle, Kennedy turned to his wife and said, "Well, Rose, this is a hell of a long way from East Boston, isn't it?"[79]

After just a couple of months in London, Kennedy felt he had acquired enough foreign policy experience to impress lawmakers back home. He suggested to Krock that "it would be a very helpful thing if agitation could be started to have me address the Senate and House Foreign Relations Committees."[80] Meantime, he used the embassy to forge alliances with visiting Americans. Any dignitary or journalist passing through London was given a generous welcome, to impress upon them that Kennedy was now not merely a politician of standing but a fully-fledged statesman.

The influential columnist Walter Lippmann was given the treatment, as was Henry Luce, the founder of *Time* magazine, and the *New York Times* owner Arthur Sulzberger. Part of the quid pro quo between Kennedy and Krock was that they should advance each other's careers at every turn. With Sulzberger a captive guest, Kennedy pressed Krock's case to be the next editor in chief of the *New York Times*.

One Roosevelt ally who passed through London and witnessed Kennedy's none-too-subtle game was Harold Ickes, on honeymoon in London with his young bride, Jane. Ickes found Kennedy "most cordial and hospitable." He was "enjoying his job" and "having the time of his life," though "he appears to have been taken in hand by Lady Astor and the Cliveden Set" and seemed "very nervous over the entire European situation."

Ickes and his wife went to a dinner thrown by the Kennedys in honor of the king's brother, Prince George, Duke of Kent, and his wife, Marina, where Ickes was pleased to see close up the by now infamous Nancy Astor. Ickes noted, "She may have been a famous beauty once but she gives no impression of beauty now. I did not care for her. She seemed nervous and fussy, quite in contrast to the English women present."[81]

There had been rumors in the American papers all spring that Kennedy was plotting a presidential run. On March 15, the ides of March, the *Washington Post* reported that Kennedy stood "an excellent chance to be the first Catholic president"[82] and noted "he has the nearest to a Rooseveltian personality among the viziers."[83] Other papers piled on. The *Boston Globe* described Kennedy as one of the most able American men, his most glaring fault being his empathy with the common man. "He is too regular to be a politician," the paper noted. "His expressed insight into human nature would probably cause a riot on the stump. But this country will either select a next President of the Kennedy type—or it will wish it had."[84]

Not to be outdone, the New York *Daily News* declared Kennedy "the Crown Prince of the Roosevelt regime—FDR's personal selection as his successor."[85] The idea that Kennedy might make a presidential run was widespread in Britain, too. In April, Ickes was told by a British member of Parliament, Colonel Josiah Wedgwood,[86] who was "quite out of sympathy with Chamberlain's foreign policy" and "doesn't think very much of Kennedy," that it was a little-kept secret in London that Kennedy had his eyes on the White House. Ickes told his diary: "At a time when we should be sending the best that we have to Great Britain we have not done so. We have sent a rich man, untrained in diplomacy, unlearned in history and politics, who is a great publicity seeker and who is apparently ambitious to be the first Catholic President of the United States."[87]

In May, an opinion poll canvassing Americans on who should succeed Roosevelt put Kennedy in fifth place.[88] The same month, a glowing piece appeared in *Liberty*, a magazine that boasted the second highest circulation in America after the *Saturday Evening Post*. Titled "Will Kennedy Run for the Presidency?," it offered a "candid close-up" of Kennedy as "a prospect that looms arrestingly large on the political horizon" and described him as the Democrats' best hope to succeed Roosevelt. While conceding that "one of his weak points" is that "he is a Roman Catholic," the author insisted that while "professional political handicappers will give heavy odds against him at this stage . . . a few connoisseurs of Presidential material are willing to make long-shot bets that the next Democratic nominee will be Joseph Patrick Kennedy."[89]

"In 1940, both the Democratic politicians and the country at large may demand a man who can make business and progressive reform pull together toward sound prosperity," the piece suggested. The author praised Kennedy's "brains, personality, driving power and the habit of success" and his foreign policy experience as ambassador in London "with the speed and untiring efficiency of a dynamo." The article added that Kennedy looked every inch a president. "European capitals have seen American diplomats who were picturesque in language or habits. Joe Kennedy isn't. He has an athlete's figure, a clean-cut head, sandy hair, clear straight-shooting eyes, a flashingly infectious smile and faultless taste in dress."[90]

It was not clear at the time to what extent Kennedy was encouraging the speculation in the American press. Certainly there were those who believed such a pitch could only be published with Kennedy's consent, if not encouragement. Roosevelt confidant and coauthor of the New Deal Hugh Johnson[91] was convinced Kennedy was behind the avalanche of speculation. "Somebody is doing one of the best recorded publicity jobs for the Honorable Joseph P. Kennedy," he remarked.[92] When Kennedy gave an interview to the *Ladies' Home Journal* saying, "I've never given the Presidency a serious thought," few gave it credence.[93]

Kennedy was one of many making plans to succeed Roosevelt, if only the president would make his intentions clear. Along with Hopkins and Hull, both of whom Roosevelt had encouraged, there was the conservative vice president from Texas, John Nance Garner, who had been backing Senator Bennett C. Clark[94] from Missouri for the presidency, until, according to Ickes, "seventeen or eighteen Democratic Senators went to Garner to tell him that he could be nominated. So it appears he has walked out on Clark."[95]

Such is the nature of presidential politics that it was in no one's interest to show his hand two and a half years before the election in November 1940, and all contenders preferred to keep their White House ambitions to themselves. Roosevelt, too, left the issue hanging, allowing colleagues to believe he would be stepping down. But until the president made it plain he was not interested in a third term, Washington and all the putative candidates lived in a state of nervous uncertainty. In such a closely guarded contest, the portrayal of Kennedy as the isolationist king across the water, waiting to be summoned to save the nation, was doing him few favors among the political class in Washington.

It was therefore with some trepidation that Kennedy boarded the *Queen Mary* on June 15. The trip was ostensibly to attend Joe Jr.'s graduation from Harvard, though Kennedy was careful to ensure that his first meeting was with Roosevelt at Hyde Park.

Krock wrote a welcome-home encomium in the *New York Times*. "Here is Kennedy back again, the rage of London, the best copy in the British press, his counsel steadily sought by statesmen of the country to which he is accredited, his influence manifest and powerful in all matters in which the United States has an interest in Great Britain," he wrote. "Here he is back again, undazzled by such a taking up socially and officially as no American perhaps has known abroad since [Benjamin] Franklin's day."[96]

When the *Queen Mary* slipped in to New York Harbor on June 20, James Roosevelt hitched a ride on a pilot's cutter to warn Kennedy that a large posse of press was waiting on the quayside and he would do well to say little or nothing about his candidacy. Forewarned, Kennedy offered the awaiting reporters the first of many denials that he was seeking the president's job. "I enlisted under President Roosevelt in 1932 to do whatever he wanted me to do," he said. "There are many problems at home and abroad and I happen to be busy at one abroad just now. If I had my eye on another job, it would be a complete breach of faith with President Roosevelt."[97] He took refuge in his home-from-home in New York, the Waldorf-Astoria.

Kennedy's interview with Roosevelt the following morning was an awkward affair, with the president, as ever, gushing an easy charm which the ambassador found disconcerting. Roosevelt asked Kennedy to convey a message to Chamberlain, urging him to stand firm in the face of the dictators and reassuring him that when the time was right he would join Britain on the side of fairness and democracy to plead for peace. The meeting over, Roosevelt conspicuously praised his ambassador to reporters and passed on "a grand line, a brilliant line": Kennedy had told him that in London he had met the same sort of rich pessimists that he came across in New York, forever moaning that the future looked bleak and that they would soon have to sell their Rolls-Royces.[98] Kennedy took strawberries with Eleanor Roosevelt, then left for the station to take the over-night train, *The Owl*, to Boston. It seemed that despite the overblown press campaign to name him Roosevelt's successor, he had escaped without a reprimand from the president.

A story on June 23 by Walter Trohan,[99] Washington bureau chief for McCormick's isolationist *Chicago Tribune*, was to alter everything. Headed "Kennedy's 1940 Ambitions Open Roosevelt Rift," it quoted "unimpeachable sources" to suggest that "the chilling shadow of 1940 has fallen across the friendship of President Roosevelt and his two-fisted trouble-shooter, Joseph Patrick Kennedy."[100] Trohan wrote that the interview between president and his ambassador at Hyde Park was held in a "frigid atmosphere because Mr. Roosevelt has received positive evidence that Kennedy hopes to use the Court of St. James's as a stepping stone to the White House in 1940."

Citing as evidence Kennedy's stream of "private and confiden-tial" round-robins sent to a select band of likely supporters, Trohan accused Kennedy of using "a prominent Washington correspondent to direct his Presidential boom from London." Close allies of the president "who once heralded Kennedy as the only representative of big business to see eye to eye with the Administration" were now condemning the ambassador's "selfishness." One of them, the presi-dent's press officer, Stephen Early, was quoted directly, saying, "Joe Kennedy never did anything without thinking of Joe Kennedy. And that's the worst thing I can say about a father of nine kids." A near-identical story appeared in the *Philadelphia Inquirer* and was soon picked up by papers coast to coast.

Kennedy was traveling from Cambridge to Cape Cod, then on to Washington, and did not read the Trohan story until June 25, the day he was due to dine with Roosevelt at the White House. When he read the stories, he felt betrayed, and recalled, "It was a true Irish anger that swept over me." At dinner, the president was his charm-ing self. Later that evening, Kennedy came to believe that the story that "heralded a series of misunderstandings . . . [and] was to plague my relationship with President Roosevelt"[101] had been planted by Early on the president's direct instructions.[102] It emerged that Krock, of all people, hoping to further Kennedy's ambition, had passed to the White House without telling the ambassador the collected "private and confidential" letters Kennedy had been sending home. It was the evidence Roosevelt needed to spring a trap.

Furious at the source of the leak, Kennedy visited Cordell Hull in the State Department and tendered his resignation, which the secretary of state declined, telling him not to take it personally; he, Hull, had been treated "twenty times as badly" by the president.[103] Kennedy confronted Early, who halfheartedly denied his part in the affair. Kennedy then insisted on seeing the president, who also denied any involvement. "In this way he assuaged my feelings and I left again for London, but deep within me I knew that something had happened," Kennedy remembered.

The hurt lasted his lifetime. In his unpublished *Diplomatic Memoir*, compiled a full decade later, Kennedy recalled the discomfort Roosevelt had caused him over his presidential ambition. The president "had a quality—a failing some have called it—of resenting the suggestion that he was to be succeeded and cooling perceptibly towards a man who might be considered by his friends a worthy successor."[104]

By letting his presidential intentions be known, Kennedy had, in biographer Michael Beschloss's ringing phrase, "like a hummingbird . . . fluttered under a glass dome, and above the dome loomed the omniscient eyes of Franklin Roosevelt."[105]

CHAPTER FIVE

LINDBERGH'S FLIGHT

*Charles Lindbergh arrives in Britain and
befriends Nazis while touring German airfields.
Kennedy and Lindbergh make a pact.
Hitler threatens the Sudetenland.*

ON JUNE 29, 1938, after two bruising weeks at home, Kennedy boarded the *Normandie* to resume his duties in London. His fellow passengers included his sons Joe Jr. and John, who would become interns at the embassy, and the financier and philanthropist Bernard Baruch, with whom the ambassador struck up a friendship.

Kennedy may have been aware of the press reports explaining that "Baruch is planning to sail to England with a group of colleagues who are in complete disagreement with the policies of Prime Minister Chamberlain. Their backing will be offered to Winston Churchill,"[1] but he did not know that Baruch's trip to Europe was also an instrument of Roosevelt's revenge against Kennedy, to undermine his position as ambassador. Bypassing Kennedy, and without informing him, Roosevelt had commissioned Baruch to assess the military dispositions of the European countries and report back.

The president no longer trusted Kennedy and was intent on keeping America's options open. The previous year, 1937, Baruch had also made a tour of European capitals and returned to warn Roosevelt that the international situation was so precarious, "anything can happen."[2] This time Baruch met Churchill, who warned, "War is coming very soon."[3] Baruch returned with a clear message to the president that, whether or not America sided militarily with the democracies against the dictators, it should for its own security rearm without delay.

Meanwhile, Europe was edging toward war, the latest subject of Hitler's aggrandizing attentions being the Sudetenland. The area bordered Germany and was heavily defended by the Czechs as it contained a great part of the country's industrial wealth. The summer days of 1938 were overshadowed by Hitler's increasingly insistent demands that the Sudeten Germans be integrated into Germany. What few outside Hitler's immediate circle knew was that the Führer had the previous November named a date for the invasion of Czechoslovakia.[4] For Chamberlain, the Sudetenland was not enough to go to war over. Kennedy returned to London prepared to back Chamberlain in appeasing Hitler and averting war. The ambassador found a kindred spirit in Charles A. Lindbergh, the first person to fly across the Atlantic single-handed, who had moved to England to escape the aggressive press attention that dogged him in America.

Until his record-breaking flight, Lindbergh had been an anonymous twenty-five-year-old US Mail pilot from Little Falls, Minnesota. In 1927, he entered a competition arranged by a New York hotelier offering a $25,000 prize ($331,046 in 2014 terms) to the first aviator from a World War One Allied country to make a nonstop flight across the Atlantic from New York to Paris or vice versa. While others combined in teams, the plucky Lindbergh decided to fly alone in a single-engine aircraft with, to save weight, no parachute, no radio, and no sextant for navigating.

On May 20, 1927, he set off from Roosevelt Field, Long Island, New York,[5] in a $10,000 Ryan monoplane, the *Spirit of St. Louis*, and thirty-three and a half hours later, navigating by the stars, he landed at Le Bourget Airport outside Paris, where a crowd of 150,000 greeted him. The feat made Lindbergh overnight the most famous man in the world. The following month, the US Post Office issued a ten-cent postage stamp featuring Lindbergh's plane and a map of the route.

Success treated Lindbergh badly. Every aspect of his life became public. Seven months after his record-making flight, Lindbergh married Anne Morrow,[6] daughter of his financial adviser, Dwight Morrow, a partner at J. P. Morgan who became ambassador to Mexico. The young couple's attempt to avoid publicity by moving to a remote farmhouse in New Jersey took a tragic turn when their twenty-month-old son, Charles Augustus Lindbergh Jr., was kidnapped and found dead.

The sensational trial of the German immigrant accused of the murder further added to the Lindberghs' grief. They concluded that they would find no peace so long as they lived in America. Hearst said he found it "extremely distressing and discouraging that this grand country of ours is so overrun with cranks, criminals, and Communists that a splendid citizen like Colonel Lindbergh must take his family abroad to protect them against violence."[7] Meanwhile, he ordered his reporters and photographers to stalk them.

Lindbergh was an early example of how an ordinary person, catapulted into fame through accident of fate, can find themselves being treated with awe and respect they barely deserve. Lindbergh was an ingenious engineer without education who desperately tried to live up to the expectations of those who, as a result of his overnight celebrity, befriended him. He became a compulsive autodidact, earnestly reading works by Tolstoy, H. G. Wells, Shakespeare, and others in order to make himself more interesting and erudite than he really was. He was naive, impressionable, vulnerable to crackpot theories and mysticism, and completely lacking in judgment. He believed in destiny and concluded that he had been chosen to become famous for a reason. He named his dog Thor, after the hammer-wielding god of thunder and lightning in Norse mythology. Notwithstanding his flimsy grasp on reality, his fame ensured he was made welcome in the most exalted of places.

In the early hours of December 22, 1935, the Lindberghs sailed for Britain, where, with their three-year-old son, Jon, they rented Long Barn, a fourteenth-century byre on the country estate of Harold Nicolson, whom Charles had met in New York with Nicolson's wife, Vita Sackville-West.[8] Nicolson had written a biography of Dwight Morrow—whom Nicolson thought "had the mind of a super-criminal and the character of a saint"[9]—for Harcourt, Brace, the publisher of Lindbergh's memoirs of his adventures in the air. The Lindberghs found peace in their retreat in the Kent countryside, about an hour by train from London, and it was not long before they received an invitation from Nancy Astor to a weekend party at Cliveden.

As the most famous aviator in the world, Lindbergh received invitations from aircraft companies inviting him to inspect their latest aircraft, and in May 1936 he visited a French airplane manufacturer. A report of Lindbergh's French tour sparked the interest of Major Truman Smith, a military attaché to the American embassy in Berlin with a watching brief to report back to Washington on Germany's rearmament program. It was known that, contrary to the Treaty of Versailles, Hitler was expanding the Luftwaffe, and Smith was charged by Washington to discover the size of the German air force.

Smith explored with officials at the German Air Ministry whether they would welcome a Lindbergh visit to German plane makers, and he was pleasantly surprised when a personal invitation to inspect military aircraft facilities was extended to Lindbergh by Hitler's air minister, the dashing World War One flying ace (but by now corpulent) Hermann Göring.[10] Because Lindbergh had in April rejoined the Air Corps Reserve and was technically a member of America's armed forces, the invitation was extended by Germany's civil airline, Lufthansa, rather than by the Luftwaffe. Smith relayed the invitation, which Lindbergh eagerly accepted, writing to his mother, "I am looking forward, with great interest, to going there."[11]

On the face of it, it seemed that the prospect of boasting about their advances in aviation engineering to the most famous flier in the world caused the Nazis to drop their guard. When the Lindberghs arrived in Berlin on July 22, they were welcomed by Göring's personal emissary, Hans-Heinrich Dieckhoff,[12] German ambassador to the United States, who had flown in for the occasion, as well as by all the American army and navy attachés in Berlin. Fifteen German bombers were sitting on the runway apron. This show of strength was misleading. According to Lindbergh biographer Leonard Mosley, "Göring, well aware that his aviation program was seriously behind schedule, had ordered factories, airfields, and flying squadrons to pack their 'shop windows' in order to impress their visitor."[13]

At Tempelhof Airport, Lindbergh was invited to pilot a Junkers Ju 52, which would become Germany's wartime medium bomber, as well as an experimental passenger craft, the *Hindenburg*. He was made welcome by the Richthofen Wing, the Luftwaffe's elite fighter squadron, and at two Heinkel plants was shown the Luftwaffe's latest dive-bombers. At the Junkers factory in Dessau, he inspected their advanced airplane engine and the assembly line pumping out medium bombers. At every works and airfield, he was met with extraordinary, seemingly foolhardy candor.

Colonel von Massow, commander of the Richthofen Wing, boasted that they were about to take delivery of Germany's newest fighter, the Messerschmitt Bf 109, the ultra-fast and easily maneuverable plane designed to be the Luftwaffe's attacking workhorse. According to Smith, the "intelligent, penetrating, firm, and affable" Erhard Milch,[14] state secretary of the German Air Ministry, "talked with extraordinary frankness and frequently gave the Americans advance data on the German airplanes and airplane engines under development."[15] Only when Lindbergh asked about rocket-propelled planes did his hosts fall silent.

The extent of German rearmament shocked Lindbergh. Living near the English Channel, which separated England from France by just 25 miles, he realized that the natural moat that had protected the English from invaders since the Norman invasion of 1066 had been made redundant by the Luftwaffe's strength, as he'd seen it. At a luncheon in his honor, Lindbergh told his German hosts:

> We who are in aviation carry a heavy responsibility on our shoulders, for while we have been drawing the world closer together in peace we have stripped the armor of every nation in war. It is no longer possible to shield the heart of a country with its army. Armies can no more stop an air attack than a suit of mail can stop a rifle bullet. . . . We can no longer protect our families with an army. Our libraries, our museums, every institution we value most, are laid bare to our bombardment.[16]

Hitler was so impressed by Lindbergh's acuity, and eager to intimidate his neighbors and deter Britain and France from halting his expansionist plans, that he ordered newspapers to print Lindbergh's speech in full. The following day Lindbergh, after giving another speech, offered a toast that would come back to haunt him: "Here's to bombers, may they get slower. And here's to pursuit planes, may they get swifter."[17]

Lindbergh was honored with a formal state luncheon hosted by Göring at his residence in Wilhelmstrasse, Berlin. Despite his obesity, Göring, described by Smith as "magnetic, genial, vain, intelligent, frightening, and grotesque,"[18] counted himself a snappy dresser. His status as Hitler's second-in-command allowed him to sport a dazzling white commander in chief's doubled-breasted dress uniform trimmed with gold buttons and gilt epaulettes and bedecked with his legion of medals, including two Iron Crosses for gallantry and Prussia's top honor, Pour le Mérite (informally known as the Blue Max).

He easily outshone his new wife, Emmy, a stage actress resplendent in a long green velvet dress adorned with a glittering emerald and diamond Nazi swastika pin. After lunch, the Lindberghs joined the Görings and, to the Lindberghs' alarm, Göring's pet lion cub, for coffee. The Görings were charming, even when the lion urinated on Göring's leg and he had to excuse himself to change his pants. Göring showed Lindbergh a map of all the military airfields in Germany, which he ominously referred to as "our first seventy." The message was clear. "From the inspection trips I had made through German factories, I knew warplanes were being built to fill those fields," Lindbergh recalled.[19]

Each morning of his German visit, Lindbergh sat down with Smith and others in the American embassy to recount what he had seen. Reports of his findings were then relayed to the General Staff and Air Corps in Washington DC. "Perhaps the most interesting feature of these informal morning meetings was the comparisons which Lindbergh frequently drew between the airplanes he had observed the day before in Germany and the comparable planes being built in France, Britain, and America," recalled Smith.[20] Through Lindbergh, American military attachés formed good working bonds with senior staff at the German Air Ministry. It seemed the German high command, perhaps even Hitler himself, wanted Roosevelt to know exactly how well armed Germany was, the better to deter him from war.

As a grand finale, the Lindberghs were invited by Göring to attend the opening by Hitler of the 1936 Berlin Olympics in Nuremberg, sitting in Göring's private box at the 110,000-capacity Olympiastadion. The Olympic spectacle, and Hitler's speech, turned the Lindberghs' heads. "While I still have many reservations, I have come away with a feeling of great admiration for the German people," Lindbergh wrote to Smith. "The condition of the country, and the appearance of the average person whom I saw, leaves with me the impression that Hitler must have far more character and vision than I thought."[21]

Anne Lindbergh was even more effusive, saying she was shocked by the "strictly puritanical view at home that dictatorships are of necessity wrong, evil, unstable and no good can come of them—combined with our funny-paper view of Hitler as a clown—combined with the very strong (naturally) Jewish propaganda in the Jewish owned newspapers."[22] She told her mother she was "beginning to feel Hitler is a very great man, like an inspired religious leader—and as such rather fanatical—but not scheming, not selfish, not greedy for power, but a mystic, a visionary."[23]

Lindbergh began alerting aviation colleagues to what he had seen in Germany. He wrote to Henry P. Davidson, a New Jersey neighbor, that Germany was "now able to produce military aircraft faster than any European country. Possibly even faster than we could in the States. . . . A person would have to be blind not to realize that they have already built up tremendous strength."[24]

Harold Nicolson recorded that Lindbergh "has obviously been much impressed by Nazi Germany."[25] By contrast, Britain was proving a disillusionment. "It was as though the Englishman's accomplishments, century after century, had become a cumulative burden on his shoulders until his traditions, his possessions, and his pride overweighed his buoyancy of spirit," Lindbergh wrote.[26] Nicolson noted that the aviator "admits that [the Nazis] are a great menace, but he denies they are a menace to us."[27]

The following year, 1937, Lindbergh made his second visit to Germany, on October 11, visiting the Focke-Wulf works in Bremen, where he was shown a vertical takeoff and landing aircraft, a forerunner to the helicopter. At the top-secret Rechlin air testing station in Pomerania, he got to see the Bf 109 up close and learned of the Luftwaffe's intention to build a Messerschmitt Bf 110 with a 1200-horsepower engine. Again, on his return to London, he helped Smith compile a report. "Germany is once more a world power in the air," it read. "Her air force and her air industry have emerged from the kindergarten stage."[28]

Although he did not meet any Nazi leaders on his second trip, his admiration for Hitler continued to increase. Lindbergh wrote to his spiritual mentor, Dr. Alexis Carrel,[29] "Hitler is apparently more popular than ever in Germany, and, much as I disagree with some of the things which have been done, I can understand his popularity. He has done much for Germany."[30]

Lindbergh's own beliefs chimed with the racial and mystical notions that underpinned Nazism. He was an elitist who believed that some races were superior to others, and he promoted eugenics, the racial theory that humanity could be "improved" through selective breeding. He judged people above all by their race and was happy to make wide generalizations about "races" and "peoples."

Lindbergh sympathized with Carrel's notion that those with white skin were superior to those of African, Latin, South Asian, and Asian descent, who had suffered from centuries of too much sunlight. "Excessive light is dangerous," Carrel wrote. "We must not forget that the most highly civilized races—the Scandinavians [like Lindbergh's family], for example—are white and have lived for many generations in a country where the atmospheric luminosity is weak during a great part of the year. . . . The lower races generally inhabit countries where light is violent."[31] Like the Nazis, Carrel urged the cleansing of the "white race" not only by selective breeding but by putting to death those deemed "inferior."

Lindbergh explored spirituality and shocked the otherwise unflappable Nicolson when he asked, "Would you know of a medium here or in London whom we could visit, so we could attend a séance?"[32] He was also a vigorous anti-Communist who thought "Europe, and the entire world, is fortunate that a Nazi Germany lies, at present, between Communistic Russia and a demoralized France."[33] He became interested in the Oxford Group, a Christian sect founded by Dr. Frank Buchman,[34] who urged "moral rearmament" in the West and met three times with Heinrich Himmler,[35] head of the Nazi paramilitary SS, to try to persuade the Nazi leaders to embrace Christ and confront Communism.

It is little wonder that Lindbergh found Germany so appealing, though that may be because he did not interest himself in the curtailment of democratic liberties, the end of the rule of law, and the officially condoned thuggery exercised by the Nazis against racial minorities and political opponents. As Lindbergh's biographer Mosley put it, "The German government had vowed that they would show him everything he asked to see, and since he did not ask to see concentration camps, political prisoners, Jews, Communists, Social-ists, Social-Democrats, or other opponents of the regime, his picture of the Nazi Reich was a decidedly favorable one."[36]

In Carrel, who won a Nobel Prize in 1912 for pioneering work in heart surgery, Lindbergh found both a kindred spirit, who encouraged him in his racial beliefs and his study of eugenics, and a substitute for his father, Charles August Lindbergh,[37] a congressman from Minnesota who had strenuously campaigned against America's entry into World War One. Commenting on Lindbergh's "suit of armor" speech in Berlin, a *New York Herald Tribune* columnist speculated, "It was from his father, whom [World War One] drove into obscurity, that he inherited both the courage and the right to speak as he did."

Lindbergh's father was a first generation Swedish American who in 1907 was elected Republican US congressman for Minnesota's Sixth District. His move to Washington DC allowed him to escape an unhappy marriage without provoking a scandal that would harm his political career. Young Charles and his mother, Evangeline Lodge Land Lindbergh, were consigned to a peripatetic life scrounging accommodation and sustenance from distant relatives.

Lindbergh Sr. was an argumentative contrarian with Midwestern views, conventional for the time, about the dangers of big government and the wickedness of the Federal Reserve. He was also anti-Semitic and believed in the genetic inferiority of African Americans. In 1913 he published *Banking, Currency, and the Money Trust*,[38] a tract railing against big business, Wall Street, and undercapitalized banks. In the presidential election of 1912, despite his isolationist, antiwar views, Lindbergh Sr. switched from supporting the Republican candidate, William Howard Taft,[39] to the bellicose Theodore Roosevelt and his hastily assembled Bull Moose Party, splitting the Republican vote and helping Woodrow Wilson win the White House.

When Wilson took America into World War One, Lindbergh Sr. joined with isolationist lawmakers to protest at the nation's involvement in a foreign war. He gravitated towards isolationists in the Senate, such as Robert La Follette of Wisconsin and William Borah of Idaho. Even when the House voted on whether to arm American merchant ships so they could defend themselves against German U-boat attacks, Lindbergh Sr. was one of the fourteen to vote against, with 403 in favor.

He wrote a pamphlet, "Why Is Your Country at War ?",[40] claiming that World War One had been forced upon Americans by a cabal of self-serving profiteers and "wealth-grabbers." He wrote, "It is impossible according to the big press to be a true American unless you are pro-British. If you are really for America first, last, and all the time, and solely for America and for the masses primarily, then you are classed as pro-German by the big press which are supported by the speculators."[41] They were words that, twenty years later, still rang true to Charles A. Lindbergh Jr.

When, on March 12, 1938, Lindbergh Jr. heard that German troops had invaded Austria, his English friends were alarmed at further evidence that Hitler was intent on war. Lindbergh, however, was lost for words. "Stories too mixed to permit any accurate conclusions," he told his diary.[42] Four days later, he still appeared unable to understand why Germany's invasion of an independent nation was causing consternation. "I cannot help liking the Germans. They are like our own people. We should be working with them and not constantly crossing swords," he wrote. "If we fight, our countries will only lose their best men. . . . It must not happen."[43] He was less impressed with the English. "It is necessary to realize that England is a country composed of a great mass of slow, somewhat stupid and indifferent people, and a small group of geniuses," he told the assistant military attaché for air at the American Embassy in London.[44]

At the beginning of April, Lindbergh took a tour of British military aircraft plants, seeing Hurricane and Henley fighter planes at the Hawker works and Wellesley and Wellington bombers at Vickers.[45] Now he understood how far behind the British were in preparations for war. The guileless Lindbergh, incapable of dissembling, did not spare his English friends his opinion that England was doomed. He told his diary:

> The contrast between an English aircraft factory and an American or German factory is un-understandable. The English simply do not seem to have equivalent ability along those lines. God! How they will have to pay for it in the next year. This country has neither the spirit nor the ability needed for a modern war. And the worst of it is that countless Englishmen will die needlessly because of lack of training and equipment.[46]

He was similarly appalled by the complacent attitudes he heard at a dinner for the explorers' Ends of the Earth Club, where old men in black tie seemed confident that America would, eventually, enter a war on the British side. Lindbergh recorded them saying, "'We know that our American cousins will always be behind us in a crisis,' etc. 'The liberty-loving peoples of the world must stand against aggressor nations,' etc.'"[47] Lindbergh became convinced that it would be a disaster for America to play any part in the impending conflict.

Instead, he advocated appeasement. "If England and Germany fought it would probably throw Europe into a chaotic condition for an indefinite period," he told his diary. "The only hope for Europe is an understanding between England and Germany."[48] In his many visits to Cliveden and to the Nicolsons, Lindbergh's gloomy prognostications agitated already frayed nerves.

"Lindbergh is most pessimistic," Nicolson wrote in his diary. "He says that we cannot possibly fight since we should certainly be beaten. The German Air Force is ten times superior to that of Russia, France, and Great Britain put together. Our defences are simply futile."[49] Lindbergh's take on the conversation with Nicolson was noticeably different. "[Nicolson] is very anti-German," he wrote. "I took Germany's side, possibly too ardently, as is usually the case in an argument of this kind."[50] By the same token, Nicolson, a staunch anti-Fascist, found Lindbergh "much impressed by Nazi Germany. He admires their energy, vitality, spirit, organization, architecture, planning, and physique."[51] Nicolson noted, "He believes in the Nazi theology, all tied up with his hatred of degeneracy and his hatred of democracy as represented by the free Press and the American public."[52]

It was telling that although Lindbergh's barn home was close to Chartwell, Churchill's country house, and that Churchill had through Nicolson extended an open invitation to visit, the aviator made no attempt to engage Britain's most articulate critic of Hitler's expansionism. He was happier entertaining Nazis like Otto Merkel, "an officer with Lufthansa Airways", with whom he could talk of "taxes and economic policies under Hitler."[53]

On May 1, the Lindberghs went to tea at Cliveden, where fellow guests included members of Chamberlain's government. Lindbergh's account gave the lie to claims that Cockburn's reports on the Cliveden Set were merely the invention of a leftist with a colorful imagination. "I sat next to Lady Astor again at tea. She is violently opposed to any commitments to France. Wants better understanding with Germany," he wrote. "I was encouraged about the feeling of most of the people there in regard to Germany."[54] They included Sir Thomas Inskip,[55] the minister charged with coordinating Britain's defenses.

Inskip asked Lindbergh to what extent America could be relied upon to help Britain in the event of war. He inquired "about the possibility of flying large bombers across the ocean in case of necessity," Lindbergh wrote in his diary. He told Inskip, "I believe the Germans can probably produce more military aircraft than the British Empire and the United States combined, with the facilities which now exist."[56] Nicolson then arranged for Inskip and Lindbergh to have tea together at the House of Commons. Again Lindbergh's message was bleak: German bombers could not be defeated and that "all fortification is useless."[57] Lindbergh took umbrage at Inskip's apparent indifference to the news and seemed offended that he was not at once employed by the British government as an adviser.

Four days later, over lunch with Nancy Astor, Lindbergh met Joe and Rose Kennedy for the first time. "Kennedy interested me greatly," Lindbergh wrote. "He is not the usual type of politician or diplomat. His views on the European situation seem intelligent and interesting. I hope to see more of him."[58] Rose was particularly taken with the boyish aviator. "He was rosy cheeked, fresh looking with very wavy hair which falls naturally without much combing," she wrote. "Has a wonderful smile which comes easily and lights up his entire face."[59] The feeling was reciprocated by Anne Lindbergh, who said that the ambassador reminded her of "an Irish terrier wagging his tail."[60]

An invitation from Kennedy for dinner at the embassy soon followed, where Lindbergh continued to offer his frank account of the defense gap between Britain and Germany. He spoke with the secretary of state for war, Leslie Hore-Belisha,[61] who asked if Britain would be able to produce airplanes fast enough in the future. "I told him that I was very much worried about the situation which now exists," Lindbergh wrote. "He suggested that it was not possible to compete with German aircraft production under the present economic system in England, that Germany was sacrificing everything to rearm, etc."[62]

Before long, Lindbergh's views about the likelihood of Britain's defeat and the need for America to keep out of war reached Roosevelt. Lindbergh had already come to the president's attention when as a pilot he became involved in a heated dispute about air mail flights for the US Post Office which had been brewing for a decade. All air mail deliveries were the responsibility of the Army Air Corps until Hoover privatized the service in 1927. However, in 1933, after Roosevelt's election, Congress accused the private airlines of fraud, corruption, and collusion with the Post Office over the awarding of contracts. The agreements were rescinded and the army resumed delivering mail.

Senior Army Air Corps officers welcomed its return to air mail duties. General Benjamin D. Foulois,[63] head of the Army Air Corps, wrote that, by resuming air mail flights, "our pilots would get some badly needed training, which had been curtailed because of the shortage of funds. . . . The problems we might have would focus national attention on the Air Corps and maybe we would then get the funds we needed for expansion."[64]

In the five years since the army stopped delivering mail, its aircraft had deteriorated and its pilots lacked experience, particularly in countering the often treacherous weather conditions they had to endure. Not long after they resumed deliveries, planes began to fall from the sky. The first three pilots assigned to air mail duty crashed and died. Four days later, a pilot was forced to make an emergency landing and another became lost, ran out of fuel, and had to abandon his plane by parachute. As the casualties mounted, protests against the switch back to Army Air Corps mail delivery gathered momentum. The Postmaster General, James Farley,[65] was accused of negligence, even murder.

Roosevelt's administration found itself under siege and the whole of the New Deal began to be questioned. As historian Arthur Schlesinger Jr. put it, "The national shock suddenly gave pent-up dissatisfaction with the New Deal a seemingly legitimate outlet."[66]

Lindbergh, who was employed as an adviser by a number of airlines, stepped into the controversy with a stinging open letter to the president, accusing the administration of punishing free enterprise. "Your order of cancellation of all air mail contracts condemns the largest portion of our commercial aviation without just trial," he wrote, asserting that "cancellation of all air mail contracts and the use of the army on commercial air lines will unnecessarily and greatly damage all American aviation."[67] Lindbergh's intervention changed the public's perception of the dispute and successfully cast doubt on the president's integrity. In the *New York Times*, Krock summed up the damage Lindbergh had wrought on Roosevelt's reputation. "For the first time since the President was inaugurated . . . his administration seems really on the defensive. . . . An impression has gone more widely abroad that even Mr. Roosevelt cannot always be right."[68]

The air mail issue only lost its venom after the Post Office re-auctioned the contracts and awarded them to many of the airlines accused of fraud, who had applied under different names. But Lindbergh would not easily be forgiven by Roosevelt. He told Early, "Don't worry about Lindbergh. We will get that fair-haired boy."[69] The president tried to buy Lindbergh's silence by offering him a place on a government review board to assess the state of the Army Air Corps. Lindbergh declined. In turn, Lindbergh made no secret of his dislike of the president. Even ten years after the air mail controversy, Nicolson recorded that Lindbergh still "loathes Roosevelt because of the latter's treatment of the airmail companies."[70]

CHAPTER SIX

PEACE IN OUR TIME

Lindbergh and Kennedy encourage the appeasers,
Chamberlain strikes a deal with Hitler at Munich,
and Roosevelt sets a trap for Lindbergh.

THROUGH LATE SPRING and into the summer of 1938, the unresolved Sudeten question dominated European politics. When in May Edvard Beneš,[1] the Czech prime minister, ordered 400,000 troops to the German border, the French, who had guaranteed Czech independence, were joined by the British in warning Hitler to back off.

On paper, the anti-Hitler countries appeared strong. Britain and France had a mutual-defense alliance and Russia was also committed to defending Czechoslovakia. Chamberlain's warning to Hitler, however, was tepid. The British ambassador in Berlin, Sir Nevile Henderson, wrote in gentle terms to the German foreign minister, Joachim von Ribbentrop, who was formerly German ambassador in London, that "His Majesty's Government could not guarantee that they would not be forced by events to become themselves involved."

Roosevelt was being urged by his ambassador in Berlin, William Bullitt,[2] to convene a conference of European leaders to find a settlement to the Sudeten question, but the president declined. He feared he had little to gain and that the summit would merely confirm that, so long as American opinion remained staunchly against war, he was powerless to act.

It was against such a tense background that Roosevelt made a second attempt to silence the world's most famous aviator. In June 1938, Lindbergh received a message from the airline entrepreneur Juan Trippe[3] in New York asking whether he would become chairman of the newly formed Civil Aviation Commission for a six-year term. Lindbergh was fearful of returning home. He was sure he would be hounded by the press and was wary of the motive behind the invitation. "I told him I did not think it advisable to move my family back to America under present circumstances," he confided to his diary. "Trippe said the request came from headquarters, which means Roosevelt. I wonder what is behind it. Political gesture? Outside pressure?"[4]

Lindbergh had other plans. Although he was convinced that France would prove incapable of resisting a German invasion, his guru Carrel encouraged him to buy a ramshackle house on Île Illiec, an isolated islet off the Brittany coast, only connected to the mainland at low tide. From his island fastness he planned trips to Germany and Russia. "I do not want war to start without having a fairly good idea of its causes and probably consequences," he wrote. "I plan on seeing as much of the European situation as possible in the next few months."[5]

One of his first ports of call was Bullitt, whom he had met at an Astor lunch. "There are not enough modern military planes in this country to even put up a show in case of war," Lindbergh told him. "In a conflict between France, England, and Russia on one side, against Germany on the other, Germany would immediately have supremacy of the air. . . . Germany has developed a huge Air Force while England has slept and France has deluded herself with a Russian alliance. It seems that the French Air Corps is infiltrated with Communism. Especially among the higher officers."[6]

On July 20, Kennedy became involved in the ongoing negotiations between Hitler and Chamberlain over the Sudetenland. The new German ambassador to Britain, Herbert von Dirksen,[7] had urged him to intercede with the British. Reporting to Hull, the ambassador said Dirksen had told him "it was now time for Britain to make a proposition to the Germans. . . . Definitely he gave me the impression that Hitler was decidedly in the mood to start negotiations."[8]

By the end of August, however, Chamberlain had become convinced that appeasement was failing and that Hitler was intent on taking the whole of Czechoslovakia. "It is the belief of Hitler that the French are not ready to fight and that Great Britain does not want to go in," Kennedy wrote to Hull. He described Chamberlain as "the best bet in Europe against war, but he is a very sick-looking man."[9] Lindbergh, too, was aware that Europe was careening toward disaster. "Rumors of Germany starting war on August 15," he wrote in his diary.[10]

On August 18, Roosevelt embarked on a second attempt to educate the American people about the dictators. At Queen's University in Kingston, Ontario, Canada, he continued where his "quarantine speech" the previous October had left off. "We in the Americas are no longer a far away continent, to which the eddies of controversies beyond the seas could bring no interest or no harm. . . . The vast amount of our resources, the vigor of our commerce and the strength of our men have made us vital factors in world peace whether we choose it or not. . . . I give to you assurance that the people of the United States will not stand idly by if domination of Canadian soil is threatened by any other empire."[11]

The implication of Roosevelt's pledge to defend Canada was plain. As a member of the British Empire and an intimate ally of Britain, Canada could be expected to declare war following any decision by Chamberlain to go to war with Hitler. Roosevelt's speech suggested that America would stand by Britain in the event of war. He also implied that any threat to trade with North America, currently protected by the Atlantic patrols of Britain's Royal Navy, would be tantamount to waging war on the United States. Roosevelt urged Kennedy to make it plain that he robustly opposed Hitler's demands in the Sudetenland and elsewhere.[12] Yet on August 30 the ambassador reassured Chamberlain and Halifax that the president had decided to "go in with" attempts at appeasing Hitler.[13]

The president "became increasingly irritated with Kennedy," recalled Treasury secretary Henry Morgenthau. "'Who would have thought the English (the Cliveden Set) could take into camp a red-headed Irishman?'" the president joked. "'The young man needs his wrist slapped.' . . . As for Chamberlain, the President called him 'slippery' and added, with some bitterness, that he was 'interested in peace at any price if he could get away with it and save his face.'"[14] Uppermost in Roosevelt's mind was the desire to avoid the errors Wilson had made ahead of World War One. He told his most loyal aide, secretary of the Interior Harold Ickes, that if Woodrow Wilson had expressed himself more vigorously before the European nations mobilized, war might have been averted.

The president was particularly aggravated when he read the draft of a speech Kennedy was to give in Aberdeen, Scotland, that included the line, "I cannot for the life of me understand why anybody would want to go to war to save the Czechs." Hull struck out the line, but Kennedy nonetheless briefed a reporter from Hearst's *Boston Evening American* that "things aren't as bad as they seem" and that "the thing to do here and in the United States is not to lose our heads."[15] On reading the report of the interview on August 31, Roosevelt cabled Kennedy saying he was "deeply disturbed" by the ambassador's words and ordered him to stop his maverick remarks. The same day, the president began plotting to circumvent US neutrality laws by arranging with Morgenthau for the delivery of gold from London and Paris against the day the British and French needed to buy American weapons.

Chamberlain's government was beginning to fray. With Eden already on the backbenches, and with Churchill ready to pounce if the prime minister made a misstep, Halifax too began to think it was time to draw a line that Hitler should not cross. Duff Cooper,[16] First Lord of the Admiralty, was even more hawkish and favored halting Hitler by any means, even war. But how would the Americans react to a firmer British line?

Halifax asked Kennedy on September 1 whether he thought Congress would amend the neutrality laws if Britain were to go to war with Germany. Kennedy said it was unlikely and told him appeasement should be given more time. The ambassador reported the conversation to Hull, who relayed it to Roosevelt, who thought Halifax was trying to paint America into a corner. If Kennedy had replied that Congress would act and the British went to war over the Sudetenland, it would seem that America had encouraged them; if Chamberlain offered concessions to avoid war, the British would argue they did so because America would not support them.

To Roosevelt's alarm, the Halifax–Kennedy meeting was leaked to the British press, who leapt on the news that the ambassador had implied that America would not come to Britain's aid. Kennedy's response was to remain silent, which angered Roosevelt, who felt that by failing to deny the reports, he had compromised the administration's studiedly ambivalent position. Roosevelt's ambiguous attitude toward German aggression, designed to leave him every option after the 1940 election should he run for a third term, had been put at risk by Kennedy "playing the Chamberlain game."[17]

The *Times* editor and Cliveden regular Geoffrey Dawson floated the notion of surrendering to German demands over the Sudetenland in an editorial in *The Times* on September 7. "If the Sudetens now ask for more than the Czech Government are ready to give," he wrote, "it might be worth the Czechoslovak Government to consider ... making Czechoslovakia a more homogeneous state by the cession of that fringe of alien populations who are contiguous to the nation to which they are united by race."

Anxious that Hitler was about to invade the Sudetenland, the French foreign minister, Georges Bonnet,[18] inquired what the British government would do if the French went to war to protect the Czechs. Halifax responded with typical pusillanimity, "While His Majesty's Government would never allow the security of France to be threatened, they are unable to make precise statements of the character of their future action, or the time at which it would be taken, in circumstances they cannot at present foresee."[19]

By chance, Lindbergh was visiting Czechoslovakia on his way back from a tour of aviation plants in the Soviet Union and he met with Beneš on September 3. Though they spoke about "modern aircraft ... the war in Spain, of the Russian air fleet, of Czechoslovakian aviation," Lindbergh failed to raise the subject of German demands that the country be dismembered. He merely noted that it was "obvious that [Beneš] had been, and was, under tension." He inspected Czech air forces and concluded that the country "is not well equipped in the air."[20]

Lindbergh even visited the Sudetenland, where he had lunch with "Prince and Princess Clary Aldringen [sic],"[21] Austro-Hungarian aristocrats stripped of their titles after 1918, who were sympathetic to Germany. They feared they were "sitting on a bomb" and worried that there were "many Communists in the territory, all armed, and that there 'wouldn't be enough lampposts to hang them by if the trouble started.'"[22] Returning to France, Lindbergh continued his chorus of alarm by telling the French air minister, Guy La Chambre, that

France's air defenses were "desperate" and that if France tried to resist Hitler's invasion of Czechoslovakia it would be "suicide."[23]

As the slow march of diplomacy proceeded toward war, all Europe was on edge to hear Hitler at the finale of the Nazis' annual rally in the Nuremberg Stadium on September 12. Hitler's speech, preceded by chants of "Sieg Heil!" ("Welcome, victory!"), was a savage, sarcastic assault upon Beneš. The dictator's threats convinced Roosevelt that war was both unavoidable and imminent. He summoned the British ambassador, Sir Ronald Lindsay, who cabled Chamberlain that the president would be profoundly disappointed if he did not stand firm.

As London prepared for war, with trenches and air raid shelters being dug in St James's Park and gas masks being issued to all residents, Chamberlain took the initiative. Without consulting his cabinet or the French, on September 15 the prime minister flew to Munich. It was the sixty-nine-year-old Chamberlain's first airplane flight and the first instance of what would come to be known as shuttle diplomacy. In a last-minute effort to boost Chamberlain's confidence and instill some resolve in the prime minister, Roosevelt sent him a two-word telegram: "Good man."[24] After a grueling seven-hour train journey, he arrived at the Führer's mountain eyrie, the Berghof at Berchtesgaden.

Exhausted by the journey, Chamberlain was shocked by his encounter with Hitler. As Duff Cooper observed, "Chamberlain had never met anybody in Birmingham who in the least resembled Adolf Hitler."[25] Hitler's crazed demeanor and intemperate language shocked the timorous prime minister. "I am prepared to risk a world war rather than allow this [Sudeten business] to drag on," Hitler said. Chamberlain retorted, "If the Führer is determined to settle this matter by force without waiting even for a discussion between ourselves to take place, what did he let me come here for? I have wasted my time." Hitler replied, "If the British Government were prepared to accept the idea of secession in principle, and to say so, there might be a chance then to have a talk."

Despite Hitler's hectoring and mood swings, Chamberlain "got the impression that here was a man who could be relied upon when he had given his word."[26] Without reference to Beneš, the rest of the Czech government, or the French, Chamberlain agreed to cede the Sudetenland to Hitler.[27] Neglected by its closest ally, the French had little option but to follow suit. Although Britain had been rearming for two years, Chamberlain felt the country was not strong enough to save landlocked Czechoslovakia from invasion. He even had little confidence that Britain itself could be defended. Hore-Belisha told the Chiefs of Staff that "to take offensive against Germany now would be like 'a man attacking a tiger before he has loaded his gun.'" [28]

Returning to London, Chamberlain told his colleagues that the Sudetenland had to be sacrificed to prevent a world conflict. He reminded them "of the horrors of war, of German bombers over London, and of his horror in allowing our people to suffer all the miseries of war."[29] On September 18, the French premier, Édouard Daladier,[30] and colleagues arrived in London to discuss the crisis and reluctantly confirmed that Chamberlain's decision to hand the Sudetenland to Hitler was the right course. Churchill was dismayed. He felt that "the British and French Cabinets at this time presented a front of two over-ripe melons crushed together; whereas what was needed was a gleam of steel." As for the Czechs, he thought "The Babes in the Wood had no worse treatment."[31]

The next day, informed of Britain's decision, Roosevelt again summoned Lindsay to the White House, telling him that if the isolationists heard what he was about to say he would be impeached. He described the breaking of the Anglo-French promise to protect Czechoslovakia as "the most terrible, remorseless sacrifice" and added he would be "the first to cheer" if partitioning Czechoslovakia proved to be Hitler's last demand, but he doubted that would be the case. He believed Beneš would reject the deal, in which case the British and French should mobilize their forces, declare a total economic embargo against Germany, and be prepared to fight a defensive war.[32] Lindsay twice sent an urgent message to London relaying Roosevelt's robust approach. Twice he received no reply.

The president still believed that isolationist sentiment was too strong for him to join the British and French in a war against Hitler, but he thought that if Germany invaded an independent nation he could perhaps persuade the American people to support economic sanctions and to let him sell arms at a discount to the British and French.

Kennedy's response to the betrayal of the Czechs was flippant. On encountering the Czech minister Jan Masaryk in the immediate aftermath of the Munich deal, he joked, "Isn't it wonderful. Now I can get to Palm Beach after all."[33] Kennedy knew he needed to propose some startling new approach to the Czech problem if he was to add anything to his dispatches to Washington, so he sent an urgent telegram to Lindbergh in Brittany asking him to come immediately. On September 21, the Lindberghs flew to London for lunch at the embassy and the conversation turned to the comparative strength of Europe's air forces.

As Rose recalled, "The Colonel gave us a rude awakening by declaring from his observations that Germany could turn out dozens of planes to England's one."[34] He went on to paint a chilling vision of the impending European war that, he predicted, would be even more devastating than the trench-bound carnage of World War One. With its fleets of bomber planes, "Germany now has the means of destroying London, Paris and Prague if she wishes," Lindbergh told Kennedy, who relayed the grim message to Hull. "For the first time in history a nation has the power either to save or to ruin the great cities of Europe," Kennedy wrote. "England and France are far too weak in the air to protect themselves."[35] Kennedy asked Lindbergh to write his opinion in a memorandum for Hull.

While in London, Lindbergh called Nancy Astor and was promptly invited to Cliveden. There, to anyone who would listen, the flier denigrated the British at every turn with remarks like, "The best Englishmen have gone either to the empire or to the sea," "The English are in no shape for war," "This is the beginning of the end of England as a great power. She may be a 'hornet's nest' but she is no longer a 'lion's den'."[36] It was a persistently defeatist view that he dared not express outside the company of appeasers.

Lindbergh was more open about his pro-German sentiments. Typical was his thought that Hitler could "bluff about as he wishes without danger. He probably enjoys having the fate of the world in his hands, especially after the way the world treated Germany after the war. I cannot blame him too much for making France and England worry a bit. . . . Hitler is a mystic and a fanatic, but his actions and results in the past do not lead me to believe he is insane."[37]

Four days later, as Chamberlain wrestled with the Czech crisis in back-to-back meetings of the cabinet, Lindbergh made his way to Hammersmith in West London to attend a British Union of Fascists rally addressed by its leader, Sir Oswald Mosley.[38] He passed through a Communist demonstration to get to the hall and, while he found Mosley's sub-Hitler address "not too intelligent," he thought it "of a much higher quality than that of the Communists. It always seems that the Fascist group is better than the Communist group."[39]

Lindbergh's somber assessment of the relative air strengths in Europe that Kennedy passed to Hull was in line with what the State Department already believed, which is hardly surprising as their view depended on information that largely originated from Lindbergh. Roosevelt's special secret emissary Baruch, however, confirmed much of Lindbergh's pessimistic diagnosis, reporting that Germany had spent 105 billion marks ($700 million in 2014 terms) on arms the previous year.

The truth, however, was very different. Lindbergh reported to Hull that Germany's air force outnumbered the British by five to one and the Americans by eleven to one, and told Bullitt and the French air minister, Guy La Chambre, that Germany was producing 40,000 warplanes a year. In fact, Germany manufactured just 8,000 warplanes in 1938 and 1939 while Britain turned out 11,000.[40] By using Lindbergh as his willing conduit, Göring misled the Americans, the British, and the French into believing that they were outgunned and that resistance to Hitler was futile.

Lindbergh emerged as an unwitting agent in a propaganda coup for the Nazis, who in 1938 won the air war over Europe without a shot being fired. Churchill was one of the few to suspect what had occurred. In a statement issued on September 21, he declared, "The partition of Czechoslovakia under pressure from England and France amounts to the complete surrender of the Western Democracies to the Nazi threat of force. Such a collapse will bring peace and security neither to England nor to France. On the contrary, it will place these two nations in an ever weaker and more dangerous situation."[41]

Kennedy was active in shoring up appeasement in its dying moments. To minimize the growing alarm about war among the British, at the request of the Foreign Office he reached out to his old contacts at Paramount to censor a newsreel interview with

A. J. Cummings, a well regarded political commentator for the liberal *News Chronicle*, who had declared, "Our statesmen have been guilty of what I think is a piece of yellow diplomacy."[42] The Paramount people complied and the remark was removed. When Kennedy's role in censoring the newsreel came to light weeks later, he became a target of abuse for those in Britain who advocated standing up to Hitler.

Aware that America remained impotent so long as isolationist feelings remained strong in Congress and the nation, Roosevelt declined a direct appeal by Beneš for him to openly demand that Britain and France stand by their commitment to protect his country. The president also turned down Kennedy's request that Chamberlain be allowed to broadcast to the American people. If he was to defeat isolationism, the last thing Roosevelt needed was for the British prime minister to go on the radio to make the case for appeasement.

On September 22, Chamberlain flew to Bad Godesberg on the Rhine to meet again with Hitler, expecting to discuss the timetable for the ordered German annexation of the Sudetenland. Instead, Hitler said, "I'm exceedingly sorry, but after the events of the last few days [the deaths of protesting Sudeten Germans by Czech police], this solution is no longer any use."[43] If the Allies did not agree to his plan to occupy the Sudetenland by September 28, the whole of Czechoslovakia would immediately be invaded by German troops. The following day, as a concession, Hitler agreed to move the deadline to October 1.

Chamberlain returned to London exhausted, bewildered, and downhearted. Daladier informed him that in the new circumstances, the French were now prepared to fight. Chamberlain had little option but to acquiesce. On September 23, poised for an imminent German invasion, Czechoslovakia mobilized its troops. On the weekend of September 24 and 25, the British Cabinet went into prolonged session and a clear rift opened between the appeasers, led by Chamberlain, and those, like Halifax and Cooper, who were appalled at Hitler "dictating terms . . . as though he had won a war."[44]

Daladier and his supreme army commander, General Maurice Gustave Gamelin,[45] flew to London on the morning of September 26 to discuss the next steps. Although the difference between what the British and French had agreed to and what Hitler was now demanding was only a matter of timing, it was belatedly decided to take a stand. Unless Hitler agreed to the Berchtesgaden terms, agreeing to take the Sudetenland but to demand nothing more, Britain and France would go to war. A joint emissary, Sir Horace Wilson,[46] was commissioned to fly to Berlin to deliver the ultimatum in person to Hitler. Hearing of the Anglo-French verdict, Roosevelt appealed for calm and, through diplomatic channels, urged Mussolini to summon a four-power conference.

The same day Horace Wilson flew to Berlin, Chamberlain addressed the British people on the radio before delivering the Anglo-French verdict to the Commons. In words that would sound through history, Chamberlain's broadcast shamelessly played down the importance of the integrity of Czechoslovakia. "How horrible, fantastic, incredible it is that we should be digging trenches and trying on gas masks here because of a quarrel in a faraway country between people of whom we know nothing," he said. "It seems still more impossible that a quarrel which has already been settled in principle should be the subject of war."

"However much we may sympathize with a small nation confronted by a big and powerful neighbor, we cannot in all circumstances undertake to involve the whole British Empire in war simply on her account," he said. "If we have to fight it must be on larger issues than that." Hitler had told him that once the Sudetenland had been ceded to Germany, "that is the end of Germany's territorial claims in Europe."[47]

Hitler, however, was in no mood to compromise. In the Reich Chancellery, as Wilson arrived to present the Anglo-French terms, the Führer flew into a rage, screaming at the British envoy that "the Germans were being treated like niggers; one would not dare treat even the Turks like that," promising "to smash the Czechs,"[48] and predicting that the world would be at war within a week.

Later that day, in a bombastic broadcast from the Berlin Sportpalast, Hitler delivered another bloodcurdling performance, making clear that he was in no mood to abandon his demands. "[Beneš] will either accept this offer and now at last give the Germans their freedom, or we will go and fetch this freedom for ourselves," he said.[49] The American broadcaster William Shirer,[50] sitting in the balcony directly above Hitler, recorded in his diary, "For the first time in all the years I've observed him, [Hitler] seemed tonight to have completely lost control of himself."[51]

Roosevelt listened to the ranting on the radio in his White House study. "Did you hear Hitler today, his shrieks, his histrionics, and the effect on the huge audience?" the president asked his young distant cousin Margaret Suckley.[52] "They did not applaud, they made noises like animals."[53] Lindbergh listened to the address at Cliveden and concluded, perversely, that Hitler "seemed to leave considerable hope that war may be avoided."[54]

Also listening to Hitler's tirade was Kennedy, who took a different view to his friend Lindbergh. The ambassador was now convinced that Britain was on the brink of war and he began thinking about evacuating his family from London. "I'm feeling very blue myself today," he wrote Krock, "because I am starting to think about sending Rose and the children back to America and stay here alone for how long God only knows. Maybe never see them again."[55] A declaration of war by Chamberlain was not in his presidential game plan.

On September 28, "Black Wednesday," the British Parliament met to consider the unfolding crisis. After Chamberlain described the chronology of events that had led Europe to the brink of war, the packed Commons watched as a note was hurriedly delivered into the prime minister's hand. A pregnant silence fell over the chamber as Chamberlain took a full five minutes to read the message.

According to Nicolson, Chamberlain's "whole face, his whole body, seemed to change. He raised his face so that the light from the ceiling fell full upon it. All the lines of anxiety and weariness seemed suddenly to have been smoothed out; he appeared ten years younger and triumphant."[56] Chamberlain looked around the House. "Herr Hitler has just agreed to postpone his mobilization for twenty-four hours and to meet me in conference with Signor Mussolini and Monsieur Daladier at Munich," he said. "I need not say what my answer will be. I will go to see what I can do as a last resort."[57]

At the urging of both Chamberlain and Roosevelt, Mussolini had telephoned Hitler proposing an eleventh-hour four-power summit between Germany, Italy, Britain, and France, to which Hitler, anxious that he might lose Italian support, reluctantly agreed.[58] At a tense and strange meeting the following day in the Führerhaus on the Königsplatz, the ceding of the Sudetenland to Germany was confirmed, with German troops allowed to march in just two days later, on October 1.

The two Czech government officials who were invited to witness their allies debating their country's fate were obliged to wait in a nearby room before being informed of the decision. Daladier poured himself a drink and Chamberlain could not stifle a yawn as a French official read out the terms of the agreement to the Czech pair, who wept as they heard the extent of the betrayal. "They don't know what they are doing to us or to themselves," said one to the other.[59] The deal, forged at gunpoint, still left 250,000 German speakers living in the remainder of Czechoslovakia, while 800,000 Czechs would wake up to find themselves German citizens living in German Sudetenland.

In a much hyped return to Britain, Chamberlain was greeted by ecstatic crowds and every member of his cabinet on the runway of Heston airfield. He waved the Munich agreement above his head. "This morning I had another talk with the German Chancellor, Herr Hitler, and here is the paper which bears his name upon it as well as mine," he said. The agreement solemnly declared, "We regard the agreement signed last night . . . as symbolic of the desire of our two peoples never to go to war with one another again."

Speaking from a window of 10 Downing Street later that evening, Chamberlain said the words for which he is still best remembered, the final self-deluding act of appeasement and the end of peace in Europe: "I believe it is peace for our time."[60] Daladier, who had a keener grasp of reality than his British counterpart, was also greeted by crowds cheering with relief when he landed at Le Bourget. "The bloody fools," he muttered.[61]

CHAPTER SEVEN

KRISTALLNACHT

Kennedy doubles down on appeasement,
Kristallnacht betrays the true nature of Hitler's regime,
Lindbergh plans to move to Berlin, Roosevelt snubs
Kennedy as America rearms.

MUNICH CHANGED EVERYTHING. Chamberlain was so traumatized by dealing with Hitler face to face that his health fast began to fade. His reputation as a peacemaker did not last long, as it became evident that Hitler had lied and the outbreak of war had merely been delayed. Appeasement was discredited and those who clung to it began to suffer, while those who proposed a more robust response to the dictators were in the ascendant.

Above all, public opinion began to shift. Lindbergh and Kennedy both reported how surprised they were that Londoners were indignant at the shabby treatment meted out to the Czechs. In Britain, the submissive spirit of Cliveden gave way to a sense of national defiance. In America, too, opinion slowly began to move toward an understanding that pulling the bedclothes up over your head in times of danger is bad policy.

In Britain, the nervous euphoria that greeted Chamberlain's return from Munich soon turned to angry shame that Britain had delivered an independent nation into Hitler's arms. On October 2, 1938, Duff Cooper resigned from the government to join Churchill and Eden on the backbenches. "The Prime Minister has believed in addressing Herr Hitler through the language of sweet reasonableness. I have believed that he was more open to the language of the mailed fist," Cooper said in his resignation speech.[1] To friends, Cooper explained, "It was 'peace with honor' I could not stomach. If he'd come back from Munich saying 'peace with terrible, unmitigated, unparalleled dishonor,' perhaps I might have stayed."[2]

In the Commons' Munich debate, Chamberlain faced the full wrath of Churchill, glowering as he delivered a coruscating condemnation of appeasement's sorry achievements. "We have sustained a total and unmitigated defeat," he declared. "I find unendurable the sense of our country falling into the power, into the orbit and influence of Nazi Germany, and of our existence becoming dependent upon their goodwill or pleasure."[3] For Roosevelt, Churchill's address was a rally to arms. As Roosevelt's biographer Conrad Black put it, "Roosevelt thought he saw, for the first time, the British leader with whom he could make a holy alliance, informal at first, against the obscene ambition of Adolf Hitler."[4]

Lindbergh explained to Kennedy's son Joseph Jr. what he thought Munich had achieved. "[Lindbergh] said [the German air fleet] would have completely wiped out all the cities in France and England," he wrote his father. "He felt that to destroy the culture of Europe for the sake of an error made in the Treaty of Versailles was ridiculous."[5] Lindbergh found Churchill's noble sentiments hard to fathom. "The English are ready to fight for their principles, throwing all judgment to the winds," he said. "I do not see how democratic prestige would gain much from an unsuccessful war."[6]

Nor did Kennedy grasp the significance of the change in British opinion. In a note to Hull, he described the president's appeal to the Europeans to find a peaceful solution to the Czech crisis as every bit as effective in chastening Hitler as the British cabinet's decision to mobilize the Royal Navy, the most powerful fighting fleet in the world. "In view of the average American's desire for non-involvement in a European war, and in order to meet any similar future crisis, we should now try to get back to a middle position where we will have as an unprejudiced neutral good offices as such to offer," he said. He was eager that America remain impartial lest "an emotional" pro-democratic stance arouse Americans "towards action which would hold nothing for them but incalculable material and personal loss."[7]

With the Munich agreement, Kennedy found his instinct for anticipating events had deserted him. Until then he had always been ahead of the game, using a rare intuitive skill to build his fortune. He sold all his stocks before the 1929 crash, arranged deals with whisky distributors ahead of the repeal of Prohibition, and backed the New Deal when other businessmen gave it a wide berth. But when it came to appeasement and gauging the danger to America of the dictators, Kennedy displayed a rare tin ear.

Kennedy insisted that Chamberlain was right to try to come to an accommodation with Hitler at Munich. He told Halifax, who was critical of the way Chamberlain had handled the crisis, that he was "entirely in sympathy with, and a warm admirer of, everything the prime minister had done."[8] Like Chamberlain, Kennedy approached international affairs with the apolitical indifference of a business-man. As peace alone could guarantee the conditions for commerce to prosper, Kennedy was opposed to war. So long as America's national interest was not affected, he saw no reason for the US to embroil itself in foreign adventures like defending the Czechs. He shared Chamberlain's view that Munich was a pragmatic if unseemly solu-tion to an intractable conflict of interests.

Chamberlain had returned from his trysts with Hitler convinced he had saved the world. Taking Hitler at his word, he expected the next step to be disarmament talks and a new post-Versailles settle-ment. He wrote to his sister, "I believe we have at last got on top of the dictators."[9]

Believing that Chamberlain was on the right track, Kennedy con-tinued to plump for appeasement. He was invited to talk at a Tra-falgar Day dinner, a hallowed date in the British military calendar that marked Lord Nelson's[10] defeat of the French and Spanish navies in 1805, a victory that had established Britain as the world's pre-eminent naval power. It was therefore undiplomatic, impolite, and impolitic to suggest to the assembled naval brass, eager for reassur-ance, that, while he found it "hard to quarrel with the decision of any nation to build up its military forces . . . nevertheless, the arma-ment burden is approaching a point, it seems to me, where it threat-ens sooner or later to engulf us all in major disaster." Worse was to follow. "The democratic and dictator countries differ ideologically, to be sure, but that should not preclude the possibility of good rela-tions between them," he told his appalled audience.[11]

The speech stoked violent criticism of Kennedy on both sides of the Atlantic, the *New York Post* declaring, "For [Kennedy] to propose that the United States make a friend of the man who boasts that he is out to destroy democracy, religion and all of the other principles which free Americans hold dear . . . passes understanding."[12] Lippmann correctly judged the address as "designed to please . . . the voters at home."[13] Unfazed, Kennedy blamed "a number of Jewish publishers and writers" for the dissent.[14] At Harvard, the young John F. Kennedy, leaping to his father's defense, came to a similar conclusion. "While it seemed to be unpopular with the Jews etc., was considered to be very good by everyone who wasn't bitterly anti-fascist," he wrote his father.

One of "the Jews" in question, who had been quietly backing Kennedy's surreptitious 1940 presidential bid, withdrew his support.[15] Roosevelt's response to the speech was left unrecorded, though the State Department view was that "no one is going to be hurt unless it be Mr. Kennedy himself."[16]

In private letters, Kennedy tried to put a gloss on his unfortunate words. "I have no more sympathy with Hitler's ideas than anyone in America, but I asked myself, what am I going to do about it?" he wrote to the Hearst organization's T. J. White. "Unless England and France are prepared to fight . . . there is no point in staying on the side lines and sticking your tongue out at somebody who is a good deal bigger than you are. As far as the United States goes, we ought to mind our own business." Adding that "75% of the attacks made on me by mail were by Jews," he urged White to pass the letter on to Hearst. "I would like him to know how I feel."[17]

The furor over the Trafalgar speech suggested to Kennedy that he had grown out of touch with domestic opinion. Notwithstanding the war fever gripping Britain, the ambassador decided to return home at the end of December, writing to Lindbergh that he was "a little dizzy watching the present international situation and want to get to the United States to see what's happening there." Kennedy's son John reported that his father was returning because he "doesn't like the idea of sitting back and letting the Jewish columnists in America kick his head off. . . . If we could possibly do without [Britain], I think Dad would speak against us being drawn into war."[18]

The Trafalgar speech continued to cause consternation at the State Department, not least because Kennedy's sometime shill, the *New York Times* Washington reporter Arthur Krock, used it to draw attention to the difference between Kennedy's isolationism and Roosevelt's guarded approach to war, a distinction he felt certain would help Kennedy in a presidential contest. Krock wrote about "the difficulty faced these days by a government with an idealistic foreign policy that cannot be applied or very clearly explained."[19] Krock was told by State Department officials that there would be no change in administration policy.

Behind closed doors, however, there had been a significant readjustment. Munich had forced a change in the president's thinking. He was too canny to admit to such a course, but it was becoming more obvious to Roosevelt by the day that war in Europe was a matter of months away. He considered how America should respond, whether America should arm Britain and France, and how soon America should prepare itself to take part in the war.

He had already let slip to his intimates that if war led to an end of democracy in most of Europe, he would throw his weight behind the remaining democracies. Warning of "an inevitable conflict within five years," he wrote to William Phillips, newly appointed ambassador in Rome, "If we get the idea that the future of our form of government is threatened by a coalition of European dictators we might wade in with everything we have to give." He believed that "ninety per cent of our people are definitely anti-German and anti-Italian in sentiment. . . . I would strongly encourage their natural sympathy while at the same time avoiding any thought of sending troops to Europe."[20]

In a private message sent to Chamberlain via Sir Arthur Murray, a former British military attaché in Washington DC who had befriended Roosevelt when the latter was assistant secretary of the navy, the president gave a secret assurance that, in the event of war between Britain and Germany, he would provide "the industrial resources of the American nation, [to the extent that] he, the President could achieve it."[21] It was a bold and unprecedented signal of support. To the president's amazement, Chamberlain did not respond to the lifeline thrown him.

In a radio address on October 26 on the implications of Munich for Americans, the president declared, "No one who lived through the grave hours of last month can doubt the longing of most of the peoples of the world for an enduring peace." But then he opened five sentences in a row with the emphatic phrase "There can be no peace if," including, "There can be no peace if the reign of law is to be replaced by a recurrent sanctification of sheer force. There can be no peace if national policy adopts as a deliberate instrument the threat of war."[22] The broadcast was interpreted as a slap in the face to Kennedy and the isolationists. The ambassador was appalled that the president should so publicly rebuke him and referred to the broadcast as "a stab in the back."[23]

Undeterred, the next day Kennedy resumed praising appeasement, bemoaning the fact that "if you see anything good in dictatorships, you alienate the democracies."[24] Horrified at Kennedy's evenhanded attitude toward the Nazis, the Austrian-born Felix Frankfurter, who had been elevated by the president to the Supreme Court, wrote to Roosevelt, "It is the traditional function of American functionaries abroad *not* to 'see anything good in dictatorships'."[25]

The rivalry between president and ambassador had again been exposed, and Kennedy's allies in the press came to his aid. "The White House has on its hands a fighting Irishman, with blazing eyes and a determination to strip the bandages of deceit, innuendo and misrepresentation bound around the eyes of American citizens," declared Boake Carter in the *New York Mirror*.[26]

With the administration's connivance, the French government began exploring how to circumvent the neutrality laws and buy some of the immense spare capacity of America's military aircraft industry. Much to Lindbergh's discomfort, the French, through Bullitt, proposed a plan conceived by the French financier and former deputy general of the League of Nations, Jean Monnet,[27] and backed by Daladier to set up plants in Canada to assemble warplanes from parts manufactured in the US.

Bullitt asked Lindbergh to lead the French effort, but Lindbergh approached the issue from an unlikely perspective. "Those who take part in the establishment of factories in Canada for the production of warplanes for France will be considered successful only in case a war is fought," he wrote in his diary. "Therefore, success would depend upon the destruction of European civilization."[28] He replied with a counterintuitive proposal: France should buy warplanes from Germany, an idea which, though greeted at first by French laughter, was not entirely ridiculous. Lindbergh assumed that Hitler would strike east to win new territory for Germans to settle and to confront Soviet Communism. As such, he imagined there would be a mutual benefit in the trade.

Instead of helping the French, Lindbergh advanced his arrangements to spend the winter of 1938–39 in Berlin, where Hitler's architect, Albert Speer,[29] was scouting houses for him to rent. To have a world-famous hero like Lindbergh settle in Germany despite the Munich agreement was deemed an enormous propaganda coup. "I am anxious to learn more about [Germany]," Lindbergh confided to his diary. "The Germans are a great people, and I believe their welfare is inseparable from that of Europe."[30] In early October, Lindbergh arrived in the German capital, which he found had "lost the air of tenseness I noticed in 1936 and now has the appearance of a healthy, busy, modern city."[31] He continued to tour German air bases, test-flying their most advanced fighters and bombers.

As soon as the 1938 midterm elections were behind him, Roosevelt switched from pandering to the Midwestern isolationists, who liked the New Deal but were wary of foreign involvements, to wooing the Southern Democrats, who disliked intervention in the economy but were prepared to support rearmament if Britain was the beneficiary. He persuaded Congress to grant $500 million toward building warplanes and warships.

Roosevelt was frustrated that America was not already armed. "Had we had this summer 5,000 planes and the capacity immediately to produce 10,000 per year, even though I might have had to ask Congress for authority to sell or lend them to the countries in Europe, Hitler would not have dared to take the stand he did," he told Morgenthau.[32]

The president welcomed Monnet to Hyde Park to expedite the plan, with or without Lindbergh's help, to construct planes in Canadian plants, and he pledged to progress the deal with Canada's prime minister, William Mackenzie King.[33] Already General George C. Marshall,[34] deputy chief of staff of the army and a protégé of John Pershing,[35] leader of the American expeditionary force in World War One, had approached Hopkins about redirecting the New Deal's Works Progress Administration toward rearming America.

On October 16, Roosevelt met with Bullitt, Hopkins, and others to sign off on the retooling of the WPA, which was given an initial target of 15,000 warplanes a year to be built in seven government-owned plants on War Department sites; the result was that output was raised from 1,200 aircraft a year to 10,000. "Hopkins [appointed commerce secretary on December 24] could build these plants without cost to the Treasury," Roosevelt said, "because it would be work relief which otherwise would have to be provided in any case."[36]

In a candid tour d'horizon to his cabinet, Roosevelt speculated that as soon as war was declared, the British navy would dominate the Atlantic and the Mediterranean, landlocking German and Italian forces and denying Germany food and essential products with a naval embargo. The president reiterated Lindbergh's mistaken belief that Germany enjoyed air superiority, had more warplanes than England, France, and the Soviet Union put together, and a capacity to make planes three times faster.

Ickes recorded the president saying, "There could be bought in this country materials, nonmilitary in themselves, such as pipes from which shells could be made, which could easily be turned into shells and bullets and airplanes," and that "even if we had to enforce our neutrality laws, there would be a large outlet by such methods for munitions to flow toward England and France by way of Canada and otherwise."[37]

Still the rump of isolationists in Congress kept up the pressure to slow American rearmament, Nye decrying cooperation between the president and "certain European powers" to provide "undue military preparedness." The fiercely isolationist Senator William Borah, the "Lion of Idaho," joined him, declaring, "The people of the United States are not interested in European boundaries. . . . They call it peace to get us in. But after we get in it is war."[38]

The president was aware that the image of the British among Americans needed to be improved if he was to forge an alliance with Britain. Since the War of Independence, the British had come to be considered deadly rivals with a rarely understood system of government—constitutional monarchy—that appeared an affront to American democracy. Roosevelt, a lifelong Anglophile and Germanophobe, believed that if only Americans could be encouraged to like the British royal family more, his job of persuading them to back Britain would be easier.

He decided to play on the widespread American interest in celebrities and acquaint the country with the new young British monarch, George VI, and his wife, Queen Elizabeth. As the Munich crisis reached its nadir, Roosevelt wrote a letter to the king which, on the president's instructions, Kennedy delivered in person. Roosevelt had neglected to tell his ambassador what the missive contained. On September 27, Kennedy drove to Buckingham Palace where the king read the letter out loud—which is how Kennedy came to hear for the first time that the royal couple were invited to visit the United States. That the king could not help noticing that the invitation took the ambassador by surprise was humiliating for Kennedy. In subsequent weeks, Roosevelt would twist the knife, neither telling Kennedy the details of the visit nor extending an invitation for him and Rose to accompany the royal couple on their American tour.

Kennedy was being made to pay for his continued pursuit of appeasement. Despite his proud and prickly Irish roots, he had been easily seduced by London society, the house party invitations from the Astors, and the easy intimacy with which government ministers had welcomed him into their midst. Above all, he had been disarmed by the effortless charm of the stammering King George.

Although Kennedy appeared socially confident, he felt that a lingering doubt hung over his family's status. The Boston Brahmins had been cruel to the Kennedys simply because they were Irish. He had moved to the wealthy Protestant suburb of Brookline, yet still they were shunned by Boston's WASPs. Talking with one of her son John's Harvard friends, Rose once asked, "When are the nice people of Boston going to accept us?"[39]

Kennedy was often made to feel second-best among the old wealthy, such as the Roosevelts. In Britain, which was ostensibly riddled with class divisions, the easy way in which he had penetrated the upper class suggested to Kennedy that he and his family had finally arrived. It was a mark of the unaffected affability of the king and queen that they were able to put the Kennedys at ease, and the ambassador had come to think of the royal couple as true friends. To be excluded from the royal visit was a cruel blow.

At the end of October, in a letter marked "For the Secretary personally," Kennedy expressed his hurt to Hull. "While I do not like to bother you with this," he wrote, "I am somewhat embarrassed by being questioned practically every day in connection with the King's trip by the King's Secretaries and the Foreign Office," he wrote. "If the President wanted me to be aware of any discussions he is having I suppose he would inform me. . . . Because I imagine my contacts and prestige here would be seriously jeopardized I hate to admit knowing nothing about it. . . . Although it is difficult I can continue to look like a dummy and carry on the best I can."[40]

Roosevelt irritated Kennedy further by arranging every last detail of the royal itinerary himself. His aim was to ensure that the usual regal pomp and circumstance, which might jar with Americans, was kept to a minimum. When the king accepted the invitation, the president replied, "In my judgment, to the American people, the essential democracy of yourself and the Queen makes the greatest appeal of all. . . . If you could stay with us at Hyde Park for two or three days, the simplicity and naturalness of such a visit would produce a most excellent effect." He concluded, "I need not tell you how happy I am that Great Britain and the United States have been able to cooperate so effectively in the prevention of war—even though we cannot say we are 'out of the woods' yet."[41]

While Kennedy was taking umbrage at being excluded from the arrangements, Lindbergh returned to Berlin, where, after touring a Junkers plant, he went to a stag dinner at the American embassy given by the new US ambassador to Berlin, Hugh Wilson.[42] Among the guests was Göring, who leapt toward him. "I noticed he had a red box and some papers in his hand," Lindbergh recalled. "He shook hands, handed me the box and papers, and spoke a few sentences in German. I found that he had presented me with the German Eagle, one of the highest German decorations, 'by order of the Führer.'"[43]

Lindbergh failed to grasp that by accepting a Nazi decoration he had been fatally compromised. Anne, however, immediately understood how an award from Hitler would play in America. Returning from the party, Lindbergh showed off the Nazi bauble to his wife, who "gave it but a fleeting glance and then—without the slightest trace of emotion—remarked: 'The Albatross'."[44]

As soon as Lindbergh's German honor was reported in the press, Ickes turned the knife. In an address to the Cleveland Zionist Society, he asked, "How can any American accept a decoration at the hand of a brutal dictator who, with that same hand, is robbing and torturing thousands of fellow human beings?"[45] The Nazi government's objections to Ickes's remarks were so vehement that they threatened to break off all diplomatic relations with the United States. Roosevelt was unmoved, telling under secretary of state Sumner Welles, "It would not hurt us if Germany should sever diplomatic relations. So what?"[46]

Lindbergh's association with leading Nazis became even more embarrassing when, on the night of November 9, hell broke loose in Germany. Two days before, a seventeen-year-old Pole, Herschel Grynszpan, had shot dead a German diplomat in Paris in protest at the way in which 17,000 Jewish Germans, including his own parents, were expelled from Germany but left in diplomatic limbo, neither allowed to remain in Germany nor, through lack of permits, to enter Poland. The murder provided a pretext for the propaganda minister, Joseph Goebbels,[47] to demand "spontaneous demonstrations" by the general population, while the head of the SS, Heinrich Himmler, ordered his troops to attack Jews and their businesses.

On what came to be known as Kristallnacht, after the broken glass strewn in the streets, thousands of Jews were set upon and dozens were killed. About two hundred synagogues were set alight, eight hundred stores were looted and burned, and Jews became subject to a punitive tax. Decrees banned Jews from cinemas, theaters, and other places of entertainment. Jewish students were barred from universities. Jews had their passports revoked, meaning that they could not leave Germany. Jewish ghettoes were established in cities. Twenty thousand Jews were dispatched to concentration camps.

Reaction around the world to Kristallnacht and its immediate aftermath was intense. "The news of the past few days from Germany has deeply shocked public opinion in the United States," Roosevelt told reporters on November 15, before ordering Ambassador Wilson home from Berlin. "I myself could scarcely believe that such things could occur in this twentieth-century civilization."[48] Chamberlain's condemnation, however, was slow in coming. Anxious to keep the British reputation for fairness intact, the better to support Britain when war came, Roosevelt asked Kennedy to urge the prime minister to issue a condemnatory statement without delay. Again Chamberlain was found wanting; instead of making an outright condemnation, he suggested that somewhere should be found for German Jews to live outside the Third Reich. Roosevelt complained to Herbert C. Pell,[49] the American ambassador in Lisbon, "Our British friends must begin to fish or cut bait."[50]

Kennedy was disturbed by the attacks on Jews because he feared this might draw America into the war. He confided to Lindbergh on November 12, "This last drive on the Jews in Germany has really made the most ardent hopers for peace very sick at heart. . . . Isn't there some way to persuade [the Nazis] it is on a situation like this that the whole program of saving western civilization might hinge?"[51]

Before returning to America for Christmas, Kennedy told American reporters in London that he was urging the president to take a more isolationist line than he was likely to follow. "I am going home to face the President and tell him what I think," he declared, "and what I think won't please him." Not for the first time, Roosevelt's inner circle urged the president to fire him. Farley told Morgenthau that Roosevelt was "terribly peeved with Joe. . . . When Joe comes back, that will probably be the beginning of the end."[52]

Lindbergh's response to Kristallnacht was one of puzzlement. "I do not understand these riots on the part of the Germans," he told his diary. "They have undoubtedly had a Jewish problem, but why is it necessary to handle it so unreasonably? My admiration for the Germans is constantly being dashed against some rock such as this." He asked himself, "By bringing up the Jewish issue and forcing German Jews into other countries, do the Germans hope to create an international anti-Jewish movement? Or is it simply an inherent German hatred of the Jews?"[53]

Trying to make sense of Kristallnacht, he noted, "Germans all seem to be anti-Jewish. I did not talk to a single person who I felt was not ashamed of the lawlessness and disorder of the recent demonstrations. But neither did I talk to anyone who did not want the Jews to get out of Germany." He concluded that "the Jew, according to the German, is largely responsible for the internal collapse and revolution following the war. At the time of the [Weimar] inflation the Jews are said to have obtained the ownership of a large percentage of the property in Berlin and other cities—lived in the best houses, drove the best automobiles, and mixed with the prettiest girls." In a Berlin movie theater, he saw the racial caricatures used to demonize Jews and recorded, without comment, how the Nazis depicted "the typical, old-country type of Jew with a long black beard, a black gown, a caricatured Jewish nose, and a hand stretched out, obviously to receive money."[54]

Among those sickened by Kristallnacht were Anne Lindbergh and her mother. It was clear to Anne that the move to Berlin was now impossible. American newspaper reports that Lindbergh had befriended the Nazi top brass and was scouting out homes in Berlin damaged his already battered reputation. "With confused emotions we say goodbye to Colonel Charles A. Lindbergh, who wants to go and live in Berlin, presumably occupying a house that once belonged to Jews," wrote *The New Yorker*. When Kennedy heard that Lindbergh had decided not to live in Berlin, he expressed his regret, "because I think you are probably the only contact the United States now has on speaking terms with Hitler."[55]

Kristallnacht gave Father Coughlin a chance to reclaim the limelight. His powers were much diminished—over time, he had been banned from the national networks—yet he still attracted an audience of millions on independent stations. He expressed his "sincere sympathy to the millions of humble, religious Jews [for a world that] does not always distinguish between good Jews and the bad Jews; a world which lashes at the pillar of persecution the innocent Jews for the misdemeanors of the guilty Jews."

"Nazism is so hostile to Jewry," he ventured to explain, because Germans blamed Jews for the misfortune "suffered by the Fatherland since the signing of the Versailles Treaty."[56] The broadcast sparked the controversy on which the priest thrived and marked a brief surge in interest in his isolationist broadcasts. The resurgence of Coughlin was not lost on the Nazi regime in Germany. "The German hero in America for the moment is the Rev. Charles Coughlin," reported a Berlin-based reporter for the *New York Times*.[57]

Another apologist for Hitler whose reputation was damaged by Kristallnacht was Leni Riefenstahl,[58] who arrived in New York aboard the *Europa* on November 4. She was in America to promote *Olympia*, her elegiac movie account of the Nazi 1936 Olympics, which American Olympics organizer and ardent isolationist Avery Brundage[59] believed was "the greatest Olympic film ever made." The American press described Riefenstahl as "Hitler's delegate in a skirt" and the "woman behind the dictator."[60] "To me, Hitler is the greatest man who ever lived," she gushed in an interview with the *Detroit News* before her arrival. "He truly is without fault, so simple and at the same time possessed of masculine strength. . . . He's really wonderful."[61] Mobbed by reporters on the New York quay, she was obliged to deny she was Hitler's lover.

Five days after she landed came Kristallnacht.[62] Riefenstahl continued her American tour unabashed, visiting Washington DC and then Chicago, where Brundage screened *Olympia* at the Chicago Engineers' Club to a group that included seven German diplomats. On November 18, she was regally entertained in Detroit by Henry Ford, who was both anti-Semitic and isolationist. Hopeful of good publicity, he gave her a Model T. Ford "praised the elimination of unemployment in our country and in general seemed to have a soft spot for [National] Socialism," she recalled, and told her he looked forward to meeting Hitler when he attended the next Nazi rally in Nuremberg.[63]

When Riefenstahl reached Los Angeles on November 24, she was met by protesters. A demonstration by the Anti-Nazi League and the Motion Picture Artists Committee caused producers, directors, and studio heads to cancel meetings with her, though some executives kept their appointments. A party thrown by the silent comedy producer Hal Roach[64] to honor her was boycotted by Hollywood's top stars, and a day after asking Riefenstahl to sign a contract for the distribution of *Olympia*, Louis B. Mayer withdrew rather than risk a boycott of MGM movies.

One who welcomed Riefenstahl was Walt Disney. As Riefenstahl recalled:

> In Hollywood, naturally, I ran into resistance from the Jews who, on my arrival, had already published a giant advertisement in several newspapers that—under the headline "There is no place in Hollywood for Fraulein Riefenstahl"—demanded a boycott against me. Numerous American film directors didn't dare to receive me because of their financial dependence on the Jewish moneymen.
>
> An honorable exception, Walt Disney, creator of *Snow White*, warmly welcomed me and showed me his extensive studios and even his latest work. It was gratifying to learn how thoroughly proper Americans distance themselves from the smear campaigns of the Jews.[65]

Like Ford, the political ingenue Disney was an admirer of
National Socialism. According to animator Art Babbitt,[66] Disney
attended meetings of the pro-Nazi Los Angeles Bund.[67] He soon
became aware, however, of how toxic Riefenstahl had become, and,
though he screened for her the Mickey Mouse "Sorcerer's Appren-
tice" episode from *Fantasia*, he declined to have a photograph taken
with her and would not allow *Olympia* to be shown on the Disney lot.

After Riefenstahl left the studio, Disney claimed not to know
who his distinguished visitor was. Disney's amnesia was not just
good politics; it was good business. As Europe descended into war
and revenues from overseas distribution dried up, Disney needed an
alternative if he was to keep his business alive. And that was to come
from an unlikely source.

The fact that Riefenstahl's Los Angeles visit coincided with
Kristallnacht proved a turning point in Hollywood's response to
Nazism. Studios began to plan movies about the prelude to war,
about the comical as well as the sinister side of Nazism, and about
the victims of the dictators. The support of movie producers and
actors was a significant factor in the success of Roosevelt's efforts
to persuade Americans to prepare for war. The unofficial leader of
the interventionists was Douglas Fairbanks Jr.,[68] who had gone to
school with James Roosevelt. Through Fairbanks and show business friends like the screenwriter Robert E. Sherwood,[69] the president was kept informed of the movies' contributions to the nascent
war effort.

Coming so fast after the Munich agreement, public revulsion at
Kristallnacht allowed Roosevelt to step up his circumvention of the
neutrality laws and defy isolationists in Congress. In November, a
Gallup poll reported that 94 percent of Americans condemned the
Nazi treatment of Jews and 61 percent approved of a boycott of German goods. Shortly after Munich, Gallup had found that 77 percent
thought German claims on the Sudetenland unjustified and 60 percent thought the agreement more likely to lead to war than peace.
Ninety-two percent found unbelievable Hitler's claim that the Sudetenland would be his last territorial demand. Roosevelt was slowly
winning the war for public opinion.

It was typical, however, that Roosevelt should continue deliberately to confuse perceptions about his privately held military

intentions by leaving in place Harry Woodring,[70] an isolationist, as secretary of war, while quietly promoting George C. Marshall as his principal agent of rearmament. At a White House meeting on November 14, Roosevelt ordered Marshall to prioritize air power to defend the Americas "from the North Pole to the South Pole," with the aim of establishing a 20,000-plane air force and annual warplane production to increase to 24,000.

Marshall was puzzled about where at short notice he could find the hundreds of thousands of trained pilots, air crews, and maintenance teams to keep these new planes in the air. As he was to discover, the president intended the aircraft to be flown not by Americans but by British and French pilots. The same applied to Roosevelt's insistence that warships be constructed with haste. He wrote to Claude Swanson,[71] secretary of the navy, "Navy Yards doing construction should be ordered—not requested—to put as many people to work on new ships as it is possible to use at any given time—two shifts or even three shifts where they are possible."[72] Again, British sailors would man the new ships.

While today Kennedy stands accused of letting his ambitions lead him to promote a policy that, in hindsight, was unhelpful to his British hosts, Lindbergh's sin was far greater. His failure to question what he saw at German airfields led to the democracies overestimating the Nazis' air strength. According to Lindbergh's estimates, the Luftwaffe had 10,000 planes and was building 800 more a month. The true figure was very different.

Even two years later, Germany's air strength was nowhere near as high. In 1940, Germany had 4,665 warplanes: 1,711 bombers, 414 dive-bombers, 354 escort fighters, 1,356 pursuit planes, and 830 reconnaissance and other planes. German plants were making just 125 fighters and about 300 bombers a month, while Britain by that time was making 325 fighters a month.[73] Yet Lindbergh's mantra that the Luftwaffe outgunned the democracies ten to one was repeated by everyone from Chamberlain to Roosevelt.

Also not evident at the time was that Hitler's ability to invade the Sudetenland had been seriously questioned by his own top brass, led by General Ludwig Beck,[74] Chief of the army general staff, who feared a German rout if Czechoslovak forces, backed by Britain and France, offered resistance. Beck insisted in a memorandum to the

Führer after the occupation of Austria in March that "the continuance of a program of conquest must lead to world-wide catastrophe and the ruin of the now reviving Reich."[75]

The German army faced up to forty Czech divisions on the fiercely fortified Sudeten border, while French forces on the Western Front outnumbered the Germans by eight to one. When Hitler refused to pledge that the Sudetenland would be his last conquest, Beck resigned, to be replaced by the more compliant General Franz Halder. According to later testimony by Halder, the German high command were prepared to arrest Hitler and impose martial law rather than put their forces to the test.[76]

"We had taken the necessary steps to immunize Germany from this madman. At this time the prospect of war filled the great majority of the German people with horror," recalled Halder.[77] According to him, the plot to oust Hitler faltered when Chamberlain requested a face-to-face talk with Hitler at Berchtesgaden on September 14. It is by no means certain the German generals would have struck—there were many plots to kill or arrest Hitler, most of which fizzled—but had Chamberlain stood firm rather than invite himself to talks about dismembering Czechoslovakia, Halder and his cohorts might well have acted. After the war, Churchill would describe the failure of the September 14 military coup against Hitler as "another example of the very small accidents upon which the fortunes of mankind turn."[78]

There were two other coup attempts planned by the German military in response to Hitler's determination to annex the Sudetenland. On September 26, a deputation of generals gave Hitler a memorandum declaring that the low morale of the German population made it impossible to sustain a general war, that the poor condition of the armed forces made war too risky, and that border defenses, particularly on the Western Front, were inadequate. In addition, Czech defenses on the German border were so strong that they would be able to resist a German offensive for at least three months, during which time the war would spread into a more general conflict involving Britain, France, and the Soviet Union.

Field Marshal Wilhelm Keitel, Germany's Supreme Commander of the Armed Forces, told the Nuremberg war crimes trials in 1946 that the military "did not believe themselves to be strong enough at that moment to break through the fortification of the Czechoslovak frontier."[79] At the same time, French generals believed they were strong enough to push through the German lines, causing the Sudeten invasion to founder. The day after the German generals delivered their assessment, Grand Admiral Raeder, commander in chief of the German Admiralty,[80] met with Hitler and made a passionate appeal for peace, causing the Führer momentarily to hesitate.

Former French premier Léon Blum[81] passed on details of the German opposition to the Sudeten invasion to Churchill in January 1939. In a letter to his wife, Clementine, Churchill wrote that "the Germans had hardly any soldiers at all on the French frontier during the crisis. . . . If the Czechs could have held out only for that short fortnight, the German armies would have had to go back to face invasion. On the other side there is their great preponderance in the air, and it depends what you put on that how you judge the matter."[82] Chamberlain had certainly depended on Lindbergh's exaggerated estimate of German air strength before he made his approach to Hitler that led to the betrayal of the Czechs at Munich.

The many disparate factors involved in the bluffs and counterbluffs surrounding Munich make it impossible, even with hindsight, to lay the blame for what transpired at one person's door. Yet it is hard not to agree with Lindbergh's biographer Mosley that "Göring had judged his man shrewdly. Once he believed what the Germans told him and showed him, Charles Lindbergh, with the utmost sincerity, fervently believing he was helping to save European civilization, set himself the job of persuading National Socialism's enemies to lay down their arms and give in without a fight."[83]

CHAPTER EIGHT

ON THE MARCH

*Roosevelt tries to have the neutrality laws
amended, Kennedy sulks in Florida,
Hitler swallows Czechoslovakia.*

ROOSEVELT'S STATE OF THE UNION address on January 4, 1939, urged Americans to face facts about the impending European conflict. To those who thought Munich was a guarantee of "peace for our time," he said, "A war which threatened to envelop the world in flames has been averted; but it has become increasingly clear that world peace is not assured."

He linked the need to counter the brutal, undemocratic force that had wrested the Sudetenland from Czechoslovakia with the need to prepare America for the trials ahead. "There comes a time in the affairs of men when they must prepare to defend, not their homes alone, but the tenets of faith and humanity on which their churches, their governments and their very civilization are founded," he said. "We know what might happen to us of the United States if the new philosophies of force were to encompass the other continents and invade our own." He took aim at the neutrality laws that inhibited his ability to help the democracies and "may actually give aid to an aggressor and deny it to the victim."[1] The following day, he requested from Congress $1.3 billion for defense out of a total budget of $9 billion.

On January 9, Kennedy appeared before both House and Senate military affairs committees and made clear that he remained an isolationist. He repeated Lindbergh's judgment that Germany's military might far exceeded that of the democracies, but said America should rearm to defend the western hemisphere. On January 12, the president requested a further $500 million from Congress for warplanes.

The same month, a French delegation arrived in Washington to finalize a deal to buy warplanes. Roosevelt contradicted the commander of the Army Air Corps, General H. H. "Hap" Arnold,[2] and instructed him to show the French a top-secret bomber, the Douglas A-20 Havoc. When Nye, at a congressional hearing, pried from Arnold the fact that, despite the neutrality laws, the president intended to sell warplanes to the French, Roosevelt countered with a declaration that the French orders would mean thousands of new jobs.

Ignoring congressional dissent, at the next cabinet meeting Roosevelt directed Harry Woodring, the secretary of war, "to proceed as before [and allow the French] to buy what they want."[3] As Roosevelt biographer Conrad Black attests, "[Roosevelt] came to believe, by 1939 at the latest, that the United States would be required as the indispensable force to rid the world of Nazism and that it would then emerge not only as a post-isolationist country but as the preeminent nation on earth."[4]

On January 31, Roosevelt invited Nye, Bennett Champ Clark, Robert Rice Reynolds, Rufus C. Holman,[5] and other members of the Senate Military Affairs Committee to the White House, where he regaled them with a history lesson, pointing out the folly of Thomas Jefferson's neutrality legislation of 1807, which, to avoid the dispute between the French and British, saw America retreat from world trade at enormous cost to the young republic's prosperity. The president stressed that the British navy's defense of the transatlantic trade routes had since the Napoleonic Wars granted America the peace to expand and prosper.

Roosevelt cast doubt on the sincerity of a speech given by Hitler to the Reichstag the day before, saying that Germany had no designs upon America North or South while hinting at closer economic ties with South American regimes.[6] He suggested to the senators that the Neutrality Acts were too inhibiting in light of the current emergency and that he would consider selling arms to the democracies on a "cash and carry" basis. Roosevelt told them he believed American interests would be threatened if the Baltic states, the Scandinavian countries, the Netherlands, Belgium, Portugal, Greece, Egypt, or Turkey "went the way of Czechoslovakia." As he left the White House, Nye told the press, "Get the uniforms ready for the boys" and wrote a report of the meeting in which he referred to Britain and France as "the so-called democracies."[7]

Roosevelt followed up the meeting by demanding from Congress a further $945,000 for coastal defenses, barracks, and National Guard camps. When Representative James Van Zandt[8] questioned whether the president was confusing domestic rearmament with supplying foreign powers, Andrew J. May,[9] chairman of the House Military Affairs Committee, assured him that Roosevelt was following Washington's policy of "peace with all nations, entangling alliances with none."[10]

The senators who had met with Roosevelt told reporters the president had said that after Munich America's eastern border had become the Rhine, prompting the *New York Times* to write that the president believed France was "the actual frontier of America in an apparently inevitable showdown between democracies and dictatorships."[11] When asked about the report, Roosevelt called it "a deliberate lie" and that "a few silly senators" had misquoted him.[12] The truth, however, was closer to the senators' account. John Cudahy,[13] the US ambassador to Ireland, reported that the "frontier on the Rhine" remark was playing well in Europe.

Although Roosevelt was in no doubt that Munich was not the end to German aggression—he told Lincoln MacVeagh,[14] the American envoy to Greece, that "Hitler and Mussolini are still on the war-path"[15]—even at this late stage he was unwilling to accept it as inevitable either that America should enter the war, or, perhaps more importantly, that America, soon to become the world's preeminent power, would have to succeed Britain as the world's policeman.

His old Harvard professor, Roger B. Merriman, a historian specializing in the Spanish Empire, sent him a whinging letter from the British historian G. M. Trevelyan[16] which Roosevelt felt typified the listless resignation of the British establishment. "I wish the British would stop this 'We who are about to die, salute thee' attitude," he wrote. He said that Lord Lothian, the new British ambassador in Washington, had told him, "The British for a thousand years had been the guardians of Anglo-Saxon civilization—that the scepter of the sword or something like that had dropped from their palsied fingers—that the U.S.A. must snatch it up—that F.D.R. alone could save the world—etc., etc.," which had infuriated him. He wrote to Merriman:

> I got mad clear through and told [Lothian] that just so long as he or Britishers like him took that attitude of complete despair, the British would not be worth saving. What the British need today is a good stiff grog, inducing not only the desire to save civilization but the continued belief that they can do it. In such an event they will have a lot more support from their American cousins.[17]

Yet Roosevelt remained devoted to British royalty. Writing to "My dear King George," on January 18, the president laid out alternative itineraries, each entailing lunch aboard the USS *Potomac* and an overnight stay at Hyde Park. He even involved himself in the king's wardrobe, suggesting "that if it is very hot, as it may be, you will both want as thin things as possible."[18]

Roosevelt's plan to persuade Americans that the British deserved better than to be beaten by Hitler was advancing apace, making him increasingly impatient with the Chamberlain government's defeatist tone. The Germans well understood Roosevelt's private intentions. Hans Thomsen, a German embassy official minding the shop in Washington after the ambassador's recall after Kristallnacht, reported the president's "pathological hatred" of Hitler, that his ultimate aim was the "annihilation of Nazi Germany and the nullification of the New Order in Europe,"[19] and that he was prepared to run for a third term to ensure that this came about.

Kennedy, meanwhile, had decamped from Washington with his son John to his high-walled seaside compound in Palm Beach to brood upon his presidential prospects.[20] He brought together a group of friends to plot his next step, what one visitor described as "a virtual publicity bureau."[21] Sitting in what he called his "bull pen," the ambassador spent most of the Christmas vacation on the telephone, sounding out supporters for a presidential bid. When he consulted with Coughlin, who had finally been driven off the air and now ran a propaganda sheet, *Social Justice*, the radio priest invited him to Royal Oak to conspire.

The ambassador also consulted with his Florida neighbor Robert McCormick, owner of the *Chicago Tribune*, who reassured him that

Americans remained solidly isolationist and in favor of appease-ment. Boake Carter was on hand to write that Kennedy had com-plained to the president about being frozen out in London "in language that Mr. Roosevelt does not care to hear" and demanded he "quit making a sucker out of me." Carter reported that Kennedy refused to resign so the president could not replace him with a war-mongering "marionette." The ambassador would stay on in London, because "he feels that he can serve America, not Mr. Roosevelt, bet-ter by sticking than in any other job."[22]

Kennedy told house guests Damon Runyon[23] and Walter Winchell[24] that it was he who was responsible for Lindbergh telling Chamberlain that German military strength could overwhelm that of Britain and France combined—a fact, he suggested, that had been pivotal in inspiring Chamberlain to deal with Hitler at Munich.

A British paper ran a story suggesting that Kennedy would not return to London, which was hotly denied by Rose, who was on a ski-ing vacation in St. Moritz, France, with most of the children. Krock sent out a feeler to Princeton University asking whether it would be prepared to award an honorary degree to Kennedy in June 1939, by which time the ambassador fully expected to have returned from London. At this time, Kennedy also enquired about becoming a part-ner at J. P. Morgan. As Pearson explained to his "Washington Merry-Go-Round" cowriter Allen, "He wants to get out but Roosevelt wants him to stay because he'd rather have Joe in England than here on his neck."[25] Meanwhile, one of the president's closest advisers, Tom Corcoran,[26] told Morgenthau that Kennedy posed a grave danger to the president's third-term prospects and that Krock was "running a campaign to put Joe Kennedy over for President, that if any promi-nent Catholic gets in the way, he's to be rubbed out . . . If anybody with financial training gets in the way, he's to be rubbed out."[27]

Roosevelt was not finished with Kennedy. Even in Florida, the ambassador posed a danger, so on February 9, Roosevelt called him to suggest that, with war looming in Europe, he should return to London without delay. Roosevelt added that Chamberlain had let it be known that he thought it strange for the American ambassador to be sunning himself in Florida when Britain was under such pres-sure. Kennedy and John F. Kennedy duly boarded the *Queen Mary* in New York, heading for Britain.

In a cable to the president on his return to London, Kennedy contradicted the pessimistic view he had expressed in Washington just a month before. After talking to Chamberlain, Halifax, the Chancellor of the Exchequer John Simon,[28] and others, his fresh assessment was that "England is on its way; that Germany will not attack; that the problem of last fall . . . is gone."[29] As to the rumors that Hitler and Stalin would sign a peace pact, a deal that would seriously alter the balance of power if war were to be declared, he reported that "Chamberlain does not take the possibility of a Russian–German alliance seriously. He says that they are both so distrustful of each other that it would never work out."[30] Hull pounced on Kennedy's poor grasp of events to argue that Kennedy was now so far removed from the administration's thinking that the president should summon him home without delay. Roosevelt, however, was receiving his own information about Chamberlain's thinking from the American naval attaché in London, a fact that was kept from Kennedy at the president's insistence.[31]

On February 13, Senator Elbert Thomas[32] introduced a bill, meant to be helpful to the White House, that would give the president power to impose an embargo on arms sales to belligerents while, with Congress's express consent, lifting the embargo on victims of aggression so that they could buy arms. Yet even this moderate measure failed to win the isolationists' backing. On the contrary, Borah introduced legislation that extended the embargo to all arms sales. Roosevelt wrote to Hull, "The more I think the problem through, the more I am convinced that the existing Neutrality Act should be repealed in toto."[33] However, Key Pittman, chairman of the Senate Foreign Affairs Committee, told Hull that so long as isolationists opposed it, repeal was impossible.

Roosevelt still wanted to send a clear signal to Hitler that America would defend the North Atlantic shipping routes currently guarded by the Royal Navy. He announced a conspicuous, large-scale, two-week naval exercise, involving a fake battle between rival forces, that entailed moving a large part of the US Pacific Fleet through the Panama Canal to the Atlantic. Always happiest when afloat, the president joined the exercise on February 16 and remained until the end.

"The weather is heavenly and I hope to get an hour or two of fishing," he wrote his mother from the USS *Houston*.[34] To Byrnes he joked, "Sincerely hope Nye, Vandenberg, and Borah will not force us into war before I get back. Charleston Naval yard needs three or four days' notice before any actual declaration."[35] Meanwhile, Roosevelt ordered the dredging of a deep harbor in Guam as an advance base in the event of war with Japan.

The isolationists did make a move in the president's absence, with the Senate Foreign Relations Committee voting against bringing to the Senate floor an amendment to the Neutrality Act backed by Senator Thomas that would have given the president discretion to allow the sale of war supplies to countries if he deemed them victims of aggression. What might be called the "battle of cash and carry" between isolationists and internationalists was joined on March 20 when Pittman introduced the bill in the Senate. After Nye had threatened to filibuster what he called an attempt "to repeal or emasculate" the existing legislation, the measure was dropped. Cash and carry remained the only legal means of aiding Britain for the next year and a half.

Polling showed that the president was slowly winning the battle for American minds. Two-thirds favored his cash and carry program, 44 percent believed Germany and Italy should be excluded from such sales, and, in the event of a European war, 69 percent said they backed all American aid to the democracies "short of war."[36] To calm fiscally conservative Democrat lawmakers anxious at the scale of rearmament spending, Roosevelt argued that making warplanes and warships meant more American jobs which led to "prosperity for this country and we can't elect the Democratic Party unless we get prosperity."[37]

Lindbergh flew back to Berlin in mid-January and met with, among other top Nazis, Hans-Heinrich Dieckhoff, the German ambassador to the United States recalled after Kristallnacht. Little of what Lindbergh said impressed Dieckhoff, who advised Hitler not to depend upon the isolationists keeping America out of the war. Unlike in World War One, he said, "in the next war, it will not be two and a half years before the United States enters; it will be much shorter."[38]

Lindbergh was more convinced than ever of Hitler's genius. "I believe the future welfare of Western civilization depends largely upon the strength of Germany and the avoidance of a major war in Western Europe," he told his diary. Although he believed American air strength should be increased, he described Roosevelt's arms program as "a hysterical rearmament" that "may easily do more damage than good."[39] He was troubled that "there seems to be a sort of plot to . . . give Germany the impression that the United States will enter a European war if one starts."[40]

Lindbergh's return to Germany sparked a round of personal abuse in the American press. A lone defender was Krock. "Criticism of any of his activities—in Germany or elsewhere—is as ignorant as it is unfair," he wrote in the *New York Times*. The flier's "individualism has earned him some personal unpopularity. But any founded on belief he has not been a patriot, and a most valuable one, is ill-founded indeed."[41]

After attending a party at Cliveden in late February, where fellow guests included Chamberlain, Kennedy, and Lothian, Lindbergh recorded that he had "a little more confidence in the sanity of German leadership than [Lothian] has," though "he agrees with me that France, England, and America are just as responsible for present conditions in Germany as the Germans are themselves."[42] The following day he dined with Kennedy, who "does not expect war this year and feels that Chamberlain has handled the situation well."[43] But he felt Roosevelt's campaign to get Americans to focus on the threat of war was paying off. "Kennedy told me that most people at home were devoting ninety-nine per cent of their attention to foreign problems," he wrote.[44]

Then, after German accusations that the Czech government had been maltreating the Slovaks, the largely rural and Catholic population in the east of the country, on March 14 Hitler ordered troops into Prague, claiming it had been a "German city" for a thousand years. Three days later, he declared the Czech provinces of Bohemia and Moravia German "protectorates." Under secretary of state Sumner Welles decried "the temporary extinguishment of the liberties of a free and independent people"[45] that now threatened world peace.

Chamberlain wriggled, claiming that because Slovakia had seceded from its union with Czechoslovakia on March 14, Britain's guarantee of Czechoslovakia's integrity was null and void. Sir Neville Henderson, the British ambassador in Berlin, who condemned "the cynicism and immorality of the German action," [46] was recalled to London. "My mission to Berlin was already a failure," he wrote, "and from that moment I had no real hopes of peace except in a miracle." [47] Halifax warned Chamberlain that unless appeasement was abandoned, the Commons would vote against the prime minister and the government would fall. Chamberlain concurred and on March 17 gave a speech that hinted at a change of course.

Lindbergh made no mention of Hitler's conquest of Czechoslovakia in his diary. A few days later he mused that "if there should be a war, of course I want to be either in the States or taking an active part of some kind over here," though what that "active part" would be, and on whose side, he did not elaborate. "The strange thing is that of all the European countries, I found the most personal freedom in Germany," he wrote. [48] He took the imminent occupation of Eastern Europe by Hitler as a given. On March 31 he wrote, "If England and France attempt to stop the German eastward movement there will be war." [49]

As Lindbergh was aware from his conversations in Berlin, Hitler was not finished with his "eastward movement." On March 20, Ribbentrop issued an ultimatum to Lithuania demanding the return of the city of Memel (known to Lithuanians as Klaipėda) which had been ceded in the Versailles Treaty. On March 22, after Britain and France failed to offer assistance, the Lithuanian government abandoned Memel to Germany and Hitler arrived (seasick) on the cruiser *Deutschland* to inspect his new prize. Nazi-run newspapers in Germany began campaigning for the German occupation of Danzig (known in Poland as Gdańsk), deemed a "free city" by the Versailles Treaty, and the Polish Corridor, which separated Germany from its isolated eastern province of East Prussia.

Everything was proceeding according to a grand plan laid down by Hitler the previous October, when he ordered his high command to bolster Germany's defenses, plot the conquest of Czechoslovakia, and occupy Memel. Three days later, he told them to plan the recovery of Danzig. He hoped to intimidate his way to victory, as he had with Austria, the Sudetenland, and the remainder of Czechoslovakia. After a meeting with Hitler on March 25, 1939, the commander in chief of the German army, General von Brauchitsch, wrote that "The Führer does not wish to solve the Danzig question by the use of force. He would not like to drive Poland into the arms of Great Britain by doing so."[50]

On March 31, Chamberlain told the Commons, "In the event of any action which clearly threatens Polish independence . . . H.M. Government would feel themselves bound at once to lend the Polish Government all support in their power."[51] The French government resolved to do the same. The prime minister wrote to his sister that the British promise to Poland was "unprovocative in tone, but firm, clear but stressing the important point . . . that what we are concerned with is not the boundaries of states, but attacks on their independence."[52] Within two weeks, Chamberlain offered similar guarantees to Romania and Greece. Hitler's response to the Romanian foreign minister was, "If England wants war, she can have it."[53] He ordered his service chiefs to prepare Operation White, the occupation of Danzig, to be carried out on September 1 "at the latest."

If Kennedy continued to believe that war could be avoided, his son John, who was visiting Poland, knew better. "The Polish people will not give up Danzig to Hitler, not without fighting for it," he wrote to his father.[54] As the war clouds gathered, Kennedy still thought Chamberlain was the right prime minister for Britain, telling doubters that the British should erect a bust to Chamberlain for Munich, as it was giving the democracies time to rearm.[55]

In mid-April, Lindbergh boarded the *Aquitania* bound for America. Alone in his cabin, he continued to express his admiration for Hitler in his diary. "Civilization depends upon [Hitler's] wisdom far more than on the action of the democracies," he wrote; "the question of right and wrong is one thing by law and another thing by history."[56] At his first dinner on board, Lindbergh was alarmed to find himself seated at a table with a young Jewish woman, a Romanian refugee, whom he genuinely felt sorry for. When he insisted the following evening that he be seated alone, he expressed concern that the woman might conclude that he had objected because she was Jewish.

As his diaries make plain—in extracts excluded from publication by the editor, William Jovanovich, head of Harcourt, Brace—Lindbergh *was* anti-Semitic. "The steward tells me that most of the Jewish passengers are sick," he wrote. "Imagine the United States taking these Jews in in addition to those we already have. There are too many places like New York already. A few Jews add strength and character to a country, but too many create chaos."[57] When he rented a house at Great Neck on Long Island, he returned to his theme. "I would not think of establishing a permanent home in New York City or on Long Island," he wrote. "I do not want to live or to have my children grow up under the set of values which exist in this section."[58]

Lindbergh's decision to return to America caused the press to salivate. There is little more appetizing to a paparazzo than a celebrity who shuns publicity. But the news also drew the attention of Sol Bloom, acting chairman of the House Foreign Affairs Committee, who contacted him on board the *Aquitania* to ask whether he would testify before the committee on newly proposed changes to the neutrality legislation. "Wonder what is behind this?" Lindbergh asked himself. Suspecting a political trap, he declined.

Bloom was leading the latest Roosevelt-inspired effort, drafted by the State Department, to amend the neutrality laws to give the president more leeway to arm those he wished. All had been going well until a last-minute amendment by Roosevelt's local New York state congressman, Hamilton Fish,[59] ensuring that arms and ammunition remained on the embargo list. "The anti-war nations believe that a definite stimulus has been given Hitler by the vote of the House," complained Roosevelt the morning after the House voted. "If war breaks out in Europe . . . an important part of the responsibility will rest on last night's action."[60] The letter, intended to be leaked to a wider audience, was part of Roosevelt's plan to pin the blame for the imminent war on the behavior of the isolationists in Congress. Meanwhile, Roosevelt wrote to his attorney general, Frank Murphy,[61] asking, "How far do you think I can go in ignoring the existing act—even though I did sign it?"[62]

On July 11, four days after the president instructed Hull to protest to the Japanese government against their aerial bombing of civilians in Manchuria, the Senate voted to postpone making a decision on the neutrality laws until the next session of Congress the following year. The president invited a number of senators, including Borah, to the White House, where he lectured them for an hour on the need for America to be flexible in the event of war. He warned that isolationism was not merely wrong but had now become dangerous. Borah insisted that neutrality was the best means of keeping America out of war.

When Hull offered to show Borah all the diplomatic cables warning that the world was on the brink of war, the Lion of Idaho declined, saying he had his own, more accurate sources of information.[63] Borah's response to Hitler's illicit territorial acquisitions is hard to credit. Rather than expressing indignation at the lawlessness, he declared admiration for Hitler's audacity. "God, what a chance Hitler has!" he said. "If he only moderates his religious and racial intolerance, he would take his place beside Charlemagne. He has taken Europe without firing a shot."[64] Roosevelt bemoaned the fact that nations could "find no better method of realizing their destinies than those which were used by the Huns and Vandals fifteen hundred years ago."[65]

As the meeting with the senators drew to a close, Garner gleefully said, "Well, Captain, we might as well face the facts. You haven't got the votes."[66] The isolationists in Congress remained beyond Roosevelt's reach. But he was more determined than ever that their insular view should not be bolstered and that the steady shift in public opinion toward aiding the democracies should not become distracted by inflammatory statements from public figures like Lindbergh, who would soon land in New York.

Lindbergh was only a day out from France when he was contacted by cable by General Arnold, who asked for a meeting as early as was convenient. A rendezvous was arranged at West Point the day after Lindbergh's ship docked, and within two days Lindbergh had agreed to join the Army Air Corps as a colonel, with immediate effect. Lindbergh did not enjoy spontaneity or lack of planning, so it must be assumed that he fully understood that, by joining the government's employ as an expert on flight engineering, he would be obliged to curtail his public pronouncements.

The first thing Arnold made him promise was that he would not testify before Bloom's committee or any other congressional hearing. "I prefer not to do so," Lindbergh confided to his diary, "but I wonder just what politics are working in [Arnold's] mind."[67] Arnold was reassured when Lindbergh told him he did not crave elected office. Not long after, Lindbergh declined an invitation to give a radio broadcast on the European situation because, he said, nothing he could say would be "of constructive value, even in a minute way."[68] Arnold—and Roosevelt—were relieved. The president's plan to gag Lindbergh appeared to be working.

As if to reward Lindbergh for remaining silent, within two days of being commissioned he was invited to the White House. It was the first time Roosevelt and Lindbergh had met. The president treated the aviator with his usual charm, though Lindbergh remained suspicious of his old air mail adversary. "I liked him and feel that I could get along with him," he confided to his diary, but "there was something about him I did not trust. . . . It is better to work together as long as we can; yet somehow I have a feeling that it may not be for long."[69] So long as Lindbergh wore a uniform and worked for the National Advisory Committee for Aeronautics, he would have to keep his isolationist views to himself. Like Kennedy, Lindbergh had flitted under Roosevelt's glass dome.

CHAPTER NINE

A STATE OF WAR

*Hitler mounts a sarcastic attack on Roosevelt
and the royal visit, Hitler invades Poland,
Chamberlain declares war on Germany.*

MUSSOLINI TOOK the next step toward world war by invading Albania on April 7. The following week, "to put the dictators on the spot," Roosevelt sent a letter to Hitler and the king of Italy (as he, not Mussolini, was head of state), asking that they pledge not to compromise the borders of thirty-one named countries for the next twenty-five years.

On the face of it, to ask for such a guarantee was a naive request, certain to be spurned. Roosevelt told Morgenthau that his appeal to the dictators' better nature enjoyed only a one-in-five chance of success. The Nobel Prize-winning author Thomas Mann,[1] living in exile from Nazism in America, recognized it as "a calculated move for reasons of domestic politics."[2] In a note to Canada's prime minister, Mackenzie King, the president revealed his true intent. If we are turned down," he wrote, "the issue becomes clearer and public opinion in your country and mine will be helped."[3]

Mussolini cursed the "absurd" demand and the president's "messiah-like messages,"[4] while Hitler summoned the Reichstag on April 28 to answer Roosevelt's plea in an address heard by hundreds of millions of listeners, including in America, Britain, and France. Flanked on either side by black swastikas and overshadowed by a vast golden eagle with a swastika in its claws, Hitler began his diatribe with a well-rehearsed catalogue of complaints against the iniquities of Versailles before calling the invasion of Czechoslovakia a "service to peace."

He accused Britain and France of trying to encircle Germany and condemned the Polish government for daring to reject his terms for Danzig and the Polish Corridor. He flatly rejected the idea that Germany was intent on invading Poland as "inventions of the international press." "The worst is that now Poland, like Czechoslovakia a year ago, believes, under pressure of a lying international campaign, that it must call up troops, although Germany has not called up a single man and has not thought of proceeding in any way against Poland," he said.

Then came a protracted sarcastic assault upon Roosevelt and, by association, all American citizens that caused his local audience to rock with laughter. It was not easy listening for the isolationists in Congress.

> Mr. Roosevelt declares that it is clear to him that all international problems can be solved at the council table, [yet] it was America herself who gave sharpest expression to her mistrust in the effectiveness of conferences. For the greatest conference of all time was the League of Nations . . . representing all the peoples of the world, created in accordance with the will of an American President. The first State, however, that shrank from this endeavor was the United States. . . . It was not until after years of purposeless participation that I resolved to follow the example of America. The freedom of North America was not achieved at the conference table any more than the conflict between the North and the South was decided there. I will say nothing about the innumerable struggles which finally led to the subjugation of the North American continent as a whole. [At Versailles, the German delegation was] subjected to even greater degradations than can ever have been inflicted on the chieftains of the Sioux tribes.

For once, Roosevelt found himself agreeing with much of what Hitler was saying. Then came the response to Roosevelt's appeal for peace.

"Mr. Roosevelt asks that assurance be given him that the German armed forces will not attack, and above all, not invade the territory or possessions of the following independent nations," Hitler said. In a *coup de théâtre,* he slowly read out the president's list of countries, causing the audience seated in front of him to roar with laughter at each successive name. Though few noticed it at the time, the nation Hitler did not read aloud was Poland. He made fun of the fact that Ireland was among the nations listed and quoted a speech by the Irish prime minister, Éamon de Valera,[5] "in which, strangely enough, and contrary to Mr. Roosevelt's opinion, he does not charge Germany with oppressing Ireland but he reproaches England with subjecting Ireland to continuous aggression. In the same way, the fact has obviously escaped Mr. Roosevelt's notice that Palestine is at present occupied not by German troops but by the English."

In his most mocking tone, Hitler said, "I should not like to let this opportunity pass without giving above all to the President of the United States an assurance regarding those territories which would, after all, give him most cause for apprehension, namely the United States itself and the other States of the American continent." He described reports that Germany had set its sights on America, North or South, as "rank frauds and gross untruths" and the concoction of "a stupid imagination."

Then came the peroration:

> Mr. Roosevelt, I fully understand that the vastness of your nation and the immense wealth of your country allow you to feel responsible for the history of the whole world and for the history of all nations. I, Sir, am placed in a much more modest and smaller sphere. . . . although for me it is more precious than anything else, for it is limited to my people![6]

Roosevelt's gamble had paid off. The scraping sound of Hitler's guttural accent and the echoing jeers from his Nazi followers sounded even more terrifying to the worldwide radio audience for the lack of pictures. To most Americans of either stripe, Hitler had not only insulted their president but had failed to answer the single question Roosevelt had asked him: would he give a guarantee not to invade any of the named countries?

It was not just Hitler who had fallen into the president's trap. Again, the isolationists were quick to misread the outcome. Senator Hiram W. Johnson, who had introduced the law forbidding foreign countries from buying arms if they owed money to the United States, wrote to his son, "Hitler had all the better of the argument. Roosevelt put his chin out and got a resounding whack. I have reached the conclusion there will be no war." Roosevelt wanted "to knock down two dictators in Europe, so that one may be firmly implanted in America," he wrote.[7] Nye was foolish enough to offer his views on Hitler's speech to reporters. "Nothing said by Hitler can be taken as an insult to the American people," he said, "and it might be that a reasonable approach to Germany by our government now would invite better understanding and bring rest to the world."[8]

Alarmed by Hitler's continued bellicosity, the British belatedly began negotiating a pact with the Soviet Union. As a businessman, Chamberlain had a visceral dislike of Communism, which prevented him from doing what had been urged on him for months by Churchill and others. Still, he left it to Moscow to make the first move. On April 17, the Soviet foreign minister, Maxim Litvinov,[9] proposed to the British ambassador a mutual defense pact between the Soviet Union, Britain, and France, to include guarantees for the defense of Poland, Romania, and Greece.

The British response on May 8 was tardy and tepid. They offered a counterproposal that, to Joseph Stalin,[10] the dictator of the Soviet Union, appeared to put the onus of waging war against Germany more on the Soviets than on the Western democracies. A Soviet counterproposal demanding that Britain, France, and the Soviet Union give "immediately all effective assistance" in the event of an attack on themselves or on Denmark, Norway, the Netherlands, Slovakia, Hungary, or Yugoslavia was delivered on July 23. Again the British waffled. The following month Roosevelt cabled Stalin, urging him to do a deal with the British and French without delay and predicting that as soon as Hitler had invaded Poland he would attack the Soviet Union. Stalin had already come to a similar conclusion.

While London and Moscow played tag diplomacy, Joseph Kennedy and Rose, hobnobbing with King George at a weekend party at Windsor Castle on April 14, could not avoid hearing about the arrangements for their US visit from the royal couple. Kennedy asked to be allowed to return to America for the event, but the State Department turned down the request. They could not, however, prevent Rose from claiming a small place in the American entourage.

While enjoying Kennedy's discomfort, the president did not lose sight of the goal he had set. As Black explained, "Nothing could be done to make the inept British political leadership more popular, but Roosevelt thought the young monarch and his queen might perform a public relations coup in the United States."[11] Eleanor Roosevelt was well aware of the importance of the visit. "There is always a certain amount of criticism and superficial ill feeling toward the British in this country," she later explained in her autobiography. "Believing that we all might soon be engaged in a life-and-death struggle, in which Great Britain would be our first line of defense, [Franklin] hoped that their visit would create a bond of friendship between the peoples of the two countries."[12]

King George and Queen Elizabeth crossed the Canadian border on June 7—the first reigning British monarch to visit America—and boarded a train to Washington DC. The following morning, they were welcomed at Union Station by the president and first lady. Crowds cheered as the royal couple were driven to the White House, and they continued to be welcomed by large numbers wherever they went. To show that there were no hard feelings about the unpleasantness of the War of Independence, the king and queen were ferried up the Potomac to visit Washington's home at Mount Vernon and they laid a wreath at the Tomb of the Unknown Soldier at Arlington Cemetery.

After visiting the New York World's Fair, where the Czech and Albanian flags were flying at half-mast, they arrived by car at Springwood, where Franklin, Eleanor, and Sara Roosevelt awaited them. The president had prepared a tray of cocktails, which his mother frowned upon, suggesting that it might be more appropriate to offer something soft to drink. When the king arrived, Roosevelt said, "My mother does not approve of cocktails and thinks you should have a cup of tea." The king said, "Neither does my mother," and helped himself to a martini.[13]

From that moment the two men got on famously, with Roosevelt adopting his best avuncular tone. They compared notes on the prospect of war—Roosevelt saying he thought war inevitable, the king still hoping it could be avoided—and the president ended the day by patting the king on the knee, saying, "Young man, it's time for you to go to bed."[14] George asked Mackenzie King, "Why don't my ministers talk to me as the President did tonight?" The following day, Eleanor threw a picnic and invited mostly Hyde Park locals with a spattering of dignitaries to eat hot dogs cooked on a barbecue accompanied by baked beans, smoked turkey, and ham, followed by strawberries.

Roosevelt insisted on driving the queen to the picnic himself. "He was conversing more than watching the road and drove at great speed," she recalled. "There were several times when I thought we would go right off the road and tumble down the hills. It was very frightening, but quite exhilarating."[15] The press, who were a key element in Roosevelt's plan, made a great deal of the queen's feigned embarrassment at plunging a hot dog into her mouth. It was the sort of absurd incident Roosevelt knew would endear the royal couple to Americans.

Eleanor concluded that "in many ways [the visit] was even more successful than [Franklin] had expected."[16] That evening, as the royal couple waved farewell from the rear platform of the train taking them back to Canada, the crowds at Poughkeepsie spontaneously broke into "Auld Lang Syne," with the president, waving from his car, joining in. As the train pulled away, the president shouted, "Good luck to you! All the luck in the world!"[17] "There was something incredibly moving about the scene—the river in the evening light, the voices of many people singing this old song, and the train slowly pulling out with the young couple waving good-by," recalled Eleanor. "One thought of the clouds that hung over them and the worries they were going to face, and turned away and left the scene with a heavy heart."[18]

The humiliation of being left out of the royal party proved too much for Kennedy. He decided he would resign in July. "I am handicapped by my position, in that I cannot say what I think and I cannot resign and say what I think until at least the situation has become more quiet," he wrote.[19] He booked one of the first flights on a new transatlantic Pan American Airways service and let it be known to friends that he would be home by midsummer. He rehearsed the reasons he would give Roosevelt for cutting his assignment short. The cost of being ambassador in London was unbearable, even for him. His business interests needed tending. His children were becoming British in their outlook and needed a good American education. He was homesick.

He kept repeating that Britain's hope that America would come to her aid in the event of war was unrealistic. "A lot of people tell me that Britain is relying on two things today," he told a British reporter. "One is God and the other is the United States. And recently you don't seem to have been counting too much on the Deity."[20] He told a dinner party attended by the columnist Walter Lippmann that war was inevitable and that Britain would be beaten. Kennedy also grew reckless in his criticisms of the president. Harold Ickes, ever eager to pounce on examples of Kennedy's disloyalty, reported to Roosevelt an account retailed by the ambassador-at-the-ready John Cudahy that Kennedy "does some pretty loud and inappropriate talking about the President. He does this before English servants, who are likely to spread the news. . . . Kennedy is vulgar and coarse and highly critical in what he says about the President. And when John cautioned him on one occasion not to talk as he was doing before the servants, Joe said that he didn't give a damn."[21]

Roosevelt was still not ready to allow Kennedy his freedom. Instead, he urged Kennedy to "put some iron up Chamberlain's backside." Kennedy's response was that "putting iron up his backside did no good unless the British had some iron with which to fight and they did not."[22] Overwhelmed by Roosevelt's charm and persuaded by his logic, Kennedy canceled his return trip and agreed to remain at his post until September.

Krock penned a piece titled "Why Ambassador Kennedy Is Not Coming Home" that blamed "young New Dealers" for Kennedy's increasingly poor reputation back home. "They engaged in a propaganda campaign against him," Krock wrote, suggesting that "he was in the White House disfavor because he wanted to make terms with the dictators, because he had 'gone British,' was a member of the Cliveden (appeasement) set in Great Britain, and spoke somewhat less than adoringly off the record of his chief." Krock declared that "None of these statements was true,"[23] despite ample evidence to the contrary.

In July, Kennedy retreated with Rose and some of the children to pass the summer in a villa near Cannes in the South of France. But even that absence from his post was short-lived. At the end of the month, he received a letter from Roosevelt. "I suppose you saw the latest 'Krock' in the *Times* about you, and I think you begin to agree with me that that particular gentleman, with his distorted ideas of how to be helpful, has done you more harm in the past few years than all of your enemies put together," he wrote. Kennedy wrote back, "Your letter made me happy—not only what you said but the whole tone of it." Then he made a fateful promise: "Regardless of any personal inconvenience, as long as I am of any assistance to you, I shall remain for whatever time you like."[24]

Roosevelt could take comfort that the royal visit was beginning to pay dividends. By the end of August, polling revealed that the percentage of Americans who supported providing Britain and France with arms had leapt from 31 to 50. John W. Boehne, a longstanding isolationist congressman from Indiana, sent the president a telegram on August 30 saying he had changed his mind about the need to amend the neutrality legislation.

The president did not wait for war to break out before he began committing American forces to the defense of the democracies. He told the British ambassador in Washington, Sir Ronald Lindsay, that he was planning, in the event of war, to declare a neutral zone extending 500 miles into the Atlantic, and that in order to provision American warships patrolling the zone he would like to lease harbor bases in Bermuda and the British West Indies. Lindsay leapt at this hard evidence that America was prepared to back Britain with force and urged Chamberlain to take up the offer without delay. Again diffidence overcame good judgment and the prime minister hid behind Foreign Office advice that the deal was "hardly within the realm of practical politics."[25] Roosevelt left the offer on the table and in mid-August ordered the navy to lease facilities from Pan American Airways in Trinidad, St. Lucia, and Bermuda. On August 17 he secretly set up the War Resources Board, comprising the military, government officials, businesspeople, and economists, to coordinate armament production.[26]

Each day of the summer of 1939 brought new frightening developments. On August 21, Ribbentrop flew to Moscow, causing Kennedy to abandon his vacation and scurry back to London. On August 23, Hitler and Stalin startled the world by announcing a ten-year nonaggression pact. Simultaneously, the Soviets, who had for years been defending against the encroachment of the Japanese on the Manchurian border, signed a truce with Tokyo. Nazism and Communism were now allies and it seemed certain that Poland, lying between Germany and Russia, would be the first victim of this hellacious ideological marriage.

Halifax told Kennedy, "The jig is up," and "England will definitely go to war if Poland starts to fight."[27] "[Chamberlain] says the futility of it all is the thing that is frightful," Kennedy wrote to Hull. "They cannot save the Poles; they can merely carry on a war of revenge that will mean the destruction of all Europe."[28] The ambassador issued a formal warning to Americans living in Britain that they should return home without delay.

On August 22, as German pressure on the Poles to buckle became intense, Chamberlain told his cabinet, "It is unthinkable that we should not carry out our obligations to Poland."[29] Three days later, Hitler offered Chamberlain a deal. In exchange for turning a blind eye to the occupation of Danzig and the Polish Corridor, he offered a disarmament treaty and a nonaggression pact that would leave the British Empire unmolested.

Chamberlain responded to Hitler on August 28, saying that he would not "acquiesce in a settlement which put in jeopardy the independence of the state to whom they had given their guarantee"[30] and proposing German–Polish negotiations. On August 29, Hitler offered Ambassador Henderson a compromise on Danzig and the Polish Corridor: he would negotiate with a Polish representative, but only if one were to arrive in Berlin the following day. The Polish government refused. The next day, Roosevelt wrote to a congressman from Missouri, "I am hoping and praying that war may be averted but if, unhappily, war comes the country will know just who is responsible for the tragic plight in which we find ourselves."[31] He blamed war on the isolationists as well as on Hitler.

On the morning of September 1, fifty-seven German divisions supported by tanks and bombers crossed the undefended Polish border. Kennedy cabled Hull, "The party is on."[32] Asked whether there was any doubt that Britain would fight, the ambassador replied, "Unquestionably none."[33] Roosevelt remarked to Bullitt, "It's come at last. God help us all."[34] At a press conference, the president sought to reassure the American people that war in Europe need not involve America. Asked whether America could stay out of the war, he replied, "I not only sincerely hope so, but I believe we can. . . . Every effort will be made by the administration so to do."[35]

However, Roosevelt made his position clear to Lothian. "There is certainly nothing neutral about the President's personal attitude toward the conflict," the British ambassador reported to Halifax.

Marshall, whom Roosevelt promoted to army chief of staff, put all American forces on alert. Two long days later, Chamberlain asked Kennedy to Downing Street and showed him the speech he intended to give in the Commons that evening. The ambassador wept as he read the prime minister's words: "Everything that I have worked for, everything that I have hoped for, everything that I have believed in during my public life has crashed in ruins."[36]

Chamberlain issued an ultimatum, which was delivered by Henderson. If Germany did not withdraw from Poland by eleven o'clock that morning, Sunday, September 3, a state of war would exist between the two countries. In a broadcast to the nation, Chamberlain explained that the deadline had passed: "I have to tell you now that no such undertaking has been received and consequently this country is at war with Germany."[37] In Berlin, on being read Chamberlain's final demand, Hitler turned to Ribbentrop and asked, "What now?"[38]

Just after four in the afternoon Eastern Standard Time, a call from Kennedy woke the president. With a catch in his throat, the ambassador broke the news that Britain was at war with Germany. "It's the end of the world," he said. "The end of everything."[39]

CHAPTER TEN

THE BATTLE OF NEUTRALITY

The Phony War, Lindbergh starts broadcasting,
Kennedy is shunned in London, Roosevelt begins
his secret correspondence with Churchill,
and the Battle of Neutrality.

CHAMBERLAIN'S DECLARATION OF WAR against Germany, with France following a few hours later, upped the stakes. For Roosevelt, hoping to reach November 1940 and gain reelection without incident, war had come too soon. For Kennedy, it offered opportunity. Even if Roosevelt intended to stand for a third term, there was now room for an isolationist or noninterventionist candidate to challenge him. The moment Lindbergh had long anticipated had arrived, which meant it was time for him to join with his isolationist allies to prevent America entering the war.

Roosevelt did not wait for war to be declared before he began to harass German shipping. He ordered a bow-to-stern search of the German passenger liner *Bremen* for hidden war supplies and prevented it from steaming out of New York harbor until the Royal Navy was in a position to sink it. For the first time, Chamberlain gave the president cause for hope. To cling to power, the prime minister was obliged to open his government to new blood, and the first person he appointed to a reshuffled cabinet was Winston Churchill, as First Lord of the Admiralty.

At the grand age of nearly sixty-five, Churchill had been vindicated by events and Chamberlain had given him his due. On hearing of the return of Churchill, Hitler was thrown into "consternation." "Göring stepped out of the door of Hitler's salon," recalled Lindbergh's friend Speer. "He dropped into the nearest chair and said wearily: 'Churchill in the Cabinet. That means that the war is really on.'" [1]

Churchill was immediately thrust into the center of the action when on September 3 a German U-boat torpedoed a British passenger liner, the *Athenia*, heading across the Atlantic toward New York. Of the 1,418 passengers, 117 were killed, of which twenty-eight were American. Churchill, in his element, was less concerned about the loss of life than with how the tragedy would play in America. "The occurrence should have a helpful effect as regards public opinion in the United States," he gaily told a hastily arranged meeting of the war cabinet. [2]

Hitler was so anxious that in the *Athenia* Roosevelt might have found another *Lusitania*, the trigger that had caused Wilson to bring America into World War One, that he ordered an immediate end of naval strikes against British and French shipping. Roosevelt kept his cool. The loss of American life would simply be added to the ledger, for use if the Axis were to strike directly at an American target. In the meantime, he explored whether he could confide in Churchill.

Churchill was no stranger to America. He was half American, with a New Yorker mother, the socialite Jenny Jerome, and had spent long stretches of time in the United States, where he enjoyed the canny political advice of his mother's friends, gave coast-to-coast speaking tours, and wrote books and journalism, for a hefty fee, for Hearst and others. He was well known in America for his writing, and he was a familiar radio voice, too, his sonorous tones offering an eloquent counterpoint to those of the increasingly pro-German statements and speeches of Father Charles Coughlin.

In the week Germany invaded Poland, Churchill's face looked out from the cover of *Time* magazine. The story inside might have been written by Churchill himself. As a mere Member of Parliament, the piece said, Churchill had little power, "But as Winston Churchill the Elder Statesman, scarred veteran of innumerable parliamentary battles, historian of the World War, novelist, biographer of his ancestors, and the most pungent and expressive critic of Prime Minister Chamberlain, he had an influence, a possible future and a voice in affairs that made his position unique."

As a fixture on London's society circuit, Churchill often encountered Kennedy and, even before he rejoined the government, was not beyond confronting the ambassador over his isolationist views. When in the summer of 1939 he was told by Lippmann that Kennedy was warning friends that "war was inevitable and [Britain] should be licked," Churchill was roused into an impromptu speech. As Nicolson recalled, on hearing Kennedy's defeatist words, Churchill, "hunched there, waving his whisky-and-soda to mark his periods, stubbing his cigar with the other hand," burst into full torrent.

> It may be true that this country will at the outset of this coming and to my mind almost inevitable war be exposed to dire peril and fierce ordeals. It may be true that steel and fire will rain down upon us day and night scattering death and destruction far and wide. It may be true that our sea-communications will be imperiled and our food-supplies placed in jeopardy. Yet these trials and disasters, I ask you to believe me Mr. Lippmann, will but serve to steel the resolution of the British people and to enhance our will for victory. No, the Ambassador should not have spoken so, Mr. Lippmann. He should not have said that dreadful word.

The next part of his riff set the British tone of defiance for the next five years.

> Yet supposing (as I do not for one moment suppose) that Mr. Kennedy were correct in his tragic utterance, then I for one would willingly lay down my life in combat, rather than, in fear of defeat, surrender to the menaces of these most sinister men. It will then be for you, for the Americans, to maintain the great heritage of the English-speaking peoples. It will be for you to think imperially, which means to think always of something higher and more vast than one's national interests. Nor should I die happy in the great struggle which I see before me, were I not convinced that if we in this dear dear island succumbed to the ferocity and might of our enemies, over there in your distant and immune continent the torch of liberty will burn untarnished and (I trust and hope) undismayed.[3]

Kennedy was aware of the danger Churchill, and the great power of his spoken prose on the radio, posed to American neutrality and was quick to try to diminish him. In a letter to Roosevelt in July, Kennedy had recounted a conversation with Chamberlain. "[Churchill] has developed into a fine two-handed drinker and his judgment has never been proven to be good," the ambassador reported. "Chamberlain is also convinced that if Churchill had been in the Cabinet, England would have been at war before this."[4] Kennedy told Rose, "Churchill has energy and brains but *no* judgment."[5] Later he was to dismiss the prospect of Churchill replacing Chamberlain as prime minister: "I can't imagine [him] adequately leading the people out of the valley of the shadow of death."[6]

More telling for Roosevelt was Churchill's grateful response to the president's guarded public support for the democracies. "Every country must judge its own interest and its own duty for itself," Churchill told a group of Conservatives, "but the understanding, goodwill and sympathy of the Great Republic and its eminent President were a very great encouragement to us in months and weeks of increasing anxiety."[7] It was clear to Roosevelt that Churchill understood the freedoms at risk if Nazism were to prevail. "This is not a question of fighting for Danzig or fighting for Poland," Churchill told a radio audience on September 3. "We are fighting to save the whole world from the pestilence of Nazi tyranny and in defense of all that is most sacred to man."[8] As far as Roosevelt was concerned, better Churchill drunk than Kennedy sober.

Frankfurter, now on the Supreme Court, spoke for Roosevelt when he wrote to congratulate Churchill on his new post. "Since you are sponsoring the cause of free men everywhere, perhaps you will not decree it the act of an impertinent outsider for me to express satisfaction that you now are where you ought to be." He added, "In thought, this country is certainly not neutral. There is a unanimity of opinion for the democracies unlike the confusion of feeling in 1914."[9]

It was a theme Roosevelt would sound in a somber fireside chat delivered the night the *Athenia* was sunk. Treading a narrow line between alarm and reassurance, he asked for national unity and bipartisanship during this time of crisis, leaving isolationists to support him or appear unpatriotic and small-minded. He invoked the memory of George Washington, declaring, "We seek to keep war from our own firesides by keeping war from coming to the Americas," though he was careful to avoid Jefferson's phrase "entangling alliances."

In a sly criticism of the neutrality laws that prevented him from fully arming Britain and France, the president said, "This nation will remain a neutral nation, but I cannot ask that every American remain neutral in thought as well. Even a neutral has a right to take account of facts. Even a neutral cannot be asked to close his mind or close his conscience." And he reiterated his personal commitment to keep America out of war as long as possible. "I have said not once but many times that I have seen war and that I hate war," he said. "I hope the United States will keep out of this war. I believe that it will. And I give you assurance and reassurance that every effort of your Government will be directed toward that end."[10]

Lindbergh thought the address "a better talk than [Roosevelt] usually gives. . . . I wish I trusted him more."[11] He speculated on the president's motives in his diary. "I am far from being sure," he wrote, "that Roosevelt would not sacrifice this country in war if it were to his own personal interests; he would persuade himself that it was also to the best interests of the country."[12] At this time, Lindbergh was so wrapped up in promoting isolationist ideas that he did not notice that his wife, Anne, had fallen in love with a French flier, Antoine de Saint- Exupéry.[13]

Keen to hear of the war's progress without the misty lens of the appeasers, Roosevelt wrote directly to Churchill, behind the backs of both Kennedy and Chamberlain,[14] thus opening a new chapter in one of the most fruitful Anglo-American relationships in history.[15] Their friendship had started poorly. They had met glancingly on July 29, 1918, as World War One was winding down, at a banquet at Gray's Inn Hall, London. Roosevelt was assistant secretary of the navy and Churchill the munitions minister in Lloyd George's wartime coalition.

Roosevelt told Kennedy that he had "always disliked" Churchill, who had "acted like a stinker" that evening and was "one of the few men in public life who was rude to me."[16] The exact nature of the offense remains a mystery. Though he was eventually to concoct a fanciful account of their first meeting, Churchill had no recollection of the incident. Whatever Churchill's purported "rudeness" was, it was probably little more than his usual brusqueness, sharpened by a sampling of Gray's Inn's capacious wine cellars, and the quarrel was short-lived. In 1933, Churchill sent Roosevelt an early copy of the first volume of his biography of his distinguished ancestor, the Duke of Marlborough, inscribed, "With earnest best wishes for the success of the greatest crusade in modern times."[17]

In reintroducing himself to Churchill in the changed circumstances of September 11, 1939, Roosevelt made no reference to their earlier meeting, though he included a belated thank-you for sending him the life of Marlborough. "My dear Churchill," Roosevelt began, "It is because you and I occupied similar positions in the World War that I want you to know how glad I am that you are back again in the Admiralty. . . . What I want you and the Prime Minister to know is that I shall at all times welcome it if you will keep me in touch personally with anything you want me to know about."[18]

Kennedy was summoned by Churchill to the Admiralty, where he read the president's letter to him, an act of good faith tinged with embarrassment that the president should use a back channel to circumvent his ambassador. Kennedy was furious, writing in his diary, "Another instance of Roosevelt's conniving mind. . . . It's a rotten way to treat his Ambassador. . . . I am disgusted."[19] Kennedy suspected, correctly, that the correspondence would further Churchill's efforts to persuade America to enter the war. "He kept smiling when he talked of 'neutrality' and 'keeping the war away from U.S.A.,'" Kennedy wrote of Churchill in his diary. "I can't help feeling he's not on the level. . . . He always impressed me that he'd blow up the American Embassy and say it was the Germans if it would get the U.S. in."[20]

Churchill was careful to pass Roosevelt's message to Chamberlain, who had received a similar note from the president, saying, "I hope and believe we shall repeal the arms embargo within the next month."[21] Chamberlain had a dim view of Roosevelt, whom he thought to be a "flashy and unreliable fellow," like Churchill, whom he dismissed along with his gaggle of cronies as the "Glamour Boys."[22] Waiving his right to be indignant that the president should address one of his own cabinet directly, the prime minister believed that the two chancers deserved each other.

Ten days later, Roosevelt made his move, launching the Battle of Neutrality by summoning Congress to an extraordinary session with the aim of amending the neutrality laws in light of the tempestuous news from Europe. The president's goal, according to remarks he made to Republican journalist William Allen White,[23] who was setting up the Non-Partisan Committee for Peace through Revision of the Neutrality Act,[24] was "to get the American people into thinking that they are going to be dragged into war."[25] The president also reached across the aisle to broaden support for his administration, recruiting Alfred Landon,[26] the Republican presidential candidate he defeated in 1936, Colonel Frank Knox,[27] Landon's vice presidential sidekick, and Henry Stimson, William Howard Taft's secretary of war.

Roosevelt's immediate predecessor, Hoover, remained beyond his grasp. While blaming the war in Europe on the Nazis, Hoover urged the president and Congress to "keep out of this war,"[28] confiding to Lindbergh that "Roosevelt definitely desires to get us into this conflict"[29] and proposing the formation of a committee to campaign to keep America out of the war.

To counter Roosevelt's push on the neutrality legislation, Borah made a radio appeal for retention of the Arms Embargo Act. Borah damned Chamberlain and Daladier for setting out on an "imperialist war" and played the George Washington card. He rejected the assertion "that we cannot be neutral, that Europe is now so near to the United States, owing to modern inventions and the mingling of business affairs, that neutrality is impracticable if not impossible. ... How near was Europe, how smotheringly close, was the European system when Washington announced his policy of neutrality and published it to an astonished and enraged Europe?"

Washington "thought neutrality both wise and practicable," Borah said. "In fact, he believed that such a policy was indispensable to a free America." He asked those intent on repeal, "Is it not your main purpose in securing repeal to enable us to furnish arms, munitions and implements of war to one group of nations and to deny them to another group of nations? . . . Is not this laying the foundation for intervention—in fact, is it not intervention—in the present European war? Is it not your purpose to take sides?"[30] Everyone knew the answer was yes, that the end of neutrality legislation meant America entering the war, however warily, on the side of the British and French.

The big gun rolled out by the isolationists the night after Borah's lackluster broadcast was Lindbergh. Until the outbreak of war, Lindbergh appears not to have understood how he had compromised his political independence by joining the army. He continued to discuss foreign affairs openly with friends, one being his old acquaintance William R. Castle, a Republican isolationist and former assistant secretary of state, to whom he spoke about Hoover's idea of "having a small group ready to jump in if a war begins in Europe, with the purpose of keeping this country out of trouble." Now he was ready to enter the fray.

Castle had introduced Lindbergh to the conservative commentator Fulton Lewis Jr.,[31] who, on August 23, the day the Nazi–Soviet pact was signed, discussed what to do if war broke out in Europe. While that question was left unanswered for the time being, they found common ground in their anti-Semitism. "We are all disturbed about the effect of the Jewish influence in our press, radio, and motion pictures," Lindbergh told his diary. "We must . . . limit to a reasonable amount the Jewish influence in the Educational agencies in this country—i.e. press, radio, and pictures. . . .Whenever the Jewish percentage of total population becomes too high, a reaction seems to invariably occur. It is too bad because a few Jews of the right type are, I believe, an asset to any country."[32]

The day German troops marched into Poland, Lindbergh had asked himself, "What stand should America take in this war?" before answering, "We have enough internal problems without confusing them with war."[33] Urged on by Castle and Lewis, he agreed to give a nationwide broadcast from the Carlton Hotel, Washington, on September 15. The famous flier was about to test whether, after years in self-exile, he could still move an American audience. According to some accounts, Roosevelt became so alarmed at the prospect of Lindbergh's broadcast that he considered imposing a ban upon him speaking in public, on the grounds that he was in the government's employ. If Lindbergh persisted in campaigning for isolationism, the president weighed recommending him as a suitable subject for an investigation by the Internal Revenue Service.[34]

To clear his lines within the army, Lindbergh showed the draft of his broadcast appealing for American neutrality to his old friend Hap Arnold, who was by now a major general and chief of the Army Air Corps. While believing the script "contained nothing which could in any way be construed as unethical," Arnold suggested that

Lindbergh give up the "inactive-active" military status that inhibited him from speaking openly. Arnold hinted that if Lindbergh persisted in his speechmaking, he could no longer be employed as a military aviation expert. Through Arnold, Secretary of War Woodring let Lindbergh know "he was very sorry because he had hoped to make use of me in the future, but didn't see how he could do so if I followed out my plans!"[35]

Even though Arnold had agreed not to show the radio script to Woodring, in case he should try to silence Lindbergh, the administration was aware of the message Lindbergh was about to deliver and tried to buy him off. Lindbergh's old Berlin buddy Truman Smith, now in military intelligence, told him that "the Administration was very much worried by my intention of speaking over the radio and opposing actively this country's entry into a European war" and "that if I would not do this, a secretaryship of air would be created in the Cabinet and given to me!" Lindbergh wrote in his diary that Roosevelt's offer "does not surprise me."[36] Without waiting for a formal offer, Lindbergh pressed on with the broadcast.

Addressing Americans "who feel that the destiny of this country does not call for our involvement in European wars," Lindbergh told his radio listeners, "We should never enter a war unless it is absolutely essential to the future welfare of our nation." Reminding listeners that George Washington "solemnly warned the people of America against becoming entangled in European alliances," Lindbergh said, "This is not a question of banding together to defend the white race against foreign invasion. This is simply one more of those age-old struggles within our own family of nations—a quarrel arising from the errors of the last war—from the failure of the victors of that war to follow a consistent policy either of fairness or of force." American entry into the war would mean "we are likely to lose a million men, possibly several million—the best of American youth," and he suggested that "by staying out of war ourselves, we may even bring peace to Europe more quickly."[37]

Lindbergh was encouraged when, the morning after the broadcast, his home in Lloyd Neck, Long Island, New York, was inundated with messages of support, including one from Arnold reporting that Woodring thought the broadcast "very well worded and very well delivered."[38] Meanwhile, tens of thousands protested to the White

House, condemning Lindbergh's connivance with America's enemies. Reading Lindbergh's speech, Kennedy concluded that the flier "had dealt the President's Campaign an ugly blow."

Then came the brickbats. Chief dissenter was Dorothy Thompson[39] of the *New York Post*, a stolid opponent of Nazism, who dismissed Lindbergh as a "somber cretin" and a "pro-Nazi." Winchell adapted Lindbergh's romantic soubriquet from his daring flying days, "the Lone Eagle," and renamed him "the Lone Ostrich." William Bullitt, the US ambassador to France, told Kennedy over the telephone that it was now evident Lindbergh wanted to be "the Fuhrer in the U.S."[40] Within days, Lindbergh began receiving threatening letters. He remained sanguine. "I feel I must do this, even if we have to put an armed guard in the house," he wrote.[41]

Lindbergh followed his broadcast with two long pieces of journalism—for the November edition of *Reader's Digest*, which was owned by the isolationist DeWitt Wallace,[42] and the *Atlantic Monthly*—that expanded on the racial theories that underpinned his creed. Europe was embarking on a war which "the White race is bound to lose, and the others bound to gain, a war which may easily lead our civilization through more Dark Ages if it survives at all," he wrote. The war would break down the "barrier between the teeming millions of Asia and the Grecian inheritance of Europe—one of those priceless possessions which permit the White race to live at all in a pressing sea of Yellow, Black and Brown."

He argued that Germany should be on the same side as Britain and France in a "Western Wall of race and arms" to guard against "the infiltration of inferior blood" that could only be avoided by the "English Fleet, a German Air Force, a French army, an American nation, standing together as guardians of our common heritage." Otherwise, he wrote, Europe would "commit racial suicide by internal conflict."[43]

Wallace was delighted with the *Digest* piece, telling Lindbergh that "no one in this country is able to exert a deeper influence on public opinion than yourself."[44] Soon after, Lindbergh agreed to meet a group of isolationist senators brought together by Senator Harry Byrd to discuss how the neutrality legislation could be kept intact.[45]

The president resumed his battle for the amendment of the neutrality laws with an address to both houses of Congress on September 21. He insisted that everyone in the chamber was "equally and without reservation in favor of such measures as will protect the neutrality, the safety and the integrity of our country and at the same time keep us out of war," but said circumstances had changed and he now regretted "that the Congress passed [the 1935 neutrality] act. I regret equally that I signed that act." He argued that there were good economic arguments for scrapping the law, thereby repatriating the jobs outsourced to Canadians and others who were assembling warplanes and ships for Britain and France.

"I give to you my deep and unalterable conviction," he said, "that by the repeal of the embargo the United States will more probably remain at peace than if the law remains as it stands today." Without mentioning Britain, France, or Germany, he ended on an ominous note: "Fate seems now to compel us to assume the task of helping to maintain in the Western World a citadel wherein that civilization may be kept alive."[46]

After the president's broadcast, Borah sounded out Lindbergh about becoming the Republican presidential candidate in 1940, an idea that had already been floated in the press. The flier declined, telling Borah that he was "not well suited for political office and that I would probably be very unhappy if I ever held one." He confided in his diary that night, "I enjoy too much the ability to do and say what I wish to ever be a successful candidate."[47] It was not false modesty. Lindbergh's shyness and his lonely approach to life made him a poor retail politician. Had he been more suited to politics, the history of America's involvement in World War Two might have been very different.

In their dueling speeches, Roosevelt and Lindbergh both appealed to Americans' patriotism, both claimed that Western civilization was at stake, both insisted that the maintenance of neutrality was essential. Yet Americans were aware that they were being offered two very different visions. Lindbergh's plea that Germany not be judged too harshly—"England and France, to be successful, had to keep Germany weak by force"—jarred with the graphic newsreel pictures coming out of Poland. Americans saw heartbreaking images of Germany's merciless Blitzkrieg[48] (lightning war), of Polish cavalry charging German tanks, of the bombing of Warsaw, of German troops herding Jews out of their homes at gunpoint.

To avoid becoming the focus of isolationist speeches, Roosevelt decided to let the Polish newsreels tell their own story. "I am almost literally walking on eggs," he told Lord Tweedsmuir, the Scottish novelist and author of *The 39 Steps* who had been made governor-general of Canada.[49] "I am at the moment saying nothing, seeing nothing, and hearing nothing."[50] He kept a vow of silence, too, about the prospect of a third term, even when Wallace declared that the outbreak of war in Europe made it essential that the president should be reelected. "It would have been kind and polite of the speaker to have consulted the victim before he spoke," Roosevelt responded via Early.[51] Quietly, preparations to counter the Nazis' aggression proceeded apace, the president exhorting his acting secretary of the navy to identify and report without delay German submarines or U-boat supply ships operating within America's exclusion zone.

Undecided senators and House members started falling in behind the president. Republican Senator Styles Bridges of New Hampshire said before the president's speech, "We must mind our own business," but after it he said he was "glad the President [admitted] he made a mistake in signing the Neutrality Act and that Congress made a mistake in passing it."[52]

The isolationists also lost a key advocate, Republican Senator Robert A. Taft[53] from Ohio, son of President Taft, who had warned that if America joined the war it would lead to "an immediate demand for arbitrary power, unlimited control of wages, prices, and agriculture, and complete confiscation of private property."[54] Nonetheless, like Bridges he became convinced that cash and carry would prevent the war from spreading to America and announced his intention of voting against the neutrality laws.

Others remained firm. Philip Fox La Follette,[55] former governor of Wisconsin, the isolationist son of the arch-isolationist Senator Robert M. La Follette Sr., tried to set up a national organization to oppose cash and carry arms sales and quickly recruited Lindbergh, Ford, Hoover, Borah, and Nye. But suspicion of La Follette's motives in trying to establish a presidential run through a third party led to the campaign faltering.[56]

The airwaves became a key battleground in the Battle of Neutrality. Churchill used his fame in America to broadcast at the height of the debate, though he took a risk when he invoked the Civil War, which, particularly for Southerners, remained a painful memory. "Of all the wars that men have fought," he said, "none was more noble than the great Civil War in America. . . . All the heroism of the South could not redeem their cause from the stain of slavery, just as the courage and skill which the Germans always show in war will not free them from the reproach of Nazism, with its intolerance and brutality."[57] The following morning, Churchill was relieved to discover that the comparison between the Confederates and the Nazis appeared not to have caused offense to the very people the president was depending on to repeal the neutrality laws.

Another broadcast from a most unlikely source also appealed for Americans to rally round the president. When Cardinal Mundelein, the principal Catholic in America, died in early October 1939, he left instructions that his plea for Congress to amend the neutrality laws be broadcast by a surrogate, Bishop Sheil.[58]

A second broadcast by Lindbergh, on October 13, proposed that America become a fiercely defended fortress. "We must be ready to wage war with all the resources of our nation if [the American continent is] ever seriously threatened," he said. "I do not believe that repealing the arms embargo would assist democracy in Europe, because I do not believe this is a war for democracy," he said. "This is a war . . . brought about by the desire for strength on the part of Germany and the fear of strength on the part of England and France."

Lindbergh blamed the war on Britain and France for not rescuing Germany's floundering Weimar Republic from Nazism. He remarked that he "would as soon see our country traffic in opium as in bombs."[59] "It is the European race we must preserve," he said. "If the white race is ever seriously threatened, it may then be time for us to take our part in its protection, to fight side by side with the English, French and Germans." Conscious that so long as he wore a uniform he was inhibited from campaigning against the war, Lindbergh declared his intention of leaving the National Advisory Committee for Aeronautics in mid-November, explaining, "I want to do other things."[60]

Yet despite Borah, Lindbergh, and other isolationists—including an intervention by Coughlin—American opinion slowly moved toward abandoning neutrality. Polling showed that at this time 84 percent wanted Britain and France to beat Germany, and 60 percent wanted the neutrality laws overturned. Pollsters concluded in October that "the overwhelming majority of voters . . . are willing to give [the Allies] every aid short of actual armed intervention," but they retained an "intense desire . . . to avoid shedding American blood."[61]

When the congressional votes were in on November 3, Roosevelt had scored a sizeable victory. The Senate revised the neutrality laws by sixty-three votes to thirty and the House by 243 to 172. Minor irritations remained in the amended Neutrality Act, such as a ban on American vessels in war zones and the need for Britain and France to haul away their arms and munitions in their own ships. This meant that eight Atlantic and Baltic sea-lanes were deemed out of bounds to ninety-two American merchant vessels, leaving Britain besieged by German submarines. "By taking our ships off the seas, the bill aided the German blockade of Britain as effectively as if all our ships had been torpedoed," wrote one commentator.[62]

In an ingenious workaround, Roosevelt pressed the constitutional limits of his executive power by embracing a plan to register American merchantmen under the Panamanian flag. When that met opposition even from the likes of William Allen White and Senator Harry Truman,[63] the president backed down, permitting instead a number of American vessels to be sold to British, French, and Belgian operators for the purpose of shipping arms. From London, Kennedy warned the president that news of the amendment of the neutrality legislation meant that "every hour will be spent by [the British] trying to figure out how we can be gotten in [the war]."[64]

Adopting his most avuncular style, Roosevelt wrote to the kings of Belgium—"I knew him when he was a mere boy"—and Norway— "My wife and I will always be happy that we had those few days with you"[65]—and the queen of the Netherlands—"I have ancestral Dutch connections"[66]—that they should count on him personally to help alleviate their personal discomfort. In particular, he offered to take in royal children and suggested safe routes to smuggle them out of Europe before Germany moved westward.

"It would probably be best for [your children] to go by train and motor to Bilbao or Lisbon and I would gladly send a cruiser there to bring them to Washington or to our country place at Hyde Park," he told King Leopold of Belgium, as if arranging a country picnic. "It would give Mrs. Roosevelt and me very great happiness to care for [your children] over here as if they were members of our own family,"[67] he wrote to Queen Wilhelmina of the Netherlands. "We should be delighted to have them with us at the White House or at our country place on the Hudson River where my Mother, who is eighty-five years old, would be very happy to take care of them."[68]

Even as the revised Neutrality Act neared approval by Congress, isolationists had begun to regroup, bolstered by the lack of immediate conflict in Europe between Germany and the allies Britain and France. They hoped Hitler's appetite might be satisfied by digesting Poland and that war in the west could be averted. Rather than facilitate the war, the isolationists and noninterventionists argued that America should call a peace conference to bring the warring sides together. Lindbergh asked in his diary, "Will there be peace now Warsaw has fallen? The lack of fighting on the Western front indicates a reasonable possibility of this."[69]

Kennedy continued to spread defeatism, telling partners at J. P. Morgan in October "that France and England would lose the war if they tried to attack Germany across the Western front."[70] The same month, he confessed to feeling strongly "that nothing is to be gained by the war continuing" and that a negotiated peace was possible. The ambassador met with King George, who told him that after the subjugation of Poland was complete he fully expected "a proposal will be made by [Hitler] to put a stop to this war and to arrive at some understanding."[71]

The king was well informed. Barely a month later, on October 6, as the battle in Congress over the neutrality law was reaching its height, Hitler gave a keynote speech in the Reichstag proposing peace talks. "I believe even today that there can be only be real peace in Europe and throughout the world if Germany and England [sic] come to an understanding," he said, before asking, "Why should this war in the West be fought? . . . Has Germany made any demands of England which might threaten the British Empire or endanger its existence? On the contrary."

Echoing the isolationists' arguments, he said, "This war in the West cannot settle any problems except perhaps the ruined finances of certain armament manufacturers, newspaper owners or other international war profiteers."[72] The Nazi press trumpeted the news that Hitler was prepared to make peace, the *Völkischer Beobachter* announcing, "Hitler's Peace Offer. No war aims against France and Britain. Reduction of armaments. Proposal of a conference."

But the offer was a sham. Three days later, Hitler called a meeting of his commanders in chief, telling them, "This does not alter the war aim. That is and remains the destruction of our western enemies."[73] He set a time and date for "Case Yellow," the invasion of the Netherlands, Belgium, and France: dawn on November 12, 1939.[74] As he explained, "Time is working for our adversaries. I shall attack France and England at the most favorable and quickest moment."[75]

Kennedy took up Hitler's false cry for a negotiated peace. Fearing for his family's lives, by mid-September Kennedy had sent all but the mentally impaired Rosemary back to America. At the same time, he was already planning a return to the United States "for a few months"[76] for the Christmas and New Year holidays and beyond. Fearful of being bombed by the Luftwaffe in his London bed, he took a lease on a sixty-room country house, St Leonard's,[77] near the royal residence at Windsor and spent increasing amounts of time there.

In letters to Roosevelt through the fall of 1939, the ambassador left a paper trail to attest to his isolationist credentials. Postulating that "if the war continued . . . it signifies entire social, financial and economic breakdown [in Britain] and that after the war nothing will be saved," he urged the president to "evolve world peace plans" and become the "saviour of the world."[78] Roosevelt told Farley that Kennedy's letter was "the silliest message I have ever received."[79] Hull told Kennedy the administration "sees no opportunity nor occasion for any peace move to be initiated" by the president, adding that "the people of the United States would not support any move for peace initiated by this Government that would consolidate or make possible a survival of a regime of force and aggression [in Germany]."[80]

Yet in mid-September Roosevelt did allow a secret feeler to be extended to Berlin to discover whether a negotiated peace was possible. An American businessman, William R. Davis, made a private approach to Göring, who was thought to be opposed to escalating the war. Roosevelt invested no personal credibility in a mission he believed hopeless from the start, and the initiative failed to progress.

Churchill told Kennedy that no peace plan would pass muster in Britain so long as he was there to oppose it. "For goodness sake don't let the President come out with a peace plan," he told the ambassador. "It will just embarrass us and we won't accept it. In fact, I would fight Chamberlain if he proposed to accept it."[81] Roosevelt, too, privately thought a true peace unlikely. "I do not want this country to take part in a patched up temporizing peace which would blow up in our faces in a year or two," he told William Allen White.[82]

Unable to persuade Roosevelt to negotiate peace, Kennedy engaged with members of the British government, asking John Simon,[83] "Just what are you fighting for now? You can't restore Poland to the Poles, can you?"[84] He reported to Roosevelt that the British "are more and more confused in their own minds just what they are fighting for and what they will attain even if they win."

"I have yet to talk to any military or naval expert of any nationality . . . who thinks that, with the present and prospective set-up of England and France on one side and Germany and Russia and their potential allies on the other, England has a Chinaman's chance," he wrote to the president. "We are all vitally concerned in what happens to the United States if the fight goes to a finish and the Allies are beaten," he said, with "the prospect of our best customer beaten and finished as a Power and the attendant difficulty of arranging our place in the world with Powers who know we hate them."[85]

Speculation in London suggested that Churchill, or perhaps Halifax, was poised to replace Chamberlain. Churchill's position, that there was no turning back from war, was well known and defined him as the isolationists' principal British opponent. "It was for Hitler to say when the war would begin," Churchill told Americans in a broadcast, "but it is not for him nor his successors to say when it will end."[86]

Kennedy dismissed the prospect of the vacillating Chamberlain being ousted as readily as he derided the prospect of Churchill taking his place. "There is no adequate person within the parliamentary ranks [who could do the job]," he told the president. "It would not be surprising if the maelstrom of war had to cast up extra-Parliamentary leaders."[87] And the ambassador continued to spread dissent, warning the president, "Churchill has in America a couple of very close friends who definitely are not on our team,"[88] though who he had in mind was unclear.

At this time, depressed and missing his family, Kennedy found his personal belief in democracy wobbling. He began referring to Britain and France, as Borah had done, as "the so-called democracies" and told Roosevelt that the war would inexorably lead to dictatorships on both sides of the Atlantic. "Democracy as we now conceive it in the United States will not exist in France and England after the war," he wrote to the president, before reiterating his belief that America's "vital interests . . . lie in the Western Hemisphere."[89] At the beginning of November, in another long letter to the president, Kennedy returned to his theme. "Make no mistake," he wrote, "there is a very definite undercurrent in [Britain] for peace."[90]

Kennedy's defeatism began to tell on his social life. "I don't see anyone anymore as of course there is no gathering anyplace," he wrote to Rose.[91] The war closed down the hectic party-giving of London high society hostesses and even when he did mix with the old crowd, he found attitudes had hardened against him. Preferring not to believe that his unpopularity was a result of his pessimistic views, Kennedy was convinced he was losing friends because the British had become anti-American, telling Rose, "You would never believe the way public opinion in this country has turned anti-American and incidentally anti-US Ambassador Kennedy."[92] Kennedy the isolationist began to feel increasingly isolated.

After a party at the Astors', he wrote to Rose, "They all wanted to know when America was coming in and of course I told them they weren't coming in. So perhaps, dear, you went home at the height of your husband's popularity."[93] The strain soon got to him. He developed stomach ulcers. Over the course of two months, his weight fell by 15 pounds. On November 29, exhausted, he flew to Lisbon en route for the United States for a complete rest and a top-to-toe medical checkup.

By December, Roosevelt was more than ever convinced that a victory for Germany and the Soviet Union would put in jeopardy the whole of Western civilization. "Our world trade would be at the mercy of the [Nazi–Soviet] combine and our increasingly better relations with our twenty neighbors to the south would end—unless we were willing to go to war in their behalf against a German–Russian dominated Europe," he wrote to William Allen White. "What worries me, especially, is that public opinion over here is patting itself on the back every morning and thanking God for the Atlantic Ocean (and the Pacific Ocean). . . . I fear most people are merely going around saying: 'Thank God for Roosevelt and Hull—no matter what happens, they will keep us out of war.'" [94]

Meanwhile, on the Western Front, there was a pronounced lack of bellicosity from the democracies, nor any suggestion that Germany was prepared to make the first move, an eerie stasis that came to be known as the Phony War. The French forces confined themselves to their concrete bunkers on the Maginot Line. The British were preoccupied with keeping the German navy penned in their home ports. They nevertheless suffered the loss of the World War One aircraft carrier HMS *Courageous*, with 500 fatalities, torpedoed by a U-boat in the Bristol Channel, and the battleship HMS *Royal Oak*, with 833 lives, when a U-boat penetrated the Royal Navy's home base at Scapa Flow. They responded when British and New Zealand warships stalked and shelled the German pocket battleship *Admiral Graf Spee*, which attempted to avoid total destruction by dropping anchor in Montevideo harbor, Uruguay.

As a holiday gift for his new best friend, on Christmas Eve Churchill sent Roosevelt a long, detailed, and colorful account of what became known as the Battle of the River Plate. Penned in Montevideo harbor, with the prospect of certain capture or sinking if it dared leave, Hitler ordered the scuttling of the *Graf Spee*. Churchill relished passing on the news to the British people, telling them in what was to become a series of Sunday night broadcasts often relayed to the United States, "The *Spee* still sticks up in the harbor of Montevideo as a grisly monument and measure of the fate in store for any Nazi warship which dabbles in piracy on the broad waters." [95]

In sinking the *Graf Spee*, the Royal Navy ignored the Monroe Doctrine of 1823, which declared all military matters in North and South America the sole bailiwick of the US government. In public, the Americans, at the prompting of a number of South American nations, complained that Britain had intruded upon the 300-mile noncombatant zone declared by the president. Anxious not to upset a potential powerful ally, Churchill quickly cabled an apology to Roosevelt for "recent incidents."

"We cannot always refrain from stopping enemy ships outside International three-mile limit when these may well be supply ships for U-boats or surface raiders," he explained, before reassuring the president that he had ordered Royal Navy ships in future "only to arrest or fire upon them out of sight of United States shore." "If we should break under load," he continued, "South American Republics would soon have many worse enemies than the sound of one day's distant seaward cannonade. And you also, Sir, in quite a short time would have more direct cares."[96] "Of course, the President is our best friend," Churchill reassured Chamberlain, "but I expect he wants to be re-elected and I fear that isolationism is the winning ticket."[97]

Roosevelt responded to Churchill's account of the Battle of the River Plate with the glee of a schoolboy winning a pencil and paper game of battleship. "Ever so many thanks for that tremendously interesting account of the extraordinarily well fought action of your three cruisers," he wrote. "I am inclined to think that when we know more about the facts, it will turn out that the damage to the *Admiral Graf Spee* was greater than reported."

He continued, "I would not be frank unless I told you that there has been much public criticism here" of the search and detention of American ships by the Royal Navy, but he reassured Churchill that he was not concerned. "That is always found to be so in a nation which is 3,000 miles away from the fact of war." The president signed off, "I wish much that I could talk things over with you in person— but I am grateful to you for keeping me in touch, as you do."[98]

CHAPTER ELEVEN

THIRD TERM FEVER

*Roosevelt avoids declaring for a
third term, Churchill succeeds Chamberlain,
Hitler makes his westward move.*

ROOSEVELT STARTED the election year of 1940 by reminding Americans in his State of the Union address that "like it or not, the daily lives of American citizens will, of necessity, feel the shock of events on other continents." He continued, "But there are those who wishfully insist, in innocence or ignorance or both, that the United States of America as a self-contained unit can live happily and prosperously, its future secure, inside a high wall of isolation while, outside, the rest of Civilization and the commerce and culture of mankind are shattered."

He tried to persuade voters to prepare for trouble ahead. "I can understand the feelings of those who warn the nation that they will never again consent to the sending of American youth to fight on the soil of Europe. . . . I can also understand the wishfulness of those who oversimplify the whole situation by repeating that all we have to do is to mind our own business and keep the nation out of war. But there is a vast difference between keeping out of war and pretending that this war is none of our business."

The president tempered his candor by insisting on his sincere desire to keep America out of the war. "The first President of the United States warned us against entangling foreign alliances," he said. "The present President of the United States subscribes to and follows that precept."[1] The following day, he asked for $1.8 billion ($30 billion in 2014 terms) to spend on defense.

In the midst of the Battle of Neutrality, the Republican presidential hopeful Alf Landon, who agreed with Roosevelt's general foreign policy position, added to the president's discomfort by suggesting that he should publicly declare he would not stand for a third term. Roosevelt kept mum and urged all his closest political allies to do the same. Although he had all but taken the decision to stand in 1940, to be sure of winning his party's nomination it was still too early for the president to clarify his intentions.

So long as Roosevelt maintained his silence, the 1940 Democratic race could not start in earnest. When asked by a reporter to respond to a senior Democrat's appeal for Roosevelt to serve a third term, the president declared, "The weather is very hot." When another asked him what his reelection plans were, the hapless journalist was told to "put on a dunce cap and stand in the corner."[2]

The failure of the president to make his position clear helped Kennedy. Until Roosevelt declared, no Democratic donors would give a dime to another candidate, as if Roosevelt ran it would almost certainly prove to have been a waste of money. Kennedy, however, needed no financial backers. He was rich enough to fund his own campaign. Roosevelt still feared a Kennedy candidacy as an outside chance, but felt that so long as the ambassador was confined to London, he would be incapable of organizing a viable campaign. He did not fear Lindbergh as a Republican presidential candidate, because the aviator was a divisive figure without charm or political experience. He was, however, anxious that Lindbergh might ally himself with an isolationist like Kennedy and make the election a referendum on whether America should stay out of the war.

Events in Europe did not suggest that now would be a good time for Roosevelt to declare. Despite the high drama of September 1939, there was little movement on the Western Front. In the east, however, the Blitzkrieg—the first use of a new, fast-moving military strategy—had quickly overcome the ill-equipped and ill-trained Polish forces and led to the partition of that country. In October, following his secret deal with Hitler, Stalin swallowed the eastern part of Poland and the Baltic states of Latvia, Lithuania, and Estonia, before, at the end of November, turning his invasion force on Finland.

Meanwhile, as "spontaneous" pro-Roosevelt third-term campaigns began to emerge in Chicago and elsewhere, potential Democratic runners began circling the paddock. In May 1939, a "Garner for President" office was set up in Dallas, Texas, to promote John Nance Garner, the sixty-nine-year-old, twice-elected vice president who had been imposed upon the president by Hearst. Roosevelt held Garner in contempt, and when the vice president was absent from a cabinet meeting was openly rude about him. Garner, in turn, was weary of being excluded from decision-making and held constitutional objections to Roosevelt serving more than two terms. His isolationist credentials were confirmed by Henry Ford, who declared, "Jack Garner would make a mighty fine president."[3] Early polling by Gallup put Garner near the top of a short list of Democratic contenders with 50 percent, but only so long as the president was not a candidate.

More popular than Garner in early polling was James A. Farley, the Postmaster General from New York, who was chairman of the Democratic National Committee and knew the party inside out. Like Kennedy, he was an Irish American Roman Catholic, which led some to suggest that his religion made him unelectable. Certainly the Catholic prelate Cardinal Mundelein of Chicago thought so. He told Farley he hoped he would "do nothing to involve the Catholics . . . in another debacle,"[4] a reference to Alfred E. Smith's[5] crushing defeat in the presidential election of 1928. Farley told Mundelein, "I am not planning to secure the nomination myself," though it was by no means clear that he meant it.

In an apparent reference to Roosevelt's suggestion the previous year that Farley run for governor of New York, which Farley interpreted as an attempt to put him off aiming for the White House, Farley told the cardinal, "I will not let myself be kicked around by Roosevelt or anyone else."[6] Mundelein told him he hoped Roosevelt would stand for a third term. Nonetheless, at the end of January 1940 Farley filed his name for inclusion in the Massachusetts Democratic primary in March.

George Earle,[7] the popular, wealthy, well-connected pro-labor governor of Pennsylvania, was, by April 1937, second in the polls to Farley, and, as a former minister to Austria, could claim some foreign policy experience. He sought Roosevelt's blessing for a run by declaring his devotion to the president in June 1937. "There are . . . no men in the Democratic party or any other party who reach knee-high in stature, mentally and morally, to Franklin D. Roosevelt," he said. "Between the third-term precedent and the welfare of the country, can any patriotic citizen hesitate as to which course he will take?" On this issue, at least, Roosevelt heartily agreed with him.

Not far behind in popularity was Senator Burton K. Wheeler,[8] a liberal centrist from Montana and, until the Supreme Court-packing drama, a fervid New Dealer. By the end of 1939, however, he had become an isolationist and fierce opponent of Roosevelt. His principal backer was the mineworkers' union leader and fellow isolationist John L. Lewis.[9] To dampen the senator's chances, the president let slip to Jim Farley, "If Wheeler should be nominated for President, I'd vote for a Republican."[10]

The governor of Indiana, Paul V. McNutt,[11] whose good looks caused Roosevelt to dismiss him as "that platinum blond S.O.B. from Indiana,"[12] was the Democratic frontrunner in the months leading up to the presidential election of 1936, until Roosevelt announced that he was seeking reelection. McNutt's record as governor, in particular calling in the National Guard to break strikes, for which he was dubbed "the Hoosier Hitler," made him unpopular among both labor unions and party activists in general. Yet by November 1939, with McNutt declaring he would run only if the president declined a third term, McNutt's campaign managers believed their man could win.

Among the no-hopers was a Houston, Texas, businessman, Jesse Jones,[13] who was favored by other Texas businessmen but by few outside the state. He was running such an imperceptible campaign that George Creel, Woodrow Wilson's head of wartime propaganda, described it as "as loud as the tramp of a timorous kitten."

To divide and rule his opponents, Roosevelt encouraged other no-hope candidates so that no one could establish a firm foothold. His close aide Hopkins, director of the WPA, was heartened to be told by Roosevelt that he was his hand-picked heir. The two had a long conversation about the chances of success, with Roosevelt reminding Hopkins that his divorce was sure to be an issue, though not perhaps an insurmountable one. He cited as a precedent President Grover Cleveland,[14] who had admitted to an illegitimate child. Apart from having to endure on the stump the constant chant of "Ma, Ma, where's my Pa?", he suffered no electoral harm from the scandal.

More seriously, Hopkins was diagnosed with cancer in the summer of 1939 and was given little time to live. After most of his stomach was removed, he recuperated at Kennedy's Florida estate, but his poor health persisted and he returned to be treated at the Mayo Clinic in Rochester, Minnesota. For Roosevelt, bolstering Hopkins's presidential hopes was a way of keeping his dear friend alive while further muddying the waters.

Among other close allies Roosevelt flattered into believing they were his natural heir was former Republican Henry Wallace, secretary of agriculture, from Iowa, and Secretary of State Hull, who was perhaps too serious-minded to enjoy the knockabout of a campaign but, having watched at close quarters the war in Europe unfolding, could at least boast extensive knowledge of foreign affairs. There were other passing flavors of the month, among them Senator Bennett Champ Clark of Missouri. At the end of 1939, polls put Garner, Farley, and Hull at the top of a long line of hopefuls.

Nothing said by Roosevelt about the presidency at this time could be taken at face value. Over lunch with Farley at Hyde Park in August 1939, the president said that the Manhattan district attorney Thomas E. Dewey[15] would be the Republican candidate and, although "arrogant and ambitious," would "make a formidable opponent." While giving Farley no encouragement, the president declared Garner "impossible," said Wallace was agreeable but felt he did not have the "it" factor, and responded to McNutt's name with a firm thumbs-down. As for his own intentions, Roosevelt whispered, "Jim, I am going to tell you something I have never told another living soul. Of course I will not run for a third term. Now I don't want you to pass this on to anyone because it would make my role difficult if the decision were known prematurely."[16]

Roosevelt's mother, Sara, appeared to confirm as much when, in September, on her eighty-fifth birthday, she said, "I don't think my son has the slightest wish for a third term. He is thinking only about the war."[17] Roosevelt, meanwhile, said the war meant he could not take a decision "until the spring, March or April."[18] In March 1940, Roosevelt was insisting that others could win the 1940 election. "I deprecate the attitude of some of our friends that unless I run, no other Democrat can be elected," he wrote to the Democratic governor of Illinois, Henry Horner.[19]

Whether the president would or wouldn't run became a national joke, Roosevelt's continuing silence eliciting a ditty from a reporter: "He's riding high, and he's riding straight / He's heading straight for the White House gate." Even Roosevelt himself began to joke about it. Laying the cornerstone of his presidential library at Hyde Park in November 1939, he paused before saying, "And may I add, in order that my good friends of the press will have something to write about tomorrow . . ." He surveyed the crowd of reporters before continuing, "that I hope they will give due interpretation to the expression of my hope that"—and he paused again—"when we open the building to the public it will be a fine day."[20] Krock reported, "Whatever Mr. Roosevelt may intend, he is obviously enjoying it."[21]

Speculation was not confined to America. On her return from her visit to Hyde Park in July the previous year, Queen Elizabeth had told Kennedy that the president had confided to her that he "absolutely does not want to be a candidate."[22] Kennedy could barely contain his delight. Yet after lunch at Buckingham Palace at the end of November, Kennedy noted that the queen still "wanted to know if Roosevelt would want Third Term. All English hope so."[23]

Frustrated by the welter of ambiguous information, the press began drawing attention to Roosevelt's dilemma by dubbing him the Sphinx, a soubriquet gratefully taken up by political cartoonists. In "Washington Merry-Go-Round," Drew Pearson summed up Roosevelt's predicament: "If the President talks now, the chances are ten to one he will take himself out of the race; whereas if he continues silent until next spring, pro-third term sentiment within the party may be stoked up to such an extent that even if he said he wasn't a candidate he might be 'drafted' anyway."[24]

A hint of the president's true intentions came when he made it known that he thought the Democratic Convention should be held in July or August, leaving new candidates little time to campaign for the election in November. Farley, for one, was not to be deterred. In January 1940, at a Jackson Day Democratic fundraiser in Washington, Farley, seated beside the president, opened his remarks with, "Fellow candidates." Landon, the titular head of the Republican Party, continued to taunt Roosevelt about his intentions. "If the President would just give the spirit of unity an opportunity to work in this country, it would be so helpful," he said. "Instead he makes it difficult by his foxy way of hiding, playing with the third-term proposition."[25]

The president betrayed more than he intended when replying to a complaint from a feminist, Mary Dewson,[26] that there were not enough portraits of women on postage stamps. Pointing out that "old Martha Washington was the only female face on letters" until his inauguration, that he had "even put Whistler's mother on a stamp," and that "if you had asked me to put Greta Garbo's face on a stamp, I might have listened," he promised that "if we inaugurate a Democratic President in 1941, I will guarantee that he will provide one new female stamp each year."[27]

Visiting the White House in December 1939, Kennedy stood on the front steps and gave a not entirely convincing endorsement of Roosevelt for a third term. Once alone with the president, however, Kennedy popped the question. "No, Joe, I can't do it," Roosevelt replied. "I'm tired. I can't take it. What I need is a year's rest. You do too. . . . I just won't go for a third term unless we are in war. Even then, I'll never send an army over. We'll help them, but with supplies."

The president then gave Kennedy his opinion of the Democratic runners, calling Hull a ditherer, McNutt unfocused, and Hopkins too unwell, before surprising Kennedy by saying, "There's your-self."[28] It was neither an encouragement nor a deterrent. Kennedy was perplexed. At the time, Farley was enjoying an early surge in Massachusetts, which was due to hold its primary on March 5.[29] Eager to undermine Farley while flushing out Kennedy, the president played on the ambassador's vanity, telling him that it did not seem fair that Farley should be romping away in Kennedy's backyard. Perhaps, he said, Kennedy should run as a "favorite son."

As if by coincidence, in January 1940 a "Kennedy for President" campaign suddenly emerged in Massachusetts, with Kennedy's fin-gerprints all over it. Krock was chief cheerleader. But to Kennedy's disappointment, the flurry of activity did not develop into a stam-pede, though it was enough of a distraction to dampen the early enthusiasm for Farley, which pleased the president.

If Kennedy was going to make a serious bid, he felt he would have to enter the race at the last minute, when and if Roosevelt declared he would not run. To jump in earlier would incur the president's wrath. He would look disloyal and ungrateful. Above all, perhaps, he would look overtly ambitious and irresponsible, leaving his London post when Britain was at war. Only if he held back would he be able to gain the president's blessing.

After meeting again with Roosevelt in February, the ambassador made an announcement. While he found the suggestion he should run "flattering," he reminded Americans, "I now occupy a most important government post which at this particular time involves matters so precious to the American people that no private consideration should permit my energies or interests to be diverted. . . . I must with positiveness state that I am not a candidate."[30] Obliged to bide his time until the president had declared his intentions, Kennedy announced that he would return to London, via Italy, on the *George Washington*.

Kennedy was far from happy at being held hostage by Roosevelt, and he could not contain his irritation. Behind closed doors in the office of Bill Bullitt, the ambassador to Paris who was back in Washington to report to Hull on the inadequacies of the French plans to resist a German invasion, Kennedy made clear his disenchantment with the president in "lurid" and "unrestrained" language. J. M. Patterson, publisher of the *New York Daily News*, and Doris Fleeson, the *News*'s Washington reporter, witnessed the outburst but did not file a report.[31]

"He began to criticize the President very sharply, whereupon Bill took issue with him," reported Ickes in his diary. "The altercation became so violent that Patterson finally remarked that he suspected he was intruding and Doris Fleeson left, but Joe continued to berate the President." Bullitt accused him of disloyalty and indiscretion, daring to criticize the president in such vulgar language in front of journalists. "Joe said that he would say what he Goddamned pleased before whom he Goddamned pleased," wrote Ickes.[32]

Even as Kennedy was berating the president, Roosevelt was making arrangements for a new slap to Kennedy's sense of self-respect. To demonstrate to Americans that he was exploring all avenues to peace, even though he had no intention of making a bargain with Hitler, in late February Roosevelt dispatched Sumner Welles on a tour of European capitals. (He ruled out sending him to visit Stalin as a protest against the Soviet invasion of Finland.) The Welles peace tour was an empty gesture and the president neither granted his special emissary discretion to make proposals nor encouraged him to believe the mission would bear fruit, telling him that the odds of his mission succeeding were a thousand to one.

Kennedy had been given no hint of the Welles peace initiative by the president and took it as another deliberate slight when he found out. Enraged, the ambassador again complained to Roosevelt for excluding him.

Welles met with Mussolini in Rome on February 26 and with Hitler in Berlin on March 1–3, after which Kennedy, traveling to London via Genoa, caught up with him. According to Kennedy, Welles said, "[Hitler] was in a mood to make a reasonable peace and the French and English somewhat in the same frame of mind."[33] In London, however, Welles changed his view after spending a late-night, three-hour session with Churchill.

Churchill, who to Welles's alarm had been sipping whiskies all afternoon, made a good impression. Welles was left in no doubt by Churchill that a negotiated peace would be a travesty and that "the war must be fought to a finish."[34] The American emissary told a British official that he was "extremely impressed" by what he had been told and considered Churchill "one of the most fascinating personalities he had ever met."[35]

Kennedy was furious that Welles had been so easily won over. When asked by the press on his return to London whether America remained isolationist, Kennedy declared, "If you mean by isolation a desire to keep out of the war, I should say it is definitely stronger."[36] It was a petulant response to once again being left in the dark by the president.

Those who hoped the Welles mission would return with an olive branch were disabused by the president in a fireside chat on March 16. Peace was desirable but should not come at any price, he said. "It cannot be a lasting peace if the fruit of it is oppression, or starvation, or cruelty, or human life dominated by armed camps. It cannot be a sound peace if small nations must live in fear of powerful neighbors."[37] The broadcast marked the end of talk in the administration of a negotiated peace. Like Churchill, what Roosevelt had in mind was not negotiated peace but German surrender and Allied victory.

The stakes on Roosevelt winning a third term climbed ever higher for the British. As Queen Elizabeth had hinted to Kennedy,

Britain dearly wanted Roosevelt to stay at his post. A new president was unlikely to be as Anglophile or as supportive as Roosevelt. Dining with Kennedy in March 1940, Churchill, too, "asked whether Roosevelt would run for 3rd term," recalled Kennedy. "I said probably if it were necessary to keep things right in U.S. He said of course we want him, but we must be careful U.S. doesn't know that."[38]

A week later, Kennedy changed his mind about the chances of Roosevelt running, writing to Rose, with whom he rarely shared political gossip, that the president would not run, "so obviously I'm out [of the administration]." If the president withdrew from the race he had not yet entered, it was still possible that Kennedy could emerge as a compromise candidate and cash in on his years of isolationist statements. "Knowing myself as I do, when I've been home 6 months I'll want to get going again," he told Rose. "Maybe old age and a bad stomach will change me. I don't know. I guess I'm a restless soul: Some people call it ambition."[39]

Ever eager to involve Roosevelt in military decisions, Churchill had asked Kennedy when visiting the White House in February to seek approval from the president for the Royal Navy to place mines in Norwegian waters, to prevent steel and iron ore from reaching German war factories. British intelligence suggested that Scandinavia would be Hitler's next conquest. There was a schoolboy element to Churchill's war games and he suggested that, to confound German code-breakers, Kennedy should send a cable saying, "Eunice would like to go to party" if the president approved the mission.[40] Roosevelt duly approved the action and Kennedy sent the cryptic message.

Hitler, too, had his eyes on the US presidential election and dearly hoped that an isolationist would win. In the meantime, lest America be brought needlessly into the war, he issued a "very strict order . . . not to do anything or say anything against the United States of America."[41]

Over dinner with Kennedy, according to the ambassador's diary, Churchill had "implied it would be almost worthwhile to stir up things by July in the war so Roosevelt would run."[42] There was no need for the British to "stir things up." Hitler needed naval bases in Scandinavia from which to launch U-boat attacks on Allied vessels. He also wanted, as the British suspected, to secure Swedish iron ore that in winter had to be ferried by sea down the Norwegian coast.[43] On April 9, without warning, he launched Exercise Weser, the invasion of Denmark and Norway.

By coincidence, Churchill had planned to invade Norway and lay mines in the sea routes on the same date. That morning, the British and German fleets steamed toward each other for an unexpected and unwelcome rendezvous in the North Sea. Before long, battle was joined. German naval losses were considerable, with three cruisers and ten destroyers sunk. But German troops, backed by air superiority and the rest of the German sea forces, arrived in Norway in merchant vessels and easily took control of Oslo, beating the British to the punch.

After a few days, the British forces that had occupied the northern Norwegian port of Narvik were obliged to make an ignominious retreat. Without remarking on the morality of the invasion, Lindbergh told his diary that the Germans' "amazing success in taking over Norway" was "a victory for air power and a turning point in military history."[44]

The failure to secure Norway was a setback for Britain and for Churchill's reputation. The first naval sortie of his much-lauded return to the Admiralty was an ill-arranged debacle, and, while not as devastating and murderous as the losses suffered in his ill-judged attempted invasion of Turkey at Gallipoli in World War One,[45] the failure of the Royal Navy to deflect the German invasion of Scandinavia proved an acute embarrassment to him and a profound shock to the Chamberlain government.

On May 7, the Commons began a two-day debate on "the conduct of the war," at which Chamberlain and Churchill both spoke. It became clear that the prime minister's party were in open rebellion and his grasp on the premiership slipping when he found himself saying, "I say this to my friends in the House—and I have friends in the House . . ."[46] Churchill took up the phrase to taunt those members who had backed appeasement. "He thought he had some friends," growled Churchill, "and I hope he has some friends. He certainly had a good many when things were going well." Watching the debate from the gallery, Kennedy felt "that [Churchill] saw in the distance the mantle being lowered for his shoulders."[47]

Two senior figures in the Commons controlled Chamberlain's

future. One was Lloyd George,[48] who as prime minister had led the country to victory in 1918. "The nation is prepared for every sacrifice so long as it has leadership," he declared. "The Prime Minister should give an example of sacrifice because there is nothing which can contribute more to victory in this war than that he should sacrifice the seals of office." But the lethal intervention was that of the veteran Conservative MP Leo Amery,[49] who, in a rousing speech cheered by both sides, borrowed from Oliver Cromwell's dismissal of the Long Parliament, the meeting of the House of Commons during the English Civil War that sat for eight years: "You have sat too long here for any good you have been doing. Depart, I say, and let us have done with you. In the name of God, go."

Although Chamberlain's government survived the vote of confidence that concluded the debate, so many of his own party either abstained or joined with the opposition to vote against him that Chamberlain knew he must resign. But who should replace him? Chamberlain preferred Halifax over Churchill, but in an awkward meeting between the three on May 9, when asked by the prime minister whether he would be prepared to serve under Halifax, Churchill remained silent. The awkward hush that followed proved one of the most important absences of sound in the history of Western civilization. "As I remained silent a very long pause ensued," Churchill would later recall. "It certainly seemed longer than the two minutes which one observes in the commemorations of Armistice Day. Then at length Halifax spoke."

Without conceding that Churchill was the better choice, Halifax told Chamberlain that as he sat in the Lords rather than the Commons, he was not best placed to become prime minister, who needed to be master of the more powerful lower house. "By the time he had finished," Churchill remembered, "it was clear that the duty would fall upon me—had in fact fallen upon me."[50] On the evening of May 10, King George sent for Churchill and asked him to form a government of national unity to include Labour and Liberal members. That morning had come the startling news that Hitler's forces were fast moving through the Netherlands and Belgium and, bypassing the Maginot Line, were crossing the French border through the dense forests of the Ardennes. The Battle of France had begun.

CHAPTER TWELVE

THE BATTLE OF FRANCE

*Churchill pleads with Roosevelt for old
destroyers, British forces retreat from Dunkirk,
German troops enter Paris.*

FOR ROOSEVELT, HITLER'S assault on the Low Countries and France was more evidence that America would not be able to keep out of the war. In a warm letter to King George, he recalled the night they had stayed up late at Hyde Park and he had "seemed pessimistic in my belief in the probability of war. More than a month after that I found the Congress assured that there could be no war, and for a few weeks I had to accept the charge of being a 'calamity-howler'," he wrote. "I certainly do not rejoice in my prophecies, but at least it has given me opportunity to bring home the seriousness of the world situation to the type of American who has hitherto believed, in much too large numbers, that no matter what happens there will be little effect on this country."[1]

Roosevelt offered a similar message to John Cudahy, US ambassador in Brussels, suggesting that "if the whole of the Mediterranean becomes involved, the good people in this country will wake up to the world situation. They are already beginning to, but have a long way to go."

On May 13, Churchill gave the first of a series of stirring speeches in the Commons to galvanize support among MPs and the British people. It was a deeply pessimistic message, but delivered in such inspiring terms that it was clear the country had taken a daring and defiant new direction. He said:

I have nothing to offer but blood, toil, tears and sweat. You ask, what is our policy? I can say: It is to wage war, by sea, land and air, with all our might and with all the strength that God can give us; to wage war against a monstrous tyranny, never surpassed in the dark, lamentable catalogue of human crime. . . . You ask, what is our aim? I can answer in one word: It is victory, victory at all costs, victory in spite of all terror, victory, however long and hard the road may be.[2]

Although Kennedy was one of Chamberlain's closest friends, he was at first made welcome in Churchill's Downing Street. For the new prime minister, even isolationists had their uses when they were the American ambassador and could help speed supplies to Britain. On May 15, after a late-night visit to Churchill, who had "a tray with plenty of liquor on it alongside him and he was drinking a scotch highball, which I felt was indeed not the first one he had drunk that night," Kennedy wrote to Roosevelt outlining the new prime minister's game plan: "It was his intention, he said, to ask for whatever airplanes we could spare right now and the loan of 30 or 40 of our old destroyers." Even if Britain were defeated, Churchill and the government would "never give up so long as he remains in power in public life, even if England were burnt to the ground." Churchill had told him, "Why, the Government will move, take the fleet with it to Canada, and fight on."[3]

Churchill's first letter to Roosevelt as prime minister, sent by cable and dated May 15, set off a long and anguished exchange in which Churchill eloquently pleaded for help and Roosevelt patiently explained why American opinion, combined with isolationist sentiment in Congress, meant that he could not help as much as he wished. "Although I have changed my office, I am sure you would not wish me to discontinue our intimate private correspondence," Churchill wrote to Roosevelt. He set out the bleak military prospects facing Britain, with France on the verge of defeat and Mussolini expected to join the war any day.

"If necessary, we shall continue the war alone and we are not afraid of that," Churchill wrote. "But I trust you realize, Mr. President, that the voice and force of the United States may count for nothing if they are withheld too long. . . . All I ask now is that you should proclaim nonbelligerency, which would mean that you would help us with everything short of actually engaging armed forces." He listed Britain's immediate requirements: "the loan of forty or fifty of your older destroyers," "several hundred of the latest types of aircraft," anti-aircraft batteries and ammunition, and American steel now that Norwegian iron ore supplies were cut off by the German occupation.

With rumors swirling that German paratroops were about to land in the Irish Free State, which neighbored Britain, Churchill asked for "a visit of a United States squadron to Irish ports." He offered, as if in return, the British naval base in Singapore for the US Pacific Fleet "to keep that Japanese dog quiet." And he raised the prospect of payment. Kennedy had told Roosevelt that Britain should first liquidate its $2 billion ($33 billion in 2014 terms) in American investments, then liquidate its gold reserves. Churchill wrote to Roosevelt, "We shall go on paying dollars for as long as we can, but I should like to feel reasonably sure that when we can pay no more, you will give us the stuff all the same."[4] Not since Churchill had written home to his mother from Harrow School had he adopted such a plaintive tone.

Roosevelt disappointed Churchill when he explained that lending the destroyers would need congressional consent and "I am not certain that it would be wise for that suggestion to be made to the Congress at this moment." Also, "from the standpoint of our own defense requirements" it was doubtful "whether we could dispose even temporarily" of the destroyers he asked for. But the president agreed to supply "the latest type" of warplanes, anti-aircraft equipment, and steel. The other matters he would consider in due course. With the reassuring message that "I hope you will feel free to communicate with me in this way at any time," he signed off with a cheery if ominous, "The best of luck to you."[5]

The German offensive, code-named Sichelschnitt ("Sickle Slash"), pressed on, charging south before turning west to encircle the French, and pinning the British expeditionary force of 300,000 men against the Channel. On May 15, French premier Paul Reynaud[6] telephoned Churchill to say, "We are beaten! The road is open to Paris."[7] On May 17, German troops occupied Antwerp and Brussels. Churchill wrote again to Roosevelt saying that he expected Britain to be attacked "on the Dutch model before very long" and that "if American assistance is to play any part it must be available."[8]

In the US, there were moves to readjust to the disastrous circumstances unfolding on the Western Front. On May 16, Roosevelt went to Congress to ask in person for $1.4 billion more for "defense." He was rapturously greeted as he entered the Senate chamber and appeared atypically nervous when he declared, "These are ominous days—days whose swift and shocking developments force every neutral nation to look to its defenses." Even the old certainties which the isolationists relied upon were made redundant by the speed of the Blitzkrieg. "The Atlantic and Pacific oceans were reasonably adequate defensive barriers when fleets under sail could move at an average speed of five miles an hour," he said, but "even in those days by a sudden foray it was possible for an opponent actually to burn our national Capitol."

He warned that technological advances meant an aerial attack on America could be mounted from Greenland, which was only six hours flying time from New England and had been invaded by German troops the previous month, and that "if Bermuda fell into hostile hands it would be a matter of less than three hours for modern bombers to reach our shores." The European democracies, he argued, had become America's first line of defense. "I ask the Congress not to take any action which would in any way hamper or delay the delivery of American-made planes to foreign nations which have ordered them, or seek to purchase new planes," he said.[9] Congress leapt to its feet almost to a man and gave the president the longest and most heartfelt ovation of his career. But the warm reception did not mean the isolationists had given up.

Two days later, Grenville Clark,[10] a Republican lawyer with whom Roosevelt had worked at the New York white-shoe law firm Carter, Ledyard & Milburn, proposed universal military service, the first peacetime conscription introduced in the history of the republic. "I am inclined to think there is a very strong public opinion for universal service of some kind," Roosevelt wrote to Clark. "The difficulty of proposing a concrete set of measures 'short of war' is largely a political one—what one can get from the Congress."[11]

Churchill kept pressing for war supplies. On May 20, he wrote to Roosevelt expressing regret that the president could not send the old destroyers he had requested, for "if they were here in six weeks they would play an invaluable part," and asking for "the largest possible number of Curtiss P-40 fighters now in course of delivery to your Army." Despite Churchill's customary impatience with those immediately around him, which prompted his wife, Clementine, in a rare intervention into his political life, to urge him to curb his "irascibility & rudeness,"[12] he always maintained a cordial if sometimes gloomy disposition when dealing with Roosevelt.

The prime minister drew attention to the plight of the British fleet, which kept the Atlantic sea-lanes free, if there was a Nazi victory. "If members of the [British] administration were finished and others came in to parley amid the ruins, you must not be blind to the fact that the sole remaining bargaining counter with Germany would be the [British] fleet," he wrote. "If this country was left by the United States to its fate, no one would have the right to blame those then responsible if they made the best terms they could for the surviving inhabitants."

With the help of Henry L. Stimson, Lewis Douglas, Bill Donovan,[13] and Judge Robert Patterson, Grenville Clark of the Military Training Camps Association, a World War One veterans group, drafted the Selective Training and Service Bill, which was introduced by Senator Edward Burke of Nebraska and Representative James Wadsworth of New York on June 20.[14] It mandated that every male American between twenty-one and thirty-six register for the draft and, through a lottery system, selected 9,000 men to train and serve in the military for twelve months. Ostensibly a measure to protect America's homeland, the bill was inevitably suspected of being a back-door way of assembling an army to fight abroad. With bipartisan support, it became law in October.

Churchill kept the lines open to Kennedy, but the ambassador soon found that he no longer enjoyed free access to Downing Street and top ministers. Kennedy was considered no fun—an important element in winning favor in Churchill's circle—not least because he always declined the cocktails offered by the prime minister, citing his gastrointestinal troubles. Above all, he was not welcome because he was a defeatist.

After a meeting with Churchill and his successor as First Lord of the Admiralty, A. V. Alexander,[15] Kennedy wrote in his diary, "A very definite shadow of defeat was hanging over them all."[16] At the height of the Battle of France, when Churchill told Kennedy to "not be too depressed," Kennedy's riposte was that he "couldn't help my inner thoughts based on facts."[17] On May 20, he wrote to Rose, "The jig is up. The situation is more than critical. It means a terrible finish for the Allies." He told her he expected "a dictated peace with Hitler probably getting the British Navy, and we will find ourselves in a terrible mess."[18]

Still Kennedy clung to the notion that isolationism would save America from a similar fate. "If God hadn't surrounded us with oceans three and five thousand miles wide, we ourselves might be caving in at some Munich," he wrote.[19] Little wonder, then, that Churchill put off meeting him, or, to Kennedy's fury, kept him waiting while he took an afternoon nap. "I expressed my resentment at this because I feel it was personal," Kennedy wrote in his diary. (He was right.) Kennedy's complaints to Chamberlain about his rude treatment only served to emphasize how they had both been side-stepped by the forceful, idiosyncratic new prime minister.

Five days after German forces invaded the Low Countries and crossed the French border, Lindbergh met with Merwin K. Hart,[20] a Fascist sympathizer who opposed the New Deal, then with a group of New Yorkers, to mount a campaign to keep America out of the war. Even as the Germans continued their Blitzkrieg, Lindbergh was planning a trip to Europe which at the last minute he was obliged to cancel. "I can do nothing [in Europe] under these conditions and feel it is essential for me to keep in close contact with developments in this country," he told his diary. "There will be greatly increased pressure for us to enter the war."[21] Hart and Carl W. Ackerman, dean of the Columbia University Graduate School of Journalism, tried to persuade him to barnstorm across America in his plane, giving speeches and meeting with donors to boost the antiwar campaign. Instead, Lindbergh agreed to give another radio broadcast.

As Amiens and Arras in northern France, just 70 miles from Calais, were surrounded by German forces, Lindbergh prepared a broadcast titled "The Air Defense of America." Secretary of War Woodring asked to see the script before it was delivered, but Lindbergh refused, calling the demand "a clumsy effort to dull the edge of my talk and turn it to the Administration's advantage."[22] The broadcast went ahead on May 19, without clearance from the War Department.

In a reference to Roosevelt's warning that the US was in danger of aerial bombing, he conceded "that bombing planes can be built with sufficient range to cross the Atlantic and return" and recommended that America should build air bases on the Mexican and Canadian borders. But he urged listeners to "stop this hysterical chatter of calamity and invasion." "We are in danger of war today not because European people have attempted to interfere with the internal affairs of America, but because American people have attempted to interfere with the internal affairs of Europe," he said. "We need not fear a foreign invasion unless American peoples bring it on through their own quarreling and meddling with affairs abroad."

> Years ago we decided to stay out of foreign wars. . . . We must not waver now that the crisis is at hand. There is no longer time for us to enter this war successfully. . . . Let us turn again to America's traditional role—that of building and guarding our own destiny. . . . Regardless of which side wins this war, there is no reason, aside from our own actions, to prevent a continuation of peaceful relationships between America and the countries of Europe. If we desire peace, we need only stop asking for war. No one wishes to attack us, and no one is in a position to do so. The only reason that we are in danger of becoming involved in this war is because there are powerful elements in America who desire us to take part.[23]

The *New York Times* editorial writers called Lindbergh "a blind young man if he really believes that we can live on terms of equal peace and happiness 'regardless of which side wins this war,'"[24] but isolationist leaders were delighted by his plain speaking. Roosevelt was left in a quandary about what to do to hush this eloquent advocate of appeasement.

Still reluctant to order Lindbergh's silence for fear of unfavorable publicity, the administration began putting pressure on those around him. Morgenthau moved against Lindbergh's military attaché friend Truman Smith, who had helped write Lindbergh's broadcasts, and pressed Marshall to fire him from military intelligence. Marshall said he was too valuable to dismiss, but in order to distance him from Lindbergh, he sent Smith to Fort Benning, Georgia. "Kay [Truman Smith's wife] says the report is around Washington that the Administration is out to 'get me'," Truman Smith told his diary. "It is not the first time, and it won't be the last."[25] Lindbergh

stopped meeting friends in the Air Corps "as I know that the politicians of this Administration make as much trouble as possible for
anyone I have contact with."[26]

Lindbergh's journalist friend John Lewis told him "that someone had started the rumor that [Lewis] had taken part in writing my radio addresses and that two of his 'sponsorships' in New
York City had been canceled as a result. Lewis had been forced to
state over the radio that he had nothing whatever to do with writing my addresses."[27] Anne Lindbergh also began feeling the strain
of supporting her husband, writing to Madame Carrel, the wife of
her husband's French guru, that he "has been gravely misunderstood, misquoted, and as usual smeared with false accusations and
motives." She "felt very badly" about being "arbitrarily labeled and
shelved on a side so opposite to all one's friends and feelings."[28] One
ally the Lindberghs were slowly losing was her mother, Elizabeth
Morrow, the acting president of Smith College, who was involved in
the Bundles for Britain aid program, made regular radio broadcasts
promoting the British and French cause, and was a member of William Allen White's committee to repeal all remaining aspects of the
neutrality laws.

The war soon worsened. The Belgian army was on the point of
surrender and, as the retreating French army fought a rearguard
action, German tanks continued to advance on Paris. With the
French generals in disarray and Reynaud's government hopping
from one provincial town to the next ahead of the German advance,
Churchill tried to slow their retreat by visiting France six times
between his elevation to the premiership and the French surrender.
Bullitt reported to Roosevelt that he expected Paris to be under German occupation within ten days. The president urgently cabled Reynaud saying they should not in any circumstances allow the French
fleet to fall into German hands.

On Sunday evening, May 26, Roosevelt delivered a fireside chat.
"There are many among us who in the past closed their eyes to
events abroad because they believed . . . that what was taking place
in Europe was none of our business; that no matter what happened
over there, the United States could always pursue its peaceful and
unique course in the world," he said. It was no longer possible to take
comfort from the fact that "hundreds of miles of salt water made

the American Hemisphere"[29] immune from attack. His message was that isolationism was finished.

Lindbergh did not agree. Hart and Ackerman suggested that he leave the Air Corps and head a committee of prominent isolationists. He demurred, but met with isolationist leaders of the American Legion, including World War One flying ace Eddie Rickenbacker,[30] and agreed to speak at one of their rallies.

Events in Europe were not kind to Lindbergh and his fellow believers. The British expeditionary force of nearly a quarter of a million men, along with 45,000 French troops, surrounded on all sides by advancing German forces and under attack from the Luftwaffe, was driven back to the Channel ports of Calais and Dunkirk. Between May 27 and June 1, something close to a miracle took place. The Royal Navy, joined by a ragbag flotilla of nearly a thousand small craft, from racing yachts to tugboats, from every port in the southeast of England, effected an audacious rescue. In total, 338,000 men—224,000 British and 111,000 French, Poles, and Belgians—were lifted from Dunkirk and the adjacent beaches, leaving just 40,000 mostly French troops to be taken prisoner.

The evacuation, however, was limited to men. Left in northern France were 2,472 guns, 20,000 motorcycles, 65,000 military vehicles, and 75,000 tons of ammunition. Now more than ever, Churchill needed America to restock his depleted arsenal. An Allied triumph snatched from the jaws of defeat, Dunkirk was a setback of sorts for Lindbergh, for it showed that, contrary to his theorizing, battles could not be won by air power alone. Within range of British airfields and with the Royal Navy's dominance of the seas, the Luftwaffe had suffered disproportionate losses at Dunkirk, with four aircraft downed for every one British plane.

On June 1, Churchill pleaded with Roosevelt for 200 warplanes. "The courage and success of our pilots against numerical superiority are a guaranty that they will be well used," he said. "At the present rate of comparative losses they would account for something like 800 German machines."[31] Roosevelt promised to restore the British army to its pre-Dunkirk strength. Within six weeks of Churchill's request, Britain took delivery of 450 field artillery guns and a million shells, 500,000 (albeit outdated) Enfield rifles, 25,000 Browning machine guns, 5,000 trench mortars, and 130 million rounds of ammunition, high explosives, and miscellaneous bombs. The administration circumvented what was left of the neutrality laws by selling the equipment to the Anglo-French Purchasing Commission, specially set up to buy arms and military equipment from America via the private U.S. Steel Corporation.

The ungainly retreat at Dunkirk turned British public opinion. By dint of his inspirational oratory, Churchill was able to portray the emergency evacuation as a heroic escape; despite overwhelming odds, Britain could beat Hitler. "Wars are not won by evacuations. But there was a victory inside this deliverance," Churchill told the Commons. With the American radio audience in mind, he declared:

> We shall fight on the beaches, we shall fight on the landing grounds, we shall fight in the fields and in the streets, we shall fight in the hills, we shall never surrender. And even if, which I do not for a moment believe, this island, or a large part of it, were subjugated and starving, then our Empire beyond the seas, armed and guarded by the British Fleet, would carry on the struggle, until, in God's good time, the New World, with all its power and might, steps forth to the rescue and the liberation of the old.[32]

Churchill's address in the wake of Dunkirk proved to be his most memorable. The fighting spirit of Dunkirk put an end to talk of a negotiated peace. Although Americans remained reluctant to acknowledge that the war would eventually involve them, rearmament and the training of forces in America began to pick up speed. Dwight Eisenhower,[33] returning home in 1940 from the Philippines, noted, "Comparatively few understood the direct relationship between American prosperity and physical safety . . . [and] the existence of a free world beyond our shores. Consequently, the only Americans who thought about preparation for war were a few professionals in the armed services and those far-seeing statesmen who understood that American isolation from any major conflict was now completely improbable."[34] By the middle of June, the regular army's strength reached 375,000, almost triple the figure a year earlier.

Mussolini's declaration of war against the democracies on June 10, and a desperate appeal from Reynaud, via Bullitt, to "declare publicly that the United States will give the Allies aid and material support by all means short of an expeditionary force,"[35] prompted Roosevelt once again to broadcast to the nation. He had concluded that the best way to keep America out of the war was to keep Britain in it. But that would require support for the British which the isolationists remained determined to deny. On the day of the broadcast, June 10, Paris was abandoned to its fate by Reynaud.

Roosevelt said that young Americans were rightly asking what the future holds for people who live under democratic forms of government. Some Americans, he said, "still hold to the now somewhat obvious delusion that we of the United States can safely permit the United States to become a lone island, a lone island in a world dominated by the philosophy of force. Such an island may be the dream of those who still talk and vote as isolationists. Such an island represents to me and to the overwhelming majority of Americans today a helpless nightmare of a people without freedom—the nightmare of a people lodged in prison, handcuffed, hungry, and fed through the bars from day to day by the contemptuous, unpitying masters of other continents."

He asserted, "Our sympathies lie with those nations that are giving their life blood" to counter "the gods of force and hate." In deploring the entry into the war of Italy on the German side, the president used a phrase the State Department had urged him not to use: "The hand that held the dagger has struck it into the back of its neighbor." In response, he announced, "We will extend to the opponents of force the material resources of this nation."[36] It was a message greeted with gratitude and relief by the British and French radio audience. The isolationists, however, were alarmed.

Listening to Roosevelt's broadcast, Lindbergh "felt [the president] would like to declare war, and was held back only by his knowledge that the country would not stand for it."[37] In Washington, Lindbergh met with a number of isolationist congressmen, including senators Clark from Missouri, Van Zandt, La Follette, Wheeler, and Reynolds. "We discussed plans for counteracting war agitation and propaganda," he told his diary. "Everyone is very much worried about Roosevelt and feels he is leading the country to war as rapidly as he can."[38]

The following day, Churchill cabled Roosevelt. "We all listened to you last night and were fortified by the grand scope of your declaration," he wrote, but he drew the president's attention to the Italian submarines that would soon make Allied merchant shipping in the Mediterranean and Atlantic more hazardous. "The ocean traffic by which we live may be strangled," he said.[39] He again begged the president for old destroyers. The next day, after visiting the French government and military leaders in Briare, near Orléans, Churchill wrote to the president again, warning that "the aged Marshal Pétain[40] . . . is I fear ready to lend his name and prestige to a treaty of peace for France. . . . If there is anything you can say publicly or privately to the French, now is the time."[41]

The French cabinet were on the run. Before they set off the following day for Tours, a further 50 miles southwest of Paris, Churchill again pleaded with Roosevelt to intervene. "Anything you can say or do to help [the French] now may make a difference," he said.[42] Kennedy told Roosevelt that "unless the United States declared war on Germany and came in, France was not going to fight."[43] Roosevelt promptly cabled Reynaud that "this Government is doing everything in its power to make available to the Allied Governments the material they so urgently require."[44]

On June 14, the day German troops entered Paris, there was a further plea from Churchill to Roosevelt, saying that he had not hesitated "to refuse consent to an armistice or separate peace [asked for by the French government]." He reported Reynaud's view "that hope could only be kindled by American intervention" and asked that Roosevelt's "magnificent message" of support for France be published. "It will I am sure decide the French to deny Hitler a patched-up peace with France," he wrote.[45]

It was left to Roosevelt to give a lesson in the practicalities of American politics to Churchill (who surely did not need one) and Reynaud (who plainly did). His message of support was not "intended to commit and did not commit this Government to military participation," he wrote to Churchill. "There is of course no authority under our Constitution except in the Congress to make any commitment of this nature." He refused to allow his message of encouragement to be made public since it was "imperative that there be avoided any possible misunderstanding"[46]—by which he meant misunderstanding by Congress and the American people.

"I understand all your difficulties with American public opinion and Congress," Churchill replied on June 15, "but events are moving downward at a pace where they will pass beyond the control of American public opinion. . . . If we go down you may have a United States of Europe under the Nazi command far more numerous, far stronger, far better armed than the New World." Roosevelt needed no reminding. Events were running faster than his ability to convert American opinion.

Churchill now asked "as a matter of life or death to be reinforced with [the American] destroyers."[47] On reading Churchill's cable, Morgenthau told Roosevelt that "unless we do something to give the English additional destroyers, it seems to me it is absolutely hopeless to expect them to keep going."[48] Churchill appealed to Roosevelt, in his second long cable of the day, "When I speak of entering the war I am, of course, not thinking in terms of an expeditionary force, which I know is out of the question. What I have in mind is the tremendous moral effect that such an American decision would produce not merely in France but also in all the democratic countries of the world."[49]

The following day, June 16, despite Churchill's cabinet's agreement to an audacious and startling plan to merge Britain with France, Reynaud resigned, to be succeeded by Marshal Philippe Pétain,[50] a hero of World War One known as the Lion of Verdun, who immediately began surrender negotiations. In a studied act of humiliation, on June 21, French ministers were obliged to sign the terms of surrender in the railway carriage in Compiègne in which the Germans signed the Armistice in 1918.

Hitler and some fellow veterans from World War One went directly from the capitulation to tour his new prize, Paris. As he looked upon the tomb of Napoleon in Les Invalides, he confided to Heinrich Hoffmann, the photographer who recorded his every triumph, that he was enjoying "the greatest and finest moment of my life."[51] The Battle of France was over; the Battle of Britain was about to begin.

CHAPTER THIRTEEN

LIFE OF THE PARTY

Roosevelt purges his cabinet of isolationists,
the Democrats meet in Chicago to pick a presidential
candidate for the 1940 election.

JUGGLING THE EUROPEAN CRISIS, battling with Congress to arm the Allies, and conducting his "softly, softly" campaign for a third term took a tremendous toll on the fifty-eight-year-old Roosevelt's health. In February 1940, his devoted assistant Missy LeHand[1] and Bullitt believed he suffered a minor heart attack over dinner in the White House, which he shrugged off as indigestion. Instead of slowing down, he quickened his pace.

In order to work at his desk longer, Roosevelt started going to bed an hour later and reduced the daily swims that eased his polio to three times a week. He appeared immune to the sweltering heat of the Washington summer of 1940, insisting, because of a recurring sinus condition, that instead of air conditioning he should loosen his tie, roll up his sleeves, and be cooled by a single electric fan.

Unable to spare the time to travel to Hyde Park, where he could best relax, and rationing trips to Warm Springs, Georgia, where he frolicked with fellow polio sufferers in the outside pool, he found he could recharge if he slept overnight on board his yacht, sailing up and down the Potomac. "As long as he has this capacity for a quick come-back, there seems to be no limit to his endurance," said LeHand.[2]

As Hitler was turning his attention to confronting Churchill's defiance, the president decided to retool his cabinet. Roosevelt and Morgenthau had hit upon a ruse to outflank the remaining neutrality laws and supply Britain and France by having the War Department return "obsolete" warships and warplanes to their suppliers in exchange for new. The out-of-date equipment, including three-year-old B-17 "Flying Fortress" bombers, could then be legally sold to Britain and France.

Woodring, however, an unrepentant isolationist, insisted that such deals be referred to the War Department for assessment, causing delays and often eliciting a verdict that as the equipment was by no means old nor surplus enough to require replacement it could not therefore be sold to the Allies. Matters came to a head on June 17, when Woodring vetoed the sending of a dozen Flying Fortresses to Britain. Roosevelt dismissed him.

In his farewell letter to Woodring, Roosevelt said he needed to make "certain readjustments" that were "not within our personal choice and control."[3] In a last gesture of defiance, Woodring leaked to isolationist senators a letter he had written to the president deploring the pressure he was being put under to supply Britain with warplanes. Roosevelt responded to Woodring, "The record shows that you have evidently some slight misunderstanding of facts and dates" and warned him off causing further trouble.

"Doubtless many efforts of mere partisanship in these days, when we should be thinking about the country first, will be directed to having you appear before Committees in order to stir up controversy," Roosevelt wrote. "Partisan efforts of such a nature not only stir up false issues but do much to retard the progress of the defense program."[4] Woodring declined the president's offer of the governorship of Puerto Rico and retreated back to Kansas.

That was not quite the end of the matter. The chairman of the Naval Affairs Committee, Senator David I. Walsh, an isolationist from Massachusetts, spurred on by the anti-British sentiments of his Irish American constituents, led Congress to amend the defense appropriations bill to ban the private sale of arms to foreign governments unless the chief of the General Staff (by this time Marshall), and the chief of Naval Operations (currently Admiral Harold R. Stark)[5] specifically deemed them of no importance to America's defense. By this ruse, the isolationists managed to interrupt the sale of twenty new torpedo gunboats to Britain.

Polls confirmed Americans' continued reluctance to enter the war on the British side, a June 25 Gallup poll finding that 64 percent of Americans thought it more important to stay out of the conflict than to help Britain.[6] In Washington, however, Lord Lothian, by now the British ambassador, sensed that the administration was about to offer Britain certain support, even if it meant going to war. It "would take very little to carry them in now—any kind of challenge by Hitler or Mussolini to their own vital interests would do it," he wrote to Nancy Astor.[7]

To wrong-foot the Republicans, just five days before they gathered in Philadelphia to pick their presidential candidate, Roosevelt reshuffled his cabinet, turning his administration into a bipartisan "national" war government. Woodring was replaced by Stimson, who had been President Taft's secretary of war and Hoover's secretary of state—a man of impeccable foreign and military credentials. Frank Knox, the Republican vice presidential candidate in 1936 and a staunch and vocal opponent of isolationism, was appointed navy secretary.

The reshuffle only added to the Republicans' difficulties. The Democratic leadership had scheduled their convention in Chicago for July, allowing them to make their pick knowing whom they would be running against. The Republican race had come down to three: the frontrunner, Thomas E. Dewey, the thirty-seven-year-old district attorney of New York who was an efficient administrator and an internationalist liberal Republican; Senator Robert A. Taft of Ohio, fifty, the staunch conservative and committed isolationist son of President William Howard Taft who had led opposition in the Senate to the New Deal; and Wendell Willkie,[8] forty-eight, a liberal Republican internationalist businessman from Indiana who was the head of the country's largest utility holding company, Commonwealth and Southern. The son of Central European immigrants, with a German-born father, Willkie was a first-class retail politician and a natural broadcaster who enjoyed an easy rapport with delegates.

According to historian Richard Norton Smith, "Willkie looked like a bear. He was a great big larger than life, rumpled, wrinkled figure who nevertheless had an aura."[9] He was a loyal Woodrow Wilson self-styled "liberal Democrat"[10] until October 1938, when his dislike of the New Deal's economic interventionism caused him to switch parties. His career as a faux-populist corporate Republican sprang "from the grassroots of 10,000 country clubs,"[11] joked Alice Roosevelt Longworth, Teddy Roosevelt's isolationist niece. Willkie was a formidable, combative campaigner and, in the words of historian Charles Peters, "the most dynamic Republican nominee since the other Roosevelt."[12]

With a strong and energetic isolationist faction among the Republican Party's rank and file, Taft should have walked away with the nomination, but he looked starchy and his stilted speaking style, so suited to the Senate chamber, failed to spark enthusiasm. Dewey's Michigan background and his successful campaigns against corruption in New York City gave him an early lead. However, his youth and lack of experience—which allowed Ickes to crack that he had "thrown his diaper into the ring"[13]—counted against him. By May of election year, 1940, the bloom was coming off Dewey's campaign and Willkie, backed by *Time* magazine's owners, Henry and Clare Boothe Luce, and the *Herald Tribune*'s Ogden and Helen Reid, started to move up on the outside.

By the time the Republican Convention opened in Philadelphia on June 24, Willkie was gathering momentum. The first ballot was indecisive: Dewey 360 votes, Taft 189, Willkie 105. Strenuous campaigning in the hall by Willkie supporters translated by the fourth ballot into a Willkie lead that by the sixth and final tally, on June 28, saw him crowned Republican champion for 1940. To balance the ticket, Senator Charles L. McNary[14] from Oregon, a progressive, largely pro-New Deal Republican, but, all importantly, an isolationist, was chosen as Willkie's running mate. Triumphant, Willkie embarked on the yacht of Roy Howard, the isolationist publisher of the Scripps-Howard newspaper chain, which ferried him lazily back to New York.

When the Democrats gathered in Chicago on July 15, Roosevelt had so confused the contest for the nomination that only a couple of competitors remained: Garner and Farley. Neither enjoyed anything like the stature, nor had the political skills, to rival the president, whose command of the party appeared absolute. His remaining aloofness from the contest served three purposes. It showed that clamor from the party, not personal ambition, drove his campaign for a third term. It demonstrated that the war in Europe had reached such a critical point that Roosevelt could not spare time for partisan matters. And it allowed the president to appear lofty and remote, ensuring that he would only accept the candidacy on his terms and with a hand-picked running mate.

A week before the convention opened, Roosevelt took the precaution of inviting Farley, as chairman of the Democratic National Committee, to Hyde Park in the hope that he would stand aside. According to Farley, the president told him, "Jim, I don't want to run and I'm going to tell the convention so." Taking the president at his word, Farley said, "If you make it specific, the convention will not nominate you." Farley told the president that he was against a third term on principle and that there were at least two good candidates ready to take his place. "The smiles were gone," recalled Farley.

"I said . . . he had permitted, if not encouraged, a situation to develop, under which he would be nominated unless he refused to run . . . [and had] made it impossible for anyone else to be nominated, because . . . leaders were fearful they might be punished if they did not go along with him." Farley said that Roosevelt should follow the example of William Tecumseh Sherman,[15] who declared in 1884, "If nominated, I will not run. If elected, I will not serve." Farley gleaned from the president's face that he had every intention of running. "Jim, if nominated and elected, I could not in these times refuse to take the inaugural oath, even if I knew I would be dead within thirty days." [16]

When the convention began in the Chicago Stadium, the largest covered arena in the world, those who backed Roosevelt simply wanted to get the deal done. Supporters of Garner, Farley, Hull, and others, meanwhile, hoped for a feisty debate followed by a series of close ballots. These opponents of the president were irritated to discover that what they were attending was not an election but a coronation masterminded by the invisible hand of Harry Hopkins from a suite in the Blackstone Hotel,[17] where he had installed a direct telephone line to the White House. The president's loosely arranged strategy team in Chicago consisted of Byrnes, Ickes, and Frances Perkins. A key player was Chicago's mayor, Edward Kelly,[18] a master machine politician who had been recruited to manipulate conditions in favor of the president.

Early on, Knox's *Chicago Daily News* began reporting that the renomination of Roosevelt was likely, but that delegates would back the president "with the enthusiasm of a chain gang."[19] Hopkins was failing to marshal the president's allies. "Harry seems to be making all his usual mistakes. He doesn't seem to know how to make people happy," said Eleanor, listening to the convention on the radio in her cottage in Val-Kill above Hyde Park.[20]

Matters took a turn when isolationist senators Wheeler, Walsh, and Bennett Clark, joined by Woodring, proposed an amendment to the party platform that "We will not participate in foreign wars and we will not send our army or navy or air force to fight in foreign lands outside of the Americas."[21] Through Byrnes, the president insisted that the senators add the key words "except in case of attack." Hopkins came to the conclusion that only the arrival of Roosevelt himself in Chicago would guarantee his selection.

Roosevelt resisted. The president "expected the convention to be a drab one and was satisfied with the way that it was going," Hopkins reported to Ickes and Byrnes. "He didn't want anything done to disturb the regular procedure."[22] But Ickes soon became anxious that the convention was careening out of control, telling Hopkins that "if the Republicans had been running the convention in the interests of Willkie, they could not have done a better job."[23]

Ickes sent Roosevelt a cable. "This convention is bleeding to death and your reputation and prestige may bleed to death with it," he wrote. "There are more than nine hundred leaderless delegates milling around like worried sheep waiting for the inspiration of leadership that only you can give them." He predicted that if "the Farley–Wheeler clique" had their way, "a ticket will emerge that will assure the election of Willkie, and Willkie means fascism and appeasement." He appealed to Roosevelt to accept his historic responsibilities. "A world revolution is beating against the final ramparts of democracy in Europe," he wrote. "No man can fail to respond to the call to serve his country with everything he has."[24]

Perkins was also anxious and called the president, telling him about "the bitterness and crossness of the delegates, about the difficulties, confusion, and near fights. I told him that if he could come out to Chicago it would be a wonderful help." Roosevelt was adamant that everything would turn out right. "How would it be if Eleanor came?" he asked. Perkins said it would make "an excellent impression." "Eleanor always makes people feel right," he said, and asked Perkins to invite his wife so that the idea did not appear to come solely from him.[25]

Farley, on his way to the hall to be nominated, was alarmed to hear that the first lady wanted him urgently on the telephone, so he returned Eleanor's call. "Frances Perkins has called me and insists that it's absolutely necessary I come to Chicago," the first lady explained. "Frances doesn't like the looks of things out there and feels that my appearance would do a lot to straighten things out. Now, I don't want to appear before the convention unless you think it is all right."

Knowing how powerful a presence the first lady could be, and what her personal intervention on behalf of the president would mean to his own chances, Farley was lost for words. Then he found himself saying, "It's perfectly all right with me." Eleanor pressed the point, saying, "Please don't say so unless you really mean it." Farley replied, "I do mean it and I am not trying to be polite." Eleanor set out for Chicago, asking a friend, C. R. Smith, head of American Airlines, to fly her there in his private plane.

Reinforcements for the president's cause also arrived in the shape of Mayor Kelly. While Farley kept close control of the gallery tickets, which set the tone of the proceedings, the Chicago police, reporting to Kelly, were responsible for securing the hall. Soon Farley and Garner supporters found it increasingly difficult to gain access to the stadium. In their stead were Kelly's loyal supporters, under strict orders to chant for the president at every turn.

It fell to Senator Alben Barkley[26] of Kentucky to read a message from the president. Craftily written by Roosevelt's chief speechwriter, Sam Rosenman, it both denied that he was seeking a third term while encouraging the delegates to demand one. At the first mention of Roosevelt's name, the stadium erupted in cheers that went on for an hour. When demanding silence, banging his gavel, and calling for order had no effect on the cacophony, Barkley claimed a doctor was needed to tend to a woman who had been struck down in the mayhem. The ruse worked and the delegates simmered down.

Barkley spoke for a further thirty minutes before reaching the finely worded message the president had asked him to deliver: "The President has never had and has not today any desire or purpose to continue in the office of President, to be a candidate for that office, or to be nominated by the convention for that office," he said. "He wishes in all conviction and sincerity to make it clear that all of the delegates at this convention are free to vote for any candidate."[27] The hall fell silent.

Then, from all corners of the stadium came the refrain, "We want Roosevelt!" Adding to the hubbub, Kelly's police band marched down the aisle in full dress uniform playing Roosevelt's campaign theme, "Happy Days Are Here Again," whose chorus was picked up by the organist on the stadium's giant Wurlitzer. Chicago firemen joined in with a stirring rendition of "Franklin D. Roosevelt Jones," a popular song from the 1938 musical *Sing Out the News*, which included the words, "How can he be a dud or a stick-in-the-mud / When he's Franklin D. Roosevelt Jones?"

This "spontaneous" display of affection and affirmation was coordinated by Kelly, a former chief sanitary engineer of Chicago, who had ordered Thomas D. Garry, the city's superintendent of sewers, sitting with a microphone in the basement, to belt out "We Want Roosevelt!" over the public address until directed to stop. The orchestrated acclamation continued for an hour.

The following morning's ballot reflected the overwhelming support for a Roosevelt third term. The president won 946 votes, Farley seventy-two, Garner sixty-one, Millard Tydings,[28] a senator from Maryland, nine, and Hull, whose name was not on the ballot, five. Eager to seem a good sport, Farley gave way and proposed making the ballot unanimous. With Garner humiliated, the interest now passed to potential running mates. Twice in the previous two weeks, Roosevelt had asked Cordell Hull. He now asked for a third time, and for a third time Hull declined. Roosevelt's second choice was a surprise: Henry A. Wallace, the secretary of agriculture from Iowa, who recommended himself to the president because, although he had been a Republican until 1936, he was a progressive and came from the Farm Belt, where support for Roosevelt was weak.

Wallace had drawbacks. He had never stood for elective office, and while he had proved an innovative agriculture secretary, he dabbled with the occult and was considered eccentric in the extreme. Party elders felt that Wallace would not boost the farm vote but was sure to alarm commonsensical northeasterners. Above all, a concern arose that, in light of the president's ailing health, Wallace was a rash choice as a president-in-waiting. Who knew whether Roosevelt would last the full term? Farley's judgment about his own suitability to be president was way off, but he remained a fair judge of character. "I think it would be a terrible thing to have [Wallace] as President if anything happened to you," he had told Roosevelt during their frosty meeting at Hyde Park earlier that year. "People look on him as a wild-eyed fellow." [29]

Others lined up to be Roosevelt's successor, among them failed presidential hopefuls McNutt and Garner, Roosevelt loyalist Byrnes, and high-ranking Democrats including Barkley, Supreme Court Justice William O. Douglas,[30] Speaker of the House William Bankhead,[31] solicitor general Robert H. Jackson, House Majority Leader Sam Rayburn,[32] and Jesse Jones, leader of the Reconstruction Finance Corporation. Wallace was so unpopular that when his name was mentioned, the convention booed. Asked whether he would support Wallace, Governor Eurith Rivers[33] of Georgia said, "Why, Henry's my second choice." Asked who was his first choice, Rivers replied, "Anyone red, white, black, or yellow that can get the nomination." [34] But Roosevelt, for reasons which even today remain unclear, insisted on Wallace, and, although Eleanor, too, thought him unsuitable, asked her to fix it.

When the first lady rose to speak on July 18, only Wallace and Bankhead remained in the vice presidential race. "We cannot tell from day to day what may come. This is no ordinary time," Eleanor declared. "No man who is a candidate or who is president can carry this situation alone. This is only carried by a united people who love their country." [35] As for Wallace, "If Franklin felt that the strain of a third term might be too much for any man and that Mr. Wallace was the man who could carry on best in times such as we were facing, he was entitled to have his help." [36]

Roosevelt became so worried he would not get his way that he asked Rosenman to write a speech saying that if he did not get Wallace, he would decline the nomination. The president's belligerent mood soon transmitted itself to Chicago. Byrnes toured the convention asking, "For God's sake, do you want a president or vice-president?" [37] On the first ballot, Wallace received only 628 out of 1,100 votes, with 459 cast for his rivals. It was barely half the votes, but it was enough. Still, opposition to Wallace remained so vociferous that he was persuaded not to give an acceptance speech lest the hostility reveal itself to the nation.

In the White House, long after midnight, a relieved Roosevelt washed, shaved, and dressed, then sat down to deliver his acceptance address by radio to the Chicago delegates. He explained why he needed to stay at the nation's helm. "During the spring of 1939, world events made it clear to all but the blind or the partisan that a great war in Europe had become not merely a possibility but a probability, and that such a war would of necessity deeply affect the future of this nation." He said it was "my obvious duty . . . to prevent the spread of war, and to sustain by all legal means those governments threatened by other governments which had rejected the principles of democracy."

"If our Government should pass to other hands next January—untried hands, inexperienced hands—we can merely hope and pray that they will not substitute appeasement and compromise with those who seek to destroy all democracies everywhere, including here," he said. As soon as the address was delivered, "everyone got out of Chicago as fast as he could," recalled Ickes. "What could have been a convention of enthusiasm ended almost like a wake."[38]

CHAPTER FOURTEEN

THE BATTLE OF BRITAIN

*Hitler prepares for the conquest of Britain, the
Royal Air Force beats off the Luftwaffe,
Roosevelt speeds up the rearmament of America,
and Kennedy finds a way to escape the Blitz.*

WHILE THE DEMOCRATS were meeting in Chicago, the war in Europe
gathered pace. At the end of June, Hitler's number two soldier, General Alfred Jodl,[1] who masterminded the invasions of Denmark and
Norway, wrote, "The final German victory over England is now only
a question of time. Enemy offensive operations on a large scale are
no longer possible."[2] Britain was alone, protected from invasion by
26 miles of sea that separates Dover from Calais.

On his return from Paris, Hitler read Jodl's paper, "The continuation of the war against England," which recommended war by sea
and air against British forces, military airfields, and Atlantic convoys, followed by "terror attacks against the centers of population."
When the onslaught caused the British government to capitulate,
troops would land on a broad front across the south of England. To
ensure air superiority for Operation Sea Lion, the invasion of Britain, Jodl insisted that "the fight against the British Air Force must
have top priority,"[3] a task that the commander in chief of the Luftwaffe, Hermann Göring, thought simple. On July 16, Hitler approved
Sea Lion.

Göring's confidence that he could clear the skies of British planes
sharply contrasted with the skepticism of Grand Admiral Erich
Raeder, who by July 29 had come to the conclusion that an invasion

of Britain was impractical. For every 100,000 troops landed along the 200-mile British front, 1,722 barges, 1,161 motorboats, 471 tugs, and 155 transport ships would be needed, he said—a feat of requisition and assembly that would take months, during which German industry would be denuded of its small ships and barges, which would cripple the domestic economy. Nor did Raeder believe that the small German navy, under bombardment from the British fleet, would be able to protect the required armada, even if the sea was calm and the weather clement. He argued that Sea Lion should be postponed a full year, until May 1941.

Hitler dismissed Raeder's reservations and on July 31 called together his top brass to finalize the plan. Raeder repeated his judgment that the invasion was too ambitious unless the Royal Air Force had been defeated. Hitler insisted, however, that Britain should be invaded on September 15. His order of August 1 declared: "The German Air Force is to overcome the British Air Force with all means at its disposal and as soon as possible."[4] It proved easier to give the order than carry it out, not least because of the inadequate assessment of aerial strengths of the two sides. Once again, Lindbergh's estimates were shown to be wanting, though this time it was his German friends who had been fooled. By suggesting so openly in London and elsewhere that the British air defenses were woefully unprepared, he had misled Hitler.

The accurate numbers showed Germany to be at a disadvantage. By mid-August, Britain was fielding 1,032 fighters against Göring's 1,011. Britain counted 1,400 pilots, Germany several hundred fewer. Yet such was the fog of war that the RAF high command wrongly concluded they were vastly outnumbered, by 16,000 pilots to 7,300. By September, Göring operated under the illusion that British Fighter Command was down to 177 aircraft when by that time, despite severe losses, it could still muster 656 fighters to hurl at successive German attacks.

The British enjoyed a geographical advantage. Because the dogfights took place largely over British soil, if hit, a Royal Air Force pilot could bail out and take a train back to his base. German pilots faced death or capture. Losses of aircraft and pilots were also persistently misjudged by the British due to "a certain understandable tendency to wishful thinking, underpinned by many fighter pilots reporting the same victim as one of their near companions, with double or treble-counting being a natural result."[5]

Churchill had put the Canadian press magnate Max Aitken, Lord Beaverbrook,[6] in charge of boosting aircraft production. During 1940, Aitken's goading lifted annual warplane manufacture from 3,602 fighters to 4,283, twice the number the Germans could produce, providing the RAF with an additional 352 planes per month at the height of the Battle of Britain.[7] Despite German bombing of aircraft factories, British warplane production for 1940 would total 9,924, compared to the Germans' 8,070.[8]

On the day Hitler ordered the invasion of Britain, Churchill wrote to Roosevelt to explain that while "we have a large construction of destroyers and anti-U-boat craft coming forward," the next few months were perilous for Britain. "We could not keep up the present rate of casualties for long, and if we cannot get a substantial reinforcement, the whole fate of the war may be decided by this minor and easily remediable factor." He again pleaded for the president to "ensure 50 or 60 of your oldest destroyers are sent to me at once." The British had their backs to the wall. "Mr. President, with great respect I must tell you that in the long history of the world, this is a thing to do now," Churchill wrote. "I know you will do all in your power."[9]

Churchill had many allies in America who were also pushing Roosevelt to make a quick decision. One group, the Century Club, centered on the gentlemen's club the Century Association in New York City, sent a detailed memorandum on August 1, the day after Churchill's cable arrived, suggesting the decommissioned American destroyers be provided to Britain in exchange for permanent US military bases in British possessions in the Caribbean and a guarantee that if Britain were occupied by German forces, the Royal Navy would relocate to Canada or an American port and resume the fight from there. The Century proposal chimed with Roosevelt's own fear that Germany would "establish a naval base in the Atlantic islands, say the Azores,"[10] from which Hitler would launch bombing assaults upon the United States.

Lothian commended the deal to Churchill, suggesting that if Britain did not voluntarily provide the bases, America might occupy the islands anyway, as a first line of defense.[11] "The United States of course is steadily drifting towards war but the constitutional difficulty of getting Congressional declaration of war unless there is a manifest attack upon American soil or its most vital interests are [sic] such that the United States is likely to find herself fighting under cover in different parts of the world long before formal belligerency is recognized," Lothian cabled the prime minister.[12]

Kennedy was keenly aware of Britain's need for warships, but also that granting the destroyers in exchange for bases escalated America's participation in the war. "England is suffering great losses on the seas," he told his son John. "The destroyer problem is a precarious one for them because they are losing them altogether too fast. . . . Germany's fast motor boats, submarines and dive-bombers are seriously handicapping the progress of imports and exports." But, anxious not to encourage Roosevelt to drift into undeclared war, the ambassador did not take it upon himself to press the president or Hull to find the hardware Britain needed.

On August 2, Roosevelt gained US cabinet support to exchange the old destroyers for bases and the same day asked William Allen White to suggest to Willkie that he persuade Republicans in Congress to allow the measure to become bipartisan. The planned deal was given a boost when a number of prominent New York lawyers, including Dean Acheson,[13] wrote to the *New York Times* saying that the destroyers-for-bases deal was an essential part of national defense and that the president did not need congressional approval because he could use an executive order, an opinion confirmed by attorney general Robert H. Jackson. By describing the deal as a piece of artful negotiation in which America came out best, Marshall and Stark could, with some justification, argue that the mothballed destroyers were surplus to requirements under the congressional ban on providing any war materiel that might be of use to America's defense. They approved the deal.

On August 13, Roosevelt asked Kennedy to deliver in person to Churchill a cable confirming he would supply fifty destroyers, some motor torpedo boats, and a number of warplanes, though they "would only be furnished if the American people and the Congress frankly recognized that in return therefor the national defense and security of the United States would be enhanced." The conditions were along Century Club lines: that the British fleet would evacuate to "other parts of the Empire for continued defense of the Empire" [14] and that America be granted ninety-nine-year leases on bases in Newfoundland, Bermuda, the Bahamas, Jamaica, St. Lucia, Trinidad, and British Guiana.

When the president came to announce the deal, he described it as "the most important event in the defense of the U.S. since Thomas Jefferson's Louisiana Purchase." [15] The American people followed Roosevelt's lead and backed the agreement, with polls showing 60 percent in favor.[16] However, to expedite the handover, Roosevelt resorted to executive order rather than putting the deal before Congress as the Constitution intimated. As he explained to King George, "There is virtually no criticism in this country except from legalists who think it should have been submitted to Congress first. If I had done that, the subject would still be in the tender care of the Committees of Congress." [17]

Churchill responded with grateful thanks. "I need not tell you how cheered I am," he wrote. "You will, I am sure, send us everything you can, for you know well that the worth of every destroyer that you can spare to us is measured in rubies." While he had Roosevelt's attention, he asked for "as many flying boats and rifles as you can let us have. We have a million men waiting for rifles." About relocating the fleet, the prime minister insisted that he and the British people had no intention of surrendering. Indeed, "Their confidence in the issue has been enormously and legitimately strengthened by the severe air fighting of the past week." [18]

Churchill told Kennedy, who was once more kept waiting while the prime minister finished an afternoon nap, "We are going to beat this man." [19] Kennedy was furious that he had first learned of the destroyers deal when Churchill read the cable to him. He told his diary, "Nothing has been said to me about it and Roosevelt's conduct in this closing phase of the negotiations was just as inconsiderate as during the entire negotiations." [20]

In a cable marked "For the president, personal and confidential," the ambassador expressed his anger at being cut out of arrangements that more than any other act drew America deeper into war. "It has been impossible for me to make any contribution to the destroyer-for-bases discussion seeing as I do not know any of the facts, except second hand," he said. "Frankly and honestly I do not enjoy being a dummy. I am very unhappy about the whole position and of course there is always the alternative of resigning." [21] Roosevelt, anxious that Kennedy stay at his post until after the election, replied, "There is no thought of embarrassing you. Don't forget that you are not only not a dummy but are essential to us both in the Government and in the Nation." [22]

In the week before the destroyers-for-bases deal was struck, the skies over England were filled with dueling British and German pilots. Luftwaffe bombers raided ports, airfields, and radar bases, but the worst was to come. What Göring called Operation Eagle, and history has come to think of as the Battle of Britain, started in earnest on August 15. Before battle was joined, the stout Reich Marshal was so confident that he enjoyed superiority both in numbers and quality of men and machines that he predicted it would take only four days before Churchill came suing for peace. He boasted that Jodl need not worry about naval support for the maritime invasion of the British Isles because the British would be so demoralized by the pounding that a forced occupation would be unnecessary.

Throughout July, the Luftwaffe had increased their pummeling, targeting British commercial vessels going through the Straits of Dover, bombing southern English ports, and mounting sorties from newly occupied airbases in Normandy to deliver mostly inconsequential damage upon targets in the west of England.

On August 12, the preliminaries to the battle began in earnest when German warplanes attacked British radar bases strung along the southern and eastern coastline. But the failure to extinguish these sources of highly accurate information about German air movements culled by a novel scientific method proved to be the first of Göring's many strategic mistakes. "It is doubtful whether there is any point in continuing the attacks on radar stations," he declared on August 15, "since not one of those attacked has so far been put out of action." [23]

Over the next two days, 1,500 German aircraft were sent to destroy British airfields, but they failed to make a permanent dent. Forty-seven German planes were lost, to the British thirteen. On August 14, in fighter skirmishes above Kent, Surrey, and East Sussex, the Luftwaffe lost seventy-one planes against the RAF's twenty-seven, many of the German losses being Stuka dive-bombers that turned out to be too slow against the nimble British Spitfires and Hurricanes. And the British enjoyed a further, paradoxical advantage in equipment. The ultra-fast but short-range Messerschmitt Bf 109 fighters performed at their best at very high altitudes, but as this was too high for the Spitfires and Hurricanes, the 109s' unique quality was of little benefit. By August 22, Churchill was able to tell Roosevelt that "the air attack has slackened in the last few days," though he stressed that "I do not think that bad man has yet struck his full blow." [24] He was correct.

A spate of bad weather between August 19 and 23—a typical English summer—gave the British time to mend their fighters, patch their airfields, rest their pilots, and gather their strength. By August 20, it was clear that Germany had lost the initiative. Churchill told the Commons a stirring tale of what had so far been achieved. He paid tribute to "the British airmen who, undaunted by odds, unwearied in their constant challenge and mortal danger, are turning the tide of the world war by their prowess and by their devotion. Never in the field of human conflict was so much owed by so many to so few." [25]

Göring's second strategic error started with an accident. When, on the night of August 23, a dozen German bombers were sent to destroy aircraft plants and oil storage facilities south of London, they became lost in fog and inadvertently dropped their lethal loads on Central and East London homes. Believing the attack to be an intentional attempt to terrorize civilians, Churchill ordered the bombing of Berlin the following evening in reprisal.

Although it was a similarly overcast night and half of the eighty-one British bombers missed their targets, it was the first time in the German capital's history that it had come under aerial bombardment, startling the population and stirring Hitler into an indignant rage. In a speech on September 4, Hitler condemned "Churchill's new brain child," night bombing, and threatened retaliation of his own. "When they declare that they will increase their attacks on our cities, then we will raze their cities to the ground," he promised an audience of women nurses and social workers screaming for retribution. [26]

Hitler's demand that Göring switch from attacking British

fighter bases to carpet-bombing Londoners' homes saved the RAF on the point of its extinction. Hitler was under the illusion that the British people would crumple and was much encouraged by Washington embassy reports that it was the view of "the American General Staff" that Britain couldn't hold out much longer.[27]

In the two weeks between August 24 and September 6, Göring launched 1,000 planes a day to destroy RAF fighter bases, and the battle slowly began to turn in Germany's favor. In that brief time, five British fighter bases were put out of action and six of the seven headquarters which translated radar intelligence into pilot orders were severely damaged. The RAF lost 466 fighters, with the Germans losing 214 fighters and 138 bombers. A quarter of Britain's fighter pilots were either killed or wounded.

On Saturday, September 7, Hitler opened the chapter of the war Londoners would dub the Blitz. A giant air armada of 625 bombers accompanied by 648 protective fighters headed up the Thames to the London Docklands in what historian William L. Shirer described as "the most devastating attack from the air ever delivered up to that day on a city."[28] The blips on radar screens of the first wave of the impending attackers triggered invasion warnings across southern England. Church bells pealed, mines were hurriedly laid, and road and rail bridges dynamited. This first crushing two-night assault on the heart of London killed 842 and maimed 2,347. It resumed at a similarly destructive rate every night for a week.

The British, meanwhile, delivered destruction of their own. German naval headquarters staff reported on September 12 that it was becoming increasingly difficult to assemble landing craft in the Channel ports of Ostend, Dunkirk, Calais, and Boulogne for the invasion of Britain "because of the danger of English bombings and shelling [from British bomber planes and warships]. Units of the British Fleet are now able to operate almost unmolested in the Channel."[29]

Then came Göring's third strategic mistake. Spurred by the success of his nighttime raids, on September 15 the Reich Marshal ordered 200 German bombers defended by 600 fighters to deliver a massive daytime bomb load on London in two giant waves. The mission proved disastrous. RAF fighters guided by radar repulsed the assault, finding the lumbering bombers easy targets in broad daylight. The Luftwaffe lost thirty-four bombers and twenty-six fighters, with twenty more damaged but able to limp back to their continental bases; the RAF lost just twenty-six aircraft. The September 15 defeat, though not in itself decisive, confirmed that the RAF could maintain its superiority in British airspace.

Another blow to Germany's plans for the invasion took place the following day, when RAF bombers destroyed a sizable portion of the invasion armada, sinking twenty-one transport ships and 214 landing craft. The following day, Hitler announced to his high command the indefinite postponement of the invasion of Britain. Halfway through October, Hitler was obliged to concede that "preparations for 'Sea Lion' shall be continued solely for the purpose of maintaining political and military pressure on England."[30] The Blitz, however, continued, with bomber fleets making raids for fifty-seven consecutive nights. Churchill reported to Roosevelt that between September 7 and November 3, 1940, 200 German warplanes bombed London every night.[31] Far from lowering British morale, however, the deaths and devastation provided a rallying point for the phlegmatic Brits.

Churchill's dogged resistance, his rousing words, and his compassion also became known to the British people, who might have otherwise dismissed him as a traditional, uncaring Tory. A bond of loyalty was forged between prime minister and people that lasted for the duration of the war.[32] Each morning, the prime minister could be found in his element, tramping the rubble-strewn streets in a bowler hat, walking stick in hand, a gas mask in a khaki canvas bag slung over his shoulder, to see the damage wrought overnight and to show that he was happy to share the danger. When, after inspecting a particularly horrible scene of carnage, he burst into tears, as he was liable to do whenever moved by events, a local woman cried out, "Look, he really cares."[33]

Rather than retreating to an air-raid shelter, every night Churchill could be found on a rooftop scanning the sky with a pair of binoculars, like a schoolboy in pursuit of a rare bird. Although the number of deaths during the Blitz reached between three and five thousand a month, he told the Commons, "It would take ten years at the present rate for half of the houses of London to be demolished."[34]

Churchill's leadership during the Battle of Britain was not lost on the American press writing and broadcasting from London.

"Churchill is causing his associates much anxiety these nights," reported James "Scotty" Reston.[35] "They can't get him to stay in the shelter at 10 Downing Street." The pluckiness of the bombarded Cockneys and the often absurd lengths to which they would go to maintain a sense of normality also played well across the Atlantic. When bombs first began falling on London at the end of July, the *New York Times* published a lyrical paean to the long-suffering Londoners, asking, "Is the tongue of Chaucer, of Shakespeare, of Milton, of the King James translation of the Scriptures, of Keats and Shelley to be hereafter, in the British Isles, the dialect of an enslaved race?"[36]

The coalition between Churchill's Conservatives, Clement Attlee's[37] Labour Party, and Archie Sinclair's Liberals was also a subject of admiration for the American reporters. "The democratization of Great Britain goes on apace," wrote Reston. "What centuries of history have not done for this country, Chancellor Hitler is doing now. He is breaking down the class structure every time his bombers come over. . . . Why, it has got so now that total strangers speak to each other on the streets."[38]

"For Americans the Blitz was supremely a radio war," wrote historian David Reynolds. Networks sent top correspondents to London to report the nightly raids, among them CBS's Edward R. Murrow,[39] and William L. Shirer. The American poet Archibald MacLeish[40] paid tribute to the skills of "the Murrow Boys," writing, "You burned the city of London in our homes, and we felt the flames that burned it. / You laid the dead of London at our doors and we knew the dead were our dead."[41]

The British government wooed American opinion with *London Can Take It*, a short movie directed for the Ministry of Information by Humphrey Jennings[42] and Harry Watt[43] with commentary by an American, Quentin Reynolds,[44] who introduced himself as "a neutral reporter." The film showed how Londoners, in "the greatest civilian army ever assembled," which included King George and Queen Elizabeth, recovered from a night of bombing. "These are not Hollywood sound effects," Reynolds intoned, "this is the music they play every night in London. The symphony of war." He observed that "the sign of a great fighter in the ring is, Can he get up from the floor after being knocked down? London does this every morning." Reynolds reported that Londoners "would rather stand up and face death than kneel down and face the kind of existence the conqueror would impose upon them." [45] Released by Warner Brothers in America in November 1940, the film was seen by 60 million Americans.

Churchill's victory in the Battle of Britain, described by his biographer Roy Jenkins as "at least as decisive in its consequences as Blenheim or Waterloo," [46] put paid to the suggestion that there was little point in arming Britain because the military equipment sent would soon fall into the hands of Hitler. It ended, too, suggestions that Churchill was not up to the job because of his drinking and erratic judgment. However difficult it was for those working with him in Downing Street, or for cabinet colleagues who had to put up with a blizzard of memoranda from him on everything from sinking the French fleet to food rationing,[47] he had displayed qualities of character and resilience that in Roosevelt's mind more than made up for the years of shilly-shallying by Chamberlain and the appeasers.

Roosevelt cited the devastating events in Europe when demanding faster American rearmament. He had already received from Congress, in response to his State of the Union address in January, $1.84 billion, a sum he said at the time was "sufficient." At the end of May, as the British were evacuating Dunkirk, he won a further $1.3 billion. The fall of France gave him the opportunity to ask for $4.8 billion more. Reiterating the promise, "We will not use our arms in a war of aggression; we will not send our men to take part in European wars," he insisted, "We cannot defend ourselves a little here and a little there. We must be able to defend ourselves wholly and at any time." [48] He recruited two million men in uniform for "selective training" and built 19,000 more warplanes. On October 8, he returned to Congress asking for an astonishing $9 billion in extra spending on defense; it was granted with barely a squeak.

The result of the Battle of Britain further diminished Kennedy's reputation. Although the ambassador worked to help American nationals leave Britain and facilitated the evacuation of 100,000 British children across the Atlantic, his own behavior was less admirable. While Roosevelt was taking in the queen of Norway, setting her up with a suite of rooms in the White House, Kennedy canceled at short notice Rose's attempt to adopt Stella Jean Gordon, an English schoolgirl friend of his daughter Jean. "I am not very much impressed with the idea of taking evacuees," he told Rose. "It is all right while the excitement lasts but having another child in your house eventually gets to be an awful bore. Incidentally, you have to assume responsibility for the child up to its 21st birthday and you have to pay all its bills because they cannot send any money out of here." Although the Gordon girl had twice been offered a refuge by the Kennedys, the ambassador told his wife, "Lets us [sic] definitely out" as "I think [it] will bring a lot of grief." [49]

There was worse. Clare Boothe Luce, the playwright wife of Henry Luce, the owner of *Time* magazine, sent Kennedy a black comic telegram, "Confucius say man who gets to be American Ambassador should make up mind first whether he looks best in pine or mahogany." [50] For all the reassurance Kennedy gave to Rose that being killed by a bomb was a million-to-one shot and "I am completely a fatalist about bombing accidents," [51] he was in fear of his life. On hearing air-raid sirens, his instinct was to be driven out of London to his mansion in Windsor, far from strategic targets.

This act of self-preservation compared unfavorably to the courage of his friends the king and queen. They insisted that as soon as the German bombers were spotted heading for London they be driven from Windsor Castle, not far from Kennedy's country hideout, to Buckingham Palace, to suffer the Blitz like the rest of the nation. One day, Churchill visited the palace to find the king shooting at a target with a rifle. He told his prime minister that "if the Germans were coming, he was at least going to get his German." [52] Churchill said that if he felt that way, he would get him a tommy gun.

On September 13, the palace received a direct hit, destroying the chapel and the conservatory, where the king liked to sit to read official papers. The bombing was warmly welcomed by the royal couple as evidence that they, too, were in the firing line. The newsreels showed pictures of the couple standing amid the rubble and reported, "Truly this is a war of all the people. We are all in it." [53] On September 24, the folly of Kennedy's flights to the country was reinforced when an incendiary bomb that exploded 250 yards from his Windsor home turned out to bear his initials, "J.P.K." [54]

Speculating on what Hitler felt about the prospect of Roosevelt winning a third term, Kennedy told his son Bobby that the Führer was hoping to finish off Britain quickly, because "[Hitler] is never sure that, once the political campaign in the United States is over in the Fall, he won't have the United States giving aid to England in ways that even we do not see now."[55] Kennedy told his son John that the risk was that "if the war lasts any length of time, that Roosevelt might get the United States into the war, even through the back door."[56] He confirmed his fear to J. M. Patterson, publisher and editor of the *New York Daily News*, writing, "We [at home] are going to be faced more and more with the argument that England is our line of defense and that will serve as a reason for every action we want to take, even up to the declaration of war."[57]

Kennedy's defeatism extended to America's ability to defend itself. Complaining that his insistence that America stay out of the war had caused "the rather bitter reception" he received when last visiting Washington, he told Rose, "You know I always felt [the Americans] shouldn't [get into the war] because I knew they couldn't lick anybody, but you can't go around telling about your country's weaknesses."

Roosevelt's failure to consult him continued to stoke his anger. "I am thoroughly disgusted with the way Roosevelt is handling the situation," he told Rose, and explained that he felt ignored by the president, who "sends people over here to get reports," and that "under ordinary conditions" he would resign.[58] In the meantime, wracked with stomach pains that caused him to resort to a diet of puréed vegetables, he hired a French chef who "could purée a bale of hay and make it taste like chocolate ice cream."[59]

Kennedy hankered to get home quickly if Churchill won the Battle of Britain. He wanted to be back to take some part in the presidential election, telling Bobby, "That will depend on how gracefully I can make an exit."[60] There was press speculation, perhaps fueled by Kennedy himself, that he would be summoned home to run Roosevelt's campaign. In a telephone call to his ambassador, "so that you will get the dope straight from me and not somebody else," Roosevelt told him that "the State Department is very much against your leaving England." The president insisted it was Hull's decision, not his, saying, "You know how happy I would be to have you in charge, but the general impression is that it would do the cause of England a great deal of harm." Kennedy did not miss the chance to tell the president he felt surplus to requirements. "I am not doing a damn thing here that amounts to anything and my services, if they are needed, could be used to much better advantage if I were home." [61]

The slights kept coming. When a new US naval attaché was appointed, the cabinet and the War Office—even American reporters in London—knew about the appointment before the ambassador did. Kennedy complained to Hull, "Now there is probably a good reason why it is necessary to go around the Ambassador in London and take up the matter with the British before he knows about it. However, I do not like it and I either want to run this job or get out." [62]

The ambassador was dealt a further blow when in late July the ailing Chamberlain was operated on for stomach cancer and three months later stepped down from the cabinet. "My poor old friend Chamberlain is finished," he wrote to Rose. "He has cancer of the bowel. They haven't told Mrs. Chamberlain yet."

The destroyers-for-bases deal had revealed how important it was for Roosevelt and Churchill to remain in step. The prime minister had alarmed the president in a speech to the Commons on August 20 gratefully acknowledging how much the president was helping to arm Britain. "We have ferried across the Atlantic, in the month of July, thanks to our friends over there, an immense mass of munitions of all kinds, cannon, rifles, machine-guns, cartridges, and shell, all safely landed without the loss of a gun or a round," he said. He even suggested that the deal was the beginning of a wider integration of efforts. For Americans, Churchill's speech of gratitude was a chilling reminder of how deeply Roosevelt had implicated them in the defense of Britain.

Even more alarming, Churchill suggested that providing military aid was the start of a more intimate constitutional embrace between the two countries. "The British Empire and the United States will have to be somewhat mixed up together in some of their affairs for mutual and general advantage," he said. "I do not view the process with any misgivings. I could not stop it if I wished; no one can stop it. Like the Mississippi, it just keeps rolling along." [63] Nor did it help the president when a former British secretary for war, Leslie Hore-Belisha, suggested it was possible that the war would hasten

America and Britain becoming a single country with "an eventual common citizenship." [64]

Even if that were a pipe dream for the half-American Churchill, he showed how well he could flatter his silent partner in the war against Hitler when he appealed to Roosevelt's sense that fate had chosen him to complete the work of Woodrow Wilson, declaring, "The right to guide the course of world history is the noblest prize of victory."

CHAPTER FIFTEEN

FORD'S PLANS FOR PEACE

Lindbergh teams with Henry Ford,
Willkie comes out punching, Roosevelt stays
aloof, the Axis Pact is signed.

KENNEDY WAS NOT ALONE in thinking that if Roosevelt won a third term he would take Americans into war. In his opening election address, even vice presidential candidate Henry A. Wallace summed up the difference between the president and Wendell Willkie by saying that the Republicans were the party of appeasement and Roosevelt the man Hitler hoped would be defeated.

Lindbergh concurred. After talking with Senator Henrik Shipstead,[1] he recalled, "We agree that the public does not want war, but that Roosevelt does and is leading us toward it as rapidly as he can."[2] He reported in his diary that, during a tour of isolationist congressmen on Capitol Hill,[3] Representative Melvin J. Maas[4] predicted that if the president were reelected he "would have us in war within thirty days."[5]

Lindbergh, as ever, remained pessimistic about the future of America. "I see chaotic conditions ahead—unrest, depressions, labor troubles, violence—even if we escape the war," he told his diary, and he disliked "the superficiality, the cheapness, the lack of understanding of, or interest in, fundamental problems."[6] He considered moving to Oregon to remove himself and his family from the danger of civil unrest.

The Battle of Britain should have been of enormous interest to Lindbergh, who correctly predicted that aerial warfare would transform the way wars were fought, even if his calculations about relative air strengths were off. The high-altitude dogfights over the English countryside might have inspired in him an affinity with the courageous pilots on both sides. In the event, however, he had little to say. In a rare comment on the day before the Battle of Britain started, he wrote, "The Germans are losing a few more planes than the English, because they are attacking."

His lack of understanding of the difference between how the British treated their enemies compared to the Nazis made this plain. "The English save every man who jumps from his plane over England, while all the Germans who jump are naturally put in concentration camps."[7] There were no "concentration camps" in Britain. Germany's first camp, at Dachau, opened in 1933, three years before Lindbergh visited Germany, had he asked to see it. Further evidence of his pro-German viewpoint and his disdain for the battle engaged by the British is revealed in his account of a conversation with the motor manufacturer Henry Ford, who, in a similar misjudgment, believed at the height of the Battle of Britain that the United Kingdom and Germany were close to agreeing peace terms.

Lindbergh first met Ford in 1927, when he landed at the Ford plant's private airport in Detroit in the plane that made him a national hero, *The Spirit of St. Louis*. To his surprise, when he asked whether Ford would like to be taken up into the sky, the car maker agreed and, although the older man had to sit in a crouching position in the one-seater plane, the flight was a great success. At the end of December 1939, they resumed their acquaintance. There was no doubting Ford's genius as an engineer, which fascinated fellow engineer Lindbergh. Although Ford was against collective bargaining and pledged that no trade union would ever set up in his plants, he paid top wages for short hours in comparatively humane working conditions. The quality of his cars, in particular the Model T Ford, transformed America.

Ford was anti-Semitic. In his newspaper, the *Dearborn Independent*—which, being sold nationwide through Ford dealerships, enjoyed a circulation of 700,000—Ford published anti-Semitic tracts, often under his own name. He published the notorious Russian tsarist forgery "The Protocols of the Elders of Zion," postulating a Jewish conspiracy to dominate the world. When challenged over the authenticity of the "Protocols," Ford stood firm, saying, "They have fit the world situation up to this time. They fit it now."[8]

Ford's anti-Semitism was well known. Hitler cited Ford as a major influence in *Mein Kampf*, published in 1925, and kept a full-sized portrait of the carmaker by his desk in the Chancellery in Berlin. Like Lindbergh, Ford had been awarded the Grand Cross of the German Eagle, in July 1938. In Germany, extracts from the *Dearborn Independent* were compiled into a best-selling book, *The International Jew, the World's Foremost Problem*. Ford, a lapsed Episcopalian, had no religion, yet he was a pacifist and had opposed America's entry into World War One, just as he now opposed American entry into the current European war.

Lindbergh got on famously with Ford from the moment they met in 1927, exchanging views on everything from the war to labor relations. "Ford is a great man and a constructive influence in this country," Lindbergh told his diary. "One cannot talk to him without gaining new ideas and receiving much mental stimulation."[9]

Lindbergh boasted about his closeness with Ford to Hart and Ackerman, who "thought it would please people to think that I was going around asking various well-known men like Henry Ford their opinion about our attitude toward the war."[10] Ford needed little encouragement to provide practical help to the isolationist cause. In June 1940, over breakfast at the Ford residence near Dearborn, outside Detroit, Lindbergh persuaded Ford to back an American Legion campaign against American involvement in the war. Later the same month, Ford overruled his son Edsel, who was now running the company, and halted a lucrative federal government contract to produce 6,000 Rolls-Royce engines for British fighter planes and 3,000 engines for American warplanes.

For inspiration, Lindbergh had been reading his father's isolationist tract, "Why Is Your Country at War?", and became involved behind the scenes to press Willkie to adopt a sterner line on keeping out of the war. He agreed to give a speech in Chicago, but soon became embroiled in controversy when the organizer, William J. Grace of the Citizens Keep out of War Campaign, reported that Mayor Kelly, who had been instrumental in Roosevelt's nomination, refused permission to use the 100,000-seat Soldier Field stadium on the date they wanted.

Lindbergh's suspicions that there was a conspiracy to prevent him from expressing his isolationist views were further roused when Senator Bennett C. Clark, who over the years had been instrumental in asking him to speak, stopped taking his calls. "Perhaps he now thinks the Chicago meeting is dangerous politically," speculated Lindbergh.[11] Eventually Clark cried off the meeting altogether, claiming, through an assistant, that he was nursing an infected foot.

Eager for Lindbergh to speak in Willkie's favor in order to attract the aviator's supporters to his cause, though perhaps not on an official platform which would suggest an endorsement of his views, the Willkie campaign approached Lindbergh to talk about one of their pet ideas: the establishment of an air force independent of the army and navy. Lindbergh declined the invitation. The notion of a separate air force was then taken up by Roy Howard, who asked Lindbergh to be interviewed by one of his journalists on the topic. Lindbergh again demurred, saying he would rather write an article but would need to talk to people in the army and navy. Such an undertaking would likely put their careers in jeopardy, which he was reluctant to do.

Lindbergh was acutely aware of how unpopular he was in some quarters and how toxic his friendship was becoming, so he took heart when, driving through Illinois, he gave a lift to a World War One veteran who did not recognize him. The old soldier said "he couldn't see any reason to fight for the British Empire" and that "this young fellow Lindbergh" had the right idea. "They call him a fifth columnist, but he ain't no more fifth columnist than I am," he said.[12]

On August 4, Lindbergh arrived in Chicago to deliver his speech and was met by Colonel McCormick's chauffeur, who took him via the *Chicago Tribune* office to the McCormick home, where he was staying overnight. He then was driven to Soldier Field football stadium (Kelly had relented), where he was introduced to the capacity crowd by the organizer of the meeting, Avery Brundage, an anti-Communist, anti-Semitic admirer of Hitler.[13]

Lindbergh opened by railing against "the agitation for our entry in the war" and the "foreign propaganda [that] was in full swing." In a swipe at Roosevelt, he said, "We have by no means escaped the foreign entanglements and favoritisms that Washington warned us against," and, "We have participated deeply in the intrigues of Europe, and not always in an open 'democratic' way. There are still interests in this country and abroad who will do their utmost to draw us into the war."

He claimed Americans were "overwhelmingly against our involvement" and that "people are beginning to realize that the problems of Europe cannot be solved by the interference of America." He dismissed as alarmist the notion that America could be invaded from Europe and that Hitler had designs on the United States. "If our own military forces are strong, no foreign nation can invade us, and, if we do not interfere with their affairs, none will desire to," he said.

He insisted he had not been duped on his visits to Germany and that Göring had not flown "airplanes from one field to another so they would be counted again and again." He resented being called "a Nazi agent" by the press and administration officials. He said he had seen Armageddon coming and "the phenomenal military strength of Germany growing like a giant at the side of an aged and complacent England." The war was not about democracy, nor Christianity; it was simply "the division of territory and wealth between nations."

He suggested that America should be realistic about the postwar world. "In the past, we have dealt with a Europe dominated by England and France," he said. "In the future we may have to deal with a Europe dominated by Germany." So long as America maintained its military strength, "whether England or Germany wins this war," war between America and the new Europe could be avoided. The alternative was "a war between us [that] could easily last for generations and bring all civilization tumbling down."

He advocated rearming and forging a treaty with the Nazis. "If we refuse to consider treaties with the dominant nation of Europe, regardless of who that may be, we remove all possibility of peace," he said. "Our accusations of aggression and barbarism on the part of Germany simply bring back echoes of hypocrisy and Versailles."

As Lindbergh reached his peroration, he made fun of a remark attributed to Roosevelt that Europe was America's last bastion of defense. "What would [our forefathers] think of the claim that our frontiers lie in Europe?" he asked. "What, I ask you, would those soldiers [of the American Revolution] say if they could hear this nation, grown a hundred and thirty million strong, being told that only the British fleet protects us from invasion?"[14] Lindbergh spoke for twenty minutes and, more used to broadcasting than public speaking, found "disconcerting" the fact that "the crowd seemed to want to applaud at every opportunity."[15]

The following day, Lindbergh traveled to Dearborn to meet with Ford, who asked him whether he would entertain a tour of Europe as a freelance peace ambassador. "[Ford] thought if anyone could help in bringing peace about, I could!" recalled Lindbergh. "I told him I was afraid England would not be willing to accept any terms Germany would be willing to offer." Nonetheless, "I said I would like nothing better than to take part in ending the war if the opportunity ever arose."[16]

Sneaking into a movie theater to see how the newsreel covered his Chicago speech, Lindbergh was expecting to be portrayed poorly "because of the Jewish influence in the newsreels and the antagonism I know exists towards me." "I take the chance that they will cut my talk badly and sandwich it between scenes of homeless refugees and bombed cathedrals," he wrote.[17] He was encouraged to discover that those who hissed whenever his face appeared were matched by those who applauded what he said.

Meanwhile, the presidential election continued apace. Roosevelt appeared to have left the Republicans flummoxed as to how to oppose him. If they were against arming Britain, they were accused of being against the creation of thousands of new American jobs. Willkie, who had never run for elected office, was caught in a bind. A devotee of Woodrow Wilson's internationalism, he held views that belied his Midwestern upbringing. His public position was identical to the president's: he was an internationalist who hoped to keep America out of the war. Like the president, he sympathized with Britain and the democracies and abhorred the dictators. He dared not speculate on whether America might be drawn into war, for on that matter Roosevelt, as the experienced, world-weary incumbent, held an enormous advantage. All appeared to turn on how Willkie set the tone of the campaign in his first major address on August 17: his acceptance speech delivered in his hometown of Elwood, Indiana.

Willkie came out punching. He quoted Churchill, that he had

nothing to offer but "blood, tears, toil, and sweat [sic]," and said that Americans could expect the same if he were elected. Weaning the nation off the New Deal's public spending was sure to be painful, but it was an essential corrective that would restore the economy to health. He challenged the president to a series of "face to face" encounters "to debate the fundamental issues." But what Willkie said about foreign policy startled the isolationists. It soon became clear that the Republicans had picked a candidate just as committed to countering Hitler as Roosevelt himself. Isolationists soon discovered the truth of historian Ross Gregory's later assessment of Willkie: "His candidacy denied isolationism the most powerful forum it could have had." [18]

Willkie made clear from the start that he was no Nazi sympathizer. "The story of the barbarous and worse than medieval persecution of the Jews—a race that has done so much to improve the culture of these countries and our own—is the most tragic in human history," he declared. He said, "Our way of life is in competition with Hitler's way of life." Referring to the "misery and suffering" of the "millions of refugees who desire sanctuary and opportunity in America," his choice of words was telling. "We are not isolated from those suffering people," he said. Reminding his radio audience of millions of "all the democracies that have recently fallen," he said that while "instinctively we turn aside from the recurring conflicts over there [in Europe]," still "we cannot brush the pitiless picture of their destruction from our vision, or escape the profound effects of it upon the world in which we live."

Directly addressing the isolationists, he announced, "Peace is not something that a nation can achieve by itself. It also depends on what some other country does." He said that three of his uncles had signed up within a month of Wilson declaring war in 1916 and he welcomed the conscription measure going through Congress. "We must not shirk the necessity of preparing our sons to take care of themselves in case the defense of America leads to war," he said.

He described Germany as "a power hostile to our way of life" and asserted that the capture of the British fleet by Germany would be "a calamity." "If we had to trade with a Europe dominated by the present German trade policies," he said, "we might have to change our methods to some totalitarian form. This is a prospect that any lover of democracy must view with consternation." He declared himself "in agreement" with Roosevelt's speech about extending America's material resources to the opponents of force. "I am glad to pledge my wholehearted support to the President in whatever action he may take in accordance with these principles," he said.

And yet, quickly rowing back from embracing the whole of Roosevelt's foreign policy, Willkie "wondered if [the president] is deliberately inciting us to war." "He has dabbled in inflammatory statements and manufactured panics," Willkie said, alluding to the president's fireside chats that persistently warned of the German danger. "He has courted a war for which the country is hopelessly unprepared—and which it emphatically does not want. He has secretly meddled in the affairs of Europe, and he has even unscrupulously encouraged other countries to hope for more help than we are able to give." Nonetheless, Willkie promised "to out-distance Hitler in any contests he choses in 1940 or after. And I promise that when we beat him, we shall beat him on our own terms, in our own American way." [19]

Delighted by the slap to the isolationists, Roosevelt commissioned Ickes to take to the radio and point out that Willkie was completely at odds with his own party. In a typically memorable phrase, Ickes dismissed Willkie as the "rich man's Roosevelt, the simple, barefoot Wall Street lawyer." The president laughed out loud when he heard the line and called Ickes to congratulate him.

Within days, the ambiguity of Willkie's war policy landed him in trouble. When asked by White to help ensure that the destroyers-for-bases deal would be bipartisan, he replied that, though he himself agreed with the deal, he had no power to make Republicans in Congress vote for the measure. On August 30, however, he promised not to oppose the agreement. Yet by September 4, under pressure from isolationists in his party to claim that the deal was nothing less than an illegal act of war, he was obliged, against his better judgment, to condemn the arrangement. At first he appeased his supporters by saying, "We must be extremely careful in these times . . . not to eliminate or destroy the democratic processes while seeking to preserve democracy." Three days later, he raised the temperature again, calling the deal "the most dictatorial and arbitrary act of any President in this history of the United States." [20]

Willkie left Lindbergh cold. The aviator listened to his acceptance speech with Anne and noted, "We had hoped for more and felt depressed and disappointed. . . . The nation was waiting for a message it did not receive; it hoped for greatness, and heard mediocrity."[21] In similar despair, isolationists suggested that the leadership they felt was missing should come from Lindbergh. Douglas Stewart and George T. Eggleston, publisher and editor respectively of *Scribner's Commentator*, asked whether he would be prepared to head up "some sort of organization—nationalist, antiwar, etc." Lindbergh told him that it wasn't his field and he was unsuited to such advocacy work, but the following week he met at Van Zandt's office with R. Douglas Stuart Jr.,[22] from Chicago's Defend America First Committee, whom he thought "a fine type of fellow," then with Frederick Libby of the National Council for Prevention of War. He also met with the arch-isolationist senator and presidential hopeful Burton K. Wheeler. Slowly, Lindbergh was drawn into the political process.

The importance to isolationists in both parties of finding a celebrity like Lindbergh to champion their cause coincided with their growing concern about Willkie. Among the isolationist leading lights encouraging Lindbergh to take a more prominent role were senators Harry Byrd of Virginia and John G. Townsend[23] of Delaware, and William R. Castle,[24] a rich Hawaiian Republican and former US ambassador to Japan. Castle told Lindbergh that "most of his Republican friends are greatly disappointed in Willkie's campaign to date," and Lindbergh asked himself, "What is Willkie's real personal attitude on the war? No one seems to know."[25] Byrd, an isolationist Democrat descended from one of the socially grand First Families of Virginia, told Lindbergh that if the president proposed war, he would rather resign his Senate seat than vote for it. Senator Arthur H. Vandenberg[26] of Michigan, an internationalist who had veered toward isolationism at the outbreak of the war in Europe, was dispatched to seek out Willkie on the campaign trail and urge him "to take a stronger antiwar stand."[27]

Meanwhile, Roosevelt began edging America into the war. He called Stark to the Oval Office and ordered him without delay to bolster US Navy surveillance of German vessels in the Atlantic. He extended the limit of American operations to the 60th meridian, a line a thousand miles east of the eastern seaboard that stretched from Newfoundland to British Guiana. The US Navy's snooping was an enormous boost to the Royal Navy's efforts to track German U-boats and the few surface naval vessels that managed to escape past the patrolling British fleet into the Atlantic. The president told Stark that "loss of contact with surface ships cannot be tolerated" and demanded that all sightings of foreign vessels be reported to base without being encoded, a ruse that allowed eavesdropping Royal Navy ships to learn the exact location of enemy vessels.[28]

As for the election, the president's strategy was to remain above the fray, not engaging with Willkie and appearing indispensable in face of the European crisis. He told Kennedy, "I am not intending to campaign at all. There is enough to be done right here."[29] "Mr. Roosevelt was faced with a dilemma," wrote *Life* magazine. "If he went on the road, people would charge him with neglecting his duties as chief executive in time of crisis; and if he stayed in Washington his opponent would tear him to pieces." The president played to his strength. Just as he had calmed American nerves by remaining cool in the depths of the Great Depression, so he let it be known that he was calmly keeping watch on those threatening America.

Before long, however, he found he was drawn into the campaign. He started traveling, touring armaments, tank, and aircraft plants, ostensibly to encourage production, telling the press that the frailty of the international situation meant that he always needed to be within 200 miles or two hours' train travel of the White House. "The places visited by me—Arsenals, Navy Yards, private plants, etc.—get a real enthusiasm and speed-up production during the days following my visit," he reported to his son-in-law John Boettiger.[30] While insisting on the fiction that he was too busy to give speeches, he made a point of addressing large crowds from the back of the caboose. At first the tactic proved successful; through August and into September, he enjoyed a five to ten point poll lead over Willkie.

Slowly, however, Willkie began to gain. His forceful, energetic speaking style gave the implicit suggestion that he would be a more dynamic president than Roosevelt, who was pictured as calm to the point of complacency. He never missed a chance to call Roosevelt "the third-term candidate," with the unstated suggestion that Washington's dying wish was being ignored by Roosevelt's aristocratic sense of entitlement.

There was another threat to Roosevelt's easy reelection: Kennedy. The ambassador smoldered about his ill-treatment at the hands of the president and was determined to return home when the Battle of Britain was decided or if Germany invaded Britain, whichever was the sooner. It was important to him, however, not to appear cowardly to American eyes. "Towards the end of [September] it should become clear whether the invasion is a possibility or not," he told Rose. "By that time there will have been enough concentrated bombing on all of us in London so that certainly nobody in America could think I had left before I had seen a big part of the show."[31] He remained as defeatist as ever, telling the dying Chamberlain, "This war won't accomplish anything. We are supposed to be fighting for liberty and the result will be to turn the last of the Democracies into Socialist, Communist, or Totalitarian States."[32]

Roosevelt was in two minds about how to handle Kennedy's pleas to be allowed home. The *Washington Star* ran a cartoon of Kennedy at the quayside in Britain reading a note from the president saying, "Stay Where You Are."[33] Rose wrote to her husband, "The Pres. does not want you home before the election due to your explosive—defeatist, point of view, as you might so easily throw a bomb which would explode sufficiently to upset his chances. I wanted to go to the W.H. as a wife, say I am worried about your health, think you have done enough—guarantee to chloroform you until after the election."[34] Henry Luce, a pro-British internationalist, wrote to the ambassador in July, urging him to "return to this country immediately and tell what you think about everything."[35] Sensing that the election was slowly turning in their favor, the Willkie camp concluded that if Kennedy backed their man, the White House would be theirs.

On the president's specific instruction, Hull again denied Kennedy permission to return, but it was feared in the White House that the ambassador was in such a sour mood he might return anyway. Kennedy told Hull, Halifax, and Welles that he had written "an indictment of President Roosevelt's administration for having talked a lot and done very little," to be published coast to coast by his assistant, Eddie Moore, "if by accident" he was not allowed to leave London by November.[36]

Despite Willkie's backing of the draft, the congressional isolationists fought a rearguard action against the Selective Service Act,

Norris claiming that once in uniform Americans "would soon be fighting with somebody," and Wheeler saying that the measure would "slit the throat of the last democracy still living." [37] Roosevelt's Dutchess County thorn, Hamilton Fish, was virulent in his opposition, trying to limit the numbers called up and pressing for voluntary rather than compulsory service. A majority of Republicans voted against the measure, which nonetheless passed both houses of Congress, and Roosevelt signed it into law on September 16.[38] All men aged between twenty-one and thirty-six were to register and would be selected for service by lottery, with the final decision about fitness and claims for deferment decided by local draft boards.

On September 27, the Tripartite Pact, a mutual defense agreement between Germany, Italy, and Japan, was signed, giving birth to the Axis. The British remained anxious at the pace of American help. "Public opinion [in America] has not yet grasped that it will have to make far reaching decisions to finance and supply us and possibly still graver ones next Spring or Summer unless it is to take the responsibility of forcing us to make a compromised peace," Lothian wrote to Halifax. "Yet owing to size of country and its constitution it is usually impossible to get important decisions taken without at least six months preparation." [39]

With the Battle of Britain won and the British Isles safe from Nazi invasion, at least for now, there was time before the Germans could regroup and try again. Six months seemed hardly enough time for Roosevelt to persuade the American people that the confrontation between the democracies and the dictators of Germany, Italy, and Japan was their fight, too.

CHAPTER SIXTEEN

THE OLD CAMPAIGNER

Anne Lindbergh steps into the isolationist debate, Willkie's campaign closes in on Roosevelt, Kennedy is recalled from London, the US election results come in.

WITH THE ELECTION fast approaching, Anne Lindbergh entered the isolationist debate with publication of *The Wave of the Future: A Confession of Faith*. Her aim was benign. "The arguments of the isolationists are so often narrow, materialistic, short-sighted, and wholly selfish—I am repelled by them," she told her mother, which is why she hoped her essay would give "a moral argument for isolationism."[1]

In the book, she described the victors of 1918 as "democracies" in inverted commas, just as Kennedy and Borah did, as if to cast doubt on whether democracy was worthwhile or genuine, and she argued that had they given "reasonable economic and territorial concessions" to Hitler, the war in Europe would never have started. She suggested that the age of democracy was over and, while she abhorred many of the methods of the dictators, "the wave of the future" had begun. The world was locked in a battle between the "Forces of the Past" and the "Forces of the Future." "There is no fighting the wave of the future any more than as a child you could fight against a gigantic roller that loomed ahead of you someday," she wrote. There was no point in Americans mounting "a hopeless 'crusade' to 'save' civilization." The only way to maintain "our way of life" was to stay out of the war.[2]

Her argument was belated, anguished, and woefully jejune. When she showed the manuscript to a friend, George Stevens, she was taken aback by his animosity. "It was presumptuous—that I had no right to write it without more knowledge of history, economics, foreign affairs, etc. That it would be torn limb from limb. That it would be called—with some justification—'Fifth Column'. That it would do C. no good and me, harm."[3] When Elizabeth Morrow read her daughter's book, she burst into tears.

The instant notoriety of the slim volume made it the best-selling nonfiction book in America, with 50,000 copies sold in two months. It "overnight became the book people loved to hate. Surpassed in modern literary history perhaps only by *Mein Kampf*," reported Lindbergh biographer A. Scott Berg. Even half a century later, "*The Wave of the Future* remained a book nobody remembered with affection— not even the author, who later recanted much of its contents, which she ascribed to her naïveté."[4] While W. H. Auden,[5] the British poet who, as a conscientious objector, had exiled himself to Brooklyn for the duration of the war, described *The Wave* as "simply beautiful,"[6] Clare Boothe Luce observed that "the world has progressed only because it has not allowed the waves to sweep over it."[7] Ickes condemned it as "the bible of every American Nazi, Fascist, Bundist and Appeaser." Even Anne Lindbergh's favorite cousin concluded that the book showed that "both you and Charles seem to me to have accepted the totalitarian definition of a democracy as a static or decayed material concept."[8] One bookseller returned his copies to Harcourt with a note saying that he thought Lindbergh and his wife should be put "behind barbed wires."[9]

"I find I am hurt, not by the reviews exactly, but by the growing rift I see between myself and those people I thought I belonged to," Anne Lindbergh confided to her diary. "The artists, the writers, the intellectuals, the sensitive, the idealistic—I feel exiled from them."[10] Lindbergh told Anne they had lost friends "like a field after a bombardment." She wrote, "I am now the bubonic plague among writers and C. is the anti-Christ!"[11]

The election continued to move in Willkie's direction. He traveled 34,000 miles by train, giving over five hundred speeches in thirty-four states until his voice became gravelly, then gave out. At every turn, he repeated the danger of electing Roosevelt for a third term. And at every opportunity he demanded that the president meet him to debate in person. In Chicago on September 13 he pledged to "not send one American boy into the shambles of a European war." He departed from his prepared text to add, "If [the president's] promise to keep our boys out of foreign wars is no better than his promise to balance the budget, they're almost on the transports!"[12] By comparison with Willkie's energy, Luce's *Life* magazine described Roosevelt's campaign as having "about as much pep as an old stock company vehicle with one star performer who disliked his role."[13]

Despite polls showing that from June 1940 on Americans believed that Germany would lose the war and that the United States would become involved,[14] Willkie's message that Roosevelt would take America into war gradually began to take hold. Reading letters, telegrams, and reports from Democratic officials pouring into the White House, Roosevelt's speechwriter Robert E. Sherwood was "horrified at the evidence of hysteria." Even Democratic-leaning newspapermen reported "mounting waves of fear throughout the country, which might easily merge into tidal proportions by election day and sweep Willkie into office." A bank implored its depositors to vote Republican and advertised in the *Chicago Tribune*, "In a last stand for democracy, every director and officer of this bank will vote for Wendell Willkie." "Even more alarming" to Sherwood were the pleas from party activists flooding into Democratic national headquarters in New York. "All the messages said much the same thing," recalled Sherwood. "Please, for God's sake, Mr. President, give a solemn promise to the mothers of America that you will not send their sons into any foreign wars. If you fail to do this, we lose the election!"[15]

The Chicago America First Committee's attempt to grow into a national organization was also gathering pace. In mid-September, Lindbergh, encouraged by Stuart and the ultra-conservative Brigadier-General R. E. Wood,[16] a senior executive with Sears, Roebuck, met with Ford at the Ford Motors plant and persuaded him to give money and serve on America First's governing committee. Lindbergh found Wood "an able man [who] carried on the discussion intelligently and with great discretion" and Stuart "alert, enthusiastic, and a hard worker."[17]

Lindbergh, Wood, Stuart, and Ford were joined by Chester Bowles of the advertising agency Benton & Bowles. A broader meeting of interested parties was held at the University Club on Fifth Avenue, New York, in which the Fascist sympathizer Merwin K. Hart, the

dean of Harvard Journalism School Carl W. Ackerman, and Lindbergh were appointed as the new organization's steering committee. Hart wanted to set up an eastern committee to complement the
thriving Chicago outfit; Lindbergh thought it best to roll out the
Chicago effort across the nation.

America First soon discovered that their attempts to buy radio
time were met with resistance. "Some of the radio stations have
taken the stand that the committee has to do with a 'controversial
issue' and therefore comes under the code they have formed against
selling time for controversial issues," wrote Lindbergh in his diary.
"It is a fine state of affairs if the question of war and peace cannot
be debated before the American people because it is a 'controversial
issue.'"[18] They were left with buying a full page in the *New York Times*
to set out their arguments.

To maintain momentum, Lindbergh gave another broadcast, "A
Plea for American Independence," on the Mutual Broadcasting System, a network amenable to "controversial" views. Anxious not to
be accused of partisanship during an election, Mutual asked Lindbergh to remove the penultimate line from his talk: "When a man is
drafted to serve in the armed forces of our country, he has the right
to know that his government has the independent destiny of America as its objective, and that he will not be sent to fight in the wars of
a foreign land." Lindbergh refused.

As he prepared to broadcast on October 13, Lindbergh felt belea-
guered. His mailbox was attracting letters threatening his life and
those of Anne and their children. "I don't know how much longer I
will be able to do this," wrote Lindbergh, "for there are many people
who would like to see me stopped."[19] He suspected that the administration was tapping his telephone. "The freedom of action and
speech that we used to know in this country seems to be rapidly dis-
appearing," he told his diary.[20]

When he made his broadcast, he began by reminding the audience of the American republic's history of keeping out of the affairs
of the Old World. "Why, then ... are we being told that we must give
up our independent position, that our frontiers lie in Europe and
that our destiny will be decided by European armies fighting upon
European soil?" Lindbergh asked. He played to his strength: his reputation as an aviator. "We do not need untold thousands of mili-

tary aircraft unless we intend to wage a war abroad," he said.[21] Then he spoke the forbidden line about an enlisted man having the right to know his government had the independence of America in mind and that he will not be sent abroad to fight a foreign war. It was a simple message that rang true among headline writers across America. The *Spokesman–Review* in Spokane, Washington, headed its verbatim report, "Let Europe Stew in Own Juice; Make U.S. Stronger."[22]

Commentary on the broadcast, however, was mixed. The *Tampa Tribune* ran an editorial titled "Shame!" saying, "We are being forced to the reluctant conclusion that Charles Augustus Lindbergh ought to be interned—or gagged—for the duration of the war." A columnist in the *Evening Independent* in St. Petersburg, Florida, rushed to Lindbergh's defense, writing that there was nothing seditious in the speech "unless it has become seditious to criticize the administration, in which case at least 20,000,000 Americans are going to vote seditiously on Nov. 5."[23]

Roosevelt's attorney general, Robert H. Jackson, fired a shot across Lindbergh's bow. "No speech, in its timing and its substance, could more perfectly have served the purpose of those who would weaken the morale of democracy and undermine the spirit of our defense effort," he told an audience of lawyers. "We are witnessing the most ominous gathering of forces against freedom and democracy that has been seen in my time."[24] Lindbergh was put on notice: if America were to join the war, his isolationist remarks would count against him.

Roosevelt was acutely aware from the tightening polls that Willkie's campaign was effective. With Democratic support flagging, particularly among Roman Catholics, in mid-October Roosevelt decided to gamble. "I know what an increasingly severe strain you have been under during the past weeks," he wrote to Kennedy, before suggesting he fly home on October 21, just three weeks before polling day. There was, however, a proviso. "No matter how proper and appropriate your statements might be, every effort will be made to misinterpret and to distort what you say," the president warned. "I am, consequently, asking you specifically not to make any statement to the press on your way over nor when you arrive in New York until you and I have had a chance to agree upon what should be said." Roosevelt asked that instead of Kennedy returning to his home in

Bronxville, New York, he travel directly to the White House, "since I will want to talk with you as soon as you get here."[25]

Kennedy was in two minds about how to respond. He would return home, certainly, but he could not decide whether to back Roosevelt. Luce left him an open invitation to treachery, asking him to lunch the day he returned with the intention of persuading him to back Willkie. Kennedy had one last grisly task to perform in London. On October 19, he said farewell to Chamberlain on his deathbed. The prime minister whose poor judgment had led to the ignominy of Munich clasped Kennedy's hand between his and said, "This is goodbye. We will never see each other again."[26] Three days later, Kennedy set off by flying boat to Lisbon, then via Horta in the Azores, and Bermuda, to New York.

Roosevelt's weekly poll numbers kept dropping. In response, the president decided to give five speeches to counter what was called "a systematic program of falsification of fact" by Willkie. The first, delivered in Philadelphia on October 23, was a piece of political knockabout. Pointing out that since July "hardly a day or a night has passed" without his having to attend to a sudden political crisis stemming from the war, the president felt the time had come to confront "the more fantastic misstatements" made by his opponents. In particular, he wanted to deny the suggestion "that the President of the United States telephoned to Mussolini and Hitler to sell Czechoslovakia down the river" and that "the election of the present Government means the end of American democracy within four years."

To whoops of delight from the packed convention hall, Roosevelt declared, "I consider it a public duty to answer falsifications with facts. I will not pretend that I find this an unpleasant duty. I am an old campaigner and I love a good fight." He addressed the isolationists' suggestion he had "secretly entered into agreements with foreign nations" and had pledged "the participation of the United States in some foreign war." He gave a "most solemn assurance": "There is no secret treaty, no secret obligation, no secret commitment, no secret understanding in any shape or form, direct or indirect, with any other Government, or any other nation in any part of the world, to involve this nation in any war."

He addressed "one outrageously false charge," that he was leading the country into war, which he described as "contrary to every fact, every purpose of the past eight years." He reminded Americans of the words of the Democratic platform: "We will not participate in foreign wars and we will not send our army, naval or air forces to fight in foreign lands outside of the Americas except in case of attack." "It is for peace that I have labored," Roosevelt said, "and it is for peace that I shall labor all the days of my life."[27]

Willkie immediately responded, highlighting the failures of the New Deal and charging that, by seeking a third term, Roosevelt was becoming a dictator. He reminded his audience that George Washington had declined a third term, "even though it was urged upon him by his countrymen at a time when discord prevailed at home and war prevailed abroad."[28]

Kennedy landed in Lisbon on October 25, the day of the president's Philadelphia address, and was met by an American diplomat with a letter from the president reminding him that he should travel straight to the White House on his arrival and say nothing to the press. In Bermuda, Kennedy received a cable from the president: "I hope Rose and you will come to Washington immediately after your arrival in New York to spend Saturday night at the White House." Kennedy telephoned Roosevelt from Bermuda who "was very pleasant"[29] but again urged the ambassador to stay mum until he had had time for a long conversation. Kennedy was still angry with the president and scribbled on an envelope, "You can't say you don't want to go to war if you listen with great intolerance to somebody like Col. Lindbergh."[30]

There was a further message from the president waiting for Kennedy on his arrival at the flying boat port on Long Island Sound.[31] "Thank the Lord you are safely home," it read. "I do hope you & Rose can come down Sunday p.m.—we expect you both at the White House." Kennedy called to say he was on his way. The president took the ambassador's call in the Oval Office, where he was conferring with Speaker Rayburn and Congressman Lyndon B. Johnson[32] from Texas. "Joe, it is so good to hear your voice," said the president. "Come to the White House tonight for a little family dinner. I'm dying to talk to you." To the delight of Rayburn and Johnson, the president was all the while passing his hand across his throat to signal he was about to cut Kennedy off at the neck.

The president was not the only one trying to reach Kennedy.

There was also a letter waiting from Wood of America First, plead-ing for the ambassador to join the movement. "The whole future of the country is at stake," wrote Wood, "and the present is one of those times in history when the truth must be told." If Kennedy knew of any secret deals between the president and Churchill, now was the time to declare them. "I believe you owe to your country and to your fellow citizens the duty of telling those facts, regardless of partisan-ship or any personal friendships," he wrote.

Kennedy ran the gauntlet of the press at the airport and, his date with Luce apparently forgotten, was ushered with Rose to a mili-tary plane waiting to fly them to the capital. During the flight, Rose reminded her husband that he should be sure to be grateful for the opportunities Roosevelt had granted him. "The President sent you, a Roman Catholic, as Ambassador to London, which probably no other President would have done," she said. "He sent you as his rep-resentative to the Pope's coronation. . . . You would write yourself down as an ingrate in the view of many people if you resign now."[33]

Arriving at the White House, Kennedy was escorted to the presi-dent's study, where the smiling Roosevelt was "shaking a cocktail shaker and reaching over for a few lumps of ice." Missy LeHand was the only other person present. Kennedy was just starting on the diatribe he had been rehearsing for days when Rose entered, with Senator Byrnes and his wife. After drinks, the party went to the dining room for a supper of scrambled eggs on toast and sausages, where Byrnes, in a carefully prepared intervention, suggested that Kennedy might like to make a broadcast to boost the president's campaign. "I didn't say Yes, Aye, or No," Kennedy reported to his diary. The president directed the full force of his charm on Rose and recounted loving stories about her father, the Boston Democratic boss "Honey Fitz."

After dinner, they all returned to the study. Kennedy surmised that the evening had been choreographed to prevent him spending time alone with the president to air his grievances. He abandoned etiquette and took the floor. "Since it doesn't seem possible for me to see the President alone, I guess I'll just have to say what I am going to say in front of everybody," he said, and began to enumerate the slights, omissions, slaps, overrulings, rudeness, and personal treach-ery that had made his life in London such a misery.[34] In an attempt to defuse the awkwardness, Rose suggested that it must be difficult to maintain good relations between friends when they were 3,000 miles apart. The president, looking red-faced and blinking throughout Kennedy's tirade, took a deep breath before speaking. He said he agreed with every word, it was all a terrible mistake, and that the following day he would reprimand those in the State Department who had so upset the ambassador. After the election there would be "a real housecleaning" to purge the administration of such wretched people. Kennedy later reflected, "Someone is lying very seriously and I suspect the President."[35]

Byrnes returned to the idea of a broadcast and put Kennedy on the spot: would he be prepared to talk to the nation? "I said that I would write the speech without saying anything to anybody and say just what I felt," Kennedy recorded in his diary. Missy LeHand telephoned the Democratic National Committee to tell them Kennedy would use the hour they had reserved on CBS the following Tuesday. As the president was returning to New York by train late Sunday, it was suggested that perhaps the ambassador would like to accompany him. Kennedy declined, saying it would undermine the surprise of the broadcast. To the reporters who had already been briefed that the ambassador would accompany the president to New York, it was clear that the meeting between president and ambassador had not gone smoothly. There was intense speculation that Kennedy was about to launch an unpleasant surprise into the campaign, a rumor that gathered strength when, the following morning, Kennedy abruptly canceled a press conference.

After traveling to New York, Kennedy spent the next two days holed up in the Waldorf-Astoria writing his broadcast. He conferred with friends and received a strong plea from Clare Boothe Luce. "When you make that radio address tomorrow night, throwing as you will all your prestige and reputation for wisdom, your experience abroad into the scales for F.D.R., you'll probably help to turn the trick for him," she wrote. "I believe with all my heart and soul you will be doing America a terrible disservice. . . . I'm so *terribly* frightened for this country."[36]

On October 28, after a campaign tour of New York's five boroughs, Roosevelt gave the second of his five speeches, in Madison Square Garden. Kennedy appeared alongside him on the platform.

As if on cue, the same day Mussolini ordered the invasion of Greece. Roosevelt confronted head-on the charge that he had jeopardized America's freedom by being slow in rearming the nation. He pointed the audience toward the pages of the *Congressional Record*. There they would discover that Republican leaders "not only voted against these efforts, but they stated time and again through the years that they were unnecessary and extravagant, that our armed strength was sufficient for any emergency."

He singled out some of those who had railed against rearmament: former president Hoover, the vice presidential candidate Senator McNary, senators Taft, Vandenberg, Nye, and Johnson, and congressmen Martin, Barton, and Fish, Roosevelt's upstate New York sparring partner. He then listed opponents of the "cash and carry" measure that allowed America to arm the democracies, "Senators McNary, Vandenberg, Nye and Johnson. Now wait, a perfectly beautiful rhythm—Congressmen Martin, Barton and Fish." The audience began to catch on. "Great Britain and a lot of other nations would never have received one ounce of help from us," Roosevelt said, "if the decision had been left to"—and the crowd joined him in reciting the trio of names—"Martin, Barton and"—long pause for maximum effect—"Fish!" The president asked for support to continue making arms to defend America and Britain. Then, without mentioning Willkie by name, he said, "The alternative is to risk the future of the country in the . . . inexperienced hands of those who in these perilous days are willing recklessly to imply that our boys are 'already on their way to the transports'."[37]

The following day, Roosevelt took a leading role in the drawing of the first draft lottery, overruling the advice of his campaign team who thought it too close to election day to draw attention to the prospect of America joining the European war. As commander in chief, Roosevelt insisted on being there. An ominous sense of history surrounded the occasion. The glass drum containing the names was the same Wilson had used to pick conscripts for World War One. War Secretary Stimson's blindfold was made from the cushions on which the founding fathers had sat to sign the Declaration of Independence. Using words sent by the first American senators to the first president, Roosevelt declared, "You have the confidence and the gratitude and the love of your country. We are all with you."[38]

While polls showed that a majority of Americans were in favor of the measure, Roosevelt was careful not to use the word "draft," instead calling it a "muster," invoking the volunteers from the farms in Lexington and Concord who fought for independence.

Roosevelt won a ringing endorsement for "selective service" from America's top Roman Catholic, Archbishop Francis J. Spellman,[39] who wrote, "It is better to have protection and not need it than to need protection and not have it. . . . We really can no longer afford to be moles, who cannot see, or ostriches who will not see. . . . We Americans want peace and we shall prepare for a peace, but not for a peace whose definition is slavery or death."[40] It was an argument as much against isolationism as it was in favor of the draft.

The following night, Roosevelt sat in his White House study with the radio tuned to CBS. It did not take long before Kennedy came to the heart of the matter. "Even the most staid isolationist is now alive to the danger facing any nation in the modern world," he said. "The realization that oceans alone are not adequate barriers against revolutionary forces which now threaten a whole civilization." He continued cautiously: "While we shall not be involved in this war, we are bound to be seriously affected by it."[41] Then he turned to "the charge that the President of the United States is trying to involve this country in the World War. Such a charge is false."[42] He continued to deny Willkie's assertion that Roosevelt was lying. "To even suggest that our boys will soon be on the transports in this kind of war," said Kennedy, "is completely absurd."[43]

The ambassador ended on a personal note. "My wife and I have given nine hostages to fortune. Our children and your children are more important than anything else in the world," he said. "In the light of these considerations, I believe that Franklin D. Roosevelt should be reelected President of the United States." Relieved, within minutes of the end of the broadcast, Roosevelt sent Kennedy a cable: "We have all just listened to a grand speech. Many thanks."[44] Kennedy's twenty-year-old daughter Kathleen sent him a congratulatory note, signing off, "Goodnight from your 4th hostage."[45]

What had changed Kennedy's mind? Although there were a number of witnesses to the encounter between Kennedy and Roosevelt in the White House, each remembered a different version of events. Some suggested that Roosevelt had showed Kennedy transcripts of his disloyal conversations in London, a tactic that does not tally with Roosevelt's usual sinuous methods. Kennedy may have blinked because he hoped for another important government post in the new administration: there were rumors that he was to mastermind the National Defense Advisory Commission, set up in May 1940 to coordinate the rearmament drive. He may even have genuinely believed that Roosevelt was the only person who could lead America through the war.

John F. Kennedy believed that Roosevelt had offered his father backing for a 1944 presidential bid, which rings true as the president was always encouraging rivals with empty promises of support. Rose's advice, however, appeared to play a key part in Kennedy's decision to stay within the Roosevelt fold. She, like him, was highly ambitious for their children and hoped they would use their great fortune to lead lives of prominent public service. Clare Boothe Luce reported years later that Kennedy had told her, "We agreed that if I endorsed him for president in 1940, then he would support my son Joe for governor of Massachusetts in 1942,"[46] though as Joe Kennedy Jr. would have been only twenty-seven in 1942, the suggestion seems fanciful. James Roosevelt believed his father threatened Kennedy and his children with the mark of Judas if the ambassador were to abandon him at this crucial stage. To become estranged from the Democratic hierarchy at such a time would seriously damage the Kennedys' prospects of establishing a ruling dynasty.[47]

Lindbergh had one last chance to help defeat Roosevelt before election day. The venue was Woolsey Hall, Yale University, at the invitation of Kingman Brewster Jr.,[48] of the school's America First Committee. Lindbergh recalled that "every seat was taken, and people were standing along the walls"[49] as he explained in his soft, carefully enunciated speech that Americans faced a stark choice. "We must either keep out of European wars entirely or participate in European politics permanently," he said. "I believe that the wisest policy would be for us to build our security upon the bed rock of our own continent and its adjacent islands, and to proceed toward the independent American destiny that Washington outlined in his 'Farewell Address.'"[50]

Just a week before election day, the polls were still moving in Willkie's favor. Five Midwestern states were shifting from Democrat to Republican. The Democratic National Committee chairman, Ed Flynn, reported that since the president's remarks about Mussolini stabbing France in the back, party workers needed a police escort when campaigning in the Italian American parts of Brooklyn.

As Roosevelt's train steamed up the eastern seaboard en route to his next speech in the isolationist redoubt of Boston, he was inundated with urgent requests from anxious Democratic leaders to repeat his promise that he would not send Americans to fight in foreign wars. "How often do they expect me to say that?" Roosevelt asked Sherwood. "It's in the Democratic platform and I've repeated it a hundred times." "Evidently you've got to say it again and again and again," Sherwood replied. So were written the words that became almost as famous as "The only thing we have to fear is fear itself."[51] The Boston line was: "I give you one more assurance. I have said this before, but I shall say it again and again and again: Your boys are not going to be sent into any foreign wars." Rosenman reminded the president that the Democratic platform included the final words "except in case of attack," to which the president responded, "Of course we'll fight if we're attacked. If somebody attacks us, then it isn't a foreign war, is it? Or do they want me to guarantee that our troops will be sent into battle only in the event of another Civil War?"[52]

On the Boston Garden stage, the president turned to his left, to where Kennedy was sitting, and paid a fulsome tribute to "that Boston boy, beloved by all of Boston and a lot of other places, my Ambassador to the Court of St. James, Joe Kennedy." For the first time, perhaps, Roosevelt's praise of Kennedy was heartfelt. The rest of the speech, to a packed audience of 14,000, was a romp. At one point a voice in the gallery cried out, "What about Barton and Fish?" Roosevelt beamed at the crowd and said, "I have to let you in on a secret. It will come as a great surprise to you. And it's this. I'm enjoying this campaign. I'm really having a fine time," and the audience roared.[53]

When he came to "Your boys are not going to be sent into any foreign wars," Willkie, listening on the radio, exclaimed, "That hypocritical son of a bitch! This is going to beat me!"[54]

CHAPTER SEVENTEEN

"OVER MY DEAD BODY"

*Election Day 1940, Kennedy tenders his
resignation then speaks his mind, a bruising
encounter at Hyde Park.*

ON THE MORNING of November 5, general election day, Franklin
Roosevelt, Eleanor, and Franklin's mother made the short trip to
Hyde Park's miniature town hall to cast their vote. Willkie cast his
at Public School 6 on Madison Avenue and 85th Street, New York
City. Lindbergh, his wife, and his mother-in-law voted in Engle-
wood, New Jersey.

Although it was not as mighty a victory as before, Roosevelt won
handily, with 27 million votes to Willkie's 22 million. The electoral
college was overwhelmingly in Roosevelt's favor, 449 to eighty-two,
and the states divided thirty-eight to ten. The defeat did not come
as a surprise to Willkie. "When I heard the President hang the isolationist votes of Martin, Barton, and Fish on me," he would later say,
"I knew I was licked."[1]

Roosevelt's win was not unexpected, but it was a relief for a president who had staked everything on steering the country through
what he thought would be America's inevitable confrontation with
the dictators. The first visitor to the White House when Roosevelt
returned to Washington on November 7 was Kennedy, to tender his
resignation. It was an awkward affair that spoiled Roosevelt's day of
triumph. The ambassador arrived at lunchtime but was not invited
to join the celebratory lunch party with Morgenthau. In the course
of his five-minute audience, the ambassador could not bring himself to congratulate the president on his victory. "Well, you've got it,"

he said. "I certainly don't begrudge you the next four years."² That charmless greeting, if nothing else, ensured there would be no job for him in Roosevelt's new administration.

Roosevelt asked Kennedy to hold fire in telling of his departure until he could find a replacement for London. Smarting from Roosevelt's chilly welcome, Kennedy marched to the State Department to see Hull, Welles, and assistant secretary of state Breckinridge Long,³ who were astonished by the ambassador's pessimism and how out of step he was with their thinking. "He thinks we ought to . . . make some approach to Germany and to Japan which would result in an economic collaboration," wrote Long. "He does not believe in the continuing of democracy. He thinks we will have to assume a Fascist form of government here."⁴

Still furious at being painted into a corner before the election, Kennedy began plotting how to continue his personal campaign for America to stay out of the war. On November 9, he granted a ninety-minute interview to Louis Lyons of the *Boston Globe*, and Charles K. Edmondson and Ralph Coglan of the *St. Louis Post–Dispatch*. The outgoing ambassador was in such an expansive mood that he did not clearly express whether the interview was to be on or off the record.

"I know more about the European situation than anybody else," he said, "and it's up to me to see that the country gets it." American involvement in the war was not inevitable. "I say we're not going in. Only over my dead body. I'm willing to spend all I've got left to keep us out of the war," he declared. "There's no sense in getting in. We'd just be holding the bag." He would lead the campaign against intervention and he stressed his close links to the isolationists in Congress. He said he was "buddies" with Wheeler and had contributed to his election campaigns. "Lindbergh's not so crazy, either."

He repeated his belief that war would lead to Fascism in Britain, even if the Brits beat Hitler. "Democracy is finished in England," he said. As Labour leaders had joined Britain's war coalition, Kennedy predicted that "National socialism is coming." Asked whether he was just talking about Britain, he said, "If we get into war it will be in this country, too. A bureaucracy would take over right off. Everything we hold dear will be gone."

Kennedy dismissed Churchill's words and the courage of the British during the Blitz as misleading. "It isn't that [Britain's] fighting for democracy. That's the bunk. She's fighting for self-preservation, just as we will if it comes to us." There was no question of America sending ships or troops to Britain. "As to ships, we haven't got any. I know about ships," he said. "We couldn't send an army anywhere now. It would be senseless to go in. What would we be fighting for?"[5] The reporters gleefully filed the scoop handed to them on a plate.

For isolationists, Kennedy's candid remarks were evidence they were on the right track. For most Americans, however, who had taken Kennedy's broadcast in support of Roosevelt at face value, the interview was a bombshell of bitterness and disloyalty directed at a president they had just overwhelmingly elected. One voter wrote to Roosevelt, "I hope you put Joe Kennedy in a bag and pull the string tight."[6]

The following day, aware of the damage he was doing to his reputation, Kennedy issued a halfhearted denial that he had ever used such words. "Many statements in the article show [the reporter did not take notes] because they create a different impression entirely than I would want to set forth," he declared.[7] But he could not deny that he had been accurately reported. Overnight came news that Chamberlain had died. When the city editor of the *Globe*, Joseph Dineen, called Kennedy at home in Bronxville for a quote about his friend's death, he asked whether the interview was accurate. "I said it," Kennedy admitted. "He didn't miss a thing."[8] When the *Globe* refused to declare the interview fiction, Kennedy canceled the advertising for his whisky import business in the paper.

Kennedy's enemies were quick to exploit the gaffe. "Joe is out to do whatever damage he can," Ickes wrote in his diary. "The President said that in his opinion the interview . . . was authentic."[9] Frankfurter piled on, sending Roosevelt a transcript of what he called Kennedy's "poisonous vapors."[10] "What is printed watered down some of the things Joe said," he wrote. "[Some of the comments] were so raw the *Globe* did not want to print them."[11] William Allen White condemned Kennedy, describing him as "an enemy of the democratic way of life."[12] Krock wrote to Kennedy, "If there is anything I can do to dispel the ill effect of that unfortunate interview, I stand ready, as usual, to do it."[13]

Kennedy's tirade was a last swipe at the British, who at first had admired him for his family's glamour but in time came to despise him for his message of despair. "While he was here his suave, monotonous style, his nine over-photographed children and his hail-fellow-well-met manner concealed a hard-boiled business man's eagerness to do a profitable business deal with the dictators, and he deceived many decent English people," wrote A. J. Cummings in the *News Chronicle*.[14] "Perhaps you were always a defeatist and never owned to it in public," wrote George Murray in the *Daily Mail*. "We can forgive wrongheadedness, but not bad faith."[15]

The *Globe* interview confirmed what Roosevelt already knew, that in frustration Kennedy had gone on the rampage and would likely use his fame, fortune, and influence to frustrate the administration's freedom to maneuver. The *Globe* reported, "He's started already on a quiet but determined and fighting crusade to 'keep us out'. He's just gone to California to see one of America's influential publishers [Hearst]. He's already seen others [Howard and Patterson] and he means to see more.... He's talked to Congressmen and Senators and means to see more."[16]

Kennedy's trip to California was partly to discover whether Hearst, by this time preoccupied with a struggle to remain solvent, needed him to fix his broken finances as he had before. But mostly the ambassador discussed with the press baron keeping America out of the war. As Kennedy had told the *Globe*, "It's all a question of what we do in the next six months."[17] He set himself a busy schedule to try to prevent Roosevelt from ushering America into war.

On the day after the *Globe* interview appeared, Armistice Day, November 11, Roosevelt paid tribute before the Tomb of the Unknown Soldier at the National Cemetery in Arlington, Virginia, to those who had fought in World War One, reminding his audience "that the danger of brutality and the danger of tyranny and slavery to freedom-loving peoples can be real and terrible."[18] It was all part of his long campaign "to talk 'educationally,' quietly but effectively with the appeasers and semi-appeasers."[19]

Asking rhetorically what World War One had achieved, the president told the audience in the National Cemetery, "The men of France, prisoners in their cities, victims of searches and of seizures without law, hostages for the safety of their masters' lives, robbed of their harvests, murdered in their prisons . . . know the answer to that question. . . . The Czechs know the answer too. The Poles. The

Danes. The Dutch. The Serbs. The Belgians. The Norwegians. The Greeks." He quoted World War One hero Sergeant York, whose life had recently been made into a pro-democracies Hollywood movie: "Liberty and freedom and democracy are prizes awarded only to those peoples who fight to win them and then keep fighting eternally to hold them." "The people of America agree with that," said Roosevelt. "They believe that liberty is worth fighting for. And if they are obliged to fight they will fight eternally to hold it."[20]

Two days later, Kennedy arrived in Los Angeles and attended a lunch of about fifty movie people hosted by Hollywood studio moguls Harry Warner, Samuel Goldwyn, and Louis B. Mayer.[21] The war had placed the studio chiefs in a quandary. Since the declaration of war by Britain and France, Europe was under siege and Hollywood movies could only make a circuitous route to the screens of the once lucrative movie markets of France and Germany. Germany had also banned a great number of Hollywood movies because of their anti-Nazi tone. As a result, all studios, even Walt Disney, whose pictures were ideologically empty, were enduring the loss of 40 percent of their prewar revenue.

American movies were increasingly unsuitable for screening in Axis-held territories as they contained pro-democracy themes and made fun of Hitler and Nazism. Movies like *Confessions of a Nazi Spy*, released in 1939, starring the ardent anti-Nazi Edward G. Robinson,[22] ridiculed the pomposity and brutality of Germans in uniform. In 1940, the stream of movies encouraging audiences to sympathize with the democracies became a torrent, led by *The Great Dictator*, Charles Chaplin's satire on Hitler, *Flight Command*, about a new recruit to the navy's "Hellcats Squadron," and *Escape*, in which a young man's quest for his lost mother leads him to a concentration camp.

Kennedy's recommendation to Hollywood was to stop making pro-British, anti-German films. According to Douglas Fairbanks Jr., he put "the fear of God" into the three studio heads, all Jewish, telling them they should "stop making anti-Nazi movies or use the film medium to promote the democracies versus the dictators." He said "the Lindbergh appeasement groups were not so far off the mark when they suggest that this country can reconcile itself to whomever wins the war and adjust our trade accordingly."[23]

What Kennedy said was so treacherous that Fairbanks, who headed the Southern California branch of William Allen White's Committee to Defend America by Aiding the Allies,[24] wrote, appalled, to Roosevelt, to say that some in Hollywood felt that because Kennedy appeared to be a loyal Roosevelt ally, the ambassador's remarks must have been authorized by the president himself. "There are many of us who do not, can not and will not believe that that is so," said Fairbanks.

Not all of Hollywood agreed. Louis B. Mayer followed Kennedy's profit-before-principle line and called in anti-Nazi actors like Melvyn Douglas,[25] warning them to stop their politicking for fear of frightening off foreign buyers. "Of course, it's all right for you to think what you please, but surely you see that you don't do yourself any good at the studio when you offend a lot of people," Mayer told Douglas. "Consider what happens to our pictures in certain parts of the world because of your activities."[26] Another who put business before morality was Arthur Loew, head of foreign distribution at MGM, who advised Myrna Loy[27] not to mix politics with acting. Loy was incensed: "Here I was fighting for the Jews and they're telling me to lay off because there's still money to be made in Germany."[28]

Roosevelt had already stepped in with government money to compensate studios for the collapse of the European market. On June 5, 1940, the Motion Picture Committee Cooperating for the National Defense[29] was formed to help inform American audiences they should start planning for war. It commissioned twenty-five short films and twelve army recruitment films and encouraged movie theaters to show films promoting the purchase of war bonds and the collection of scrap metal. The committee also urged distributors to screen movies made by federal agencies to prepare Americans for war, including the Tennessee Valley Authority's *Power for Defense*, the Civilian Conservation Corps's *Army in Overalls*, and the Office of Emergency Management's *Bomber*.

Having done his best to deter Hollywood from promoting intervention in the war, Kennedy headed to Hearst's late mother's Northern California estate, Wyntoon, a half-timbered Bavarian schloss designed by the same architect as his fantasy castle San Simeon. Kennedy wanted to ensure the appeasement campaign he was about to embark upon would receive the backing of Hearst's papers. A fellow guest for the weekend was the president's daughter Anna and her husband, John Boettiger, who before long found himself in a heated argument with Kennedy. "What right have you to go against the principles of my father-in-law?" Boettiger asked. "Now, wait a minute," Kennedy replied. "I have not in any way said I'm not in accord with what your father-in-law says. Let's not argue now." When Boettiger persisted, Kennedy said, "I'm not going to stoop to argue with you." "We let them fight it out," Hearst's mistress Marion Davies recalled.[30] The following day, Boettiger wrote to the president expressing his anxiety about Kennedy's "fascist leanings."[31]

Ickes, too, was concerned that the ambassador, backed by Hearst, Howard of Scripps–Howard, and Patterson of America's best-selling daily, the *New York Daily News*, "would make a powerful combination. Kennedy has lots of money and can probably raise all that he needs. The Hearst chain and the Howard chain together comprise a lot of newspapers." With the avid support of the *News*, the Washington *Times–Herald*, and the *Chicago Tribune*, Kennedy was, Ickes believed, "out to do whatever damage he can."[32]

Roosevelt decided to try his charm on Kennedy once more, and asked Eleanor to invite him to Hyde Park. "Let's have him down here and see what he has to say," said the president. Kennedy arrived by train mid-morning on November 23 and Eleanor ferried him to Hyde Park, where the president welcomed him into the parlor. After ten minutes, the president urgently asked an aide to summon Eleanor. "There was Franklin, white as a sheet," recalled Eleanor. "He asked Mr. Kennedy to step outside and then he said, and his voice was shaking, 'I never want to see that man again as long as I live.'"[33]

Eleanor reminded him that Kennedy had been invited for the weekend, that there were guests coming for lunch, and that the New York train did not leave Rhinecliff until two. "Then you drive him around Hyde Park and put him on that train," ordered the president. Over lunch at her cottage at Val-Kill, in what Eleanor later told Gore Vidal was "the most dreadful four hours of my life,"[34] the ambassador regaled Eleanor with lurid details of the damage the German air force could wreak on American cities.

On December 1, Kennedy visited Roosevelt in the White House, hoping to be quickly freed from his government position so that he could start to campaign in earnest. There was little time to talk, and Kennedy was squeezed between more pressing appointments with Morgenthau and Welles. The president, apparently recovered from his apoplexy at their previous meeting, was still eager to keep Kennedy sweet and affected to listen with interest to the ambassador's by now routine assessment that Britain was doomed. "Churchill is keeping this fight going only because he has no alternative," Kennedy said, "but his real idea is that he'll get the U.S. in and then the U.S. will share the problems." In a vain attempt to put the president and prime minister at each other's throats, he added, "Churchill has no particular love for the U.S. nor in his heart for you." Roosevelt pretended to agree, telling Kennedy, "I know. He is one of the few men in public life who was rude to me."

Kennedy insisted that British defeat was imminent and that there was no point in America holding out alone: "With England licked, the party's over." In that case, Kennedy said, Roosevelt must either "become greater than Washington or Lincoln or become a horse's ass." Roosevelt replied, "I have a third alternative; to be the one responsible for making the U.S. a small and unimportant power."[35]

On leaving the White House, Kennedy issued a statement announcing his resignation as ambassador. "My plan is . . . to devote my efforts to what seems to me the greatest cause in the world today, and means, if successful, the preservation of the American form of democracy," he wrote, before adding, without apparent irony, "That cause is to help the President keep the United States out of the war."[36] Syndicated political gossip columnists Joseph Alsop and Robert Kintner wrote, "He really meant he was going to talk appeasement all across the United States."

When, after the ambassador's meeting with the president, Early was asked whether Kennedy could expect an appointment in Roosevelt's cabinet, he gave a faint smile as he said, "I don't see anything like that in the picture right now."[37] The same day, a report in Knox's *Chicago Daily News* alleged that Kennedy was involved in a plot to negotiate a peace with the Axis powers. According to the report, Bernard E. Smith,[38] one of Kennedy's Wall Street speculator friends, made an approach to Hitler via the leaders of Pétain's collaborationist government in Vichy. An account of the conspiracy relayed the following week by the foreign editor of the *News*, Carroll Binder,[39] said the peace proposal had been intercepted by the American ambassador to Vichy, Admiral William Leahy, who convinced Pétain's aides that Smith would be wasting his time.

In light of Kennedy's unconvincing disavowal of his *Boston Globe* interview, his denial suggested that he was certainly involved.[40]

CHAPTER EIGHTEEN

HIGH NOON

*Britain runs out of cash, Morgenthau
eyes British companies and gold reserves,
Roosevelt ponders how to supply Churchill without
involving Congress, "The Arsenal of Democracy."*

FRESH FROM HIS election victory, Roosevelt was exhausted and needed a break. At the end of November, Lothian found him "in a fatigued and depressed state of mind, unresponsive to any new ideas for action."[1] Churchill, too, was disappointed at his lack of urgency and told colleagues he was "rather chilled"[2] by Roosevelt's drifting attitude. The president found a pretext to spend a few nights at sea in the need to inspect the new US facilities in the British West Indies won in the destroyers-for-bases deal. In the final cabinet meeting before he set sail on his ten-day Caribbean cruise, he set his colleagues a question.

He was already speeding supplies to Britain. As soon as the election was won, he announced that half the planes and war supplies made in America would now go straight to Britain. There was, however, a question of how Britain could continue to pay for the war goods. It was no secret that Britain was running short of dollars. Anxious that Britain might default, American exporters of food and other supplies had begun asking for cash up front. By the end of 1939, British gold and dollar reserves stood at $545 million and were diminishing at the rate of $200 million a year. Since war was declared, Britain had spent $4.5 billion in cash with American arms manufacturers and had only $2 billion left in total dollar and sterling cash reserves, which would last until the middle of 1941.

Roosevelt told his cabinet that Britain "still has sufficient credits and property in this country to finance additional war supplies. . . . [and that the $2.5 billion in assets remaining] ought to be spent first, although the British do not want to liquidate their American securities." But, he added, according to Harold Ickes's diary account, "the time would surely come when Great Britain would need loans or credits. He suggested that one way to meet that situation would be for us to supply whatever we could under leasing arrangements . . . ships or any other property that was loanable, returnable, and insurable."[3]

Lothian gave the New York press a more exaggerated account of Britain's financial embarrassment when he arrived on a flight from London on November 23. "Britain is bust," he said, before explaining that matters were "becoming urgent" and that "available gold and securities had been virtually used up."[4] Lothian's remarks annoyed Roosevelt because they suggested a mercenary side to the president and encouraged the congressional isolationists. Nye declared that he and the rest were "ready to battle to the bitter end against any attempt to extend financial aid to the British" and that loans would "mean actual entry into war."[5] It was a reminder that the Johnson Act of 1934, which outlawed loans to any country "delinquent in its war obligations," remained in force.

Britain's cash shortage also revealed the anti-imperialist undercurrent to what was fast becoming an Anglo-American military alliance. Roosevelt and Churchill came from aristocratic backgrounds with many superficial similarities. Churchill, as the tenth-generation descendant of John Churchill, Duke of Marlborough, victor of the Battle of Blenheim (1704), enjoyed a clear edge in the social grandeur stakes over the relatively nouveaux riches of the mercantile Roosevelts. Roosevelt, however, benefited from inherited wealth which gave him complete independence of action, while Churchill was obliged to work as an author and journalist in order to feed his family and his extravagant lifestyle.

What the pair shared in their inherited privilege, however, did not translate into identical views. Churchill saw the British Empire as a dignified, patrician, and benevolent institution; Roosevelt thought it exploitative, unfair, and unkind. Some left-leaning Democrats even expressed the view that there was "a moral equivalency between Germany's war of conquest and England's [sic] efforts to protect the empire."[6]

Roosevelt had learned from Wilson that America, as the world's mightiest economy since the early years of the century, should take up the responsibilities that accompany such good fortune and treasure. With Britain rapidly spending its vast accumulation of imperial wealth on fighting Nazism, Roosevelt grasped the chance to seal the fate of the wobbling empire, which held by force of arms much of the Middle East, Africa, and India. The legitimacy of the empire was already being tested by freedom movements. So long as the isolationists insisted that Britain should not be helped, Roosevelt was able to press Churchill for the speedy liquidation of British assets. By the turn of the year, however, he was beginning to question whether insisting on full payments from an ally spending its fortune on a shared noble cause would jeopardize the goodwill necessary for their joint venture.

On December 1, Morgenthau showed the president Britain's balance sheet. Roosevelt glanced briefly at the figures before throwing them on the desk, saying, "Well, they aren't bust. There's lots of money there."[7] The same day, Roosevelt told Kennedy the same. "I've gone over their financial position and they're all right for quite a while," he said. "They've got plenty in the [sic] South [Africa] and holdings all over the world." Three days later, Sir Frederick Phillips,[8] a British Treasury official, returned to Washington[9] to resume meetings that had been going on with Morgenthau for some months to establish "a factual basis of British financial resources and war supply expenditures."[10] Phillips was working to a brief written by the British economics genius John Maynard Keynes.[11] It soon became clear in London that it would have been better if the silver-tongued Keynes, rather than the lackluster Phillips, had argued the British case.

Keynes provided Phillips with a robust response should Roosevelt and Morgenthau demand that Britain divest itself of all foreign investments before America provided direct military aid: Britain's investments were essential to the country's ability to pay its way after the war. A fire sale of assets would not provide Britain with their true value. Keynes had learned from his loan negotiations with American bankers to finance the Allies in World War One, and insisted that this time financial aid from America should be gifts, not loans. Britain would not "accept the dishonor and the reproaches of default whilst allowing to the U.S. all the consequent conveniences to their trade." If Britain were deliberately beggared, he foresaw "revolutionary changes in the commercial relations" between the two countries that would involve the closure of British and empire markets to American exporters as soon as the war was won. "America must not be allowed to pick out the eyes of the British Empire," he wrote.[12]

"Suave, balding Sir Frederick Phillips," as *Time* magazine described him, was an old-school civil servant who had been given a near-impossible task. Roosevelt and Morgenthau were daunting when working in concert, and they needed to be able to reassure Americans in general, who were still distrustful of Britain's failure to pay its World War One debts, and the isolationists in particular, who did not want to give any aid to Britain, that they had squeezed the British until the pips squeaked. Morgenthau put pressure on Phillips to liquidate national assets, such as British ownership of South American railroads and tin mines, and rubber plantations in Malaya. At one point, the president asked Phillips straight out, "How about selling some of those securities you have in Argentina?"[13] Morgenthau wanted to get American hands on British-owned companies in America, such as Shell Oil, Lever Brothers, and Brown & Williams Tobacco. At the insistence of Morgenthau, Courtaulds, the giant plastics and chemicals company, was sold in 1941 to American buyers at a fraction of what it was worth. Britain had had its pockets picked.

Roosevelt and Morgenthau also wanted Britain's gold. British reserves in Canada were already depleted to pay for war production in other parts of the empire. Britain had requisitioned French gold reserves and shipped them to Canada when the Reynaud government collapsed, but the gold could not be spent for fear of sparking a hostile reaction from the French Québécois. Nonetheless, Roosevelt and Morgenthau pressed their advantage, insisting that a warship be sent to Cape Town to pick up $50 billion ($800 billion in 2014 terms) in British gold holdings there. Picking over their financial bones was humiliating to the British, one minister complaining "that the Americans' love of doing good business may lead them to denude us of all our realizable resources before they show any inclination to be the Good Samaritan."[14] Churchill drafted a letter to Roosevelt saying that the American gold grab "would wear the aspect of a sheriff collecting the last assets of a helpless debtor."[15] For fear of offending the president, the note was never sent.

Eventually, as 1941 progressed, Roosevelt ran out of British assets to take. And from that moment he came face to face with the burdens of empire. In a memorandum to Hull, the president explored whether America should demand territory in return for armaments. He speculated about confiscating Bermuda, the British West Indies, British Honduras, and British Guiana. He could not decide whether acquiring poor colonies would be "something worthwhile or as a distinct liability. If we can get our naval bases, why, for example, should we buy with them two million headaches, consisting of that number of human beings who would be a definite economic drag on this country?" Similarly with a number of small British dependencies in the Pacific: "the islands south of Hawaii (Canton, Enderbury, Christmas, the Phoenix group, etc. down to Samoa) and the islands southwest of Hawaii and south of the Japanese mainland." "If we owned them," Roosevelt told Hull, "they would be difficult to defend against Japan."[16] For the first time, it seems, the president began to understand the burdens as well as the benefits of leading an empire that stretched around the globe.

By Thanksgiving 1940, Roosevelt faced a political and moral dilemma. He asked his cabinet to ponder in his absence how America could continue to supply the last bastion of democracy against the dictators without having to run the gauntlet of Congress, which would find endless reasons to delay the provisions. Taking with him his close aide Hopkins and a couple of other chums to make up a hand of cards, Roosevelt, in Frankfurter's words "in a deep Lincolnesque mood,"[17] departed Washington for the naval dock in Miami to sail the high seas aboard the USS *Tuscaloosa*.

Roosevelt fished by day, played poker by night, and otherwise let it be known that he wanted time alone to think. There were minor distractions, such as a stop at Guantánamo Bay, Cuba, to pick up Havana cigars, and lunch on board with the Duke of Windsor, George VI's feckless brother. The duke, a vacuous playboy ordered by the British government to live in exile since he abandoned the throne in 1936, had, much to British dismay, paid Hitler a visit the following year. The moment war was declared, he was appointed governor of the Bahamas to keep him away from further trouble. There were rumors that if Hitler succeeded in conquering Britain, he would reinstall the duke on the throne as a Nazi stooge. Roosevelt found the fallen monarch an intriguing curio, though "more pessimistic about the progress of the war than seemed suitable."[18] Noblesse did not always oblige.

A naval flying boat delivered mail to the *Tuscaloosa*, and on December 11 a long dispatch arrived from Churchill. The president retreated from the rest of the party for the duration of the cruise. For two days he lolled in a deck chair, reading and rereading the letter that Churchill believed was "one of the most important I ever wrote."[19] It suggested that Roosevelt's reelection confirmed that "the vast majority of American citizens" now believed that "the future of our two democracies and the kind of civilization for which they stand are bound up with the survival and independence of the British Commonwealth" and that "control of the Pacific by the United States Navy and of the Atlantic by the British Navy is . . . the surest means to preventing the war from reaching the shores of the United States."

Until America and Britain were fully rearmed, which Churchill thought would take at least two more years, it had fallen to Britain "to hold the front and grapple with Nazi power until the preparations of the United States are complete." Churchill asked for four specific favors: for America to maintain the freedom of the seas; to provide "escorting battleships" to keep Atlantic convoys safe from marauding Nazi submarines; that if convoying by American vessels proved impossible, to provide "the gift, loan, or supply" of warships so the Royal Navy might protect the Atlantic supply route; and, to that end, to encourage the Irish Free State government to grant Britain naval bases on Ireland's western and southern coasts. In addition, Churchill asked for many more merchant ships, 2,000 combat aircraft a month, and machine tools that would allow the British to make their own ammunition and small arms.

Then came the nub. "The more rapid and abundant the flow of munitions and ships which you are able to send us, the sooner will our dollar credits be exhausted," Churchill wrote. The current orders for arms "many times exceed the total exchange resources remaining at the disposal of Great Britain. The moment approaches when we shall no longer be able to pay cash for shipping and other sup-plies." While Britain was happy to foot the bill, he hoped the presi-dent would agree that "it would be wrong in principle . . . if, at the height of the struggle, Great Britain were to be divested of all sale-able assets so that after victory was won with our blood, civiliza-tion saved, and time gained for the United States to be fully armed against all eventualities, we should stand stripped to the bone."

The prime minister ended his plea: "If, as I believe, you are con-vinced, Mr. President, that the defeat of the Nazi and Fascist tyranny is a matter of high consequence to the people of the United States and to the Western Hemisphere, you will regard this letter not as an appeal for aid, but as a statement of the minimum action necessary to the achievement of our common purpose."[20] Roosevelt agreed with Churchill. But what to do? When helping draft Churchill's missive, Lothian purposely played on the president's acute sense of personal responsibility and sense of history. He was aware that "the knowledge that some day [the letter] might be published would act as a continual spur in meeting our requirements for fear lest it should be said in years to come, 'He knew, he was warned and he didn't take the necessary steps.'"[21] Roosevelt and Churchill were engaged in a game of chicken. Both believed that America, Britain, and Western democracy were at stake in the war, yet the president was incapable of persuading the isolationists in Congress to fund Britain's arma-ments, and the prime minister was short of dollars but reluctant to let Britain go bankrupt. Unless he found a means to help Brit-ain, the president would stand accused of dismantling the British Empire at the point of a German gun and bankrupting America's closest ally at the moment of its direst need. The shortage of British dollars also affected the pace of American rearmament. By the end of 1940, Britain had invested $2 billion in American arms compa-nies, including $880 million constructing state-of-the-art warplane plants. Roosevelt worried that Britain would no longer be able to invest in new war equipment factories and the consequent American jobs if they were to go broke.

Lothian made his final contribution to the debate on Decem-ber 11, the day before he died. He had been doubly cursed by Nancy Astor. She had, first, invited him to her weekend house parties at Cliveden, which had caused him to be dubbed, not entirely unfairly, an appeaser and, less fairly, a defeatist. He recovered from that taint by waging a strenuous campaign in Washington to encourage America to arm Britain. But in her second curse, Astor had converted him to Christian Science, which proved fatal. He contracted a liver complaint in early December and refused the medical attention and blood transfusions that would have saved his life. His last speech was read out while he was lying on his deathbed. It was addressed to Roosevelt: "If you back us, you won't be backing a quitter."[22]

It was a mark of how central Churchill now believed Anglo-American relations to be that at first he suggested as Lothian's replacement David Lloyd George, the larger-than-life World War One prime minister who had been a principal figure in shaping the Treaty of Versailles. However, Lloyd George's advanced age, seventy-seven, and the receipt of a number of skeptical letters from Commonwealth leaders caused Churchill to change his mind and he decided instead to send the foreign secretary, Halifax, whom he had beaten to the premiership. Churchill was glad to be rid of Halifax, who, as a rare remaining holdout from the Chamberlain cabinet, was still liable to argue from time to time for a negotiated peace.

Roosevelt returned to the White House on December 14, refreshed and ready for action. Awaiting him was a belatedly delivered letter of congratulation on his election victory from a much relieved Churchill, carefully tailored to flatter Roosevelt's growing sense of his place in history. "We are entering upon a somber phase of what must evidently be a protracted and broadening war," the prime minister wrote. "Things are afoot which will be remembered as long as the English language is spoken in any quarter of the globe."[23] The letter's subtext stressed their shared Anglo-Saxon heritage while at the same time alluding to the alternative: a world in which the world's common tongue was German.

It was time for Roosevelt to unveil what biographer Conrad Black judged "one of the most brilliant ideas of his career."[24] With this ingenious notion, the president managed to square the circle. It would help Britain, continue American rearmament at full throttle, avoid proposing a measure that Congress would not pass, was unlikely to be subverted by the isolationists, yet would continue to placate them by keeping America at arm's length from the war. Like the New Deal, it was Roosevelt at his most imaginative and practical. In an act of political genius, he slipped it out as if it were hardly worth mentioning in a routine press conference called after his Caribbean absence.

"I don't think there is any particular news, except possibly one thing that I think is worth my talking about," he told the assembled reporters.

> There is absolutely no doubt in the mind of a very overwhelming number of Americans that the best immediate defense of the United States is the success of Great Britain in defending itself and that, therefore, quite aside from our historic and current interest in the survival of democracy in the world as a whole, it is equally important from a selfish point of view of American defense that we should do everything to help the British Empire to defend itself.

He reminisced about the time, at the outbreak of World War One, when he met some friends in the smoking car of the Bar Harbor Express, all "eminent bankers and brokers," returning from their holiday homes in Maine. They all insisted there was not enough money in the world for the war to continue beyond three months, or maybe six months at most, and Roosevelt disagreed. He even put bets of five dollars here and there that the war would last far longer. "I must have made a hundred dollars," he said. "I wish I had bet a lot more." The anecdote was to show that "no major war has ever been won or lost through lack of money."

Talking "selfishly, from the American point of view, nothing else," he said that orders for military equipment from Britain helped America's defense "because they automatically create additional facilities." At first, he thought the only way to allow Britain to continue investing and ordering supplies from American factories was to repeal the neutrality laws and lend the Brits cash, either through banks or from government coffers. An alternative would be for America to make a gift of "all these munitions, ships, plants, guns, et cetera." He ruled that out. "I am not at all sure that Great Britain would care to have a gift from the taxpayers of the United States," he said.

But there was another way, he said, that did not involve money or mortgages or gifts. "What I am trying to do is to eliminate the dollar sign," he said. "Get rid of the silly, foolish old dollar sign."

Suppose my neighbor's home catches fire and I have a length of garden hose four or five hundred feet away. If he can take my garden hose and connect it up with his hydrant, I may help him to put out his fire. Now, what do I do? I don't say to him before that operation, "Neighbor, my garden hose cost me $15. You have to pay me $15 for it." . . . I don't want $15. I want my garden hose back after the fire is over.

If it goes through the fire all right, intact, without any damage to it, he gives it back to me and thanks me very much for the use of it. But suppose it gets smashed up—holes in it—during the fire. We don't have to have too much formality about it, but I say to him, "I was glad to lend you that hose. I see I can't use it any more. It's all smashed up." . . . He says, "All right, I will replace it." Now, if I get a nice garden hose back, I am in pretty good shape.[25]

Thus, Lend-Lease was born. As Roosevelt knew, there was little chance that Britain would ever pay for the war supplies they were about to be lent. His hosepipe banter was the most elegant and fanciful piece of American fiction since Mark Twain penned *Huckleberry Finn*.

When it came to drafting what Roosevelt liked to call the "Aid-for-the-Democracies bill," he was eager to be aboveboard. "We don't want to fool the public, we want to do this thing right out and out," he told Morgenthau,[26] who was set the task of wording the legislation. The two bills were drafted by Frankfurter, by now a Supreme Court judge, the screenwriter Ben Cohen,[27] and two of Morgenthau's most trusted aides, Edward H. Foley and Oscar S. Cox, to the president's specific brief to provide legislation "in the blank check form."[28]

The draft presented to the Senate and the House asked that the president, "notwithstanding the provisions of any other law," be given powers to "sell, transfer title to, exchange, lease, lend, or otherwise dispose of" any "defense article" to "the government of any country whose defense the President deems vital to the defense of the United States" and to accept in eventual payment for the supplies "any other direct or indirect benefit which the President deems satisfactory." The "any other law" line was included to circumvent the neutrality laws that Roosevelt had found it so hard to repeal. No president had asked for such wide-ranging powers outside of wartime.

British reaction to the wording was one of joy and amazement. Unnamed "British political leaders" were quoted as saying it was "the absolute ultimate" they could have hoped for. The whole tone of the bill "demonstrated to the world the tremendous lengths to which the United States was prepared to go to supercharge Britain's war machine." The *New York Times* reported that the bill "was assured a reception by the man in the [London] street no less enthusiastic than if an important British military victory had been announced."[29]

THE SCENE WAS NOW set for a pitched battle over Lend-Lease that extended far beyond the set-piece skirmishes staged in the House and Senate. America was as deeply divided over Lend-Lease as it had been over any issue since emancipation. On one side stood the interventionists centered around the president and his entourage, seconded by well-connected Century Club members, backed by the massed ranks of William Allen White's Committee for Peace through Revision of the Neutrality Act, the Committee to Defend America by Aiding the Allies, and similar pro-British, pro-Greek, and pro-democracy groups, along with the *New York Times*, the *Christian Science Monitor*, and the *Herald Tribune*.

Lined up against them was America First led by Wood—only founded in September, but picking up considerable public support—as well as a coalition of pacifist, socialist, Communist, and nationalist groups, given supportive column inches by McCormick's papers led by the *Chicago Tribune*, and the Hearst press including the *San Francisco Examiner*. By the end of February 1941, America First had 650 local groups distributing 1.5 million leaflets, 750,000 campaign buttons, and 500,000 bumper stickers. Money came from large donors and small. Kennedy's son John, in his senior year at Harvard, sent a $100 check with a note, "What you are all doing is vital."[30] He was joined by future president Gerald R. Ford and the future Peace Corps director Sargent Shriver.[31]

Roosevelt told senators Barkley, Harrison, and Byrnes on January 3 that he would present them with "a comprehensive plan for all-out aid to Great Britain 'short of war'."[32] Both sides began scouring the nation to find suitably persuasive witnesses to put their cases before the congressional hearings that would start in a couple of weeks.

Most of the big guns were on the side of the interventionists, starting with the president himself. There could be no more eloquent advocate for helping Britain than Roosevelt, and he was prepared to use without restraint the persuasive might of his office in what Theodore Roosevelt had called "the bully pulpit."[33] The anti-interventionists, like Henry Luce, who were internationalists but still wished to keep out of the war, and the all-out isolationists found it more difficult to recruit first-rate campaigners.

By 1940, Lindbergh had been devoting most of his time to trying to help isolationists organize. He was in at the birth of America First, which was based in Chicago with its large German American population, and the No Foreign War campaign, which worked out of the Lexington Hotel in New York. Lindbergh's diaries through that summer and into the winter are littered with rendezvous in hotel rooms or at the Engineers' Club, New York. Pressed to take a personal lead, he persuaded his fellow campaigners that he could more effectively promote their cause if he maintained his independence from individual groups.

But that was not the only reason. He was aware that his co-conspirators were mostly third-rate characters, naive and callow students, businessmen with plenty of money but without experience of public speaking or organizing, and self-seeking egomaniacs hitching a ride to national fame on a nascent political movement. Lindbergh was happy to plan endless rallies, mail shots, and newspaper publicity campaigns, but he was always sure to keep himself at a safe distance from them.

"The people who stand against our involvement in the war are badly organized at this time, and I believe we are rapidly approaching a crisis," he wrote on December 12, 1940.[34] The following day he reported, "Up to the present time there has been too large a percentage of cranks and people with strange ideas."[35] Even prominent supporters of isolationism were downhearted, Wesley Stout of the *Saturday Evening Post* telling Lindbergh that he expected his paper would continue opposing intervention "but that it looks 'like a losing fight.'"[36]

As 1941 approached, and Americans waited on Roosevelt's fireside chat that would explain why he was asking for Lend-Lease, Lindbergh, too, felt victory slipping away. "The country—or is it the newspapers?—blows hot and cold on the war," he wrote. "People do not understand either the issues or the conditions which now exist."[37]

Every now and then, he attended meetings to discuss the prospect of America entering the war only to discover that he was surrounded by prowar zealots. After one such encounter at Princeton, he wrote, "During many of the conversations it was taken for granted that the most desirable course of action for this country was that which would be of greatest aid to England, whether or not it involved us in war! . . . In other words, the prime concern of the conference seemed to be the future welfare of England rather than of the United States! . . . I kept wanting to remind them that we were in *America* and not *England*."[38]

Lindbergh had intentionally kept away from Kennedy, for fear the ambassador might be embarrassed by being associated with such a prominent opponent of Roosevelt, but on November 29 he and Anne were invited at short notice to meet with the ambassador in his suite at the Waldorf Towers. "He feels, as we do, that the British position is hopeless and that the best possible thing for them would be a negotiated peace," wrote Lindbergh. "He said the damage done by bombs was far greater than had been admitted and that the British could not continue for long to stand the present rate of shipping loss. He said that war would stop if it were not for Churchill and the hope in England that America will come in."

Kennedy believed that the German submarine war against merchant shipping in the Atlantic was proving so effective the British had just two months' food before being starved into submission. "Kennedy says he intends to fight to the limit American entry into the war, that he thinks our entry would be unsuccessful and do nothing but damage," wrote Lindbergh.[39]

A few days later, in a further attempt to find a charismatic leader to be the isolationists' champion, two leading lights of America First, Douglas Stuart and Hanford MacNider,[40] flew to meet Kennedy in West Palm Beach. They explained that Wood wanted to take a less conspicuous part in the movement and asked the ambassador whether he would become chairman and principal spokesman. Kennedy was encouraging but noncommittal.

On December 19, the day after the president announced Lend-Lease, the pair wrote formally offering Kennedy the position. He replied on the 23rd, saying that he would like to help but as he was still technically an ambassador he was inhibited from joining any political group.[41] He said he supported their cause but would probably wait until "sometime in January," when it became clear what the president was proposing, before he joined the debate. He signed off "with warmest personal regards."

Wood thought Kennedy's rejection an act of cowardice and wrote a stinging note. "You are the one man who can speak with authority," he said. "I believe that if you made some speeches or wrote some articles explaining why it would be disastrous for this country to get into the war, it would turn the tide. I believe it is your duty to do so."[42]

The battle of Lend-Lease opened with Roosevelt in a strong position and the isolationists scrabbling to find a true leader. Then came a bombshell. William Allen White, the populist owner and editor of the *Emporia Gazette*, in Kansas, and national chairman of the interventionist Committee to Defend America by Aiding the Allies, abruptly resigned to join the non-interventionists, claiming in his resignation letter that the committee contained members "ghost-dancing for war." He sent the letter to Howard, who published it with great glee in full in the *New York World–Telegram*.

"White says, among other things, we should stay out of this war, that we should not carry contraband into the war zones, that we should not repeal the Johnson Act, or use the Navy to convoy," reported a delighted Lindbergh. "He says that if he were making a motto for the use of his committee . . . it would be 'The Yanks Are Not Coming.'" Lindbergh was encouraged. "The antiwar sentiment seems to be gaining, at least momentarily, in this country."[43] He fired off a public statement of congratulation to White, the first press notice he had issued since his baby son was kidnapped eight years before.

Eager to grasp the initiative delivered him by White's defection, Wood, despite his wish to desert the front line, fired a salvo, sending a telegram to the president on December 28, the day before Roosevelt was to deliver his Lend-Lease fireside chat. Wood told the president he was "confident that you will impress upon the nation your pre-election statements that under no conditions will you involve our nation in war abroad."[44]

Roosevelt was aware that his broadcast was the key to winning

American support for Lend-Lease. Having scored a hit with his hosepipe analogy, Roosevelt cast his net wide among his intimates asking for other ingenious, striking phrases to inspire the nation. The key words emerged from an unlikely source. Over lunch with Frankfurter, the Free French official Jean Monnet, now a member of the British Supply Council arranging the purchase of war supplies for Britain, summed up America's role in a single, simple phrase. As soon as Frankfurter heard it, he ordered Monnet not to repeat it to anyone until the president had considered using it. When Roosevelt heard the soubriquet he immediately made it his own. It proved one of the most memorable and evocative catchphrases of the war: America was to become "The Arsenal of Democracy."[45]

When he began his broadcast from his desk in the White House, Roosevelt met Wood's point head on. "The whole purpose of your President is to keep you now, and your children later, and your grandchildren much later, out of a last-ditch war for the preservation of American independence," he said. The Axis nations had threatened "that if the United States of America interfered with or blocked the expansion program of these three nations—a program aimed at world control—they would unite in ultimate action against the United States." He quoted Hitler's menacing words and paid tribute to the British and the Greeks who were fighting to keep Nazism away from America's shores.

Then he directed his fire at the isolationists. "Some of our people like to believe that wars in Europe and in Asia are of no concern to us," he said. "But it is a matter of most vital concern to us that European and Asiatic war-makers should not gain control of the oceans which lead to this hemisphere." America only remained free because the British navy stood in the way of Hitler. "If Great Britain goes down, the Axis powers will control the continents of Europe, Asia, Africa, Australia, and the high seas—and they will be in a position to bring enormous military and naval resources against this hemisphere," he said. "It is no exaggeration to say that all of us, in all the Americas, would be living at the point of a gun."

"Some of us like to believe that even if Britain falls, we are still safe, because of the broad expanse of the Atlantic and of the Pacific," he continued. "But the width of those oceans is not what it was in the days of clipper ships." The distance between Africa and Brazil was less than a five-hour flight by a modern bomber plane. One of the telegrams he had received "begged me not to tell again of the ease with which our American cities could be bombed by any hostile power which had gained bases in this Western Hemisphere. The gist of that telegram was: 'Please, Mr. President, don't frighten us by telling us the facts.'" He reminded appeasers that even nations that had signed nonaggression pacts with Hitler found themselves overrun by Nazi troops.

He warned of "American appeasers" and "secret emissaries" who spread defeatism and dissension to make it easier for Hitler to conquer America.

> There are also American citizens, many of then in high places, who, unwittingly in most cases, are aiding and abetting the work of these agents. I do not charge these American citizens with being foreign agents. But I do charge them with doing exactly the kind of work that the dictators want done in the United States.
>
> These people not only believe that we can save our own skins by shutting our eyes to the fate of other nations. Some of them go much further than that. They say that we can and should become the friends and even the partners of the Axis powers. Some of them even suggest that we should imitate the methods of the dictatorships. But Americans never can and never will do that.

He warned against clamor for a negotiated peace. "Is it a negotiated peace if a gang of outlaws surrounds your community and on threat of extermination makes you pay tribute to save your own skins?" he asked.

> The people of Europe who are defending themselves do not ask us to do their fighting. They ask us for the implements of war, the planes, the tanks, the guns, the freighters which will enable them to fight for their liberty and for our security. Emphatically we must get these weapons to them, get them to them in sufficient volume and quickly enough, so that we and our children will be saved the agony and suffering of war.

"We must be the great arsenal of democracy," he said. "For us this is an emergency as serious as war itself."[46]

It was a powerful and passionate address heard by three-quarters of all Americans, the highest number ever to listen to a broadcast by Roosevelt. Of that number, polls recorded 80 percent agreeing with the president and only 12 percent disagreeing. Previous polls had shown that until then, 61 percent favored helping Britain even if it led to war.[47]

The "arsenal of democracy" broadcast immensely pleased Churchill, listening on the night that Hitler's bombers were laying waste to the City of London, the capital's financial district. He wrote to Roosevelt, "I thank you for testifying before all the world that the future safety and greatness of the American union are intimately concerned with the upholding and the effective arming of [Britain's] indomitable spirit."[48] He confided to an aide that Lend-Lease "is tantamount to a declaration of war."[49]

Roosevelt's broadcast was going to be a hard act for the isolationists to follow. Wood described Roosevelt's words as "virtually a personal declaration of undeclared war on Germany," which was a feeble and inadequate response in light of the atmosphere of crisis Roosevelt had managed to convey. In this, the first skirmish that led to two months of hard pounding, the isolationists had been outgunned. On January 3, Roosevelt told senators Barkley, Harrison, and Byrnes that he would submit to Congress "a comprehensive plan for all-out aid to Great Britain short of war."[50]

CHAPTER NINETEEN

THE BATTLE OF
LEND-LEASE

Isolationists launch "the Great Debate,"
Kennedy keeps his powder dry, both sides
suffer prominent defections.

PREPARATIONS WERE SOON under way for the legislative battle of Lend-Lease. The isolationists in Congress were not the same people as when Roosevelt had begun his presidency. A number of older figures from the Senate had faded from the scene.

William E. Borah, the Lion of Idaho, had died in January 1940. Ernest Lundeen was killed in August 1940 when his plane was struck by lightning. James Couzens lost a primary election in 1940 and died shortly afterward. And Lynn J. Frazier lost his Senate seat the same year. Old isolationist campaigners Hiram Johnson, aged seventy-four, and Arthur Capper, seventy-five, had run out of steam and played little part in events.[1] Others had changed their minds. George W. Norris, founder of the New Deal's Tennessee Valley Authority, was once a fierce isolationist but, horrified by photographs of the Japanese atrocities in Manchuria, had changed his tune by 1940.

A new generation of isolationists had taken their place.[2] In the Senate, Nye led a formidable group on the powerful Foreign Relations Committee. Fish, the butt of Roosevelt's election speeches, was the ranking member on the House Foreign Relations Committee.[3]

Thus, the scene was set for what isolationists called "the Great Debate." Though there were passionate arguments in homes and bars throughout America, the action was soon focused on Congress, its speeches and hearings from expert witnesses. For once, the whole discussion about whether to intervene in war came together in one place. Every major figure who had taken a position was prominently involved in the battle.

As so often happens in politics, the debate appeared to be cast upside down. Roosevelt led the war party, albeit a party reluctant to go to war, and the Lend-Lease bill was evidence that the president and his administration were convinced that war was imminent and it was time to prepare. The end of Britain's independence would put America next on the Axis conquest list. Yet throughout the debate, Democrats and administration supporters insisted that Lend-Lease would not facilitate America's entry into the war but instead help keep it out.

The isolationists and non-interventionists in Congress were the peace party, yet they saw clearly that Lend-Lease was not a measure to maintain peace but was tantamount to a declaration of war against the Axis. As Taft put it, "I do not see how we can long conduct such a war without actually being in the shooting end of the war as well as in the service-of-supply end which this bill justifies."[4]

The ambiguity suited Roosevelt. Ambiguity was central to his nature, and he reveled in his ability to manipulate others by saying one thing while doing another. The division in his mind appeared to perfectly complement the paradox at the heart of the American people, of whom 85 percent were against military intervention, while 65 percent wished to "aid Great Britain, even at the risk of war." Lend-Lease was an ingenious means to allow Americans to follow these incompatible paths simultaneously.

Those who took part in the Lend-Lease debate did so without benefit of hindsight. The trigger that would eventually draw America into war could not have been imagined at that time. Yet some saw more clearly than others what the future might hold and most of those were conscious that, with or without Lend-Lease, America was already well on the way to war.

Most were aware that the defeat of Lend-Lease would not prevent war unless America was prepared to make its peace with Nazism. For some, even that alternative was better than war. The most pivotal debate on America's involvement therefore emerged as something of a fait accompli, with the characters performing as if in a play, reciting lines that revealed their impotence in the face of a war that, thanks to Hitler's territorial ambitions, was knocking on America's door.

The motive that led Roosevelt to demand a war bill in the guise of a peace bill was his continuing fear of American public opinion, particularly when that opinion was expressed and amplified through Congress. It had been forty months since Roosevelt delivered the "quarantine speech," his initial attempt to educate Americans that conflict might be coming, however much they might wish to remain at peace. Although granted an unprecedented third term, the president had toyed with the voters by telling them what they wanted to hear: that he would not send Americans into a foreign war, even though he knew it was most unlikely that he would be able to fulfill his promise.

He believed war was coming, whatever he promised. But to tell the truth would invite America's defeat as well as his own. Instead, he chose to play an elaborate game of subterfuge, disguising the foreboding that had preoccupied him for years with his stock-in-trade, a well-rehearsed jocularity that, to many isolationists and pacifists, appeared to reveal his true cynicism, cruelty, and deceit.

As the debate in Congress began, the isolationists were in the minority and on the defensive: polls showed that 61 percent of Americans were in favor of Lend-Lease. Gallup suggested that the Southern states were even more in favor of "all-out" aid to Britain than the Anglophile East Coast states. Isolationist strength was concentrated in Chicago and the Midwest. The isolationists were also divided and poorly organized. Bickering at the top of the No Foreign War Committee ensured that its influence on the debate was feeble. Although America First had gathered a great number of supporters opposed to America entering the war, the isolationist movement suffered for lack of a clear and charismatic leader.

Had Kennedy, a well-liked Democrat with ample private funds, agreed to become America First's leader, the debate might have taken a different turn. He might have been able to persuade some Democrats in the House to change their minds and Lend-Lease might have been defeated. But as he remained an ambassador until February 1941, when the president finally named his successor, Kennedy was tied to Roosevelt.

Wood's exasperation at Kennedy's vacillation over whether to head America First was heartfelt; the movement was day by day losing momentum. So long as no replacement could be found, Wood was obliged to remain at the helm. Ill-equipped for such a prominent public role, but undeterred, Wood launched an assault upon the president's expanded powers, picking up on the blank check analogy Roosevelt had privately used when crafting the bill. "He wants a blank check book with the power to write away your manpower, our laws and our liberties," Wood declared.[5]

With Kennedy keeping his powder dry, isolationism's uncompromising star turn was Lindbergh, though he still held no official position in America First and declined repeated invitations to join the No Foreign War Committee. When the committee's chairman, Verne Marshall, nonetheless repeatedly cited Lindbergh as a friend and supporter, the flier was obliged to deny he was involved. "I found myself unable to support its methods and policies," he wrote. Lindbergh's fierce individualism, combined with his need to control every aspect of his life, made him reluctant to work with others even if they wholly agreed with him.

The differences between the two sides in the debate were fundamental, yet less profound than at first appeared. Many isolationists were pro-British and favored American rearmament as well as arming Britain, short of war. Typical was the No Foreign War Committee, which took radio time on New Year's Day for Marshall to declare, "Let no one try to smear us with the brush of the anti-British," for there was nothing in the organization's objectives "which would in the slightest degree hamper or seek withdrawal of full and legal help to our sister English-speaking nation."[6] The committee was, however, alarmed at the Lend-Lease bill as written, giving sweeping powers to the president and depriving Congress of the power to decide when war began.

The issue of convoying was a key difference. Not only would convoying of British merchant ships by the US Navy threaten American lives, it would most likely draw America into direct conflict with German vessels which might in turn trigger general hostilities. Yet how else would the supplies cross the Atlantic safely? As historian Charles A. Beard, sympathetic to the non-interventionists and highly suspicious of Roosevelt's motives, put it, "It would seem strange for the United States to manufacture huge quantities of supplies for Great Britain, turn them over to British ships in American harbors, and then quietly allow German submarines to send them all to the bottom of the sea."[7] Roosevelt scoffed at suggestions in the press that American ships would soon be accompanying British merchant vessels across the Atlantic. "I have never considered using American naval vessels to convoy ships bearing supplies to Great Britain," he insisted.[8]

For all the questions about how much Lend-Lease would cost and whether it removed Congress's constitutional role in declaring war, the principal argument against Lend-Lease boiled down to a simple contention: a measure designed to keep America democratic and safe from war would lead to dictatorship at home and Americans fighting abroad.

One substantial figure did emerge to rally the isolationist cause, but he, too, felt unable to accept the leadership of the opposition to Lend-Lease: the former president Herbert Hoover. He was not an ideal champion. Few former presidents find it easy to rekindle interest in their ideas after they leave the White House. Voters feel they have had their turn and should make way for new blood. The earnest, able administrator Hoover still suffered from the taint that as president he presided passively over the stock market crash of 1929 and did little in his remaining years as president to counter the mass unemployment and general misery of the ensuing Great Depression.

Hoover was reluctant to rekindle the bruising head-to-head contest with Roosevelt that saw him ejected from the White House in 1932 after a single term. However, Hoover's sense of self-importance and public duty encouraged him to press his personality upon public policy. Willkie called him "the real brains" behind opposition to Lend-Lease.[9] Lindbergh had a more sober view of his movement's tacit leader. "He has stability and, I think, integrity," he wrote. "But he lacks that intangible quality that makes men willing to follow a great leader even to death itself."[10]

As one of Wilson's team during the Paris peace talks in 1919, Hoover had helped to unravel the diplomatic tangle that prevented vast numbers of defeated Germans and Austrians being adequately fed as a result of the Allies' continuing trade embargo. In September 1939, as Europe once again went to war, Hoover had picked up where he left off, urging Roosevelt to persuade Churchill to ease the embargo on all supplies, including food and medicines, imposed by the British upon German occupied territories. Britain was itself under siege and under threat from German occupation. But its over- whelming naval strength ensured it could still freeze ocean-going trade with Germany and its new, hungry European conquests, deprived by their occupiers of food supplies to ensure that Germans were adequately fed.

So long as the Royal Navy dominated the Atlantic sea routes, America was powerless to halt Britain's siege of continental Europe. Lend-Lease offered an opportunity for Hoover to argue for a quid pro quo: the British could have all the war equipment they asked for if they would allow food and humanitarian supplies to reach the vanquished nations. Churchill and Roosevelt viewed Hoover as a naive meddler whose good intentions were jeopardizing their desire to contain Hitler in Europe. Hoover's humanitarian pleas were ignored.

Hoover began to formulate arguments to be marshaled against Lend-Lease in the congressional hearings and to provide rigorous thinking to a campaign conspicuously lacking in brainpower. After a campaign tour against Lend-Lease that took him to a number of cities, Hoover reported to William R. Castle, who had first recruited Lindbergh to become active in the antiwar cause, that Americans still widely misunderstood the purpose of the proposed legislation. "It is a war bill, yet 95 percent of the people think it is only aid to Britain," he wrote.

Hoover thought the bill would award Roosevelt the sort of dic- tatorial powers only granted to a leader in time of war. "The bill: surrenders to the President the power to make war," he said. "Any subsequent action by Congress will be rubber stamp work; empow- ers the President to drive the country still further toward a national socialistic state; [and] empowers the President to become [the] real dictator of opposition policies to the Axis. He can determine who, in what way and how much aid any nation may receive from the United States." [11]

Shortly after the Lend-Lease bills were published in both houses of Congress, Hoover issued a statement questioning the "enormous surrender" of congressional oversight ceded by the new law.[12] He began rallying opponents of Lend-Lease and urged them to speak up. "We have secured a continuous stream of able radio speakers and have more coming up," he wrote. "I think we are going to defeat the big issue in this bill, that is giving the President the power to make war."[13] Beyond questioning Roosevelt's intentions, Hoover also offered advice on how to make the isolationist message better understood. Yet for all his ideas and energy, the former president persistently declined invitations from America First to broadcast for them.

Hoover wrote to Taft, saying that, while he supported helping Britain, questions should be raised about British payments for materiel already contracted and payments made for future supplies. Would they still stand? Or were they to be part of the new arrangement? Hoover also suggested that Britain's war aims should be explored. After its initial goal, to prevent a German invasion of the British Isles, what next? What exactly was America signing up to? When the war was over, how should disarmament and a permanent peace be brought about? Hoover pointed to a profound omission in the president's war plans: if America was drifting into war with other nations, what did Roosevelt hope to get out of it? And what part did he expect America to play in the postwar world? What was the endgame?

A tart early shot at the president came from Wheeler, who hit at the heart of the moral argument about lending rather than giving aid to Britain, considering that the British were the front line of America's defense against the common enemy of Nazism. "If it is our war," Wheeler asked, "how can we justify lending them stuff and asking them to pay us back? If it is our war, we ought to have the courage to go over and fight it. But it is not our war."[14]

At the president's State of the Union address on January 6, Prince Olaf of Norway, driven from his country by the Nazi occupation, sat with Eleanor in the Senate gallery. "The United States as a nation has at all times maintained clear, definite opposition to any attempt to lock us in behind an ancient Chinese wall while the procession of civilization went past," Roosevelt said. "We oppose enforced isolation for ourselves or for any other part of the Americas. . . . The future and the safety of our country and of our democracy are over-whelmingly involved in events far beyond our borders."

He pointed the finger at Lindbergh, Kennedy, and their sort: "We must always be wary of those who with sounding brass and a tinkling cymbal preach the -ism of appeasement. We must especially beware of that small group of selfish men who would clip the wings of the American eagle in order to feather their own nests." As for Lend-Lease, "We are committed to full support of all those resolute peoples, everywhere, who are resisting aggression and are thereby keeping war away from our Hemisphere."[15]

Roosevelt's strictures upset Lindbergh, who wrote in his diary, "The pall of the war seems to hang over us today." His dislike of Roosevelt was intense. "I have tried to analyze his thinking," he wrote, "but it is extremely difficult, for the man is so unstable . . . I feel sure he would, consciously or unconsciously, like to take the center of the world's stage away from Hitler. I think he would lead this country to war in a moment if he felt he could accomplish this object."

Lindbergh realized the stakes were high for both the president and America. "If Roosevelt took this country into war and won, he might be one of the great figures of all history," Lindbergh wrote. "But if we lost, he would be damned forever." He tried to make sense of paradoxical polling that showed Americans in favor of helping Britain while wishing to stay out of the war. "In other words," he wrote, "we seem to want to have Britain win without being willing to pay the price of war."[16]

Roosevelt's State of the Union promised "to change a whole nation from a basis of peacetime production of implements of peace to a basis of wartime production of implements."[17] The president did not wait for Congress to pass the Lend-Lease legislation before demanding a budget of $17.5 billion, of which 62 percent ($10.8 billion) was ear-marked for defense. The 1,000-plus pages of the budget spelled out how the money would be spent: the army would increase its manpower from its June 1940 figure of 250,000 to 1.4 million by 1942 and would be "equipped with the most modern devices of motorized and mechanical warfare"; the navy would increase by 42,000 sailors to 232,000 and be divided into the Atlantic, Pacific, and Asiatic fleets; and it revealed that "behind the lines a whole new defense industry is being built" with federal money, including 125 new plants. Roosevelt appointed labor leader Sidney Hillman[18] and industrialist William S. Knudsen[19] to head the federal Priority Board, to hasten the manufacture of war materiel and commission car makers such as General Motors and Ford to build warplanes. Late in 1940, the government contracted with Ford to begin producing Pratt and Whitney engines, and the following year contracted him to make B-24 bombers. The budget did not include the cost of aid for Britain if Lend-Lease were approved.

Roosevelt worked best one-to-one with political friends and felt he did not quite grasp Churchill's personality or the exact nature of the shortages facing Britain. Churchill was a Falstaffian figure to whom Roosevelt would have to play both Henry IV and the young Prince Hal—a louche fellow who outspent the considerable earnings he made from his prodigious pen. This did not in itself alarm Roosevelt, but until he could effect a face-to-face meeting, he needed to know the man he was dealing with.

There were reports that Churchill, notwithstanding his American mother, was privately anti-American and that, despite the warmhearted letters he wrote to the president, he held Roosevelt in low regard. "You know, a lot of this could be settled if Churchill and I could just sit down together for a while," Roosevelt told Hopkins, which allowed his closest aide, in the absence of an ambassador in London, to volunteer to fly to London and arrange a summit between the two leaders. With some reluctance, Roosevelt agreed.

Since contracting stomach cancer in 1937, Hopkins had taken permanent refuge in the White House, having stayed over one night after dinner and then failed to move out. In the intervening years, he had established a pivotal role in Roosevelt's life as his principal confidant and fixer, a worthy successor to Louis Howe, who had so ably managed Roosevelt's early political career.

Roosevelt told reporters on January 3 that he would be sending Hopkins to London but refused to be drawn on the purpose of the visit. Asked whether Hopkins had been given any special brief, the president said, "No, no, no." Asked whether Hopkins would be given a title, he replied, "No, no." Asked whether Hopkins would travel alone, the president said, "No, and he will have no powers."[20] So, on January 7, Hopkins boarded a Pan Am Clipper bound for Lisbon to discover exactly what Churchill was like and what Britain most urgently needed. Roosevelt told Ickes that he wanted Hopkins to get properly acquainted with the prime minister "so that [Hopkins] can talk to Churchill like an Iowa farmer."[21]

Two days after the State of the Union, on January 8, a second defection rocked the Lend-Lease debate, a desertion far more significant than William Allen White's switch to the non-interventionists. Wendell Willkie, who throughout the election had adopted a robust non-interventionist stance, told a meeting of the Women's National Republican Club at the Hotel Astor, New York, that "America cannot remove itself from the world.... If Britain falls before the onslaught of Hitlerism, it will be impossible over a period of time to preserve the free way of life in America." He issued a warning: "If the Republican party . . . makes a blind opposition to [the Lend-Lease] bill and allows itself to be presented to the American people as the isolationist party, it will never again gain control of the American government."[22]

The next day, January 9, from his headquarters at the Hotel Commodore, New York, Willkie declared his unequivocal support for Lend-Lease. He agreed that power to administer the scheme should be vested in the president alone, "because democracy could defend itself from aggression only by giving extraordinary powers to the elected executive," and he warned against "appeasers, isolationists, and lip-service friends of Britain" who would seek to sabotage the bill.[23]

Some slight differences with the administration remained. Willkie insisted on "thorough debate" of Lend-Lease in Congress, while the White House wanted it passed with minimum delay. Willkie also wanted a time limit set on Lend-Lease powers, allowing Congress at regular periods to decide whether to continue them.

There was talk of complicity between the president and his former rival when it was revealed that Willkie, like Hopkins, was also going to London to meet Churchill. This sense of collusion was heightened when Willkie traveled to Washington to be personally briefed by Hull for two hours on the state of the war, then met alone with Roosevelt, who gave him a personal letter of introduction to Churchill.

The president took a piece of headed paper and wrote, "Wendell

Willkie will give you this—he is truly helping to keep politics out over here." Until that moment, even in the heat of the election, the president had not once mentioned Willkie by name. Then, noting that "I think this applies to you people as it does to us," he wrote from memory some lines by Longfellow.

> Sail on, O Ship of State!
> Sail on, O Union strong and great!
> Humanity with all its fears,
> With all the hopes of future years,
> Is hanging breathless on thy fate![24]

After a time, Churchill responded with some verse by Arthur Hugh Clough.

> For while the tired waves vainly breaking
> Seem here no painful inch to gain,
> Far back, through creeks and inlets making,
> Comes silent, flooding in, the main.
> And not by eastern windows only,
> When daylight comes, comes in the light,
> In front the sun climbs slow, how slowly,
> But westward, look! the land is bright.[25]

Willkie's defection set off a wave of recrimination among Republicans. Willkie's immediate predecessor, Landon, who had been roundly defeated by Roosevelt in 1936, asserted that Willkie would not have been nominated by the Republicans in 1940, nor would Roosevelt have been elected, if voters had known that the two men agreed on American involvement in the war. "There is no essential difference between Mr. Willkie's position and Mr. Roosevelt's position, which is to go to war if necessary to help England [sic] win," Landon declared.

Isolationists felt duped, and reminded one another that Willkie had been foisted on them by rich eastern seaboard Republican bigwigs. They convinced themselves that Willkie's desertion would not affect a single vote in Congress. But their claim that, having so recently been a Democrat, Willkie was no longer the Republican leader was somewhat confused by a declaration by Senator Warren R. Austin,[26] acting head of the party, that he would support

Willkie on Lend-Lease so long as the president's powers were kept in check. McCormick, however, was furious at Willkie's treachery. "Mr. Willkie entered the Republican party as a mysterious stranger," his *Chicago Tribune* wrote. "He may take his leave, quite as suddenly, still a stranger to the party's principles, although no longer mysterious."[27]

The day Willkie defected, the president invited congressional leaders to the White House to discuss management of the bill through Congress. No Republican was invited. The bill was to be launched in both houses simultaneously on January 17. Frankfurter came up with the title, "a bill further to promote the defense of the United States, and for other purposes," and the House parliamentarian, Lewis Deschler,[28] artfully numbered it HR 1776, the year of America's declaration of independence from British rule.

Fish, leading the charge against the bill in the House, took aim at his old tormentor. "It looks as if we are bringing Nazism, fascism, and dictatorship to America and setting up a Führer here," he said. John M. Vorys, a Republican from Ohio, judged the bill little more than "a streamlined modern declaration of war."[29]

In the Senate the next day, the arch-isolationist Hiram Johnson, ranking member of the Foreign Relations Committee, who had lent his name to the bill forbidding arms sales to belligerents, was quick off the mark. "I am neither an appeaser nor a Hitlerite. I want to see Hitler whipped and Britain triumphant," he said. But the bill was "monstrous." "I decline to change the whole form of my government on the specious plea of assisting one belligerent." He said the bill would make America a dictatorship and "a member of the totalitarian states."

Taft said the bill "combines all the faults of the worst New Deal legislation, including unlimited delegation of authority and blank-check appropriations." Only a "rubber-stamp Congress" would agree to such terms. Clark summed up the general feeling among isolationists, that they were being presented with "a bill to authorize the President to declare war abroad and a totalitarian government at home."[30]

Landon made an early entry into the debate, dismissing Lend-Lease as a typically "slick scheme" of Roosevelt. He, too, claimed to support sending arms to Britain, but drew a line close to America's borders for where help should cease. "Those who really mean all aid to England [sic] short of war should specifically say: no convoying, no American ships in war zones," he said. "The minute an American ship is sunk and the American flag is fired upon and Americans are killed, we are then in the war, as we should be, with men."

Like Kennedy, he doubted that a British victory was, as Roosevelt contended, essential to America's national interest. "If Hitler wins, it will be a 'new and terrible era' for a time," he said. "But in the end free labor will always whip forced labor, and without going to war to do it." He recommended direct subsidies to Britain, an option that "runs no risk of involving us in war." As for the hosepipe comparison, "The lending of war material, the garden hose scheme, might better be compared to lending a cake of ice in July in Kansas, with the same hope of recovery."[31]

Before the debate opened in Congress, Senator Wheeler of Montana had invited Johnson and eight other leading non-interventionists to plot opposition to the president's measure in both houses. When Johnson declined the leadership, Wheeler stepped up. Wheeler, who was unwell the day the debate opened in the Senate, sent a message saying he would address Lend-Lease in a broadcast the following Sunday.

His was a more complex position than many opponents of intervention, as befitted his colorful personal history. Born in Massachusetts and finding work first in Boston, Wheeler's life might have turned out differently had he not broken a journey in Butte, Montana, lost everything to card sharks playing poker, and stayed on to practice law. He became a progressive, left-leaning, pro-labor Democrat dubbed "the Yankee from the West." He stood against Roosevelt in the 1924 election as the Progressive Party's vice presidential candidate, with Robert La Follette Sr. at the top of the ticket. He became a putative presidential candidate himself in 1940 when the powerful anti-Roosevelt labor leader John L. Lewis, a staunch isolationist, led a "Draft Wheeler" campaign.

Wheeler may have looked mild, with a soft face, wire-framed spectacles, and thinning hair, but his political style was anything but. Although he had been in favor of the New Deal, he parted ways with Roosevelt when the president tried to pack the Supreme Court in 1937. Wheeler's much-heralded Sunday evening broadcast on January 12 alluded to the New Deal's Agricultural Adjustment Act, known simply as "Triple A." To lift cotton prices, Triple A paid farmers generous subsidies to destroy a quarter of their cotton crop and plow it under.

Wheeler found in the Lend-Lease bill a headline-grabbing comparison he knew would inspire isolationists in the Midwest, who had benefited most from the New Deal. He called Lend-Lease "the New Deal's 'Triple A' foreign policy" that would "plow under every fourth American boy." If Americans wanted to back Britain, he said, "then we should lend and lease American boys. . . . Our boys will be returned. Returned in caskets, maybe. Returned with bodies maimed. Returned with minds warped and twisted." The analogy may have been apt, but Wheeler's blunt words were widely considered a tasteless slur on the president's intentions.

Wheeler further charged:

> Never before have the American people been asked or compelled to give so bounteously and so completely of their tax dollars to any foreign nation. Never before has the Congress of the United States been asked by any President to violate international law. Never before has this nation resorted to duplicity in the conduct of its foreign affairs. Never before has the United States given to one man the power to strip this nation of its defenses. Never before has a Congress coldly and flatly been asked to abdicate.[32]

Wheeler's brutal description of what war would mean to American families set the tone for the rest of the battle. Roosevelt usually met criticism with a grin and a smart remark. But he was so aghast at being pictured as a butcher that he told White House reporters he was disgusted by Wheeler's contribution, accusing him of saying "the most untruthful, the most dastardly, unpatriotic thing that has ever been said. That really is the rottenest thing that has been said in public life in my generation." For once the president insisted, "Quote me on that."[33]

Wheeler was not done. The following week, he accused Roosevelt of diplomatic skullduggery, charging that Churchill had secretly demanded "a declaration of war by this country" and that Hopkins's mystery mission to London was to discover "what immediate steps can be taken [by America] short of a war declaration." He claimed that the British government was demanding far more than the president was admitting. "They not only want planes and ships at this time, but they also want pilots to man the planes and sailors to man the ships," he said. "Every American ought to realize that Mr. Roosevelt is leading us down the road to war, not step by step but leap by leap."[34] Wheeler felt that by calling him out on the prospect of American boys dying in the field of battle, he had disturbed Roosevelt's eternally calm demeanor. "Apparently the President lost his temper," he remarked with glee.[35]

Isolationism was not merely a conservative phenomenon, as a rally of 20,000 Communists in Madison Square Garden, New York, in January 1941, to mark the death of Lenin, dramatically attested. Earl Browder, the Communists' general secretary, declared that America was already "in the war." Wilson had been modest in his ambition to "make the world safe for democracy"; Roosevelt "proposes to take his brand of democracy and that of Winston Churchill and make it supreme over the whole world." Israel Amter, who presided over the convention, said, "Roosevelt tells us that the war is being forced upon us. But is it not a strange fact that the Soviet Union lies next door to Germany and yet it cannot be forced into the war?"[36] Each mention of the president's name sparked a round of booing.

Roosevelt met with humor the accusation that he was demanding more powers for himself so that he could become a dictator. On January 17, he was asked whether it was true that under the bill he would be able to give away the American navy or buy the Royal Navy. "The bill does not prevent the president from standing on his head," Roosevelt replied, "but the president does not expect to stand on his head."[37] He suggested that perhaps the bill would be worded to allow him to buy the German navy, which would certainly solve one pressing problem. Asked whether he had consulted over Lend-Lease with the Vatican, Roosevelt roared with laughter and quipped that perhaps he should buy the Vatican navy.

Meanwhile, the disparate isolationist leaders lined up the historian Beard, the president's perennial critic, and McCormick, publisher of the *Chicago Tribune*, to persuade Lindbergh and Kennedy to appear as star witnesses in the congressional hearings.[38] On January 10, Fish had sent a telegram to Lindbergh, urging him to testify against the "most important and far reaching Administration bill ever presented to Congress." Lindbergh agreed to testify on January 23.

On January 14, Fish cabled Kennedy and asked him to take pride of place as the first to testify. Kennedy, who as an ambassador remained under his obligation to refrain from criticizing administration policy so long as Roosevelt delayed naming a successor, consulted with Welles. Out in the cold, Kennedy was still angry at the president but needy for his attention. He felt that his reputation had been damaged when Luce's *Life* magazine ran a display of Roosevelt's top "foes" in the Lend-Lease battle, with himself prominent among them, alongside Charles and Anne Lindbergh, and described as "defeatist about Britain, in favor of a quick peace."[39] "I am sick and tired of being attacked by both sides and think I am at least entitled to state my position clearly," Kennedy told Welles, adding, as if there were any doubt, "I'm sore." Kennedy bought radio time to put the record straight, and agreed to appear before the House committee. Hoover, like Kennedy, lived in the Waldorf Towers and made a neighborly visit to the ambassador, who read out a draft of his impending broadcast. Hoover declared it "one of the finest speeches he had ever heard."

Hoover was bullish about the chances of defeating the bill, telling Kennedy that "the Republicans were going to stand quite solidly against the bill and if the Democrats could marshal 50 or 60 votes against the bill they would kill it."[40] Hoover hoped Kennedy would come out cleanly against Lend-Lease and spur a Democratic revolt in the House.

Alarmed at the damage Kennedy might inflict, Roosevelt summoned the ambassador to the White House. Although it was midmorning, Roosevelt, dressed in pajamas, welcomed Kennedy into his bathroom, invited him to perch on the toilet seat, and started to shave. Kennedy told the president he was "for all aid to Britain short of going to war," but warned that if Lend-Lease were forced through Congress against the opposition of people like him, "it would leave a very bad taste."[41] Kennedy urged the president to allow Democrats to make changes to the bill, and Roosevelt said he was prepared to allow an amendment proposed by the Republican James Wadsworth to set up a joint House/Senate oversight committee to monitor implementation of Lend-Lease.

As he left the White House, Kennedy made an ominous remark to reporters, hoping to draw maximum attention to his impending broadcast. "For once, I am going to say for myself what I have in my mind," he told them.[42] Before returning to New York, the ambassador discreetly consulted Wheeler, who said he was "delighted" that the president had condemned his "plow every fourth boy under" remark because it showed the isolationists "were making headway."[43]

Kennedy made his broadcast on January 18. "Many Americans, including myself, have been subjected to deliberate smear campaigns merely because we differed from an articulate minority [that favors arming Britain]," he said. He denied he was or had ever been a defeatist. When he reported from London "the seriousness of the problems that faced the British," he was telling the truth, as was his duty as an ambassador. "A prediction now of England's [sic] defeat would be senseless," he said. "One can recognize the enormous difficulties facing Britain without foreseeing its defeat."

He said he resented being labeled an appeaser by "certain citizens who favor keeping America out of the war." But "if I am called an appeaser because I oppose the entrance of this country into the present war, I cheerfully plead guilty." Helping Britain would give America time to rearm, but "aid should not and must not go to the point where war becomes inevitable."

As for neutrality, "This country certainly has committed acts sufficiently un-neutral to justify a less despotic tyrant than Hitler to declare war," he said. "The American people obviously have not the slightest desire to remain neutral in the face of the aggression of the Axis powers." He asked, who wanted war? "Certainly the isolationists (with whom I cannot sympathize) do not want war," he said. "The President has declared on many occasions that he does not want war. Congress surely is dedicated to the task of keeping us at peace. Why, then, all the shouting?"

America was unprepared for war. "If I could be assured that America, unprepared as she now is, could by declaring war on Germany within the space of say a year end the threat of German domination, I would be in favor of declaring war right now. The inescapable point, however, is that we are not prepared to fight a war—even a defensive one—at the moment." The war in Europe was not America's war. "England is not fighting our battle. This is not our war. We were not consulted when it began. We had no veto power over its continuance," he said.

Finally, he declared himself wholly against Lend-Lease. "I am unable to agree . . . that it has yet been shown that we face such immediate danger as to justify this surrender of the authority and responsibility of the Congress," he said.[44] But if the law passed, Americans should fall in behind the president.

Kennedy's broadcast was a confused, self-contradictory, inconsistent, ill-argued mess that failed to impress either side in the Lend-Lease debate. Where was the decisive, snappy, combative Kennedy of the *Globe* interview? The ambassador was diagnosed by observers as suffering from personal distress at being shunned by the president, yet unable to break free of Roosevelt's embrace. "Mr. Kennedy evidently felt himself to be virtually on trial, charged with disloyalty to the President," was the *Christian Century*'s conclusion. The following night, on the eve of his appearance before the House committee, Kennedy spoke off the record to a small group of Washington reporters, all of whom were left feeling that the next day the ambassador would stop shilly-shallying and launch a blistering assault on Lend-Lease.

In the morning, confident that Kennedy was about to hole Lend-Lease below the waterline, Fish leapt to his feet when the ambassador entered the committee room and shook him vigorously by the hand. Kennedy was happy to be back in the limelight and exuded confidence as he answered questions for five hours. Yet for all the thousands of words he uttered, he only succeeded in magnifying the confusion sown by his broadcast. His most definitive statement was, "I do not want to see this country go to war under any conditions whatever unless we are attacked." Otherwise he appeared muddled, poorly briefed, under-rehearsed, and out of his depth.

He wanted amendments made to the bill but could not say exactly what they should be. When asked point-blank what he wanted to change, he confessed, "I cannot express an opinion on that. I am not an expert on that at all. I have no experience drafting bills. I am afraid I am one of those critics that only becomes constructive after he sees what the other fellow has done." He admitted, "I do not want to make any suggestions, because I do not know what I am talking about."[45] As the daylong testimony came to an end, Fish put a brave face on the confusion, lauding Kennedy as "the one man who, more than any other, is trying to keep the United States out of this war." But few thought Kennedy had lived up to his carefully constructed reputation for talking truth to power.

Kennedy was aware that he had pleased neither side and wrote a self-pitying letter to Roosevelt's son-in-law Boettiger complaining that "if my statements and my position means that . . . I am to be a social outcast by the administration, so be it." The president told Boettiger, "It is, I think a little pathetic that he worries about being, with his family, social outcasts. As a matter of fact, he ought to realize of course that he has only himself to blame for the country's opinion as to his testimony before the Committees. Most people and most papers got the feeling that he was blowing hot and blowing cold at the same time—trying to carry water on both shoulders."[46]

CHAPTER TWENTY

LINDBERGH'S BEST SHOT

*The battle of Lend-Lease continues, Lindbergh
and Kennedy testify before Congress, Roosevelt
asks the FBI to investigate Lindbergh.*

ROOSEVELT'S THIRD INAUGURATION offered a further chance for
the president to win the American people to his side. He used the
address to counter those, such as Anne Morrow Lindbergh, who had
written that democracy was finished and that Nazism and Fascism
represented a "new wave" of politics. He said:

> There are men who believe that democracy, as a form of government
> and a frame of life, is limited or measured by a kind of mystical and
> artificial fate that, for some unexplained reason, tyranny and slav-
> ery have become the surging wave of the future—and that freedom
> is an ebbing tide. We Americans know that this is not true.[1]

Three days later, on January 23, Lindbergh sat before the horse-
shoe-shaped desk populated by the House Foreign Affairs Committee. The gallery was filled with more than a thousand spectators,
eager to catch sight of the celebrity flier. This was the first time press
photographers had been given a prolonged look at Lindbergh up
close since the murder of his baby son in March 1932. Now, subjected for two and a half hours to whirring newsreel cameras and
photographers' flashing bulbs, he felt surrounded by "all the things
I dislike and which represent to me the worst of American life."[2]

Lindbergh did himself no favors when, asked point-blank whether
he was sympathetic to Britain's wish to defeat Hitler, he replied, "I
am in sympathy with the people on both sides." Asked whether he

did not think it was important, in terms of America's defense, for Britain to win, he answered, "No, Sir. I think that a complete victory, as I say, would mean prostration in Europe and would be one of the worst things that could happen." He insisted that America's best interests would be served if there were a negotiated peace. He added that if America were to enter the war, it "would be the greatest disaster this country has ever passed through."[3]

Perhaps because Representative Bloom profusely thanked Lindbergh for being "one of the best witnesses that this committee has ever had,"[4] Lindbergh felt he had performed well. "One or two of the Congressmen were a little unpleasant, but not for long," he reported to his diary. "To my amazement, I found that the crowd was with me. They clapped on several occasions!" As always, however, Lindbergh had only seen what he wanted to see. He despised moderation and got a thrill from articulating unpopular thoughts. "I have no apology to make for the fact that I prefer adventure to security, freedom to popularity, and conviction to influence," he wrote.[5]

The day after Lindbergh's appearance, Hitler made a clumsy intervention in the Lend-Lease debate, claiming that Germany had no intention of waging war on America. "There exists no territorial, strategic, economic or political point of conflict," read the release from the German Foreign Office. "The declaration of the American President that Germany intends to attack the United States is in every way without qualification an invention." It bolstered Lindbergh's claim that America was not vulnerable to attack by long-range bombers because "broad oceans render technically impossible warlike actions by one continent against another."[6]

Hitler might have done better to consult with William R. Castle, Hoover's under secretary of state, who had concluded that after Lend-Lease was passed the Führer would find in Roosevelt a new and wily opponent. By dint of his control of war supplies through Lend-Lease, it would be Roosevelt rather than Churchill who directed the democracies' war strategy. The war was about to become a duel between Roosevelt and Hitler.

After a hectic month of campaigning for and against Lend-Lease, Gallup reported at the end of January that Roosevelt's personal popularity was higher than at any time in his eight-year presidency, with 71 percent approving and 29 percent disapproving. Most telling, 38 percent of those who had voted for Willkie just two months before now approved of Roosevelt as president.[7] The Lend-Lease debate was both educating Americans about war and winning the argument in Roosevelt's favor.

Sometimes the artlessness and naïveté of the isolationists surprised even the president's allies. On January 26, when the Senate committee began three weeks of public hearings, Nye demanded that Roosevelt personally canvass Hitler and Mussolini to discover their war aims and whether they were party to secret treaties. Only in this way, he said, could America avoid playing the "sucker part" in settling the "age-old disputes of Europe," as it had done in World War One. Such simplistic, solipsistic solecisms were hardly helpful to the isolationist cause. As Senate Majority Leader Alben Barkley reminded Nye, it was "rather silly" for those who encountered a man with a knife to another's throat to ask what the fight was about before helping the victim.[8]

On February 6, Lindbergh returned to Washington to appear before the Senate committee. Despite his father's congressional career, Lindbergh had only a bare grasp of how politics on Capitol Hill worked in practice. He expressed surprise that, while much of the senators' questioning was robust and "antagonistic," during the break in proceedings his inquisitors were charming and friendly. "[Senator] Pepper has called me everything from a fifth columnist on down," Lindbergh wrote in his diary, "but he was smiling and good-natured during the lunch hour. In a sense it demonstrates a dangerous irresponsibility in the speech of public men."

Lindbergh's opening statement to the senators allowed him to modify remarks made to the House committee that had, he felt, been misconstrued. He described his opposition to Lend-Lease as twofold: it was "a step away from the system of government in which most of us in this country believe," and it would weaken rather than strengthen America. Speaking "with the utmost frankness," he said he did not believe it "either possible or desirable for us in America to control the outcome of European wars." He favored a negotiated peace because a British victory "would necessitate years of war and an invasion of the Continent of Europe" that would lead to "prostration, famine, and disease in Europe—and probably in America."

Lindbergh did not believe that Britain could win. "If she does not win, or unless our aid is used in negotiating a better peace than could otherwise be obtained, we will be responsible for futilely prolonging the war and adding to the bloodshed and devastation in Europe," he said. While Lend-Lease might buy time for America to rearm, "instead of consolidating our own defensive position in America, we are sending a large portion of our armament production abroad. In the case of aviation, for instance, we have sent most of it."

He returned to his favorite theme, relative air force strengths. He had concluded from tours of European military airfields in 1936, 1937, and 1938 "that Germany was the natural air power of Europe, just as England [sic] is the natural sea power." This judgment was not simply based on what he had seen but on "a combination of factors including geographical and meteorological conditions; national psychology; ability in the design, manufacture, and operation of aircraft; and upon a comparison of existing European air forces and manufacturing facilities." He thought that America could not supersede Germany in air strength "in less than several years."

With Lend-Lease sending warplanes to Britain, Americans would have "England as a bridgehead in Europe. And, one might say, with the American neck stretched clear across the Atlantic. . . . What we are doing . . . is giving up an ideal defense position in America for a very precarious offensive position in Europe." He concluded by saying, "I do not believe that the danger to America lies in an invasion from abroad. I believe it lies here at home in our own midst, and that it is exemplified by the terms of this bill—the placing of our security in the success of foreign armies and the removal of power from the representatives of the people in our own land."[9]

After a jokey start, in which Senator Pepper failed to see the humor in Lindbergh's deadpan response to the question, "When did you first visit Europe?"—"1927, Sir," the year he famously flew solo across the Atlantic—the world's most famous flier was pressed on why he had remained silent on German aggression and atrocities. "Nothing is gained by publicly commenting on your feeling in regard to one side of a war in which your country is not taking part," Lindbergh replied. Five hours of questioning failed to budge him from his mantra that Lend-Lease would "lead to failure in war, and to conditions in our own country as bad or worse than those we now desire to overthrow in Nazi Germany." [10]

Lindbergh's nonchalant disregard of the miseries and outrages inflicted by the Nazis did not bolster the isolationist cause. His views appeared cold and dispassionate when every night radio reporters in Britain told stories of the heroism of ordinary Brits enduring the Blitz. The *Richmond News Leader* wrote, "Millions would vote today to hang Lindbergh or to exile him. . . . Half the letters that have come to newspapers during the past few days have been abuse of him. Some of the communications have been so scurrilous that they could not be printed." The author advised the flier that if he wanted to boost Nazism and keep America out of the war, he would be more effective by "keeping away from the committee room and plotting in the background." [11]

The appearances before the committees of Lindbergh and Kennedy were the dramatic highlights of the Lend-Lease debate, but a great deal of the heavy lifting was done by administration members called to explain how Lend-Lease would work and by congressmen, aware that in the nation's history few debates in Congress were as important as this. Roosevelt was eager to keep his top officials away from the close questioning of the committees, but that was not always possible. At first, the administration tried to prevent Republican members from questioning Marshall, Stark, Knox, Stimson, and George H. Brett, acting chief of the Air Corps, but they were all eventually allowed to testify.

Knox found himself playing cat and mouse with Nye, who asked about convoying. "You stand very much opposed to the idea of convoying merchantmen across the Atlantic?" Nye asked. Knox agreed. "You look upon it as an act of war?" Knox again agreed, though in later testimony he said he was bound by the president's orders as commander in chief and would obey any order given. [12] The isolationists were delighted to discover that Stimson took a different view. He thought supplies could be sent across the Atlantic "if necessary in our own ships and under convoy." Pressed to explain why convoying in these circumstances would not be either illegal under international law or an act of war, Stimson cited resolutions passed at the International Law Association in Budapest in 1934, an argument that would have been more convincing had America ever agreed to them.

The Knox–Stimson double act continued over sea defenses. "We can keep non-American military power out of our hemisphere only through being able to control the seas that surround our shores," Knox maintained. "Once we lose the power to control even a part of those seas, inevitably the wars of Europe and Asia will be transferred to the Americas. We need time to build ships and to train their crews. . . . Only Great Britain and its fleet can give us that time."[13]

In his cross-examination of Stimson, however, Fish drew attention to the moral dilemma raised by Wheeler: if the war Britain was fighting was also America's war, why were we not already at war? "If our Navy is not our first line of defense, and if Great Britain is our first line of defense, then it is our war, and it would be craven not to be in it. But I believe the American Navy is our first line of defense, and always will be, and we do not have to depend on anyone else," said Fish. Stimson replied that he was in favor of helping Britain maintain her fleet. "At present, she, being at war, is providing for the defense of the North Atlantic, and we are vitally interested in that defense."[14]

Later, Stimson suggested to the committee that all America was doing was buying time from "the only nation that can sell it"— Britain—and that the Lend-Lease bill was "about the last call for lunch."[15] He also put to rest a recurring isolationist argument: that to avoid a dictatorship, Congress needed to control the president's actions, even in wartime. Stimson riposted that a "government of law which is so constructed that you cannot trust anybody with power will not survive the test of war."[16] Bullitt also believed that Lend-Lease would give America time to rearm. "Should the British Navy be eliminated and should the Panama Canal be blocked before we are prepared, invasion of the Western Hemisphere would be almost certain," he said.[17]

Morgenthau, who appeared before the Senate committee on January 28, found himself fencing with Johnson, though neither drew blood. In fact, the to-and-fro was remarkably agreeable, even if the irony in the exchange may have been missed by those who read it the following day. Johnson said there was one thing he wanted above all and that was "to keep this country out of war."

Morgenthau replied, "You and me both."

"Do you too?" asked the senator.

"Most fervently."

"I will shake hands across the table," said Johnson, "because there are a great many people in this audience and in this city and in this country at present who want nothing better than to stick us into some war and with all of its bloody consequences."

The Treasury secretary insisted, "It is my fervent prayer that we stay at peace." To which Johnson responded, "We will play ball together."[18]

To head off arguments that there was no need for Lend-Lease because Britain could afford to pay for its own armaments, the president asked Morgenthau to open the British books for inspection by the House committee. "So far as I know, this is the first time in history that one government has put at the disposal of another figures of this nature," said the Treasury secretary. He explained that Britain had so far spent $1.33 billion on American war supplies and could probably afford $1.4 billion more during 1941 for existing orders. Otherwise, Britain had just $1 billion left in dollar reserves. Its $8 or $9 billion in worldwide assets were being used to buy war materiel and support its defense efforts elsewhere.[19]

When Secretary of State Hull was called before the House committee, Roosevelt helped draft his statement to ensure that Hull concentrated on the defensive nature of Lend-Lease, rather than on whether it would tip America into war. The bill needed to be passed to keep the war away from America's shores, insisted Hull in camera before the Senate committee on January 27. His evidence to the House was much the same, but "more frankly and bluntly stated."[20] He expanded the debate to the rest of the world, warning that the Japanese wanted to establish an empire of a billion people that included India, the jewel of the British Empire.

After all of his work behind the scenes of the isolationist movement, Hoover's contribution before Congress disappointed. He told the House committee that his preference was not to stand on the sidelines and watch the British sink but to give them "all of our accumulated defense material which we could spare" and "an appropriation of anywhere from two to three billions [of dollars] with which to buy other things," allowing them "to spend the money directly themselves and to conduct their own war in the way that seems to them to be the wisest."[21]

The discussion about whether Lend-Lease was a defensive or offensive measure was addressed by Democrat John W. McCormack, Majority Leader of the House.[22] "Suppose," he asked, "the people of America should read of the defeat of Britain, what do you suppose would be their feelings? Will it be one of calmness, of safety and security, or will it be one of alarm, one with the feeling of fear, or impending danger? Would not their feelings be properly summed up in the words, 'We are next!'"[23]

Representative E. V. Izak, a Democrat from California, recalled, "I lost all patience with my people when they came to me during the last campaign and said, 'Please don't get us into war.' I said, 'Don't look at me. I am not getting you into war. But there is one man who has the power to do that and that is Mr. Hitler."[24]

Senator J. W. Bailey, a Democrat from North Carolina, was candid. "Some say what is proposed by the bill is intervention," he said. "It is. . . . It is not neutrality. It is the reversal of the policy which we laid down in the neutrality act." He continued, "It is said the passage of the bill will lead to war. . . . I think those who predict that it will lead to war are in a pretty safe position, because there is a great deal of probability that war is coming, either course we take."[25]

Always ready with a colorful quote, Barkley painted a bleak picture of American life if Britain were defeated. "We run the risk of being hemmed in and fenced off as a sort of unilateral concentration camp," he said. "We run the risk of seeing the rest of the world overrun, and then being compelled to fight a hostile world or be overrun ourselves." Asked about the shape of the postwar world, he said, "You might with equal propriety ask a peaceful citizen who is under the heel of a highwayman with a knife at his throat what use he will make of his life if you help him to preserve it."[26]

Anxious that the bill might be lost in the final stages, Hull cabled Willkie in London, where he had met with Churchill three times, and urged him to return to testify before the Senate committee. Appearing on February 11, Willkie was immediately quizzed, in light of his strong support for Lend-Lease, about his opposition to the destroyers-for-bases deal. He explained that he had been against the deal for legal reasons. Willkie said that America had little option but to help Britain. "I really do not think we have any chance of keeping out of war if we let Britain fall," he said. "My judgment is that if Britain collapses tomorrow we would be in a war in a month."[27]

Republican senators relished taking Willkie to task for changing his mind about helping Britain, as the platform on which he had fought the presidential election stated clearly that he did not support America becoming involved in foreign wars. They pressed him on how, in less than three months, he could so swiftly alter his view about the president and his war policies. "I tried as hard as I could to defeat Franklin Roosevelt," said Willkie, "and I tried not to pull my punches. He was elected president. He is my president now." Nye pushed further, reminding Willkie that he had said that if Roosevelt were elected America would be at war by April. What did he think of that prediction now? Willkie smiled. "It was a bit of campaign oratory," he said. The audience roared with laughter.

Willkie failed to find a place in the hearts of either Democrats or Republicans, interventionists or isolationists, but his role was not underestimated by either Franklin or Eleanor Roosevelt. In her newspaper column, "My Day," Eleanor said she was "thankful beyond words" for Willkie's bold intercession.[28] When Hopkins, eager to please the president, began to slur Willkie, he was met with a tart response. "Don't ever say anything like that around here again," Roosevelt said. "We might not have had Lend-Lease or Selective Service or a lot of other things if it hadn't been for Wendell Willkie. He was a godsend to the country when we needed him most."[29] For Hull's top aide Carlton Savage, Willkie was "the real hero" of the battle of Lend-Lease.[30]

To expedite passage of the bill, the administration agreed a number of changes. On January 24, Hoover had sent Vandenberg amendments which would deprive the president of the power to authorize the convoying of British ships by the American navy, forbid the repairing of ships of belligerent nations in American docks, and ban the transfer of American naval vessels to other nations. Only the first amendment was adopted.

A bipartisan conference of congressional leaders was convened at the White House three days later. McCormack told the president that he expected Lend-Lease to pass the House with an "overwhelming" majority in favor, but that certain changes should be made "strictly in the interest of speed and harmony."[31] It was agreed that Lend-Lease should expire on July 1, 1943, pending renewal; that the president was obliged to report to Congress on Lend-Lease every ninety days; and that an upper cost limit to Lend-Lease be set at $7 billion. A more troubling amendment for the administration from anti-Communist House member George Tinkham of Massachusetts, which sought to limit aid to a list of countries including the Soviet Union, was resisted.[32]

On January 30, the House committee reported out HR 1776 by seventeen votes to eight, and on February 8 it passed the House 260–165. The following day Churchill broadcast an impassioned plea for Lend-Lease to pass the Senate.

> A mighty tide of sympathy, of good will and of effective aid, has begun to flow across the Atlantic in support of the world cause which is at stake. Here is the answer which I will give to President Roosevelt: Put your confidence in us. Give us your faith and your blessing, and, under Providence, all will be well. We shall not fail or falter; we shall not weaken or tire. Neither the sudden shock of battle, nor the long-drawn trials of vigilance and exertion will wear us down. Give us the tools, and we will finish the job.[33]

Ever the grateful supplicant, Churchill had told the Americans what they wanted to hear. As Churchill biographer Roy Jenkins explained, the "give us the tools" speech was "a piece of tactical phrasing. . . . The most that he really meant was 'give us the tools and we will hold on long enough for you to take your time about coming in.'"[34]

Only late in the day did the White House invoke the FBI in its attempt to defeat the opponents of Lend-Lease. In February 1941, Roosevelt, brandishing a leaflet describing Lend-Lease as the "War Dictatorship Bill," asked Early, "Will you find out from someone— perhaps the FBI—who is paying for this?"[35] On March 1, J. Edgar Hoover[36] returned with an eight-page report, dated February 7, 1941, that credited the pamphlet to America First but offered little new insight into the organization. Its main donors were Wood, Henry Ford, J. C. Hormel, president of the Hormel Meat Packing company in Minnesota,[37] and J. Sanford Otis, of the Central Republic Bank of Chicago.

The names the FBI linked with America First were eminently respectable, among them Teddy Roosevelt's daughter Alice Roosevelt Longworth; Clay Judson, an attorney with a white-shoe Chicago law firm; Dr. Anton Julius Carlson, a professor at the University of Chicago and a member of the American Civil Liberties Union, whom the report described as "extremely liberal"; Janet Ayer Fairbank, a former Democratic National Committee member; Thomas McCarter, former attorney general of New Jersey; and John Flynn, the resident critic of the president at the liberal *New Republic*.

In the covering note attached to the brief report, Hoover wrote, "If it's the President's wish that a more exhaustive investigation be made relative to the means by which the America First Committee is financed, I hope you will not hesitate to call upon me." Although the FBI kept a watching brief on America First, despite 2,900 pages of investigations the Bureau found nothing untoward. Lindbergh, convinced that his phones were tapped by FBI agents, declared that "if there was anything they didn't understand in my phone conversations, I would be glad to give them additional information."[38]

On March 8, the Lend-Lease bill passed the Senate by sixty votes to thirty-one. Although the division in Congress was roughly along party lines, 15 percent of Republicans in the House and 30 percent of Republican senators voted in favor. When news of the Senate vote reached Hopkins, he telephoned Churchill at Chequers, the British prime minister's country residence, where it was early morning. The moment Churchill woke, he was given the message and called Hopkins, telling him, "The strain has been serious, so I thank God for your news."[39]

With the passage of Lend-Lease, Roosevelt could afford to congratulate himself on a job well done. As his biographer Black explained, "He had in eighteen months, with the help of British heroism, Churchill's leadership, and Hitler's butchery, brought American public opinion along from opposition to any departure from neutrality to a blank check to the President to give all aid short of war."[40]

JESUS CHRIST!
WHAT A MAN!

Roosevelt welcomes Halifax to America,
the US and Britain begin joint military talks,
Hopkins meets Churchill, the Battle of the
Atlantic begins in earnest.

AWARE OF ROOSEVELT'S PASSION for everything to do with the sea and the navy, on January 21 Churchill had sent an innocuous invitation to the president. "You probably know that Lord Halifax will arrive at Annapolis in our new battleship HMS *King George V*," he wrote. "I do not know whether you would be interested to see her." The new battleship, the pride of the British fleet, would arrive in Chesapeake Bay at 7 a.m. on January 24.

The president needed a break. Cooped up in the White House during the long Lend-Lease battle, he had been on edge and was angered by the language used and the deliberate misunderstandings bandied about during the debate. To clear his mind, he dictated notes for a long, vituperative speech, never delivered, that listed all the "many deliberate attempts to scare the people."[1] A day on the sea inspecting a spanking new warship would calm him.

With the puzzled press in tow, Roosevelt set off for the Naval College dock at Annapolis early on January 29, boarded the *Potomac* and set off to see Churchill's new toy. Much to his disappointment, the sea was too choppy for him to be manhandled aboard the 42,200-ton warship. While two American admirals were piped aboard to make a close inspection, he contented himself with having the

Potomac circle the *George V* so that he could see her from every angle. The Halifaxes joined him and, chatting all the way, he drove them to the British ambassador's residence.

It was an extraordinary precedent for a president to take such care in welcoming a representative of another government. As the *New York Times* observed, "It was the first time in American history that a President had left the White House and the capital to meet an Ambassador from a foreign power."[2] Nor was this conspicuous act of kinship lost on Churchill. "There was considerable meaning in this gesture of the President," wrote Halifax's biographer, Lord Birkenhead. "With that sense of timing which [Roosevelt] could at times so brilliantly exhibit he intended to certify to the world in a manner at once dramatic and unmistakable his sympathy with the cause of embattled Britain."[3]

Roosevelt and Churchill were too well brought up in the English style to admit that their friendship contained an element of sentimentality, and both were far softer than they liked to appear to outsiders. A rare glimpse of their closeness at this stage, even before they had met face to face, was contained in a note Churchill had sent in response to Roosevelt's "Ship of State" missive. "[I] was deeply moved by the verse of Longfellow's which you had quoted," wrote Churchill. "I shall have it framed as a souvenir of these tremendous days, and as a mark of our friendly relations, which have been built up telegraphically, but also telepathically under all the stresses."[4]

The arrival of the *King George V* marked the start of direct military collaboration between America and Britain. The previous November, while the Lend-Lease debate was at its height, Chief of Naval Operations Stark had sent a memorandum to the president expressing anxiety about the lack of defense planning. Writing that America's security depended on "the continued existence of the British Empire," he averred "that Great Britain requires from us very great help in the Atlantic, and possibly even on the continents of Europe and of Africa, if she is to be enabled to survive."

His proposal was that America should take the offensive against Germany in the Atlantic while fighting a defensive campaign against the Japanese. He asked permission to begin talks with British military and naval top brass. Without committing himself to Stark's Atlantic-first policy, Roosevelt agreed to let the conversation begin.

King George V did not just deliver Halifax and his wife but five senior British military officers dressed as civilians, traveling under the guise of "technical advisers" to the British Purchasing Commission. The Pentagon was two years away from completion, so the five met with their American counterparts[5] to establish a joint strategy at the US Department of War's temporary home in the Gregory Building on Constitution Avenue on the National Mall.

They quickly approved Stark's plan to divide the war into two theaters, the Atlantic/Europe and the Pacific/East Asia, and that priority be given to Hitler's defeat. While details remained unresolved, by March 27 the Anglo-American team had come up with a plan, codenamed ABC1, short for "American–British Conversations," to be followed if and when America entered the war. What Sherwood called America's "common law alliance" with Britain had been consummated, and what would come to be called "the Grand Alliance" had begun.

The ABC talks failed to resolve an apparent contradiction between the president and prime minister on how to proceed. Churchill, used to running his own show, was convinced that there would be no need for the Allies to launch an invasion of mainland Europe. Unlike World War One, this war "would never see great land forces massed against one another," he said.[6] So long as Britain was able to defend itself from invasion, which with twenty-five army divisions assembled in the south of England seemed assured, it could wait until either the oppressed citizens of the Third Reich and its subservient empire rose against Hitler or until Hitler inevitably turned on Stalin to gain access to Russia's great untapped resources of land, people, and minerals.

Roosevelt knew that American impatience would not allow a waiting game. Americans expected results, and the constant need to keep them pleased guided the president's military strategy as it had done his backdoor entry into the war. The president bided his time, leaving it to Marshall to take the initiative in early June to make American dispositions according to the ABC plan and its derivative, the Rainbow 5 report. Marshall told Stimson, Knox, and Hull that they should interpret the president's silence as assent.

Hitler was in no mood to declare war against the United States, even though the US needed perhaps two years to be fully prepared to counter German aggression. Nor would Lend-Lease appear to have made much difference to Hitler's calculations. As a number of witnesses in the Lend-Lease debate had argued, Hitler already had plenty of grounds to go to war with America if he wished.

A key element in ensuring the swift amalgamation of American and British military efforts was the friendship that grew up between Churchill and Hopkins. On his arrival in Britain on January 9, Hopkins had confided to Edward R. Murrow, "I've come to try to find a way to be a catalytic agent between two prima donnas. I want to get an understanding of Churchill and the men he sees after midnight."[7]

For his part, Churchill understood the nature of Hopkins's mission and was determined to charm him. Churchill's equivalent to Hopkins, Brendan Bracken,[8] was in no doubt that Hopkins was "the most important American visitor to this country we have ever had."[9] But, from what Churchill had gleaned about Hopkins's modest upbringing and his concern for the poor and downtrodden, the prime minister was by no means sure how best to win him over.

In a Foreign Office brief for the prime minister, Hopkins was described as "the old conscience of Victorian liberalism arisen in our midst. He does not believe that a world in which some live in the sun and others in the shadow makes sense. He is sincerely interested to find out if we have similar views and aspirations."[10] There was some amusement to be had in Washington in imagining how Hopkins, a convinced egalitarian and perhaps the most committed New Dealer of all after Roosevelt himself, would get along with the hedonistic son of a duke who swore like a trooper, stayed up until all hours, surrounded himself with what starchy British Tories dismissed as "the Glamour Boys," and downed champagne as if it were Coca-Cola.[11]

When Bracken went to welcome Hopkins off the British Overseas Airways Clipper from Lisbon, he found him on board "still sitting, looking sick and shrunken and too tired even to unfasten his safety belt."[12] By the time Hopkins met Churchill, at 10 Downing Street, he had recovered from the grueling flight across the Atlantic. "A rotund—smiling—red faced, gentleman appeared—extended a fat but none the less convincing hand and wished me welcome to England," Hopkins wrote to Roosevelt from Claridge's Hotel. "A short black coat—striped trousers—a clear eye and a mushy voice was the impression [I got] of England's leader." Hopkins told Churchill, "The president is determined that we shall win the war together. Make no mistake about it. He has sent me here to tell you that at all costs and by all means, he will carry you through, no matter what happens to him."[13]

Churchill remained on best behavior and trimmed his promises about life in Britain after the war to flatter Hopkins's progressive views. In an altogether unlikely lyrical flourish, the prime minister regaled his American visitor with how he hoped, when peace returned, to provide all British homes with electricity, indoor plumbing, and a strong sense of social security.

"As the humble laborer returns from his work when the day is done, and he sees smoke curling upwards from his cottage home in the serene evening sky, we wish him to know that"—Churchill rapped on the table—"no rat-a-tat-tat of the secret police upon his door will disturb his leisure or interrupt his rest." Churchill looked for a response from Hopkins. "What will the President say to all this?" he asked.

"Well, Mr. Prime Minister," Hopkins replied, "I don't think the President will give a damn for all that. You see, we're only interested in seeing that that goddam son of a bitch Hitler gets licked."[14]

Hopkins's first task was to make arrangements for Roosevelt and Churchill to meet in April. Churchill said he was sorry that the rendezvous could not be in Bermuda because "the climate was nice." His idea of the summit was to "bring a small staff—board a cruiser and by accident meet the President at the appointed place—and discuss our problems at leisure." Hopkins quizzed Churchill on whether it was true, as reported by some in Washington, that he was anti-American and disliked Roosevelt. "This set him off on a bitter tho' fairly constrained attack on Ambassador Kennedy who he believes is responsible for this impression," Hopkins wrote to Roosevelt.[15]

Roosevelt had told Hopkins to discover exactly what Britain needed to keep Hitler's forces from invading the Americas. Herschel V. Johnson, the State Department official filling in as ambassador until Kennedy's successor arrived, was grateful that Hopkins was different from Kennedy and others from the administration who had visited Britain. "Some other Americans who had come to London devoted themselves to investigations to determine if the British really needed the things they were asking for," recalled Johnson.

"Harry wanted to find out if they were asking for enough to see them through."[16]

Having decided that Hopkins was both a friend and a good ally, and that he was not averse to having a good time, Churchill treated his American guest to the full wonders of his extraordinary life. This meant weekends in the country, come what may. No military disaster or emergency was too great to prevent Churchill spending time at either Chequers, his official residence, or, when the full moon meant that Chequers was visible to night bombers, Dytchley House, the country estate of Bracken's assistant, Ronald Tree, who had inherited much of his grandfather Marshall Field's department store fortune.

Hopkins witnessed Churchill in full flow at the dinner table, casting his conversational net wide with colorful memories, vivid assessments of wartime strategies, and soaring visions of how victory would be achieved, backed by a vast hinterland of knowledge about history and culture. He learned of Churchill's incessant energy, his short afternoon naps that allowed him to continue working until three in the morning, and his relentless regime of dictating memos, letters, and speeches, all the while sipping champagne, brandy, or Scotch whisky and chomping on a Havana cigar. Hopkins learned how Churchill took in his stride the rhythm of war, waiting for plans to work out and accepting without complaint the nasty surprises the Germans dealt.

Churchill's style was quite different from the calm in which Roosevelt preferred to make decisions. But Hopkins recognized in Churchill a partner of extraordinary drive and focus that belied the character studies provided by those who could not see beyond Churchill's bombast, booze, and bluster. As Hopkins told the British cabinet minister Oliver Lyttelton after a typical late-night session with Churchill, "Jesus Christ! What a man!"[17]

The affection and trust Churchill showed Hopkins was completely reciprocated. Churchill told the president, "It has been a great pleasure to me to make friends with Hopkins who has been a great comfort and encouragement to everyone he has met. One can easily see why he is so close to you."[18] "He was the most faithful and perfect channel of communication, slim, frail, ill but absolutely glowing with refined comprehension of the Cause," wrote Churchill.

"He was a crumbling lighthouse from which there shone the beams that led great fleets to harbor."[19]

"Churchill is the government in every sense of the word," wrote Hopkins. "He controls the grand strategy and often the details. Labour trusts him. The army, navy, air force are behind him to a man. The politicians and upper crust pretend to like him."[20] As Elliott Roosevelt recalled, "Hopkins' mission was only supposed to last two weeks, but he was getting on so famously with Churchill and learning so much that he cabled for permission to stay."[21] Hopkins proved Churchill's most appreciative audience, and officials found that when together they forgot time. "Hopkins was lunching with the P.M. and they were so impressed with each other that their tête-à-tête did not break up till nearly 4.00," John Colville complained to his diary.[22]

Most importantly, Hopkins reported back to Roosevelt that the supplies given to Churchill would not be wasted. "They need our help desperately and I am sure you will permit nothing to stand in the way," he wrote. "I am convinced this meeting between you and Churchill is essential—and soon—for the battering continues and Hitler does not wait for Congress. . . . This island needs our help now Mr. President with everything we can give them."[23]

At a dinner in Glasgow, after Churchill and Hopkins had seen Halifax set off on his journey aboard the *King George V*, to show his solidarity with Churchill Hopkins quoted the book of Ruth. "Whither thou goest, I will go . . . even to the end."[24] Hopkins told a clutch of newspaper editors "the President and those around him were convinced that America's world duty could be successfully performed only in partnership with Britain," and he added that "although America was not yet in the war, she was marching beside [the British], and that should we stumble she would see we did not fall."[25] Beaverbrook confided to Sherwood that Hopkins's words of encouragement at this time "provided more tangible aid for Britain than had all the destroyers and guns and rifles and ammunition that had been sent previously."[26]

Before Christmas, Hopkins had sent a long missive to Roosevelt, listing all of Britain's immediate needs and offering his assessment of the war. "Most of the Cabinet and all of the military leaders here believe that invasion is imminent," he wrote. They were working toward an invasion "not later than May 1" and expected "an all out attack, including the use of poison gas" but that "the Germans will have to do more than kill a few hundred thousand people here before they can defeat Britain." He concluded, "If Germany fails to win this invasion then I believe her sun is set. I am convinced that if we act boldly and promptly on a few major fronts we can get enough material to Britain within the next few weeks to give her the additional strength she needs to turn back Hitler."[27]

Roosevelt did not hesitate. As soon as Lend-Lease passed the Senate, on March 8, Roosevelt cabled Churchill, "Confidentially, I hope to send estimates for new orders and purchases under the bill to the House on Wednesday [March 12]."[28] Lend-Lease completed its passage through both houses of Congress on the afternoon of March 11 and was signed into law by the president half an hour later. The following day, while paying tribute to Roosevelt's "generous and far-seeing statesmanship," Churchill told the Commons that Lend-Lease was more than just a helping hand; it represented "a new Magna Carta" that laid down "the rights and laws upon which a healthy and advancing civilization can alone be erected" and described "the duty of free men and free nations, wherever they may be, to share the responsibility and burden of enforcing them."[29] It was an acknowledgment from the most imperialistic of prime ministers that from that moment Britain was prepared to share with America responsibility for maintaining order in the world.

A week later, Roosevelt responded to Churchill's challenge when addressing the White House correspondents' annual dinner. "America is not a country which can be confounded by the appeasers, the defeatists, the backstairs manufacturers of panic," he said. The great debate over Lend-Lease that had taken place "in every newspaper, on every wave length, over every cracker barrel in all the land" was over. The result was "binding on us all." "This decision is the end of any attempts at appeasement in our land, the end of urging us to get along with the dictators, the end of compromise with tyranny and the forces of oppression." He declared that "every plane, every other instrument of war, old and new, every instrument that we can spare now, we will send overseas" to "the battle lines of democracy." And he added that when the war was won "our country must continue to play its great part in the period of world reconstruction for the good of humanity."[30]

Roosevelt duly signed an appropriations request for $7 billion on March 27. On his return to Washington, Hopkins was placed in charge of the committee advising how best to expedite help to Britain. To the amusement of both Roosevelt and Churchill, the first shipment of Lend-Lease aid contained 900,000 feet of fire-hose.

The handover of power from the British Empire to America came at a crippling cost to Britain. Even after Lend-Lease had passed Congress, Roosevelt kept up his demands that all available British dollars be handed over. Negotiations over the American naval bases in the British West Indies proved troublesome. Churchill urged the British to fall in with America's wishes. "The United States has now openly espoused our cause and has virtually promised us financial help of inestimable value," he told the cabinet on February 6. "We must do what we can to meet American difficulties."[31]

Two weeks later, Halifax cabled Churchill that "it was of the utmost importance that we should without delay hand over to America our remaining resources in that country." Churchill told the cabinet, "We shall have to resign ourselves to meeting American wishes. . . . It is clear we shall receive from America far more than we could possibly give." He said, however, that he would send a private telegram to Roosevelt asking him not to sell British securities "at knock down prices."[32]

Undeterred, Roosevelt had pressed Halifax to put all British investments and businesses in America into the hands of a joint United States and British board. Churchill wrote a pained note to Hopkins: "Is this really necessary? It will place us in great difficulties here."[33] Nonetheless, he complied. By mid-March, when Lend-Lease was the law, Churchill had become a little less patient with Morgenthau's incessant demands. "I am clear that this is no time to be driven from pillar to post," he wrote to Halifax. "Although they may not all realize it, their lives are now in this business too. . . . I refuse altogether to be hustled and rattled. God knows we are doing our bit."[34]

The conclusion of the Lend-Lease bill coincided with a series of setbacks for Britain in Europe and North Africa. At first, in 1941, the democracies did well. The Greeks drove out the invading Italians, which encouraged Churchill to send to Greece some of his North African forces, who were keeping the Italians in Libya from occupying the Suez Canal and reaching the oil-rich sands of the Middle East. But Italian insouciance caused Hitler to take command of the Mediterranean Axis campaign, and before long German forces had occupied Yugoslavia, retaken Greece, and invaded Crete. Even more threatening, he sent his top general, Erwin Rommel,[35] to Tripoli to drive the British from Egypt, and he waged a punishing bombing campaign against the heavily fortified island of Malta, an essential British strategic redoubt in the middle of the Mediterranean, halfway between Sicily and Libya.

The main danger to Britain, however, was the threat to its lifeline across the Atlantic, through which all supplies needed to pass. Frustrated at not being able to invade Britain, Hitler adopted the plan of Grand Admiral Erich Raeder, commander in chief of the German navy, to wage an intense U-boat campaign to disrupt shipping and deny Britain the seaborne deliveries it needed. Ignoring the ban on convoying in the Lend-Lease Act, Stark set about converting the mostly old patrol vessels operating in the Atlantic into a full-scale aggressive Atlantic fleet. In mid-February, he ordered that American warships should be prepared from mid-March to escort British vessels across the Atlantic.

The losses of British ships ferrying supplies to Britain were becoming acute. By March 6, Churchill conceded that Britain was losing the Battle of the Atlantic and appealed again to Roosevelt for immediate help. Drawing upon his experience when assistant secretary of the navy, the president arranged for British merchant ships to be repaired in American ports. As historian Kenneth Davis wrote, "Almost [Roosevelt's] every word, deed, gesture—his every act or refusal of action in response to a specific challenge—had worldwide consequences."[36] The president now fully understood that he was at the helm of the Allied war effort, even though America was not at war.

The Battle of the Atlantic would prove to be the longest-running battle of World War Two, fought on the Allied side largely by merchant seamen under some of the worst conditions imaginable, mostly in the 3,000-mile stretch between Halifax, Nova Scotia, and

Liverpool in the United Kingdom. British and Canadian ships were under attack from "three-dimensional warfare": German surface ships, U-boats, and Focke-Wulf long-range bomber planes, matched by intense bombing of British Atlantic ports.

Britain countered this debilitating assault by bombing German U-boat bases, mostly in the Baltic but also in French, Belgian, Dutch, and Norwegian ports, by mining coastal waters, by patrolling by ship and airplane, particularly in the western approaches to the British Isles that marked the outer reach of Germany's U-boats and warplanes, and by convoying, the bundling together of up to eighty ships with Royal Navy and Royal Air Force escorts until safely out of German range.

Slow ships awaiting protection from warships assembled in Halifax, Nova Scotia, and Bermuda and traveled together, meeting up with others at rendezvous points in the eastern Atlantic before running the gauntlet on their way to Glasgow, Belfast, Liverpool, and Bristol. In that way, hostile raiders were obliged to come under considerable fire if they were to attempt to sink shipping. Allied ships capable of traveling faster than the maximum speed of U-boats, i.e. more than fourteen knots, journeyed alone. Most of the action took place where the sea route narrowed between Scotland and Ireland. Ireland's refusal to allow Britain naval bases proved costly in lives and naval losses.[37]

Since the war began in September 1939, German warships had sunk 5.8 million tons of British, Allied, and neutral shipping. Germany had lost 178 submarines. In April 1941 alone, 488,000 tons were sunk. With Lend-Lease passed into law, the way was open for America to help Britain as never before. But there was still the problem of protecting British ships when the Lend-Lease Act specifically outlawed convoying by American vessels. Convoying soon became the new battleground on which isolationists waged a rearguard action.

WE'VE GOT OURSELVES
A CONVOY

*Isolationists turn their fire on convoying,
Roosevelt attacks the Copperheads, Lindbergh
resigns from the army, Willkie backs the president,
the Royal Navy sinks the Bismarck.*

HALIFAX HAD a tin ear for public opinion and little grasp of American politics, which is why he believed isolationism was finished. "With the passage of the [Lend-Lease] Bill, it can be said that except for a small number of irreconcilable isolationists the whole country is united in its support of the Allies against the totalitarian powers," he wrote home.[1] He declared that the chronic insularity in America that had caused the Senate to refuse to ratify the Versailles Treaty had been roundly defeated.

Hopkins had a clearer view. He told Churchill that the 10–15 percent of Americans who said they supported neutrality were Nazi or Communist sympathizers who, like Lindbergh, prayed for Hitler to succeed; that a further 15–20 percent, led by Kennedy, wanted to help Britain but not if it meant going to war; that 10–15 percent believed, like Knox, Stimson, and most of the military officers, that war was now inevitable and that war should be declared against the Axis; and that Roosevelt, like 50–60 percent of Americans, wanted to give Britain as much help as it needed, even if this meant that America would be dragged into war. As the president was backed by the Knox–Stimson group and also represented a fair proportion of Kennedy's supporters, Hopkins estimated support for Britain at about three-quarters of the country.[2] Gallup confirmed that 72 percent favored the president's support for Britain.

Still reeling from their Lend-Lease defeat, the isolationists regrouped and returned to the attack. On April 1, seventy-one isolationist members of Congress met to discuss how best to continue their opposition to the president. The suggestion that the US Navy should escort British merchant vessels provided a perfect opportunity. Their intransigence gave credence to a view circulating in the British Foreign Office that, even with Lend-Lease now the law of the land, America might still find a way to duck out of playing its part in defeating Fascism.

It was an opinion propounded by the Foreign Office official and later Harvard Business School professor T. North Whitehead, who, after more than a decade in Cambridge, Massachusetts, had returned to London to advise on American attitudes. The Americans, he said, were "a mercurial people." "Until they are finally committed to actual warfare, it would be unwise to assume that, in certain circumstances, the Americans would be incapable of checking their present helpful trend," he wrote. "The Americans are coming on well, but they are not yet in the bag."

It was a view shared by Sir Robert Vansittart,[3] the veteran Foreign Office official whose suspicion of Hitler from the early 1930s had sat oddly with having to lead the British foreign service during appeasement. "Many here have an uneasy feeling that, if we study America, she may in her turn yet rat on us," he wrote. "My country is, for the second time, doing America's fighting for her."[4] His view coincided with that of Fish, who had asked in the Lend-Lease debate, "Is it not rather cowardly of us, if England [sic] is fighting our battle, not to go into the war?"[5]

The isolationists had pressed for a ban on convoying in the Lend-Lease Act. The key line was, "Nothing in this Act shall be construed to authorize or to permit the authorization of convoying by naval vessels of the United States." During the Senate hearings, Nye had extracted a statement from Knox that convoying was an act of war. For opponents of the war, convoying became the key test of the president's sincerity when he said he had no intention of America entering the fray. His remark, made at a press conference on January 21, that convoys would bring America "awfully close to war"[6] was simplified by isolationists into "Convoys mean shooting, and shooting means war" and repeatedly thrown back at him.

After Lend-Lease became law, throughout March the president batted increasingly aggressive questions about convoying. In his speech to the White House correspondents on March 15, he spoke of "the survival of the vital bridge across the ocean—the bridge of ships which carry the arms and food for those who are fighting the good fight,"[7] which suggested convoying. The next day, Senator Carter Glass[8] said he favored convoys, if that is what was needed. The next day, the Committee to Defend America by Aiding the Allies announced its support for convoys. On March 19, a motion was introduced into the House to reinforce the ban on convoying, and on March 31, the Senate debated a proposed ban led by isolationist Charles W. Tobey of New Hampshire. Polls showed, as Whitehead and Vansittart had predicted, that a majority of Americans were not in favor of the US Navy protecting British ships, despite their notional support for Britain against Hitler.

By mid-April, rumors in Washington that "battlecraft of the Navy and Coast Guard are now giving armed escort to munition-laden British merchantmen leaving Atlantic ports for the European battlefront"[9] were swiftly denied by Stark. Early told the press that the president was obliged to protect American shipping and might issue "a sensational announcement that if New York City were attacked by an enemy it will be defended."[10]

The next day, Early confirmed that American vessels were "on neutrality patrol" in the Atlantic and if they encountered "alien ships" they would report the sighting by unscrambled radio message, meaning that anyone, including the Royal Navy, could listen. Roosevelt had gradually extended the reach of naval patrols. In September 1939, the limit was just three miles from the American shore. By November 1940, that had been extended to 1,000 miles. In the spring of 1941, it reached 1,200 miles.

Tobey increased the heat on the White House when he published a letter from an anonymous mother of an American sailor alleging that "the United States has been convoying ships for about 1 month." The accusation was true, in that American naval vessels were accompanying British ships. The administration then made it clear that they were indeed prepared to convoy British ships, however convoying might be defined. On April 24, Knox declared, "We cannot allow our goods to be sunk in the Atlantic—we shall be beaten if they do. We must see the job through. . . . This is our fight."[11] The same day, Hull confirmed that "aid [to Britain] must reach its destination in the shortest time and in maximum quality. So ways must be found to do this."[12]

Into this confusion came Lindbergh, who had finally agreed to join the committee of America First, but had declined the chairmanship. He continued to campaign as if Lend-Lease had not become law and could be repealed. Before "an enthusiastic crowd" of "11,000 inside and about 4,000 outside"[13] at the Chicago Arena on April 17, he claimed that America First represented "the hundred-odd million people in our country who oppose sending our soldiers to Europe again." His aim was "to make America impregnable at home, and to keep out of these wars across the sea." He believed that "sending of arms to Europe was a mistake" and insisted, "Whether or not America enters the war is within our control."

He thought it would be "a tragedy to the world—a tragedy even to Germany—if the British empire collapses. But I must tell you frankly that I believe this war was lost by England [sic] and France even before it was declared, and that it is not within our power in America today to win the war for England. . . . We will not be able to transport an army across the ocean large enough to invade the continent of Europe successfully."[14]

Six nights later, in the Manhattan Center, New York, he told a capacity crowd of 10,000 much the same, but elicited some of the most savage criticism he had yet received. Columnist Walter Winchell reported that "every hate spreader they could find showed up." The newspaper *PM* described the audience as "a liberal sprinkling of Nazis, Fascists, anti-Semites, crackpots and just people. The just people seemed out of place." Rex Stout, chairman of the prowar Friends of Democracy, said that Lindbergh "would be acceptable to Hitler as an American gauleiter."[15]

The following day, Roosevelt insisted to the press that American ships were "patrolling" the Atlantic rather than "convoying" British ships. The words meant very different things, he said. "I think some of you know what a horse looks like. I think you also know what a cow looks like," he said. "You can't turn a cow into a horse by calling it something else. Calling it a horse, it is still a cow." He used the analogy of Western wagon trains that employed scouts to discover whether there were dangers ahead. "It didn't move across the plains unless it got reports from a long ways—200 to 300 miles off," he said. "It was not felt safe to wait until the Indians got two miles away before you saw them."

Then he turned his fire on Lindbergh. Asked why the army, which needed experienced fliers, had not called up Lindbergh from the reserve, he replied, "There are people in this country . . . who are adopting a rather curious attitude." There was "this mythical person in our midst who takes the attitude that dictatorships are going to win," he said, which was "dumb." If anyone doubted that the "mythical person" the president had in mind was Lindbergh, Roosevelt reminded the reporters of the Civil War Democratic leader Clement Vallandigham,[16] leader of the "Copperheads," opponents of the war who constantly demanded that Lincoln sue for peace with the Confederacy.

"Vallandigham, as you know, was an appeaser," said the president. "He wanted to make peace from 1863 on because the North 'couldn't win.' Once upon a time there was a place called Valley Forge and there were an awful lot of appeasers that pleaded with Washington to quit, because he 'couldn't win.'"[17] He commended to the reporters what Thomas Paine had to say about "the summer soldier and the sunshine patriot."[18]

To be attacked directly by the president was too much for Lindbergh. "Roosevelt had implied treason in connection with my name," he wrote in his diary. "The President's attack was more than just a political attack, for he did so in connection with my commission in the Army. . . . A point of honor is at stake." He thought he would have to resign from the reserve. For once, he considered his paradoxical position. "Here I am stumping the country with pacifists and considering resigning as a colonel in the Army Air Corps, when there is no philosophy I disagree with more than that of the pacifist, and nothing I would rather be doing than flying in the Air Corps."

Two days later, he decided to resign, lest "I would lose something in my own character that means even more to me than my commission in the Air Corps."[19] Everywhere he saw conspirators working to do him and America ill. "Most of the Jewish interests in the country are behind war, and they control a huge part of our press and radio and most of our motion pictures," he wrote. "There are also the 'intellectuals,' and the 'Anglophiles,' and the British agents who are allowed free rein, the international financial interests, and many others."[20] Two days after Lindbergh's resignation from the armed forces, isolationists suffered another blow when the Senate Foreign Relations Committee dismissed an attempt to pass a reinforced ban on convoying.

By the start of May, Lindbergh had recovered his composure and, at an America First rally in St. Louis on May 3, explained why he had resigned his commission. It was because "our country should not enter the war in Europe, while the President . . . believe[s] we should take part in that war." He reassured his audience that America was not in real danger, saying, "Bombing planes can be built to fly across the ocean, but their cost is too high and their effectiveness too low to make them a serious menace to this country."[21]

The same day, Willkie made a dramatic reentry into the national debate by writing to the president saying that the Atlantic patrols were inadequate and that he would support convoying. "If I were President," Willkie told reporters, he would ask the armed services the best way to ensure that the supplies reached Britain. "I do not believe the present use of the Navy for patrolling is enough to prevent our production from going to the bottom," he said. He thought Roosevelt's comparison of Lindbergh to a Copperhead ill-advised. "The best way to dissipate Colonel Lindbergh's influence is to show the fallacy of his arguments, not to attack him personally," he said.

Three days after Lindbergh spoke, Stimson, at Roosevelt's urging, told a national radio audience, "So long as [the Atlantic and the Pacific] are under our own or of friendly control their broad waters constitute an insuperable barrier to any armies." He reminded his listeners that "for over one hundred years" the British fleet had protected America, which had allowed America to do without "large standing armies. We have built populous cities upon our seacoast which are easily vulnerable to attack" and "adopted a mode of national life" dependent on the British, whom Americans did not fear.

But Britain was now besieged by Hitler and America still needed two years to rearm. If the US Navy "should make secure the seas for the delivery of our munitions to Great Britain," it would help preserve America's freedom. "Unless we on our side are ready to sacrifice and, if need be, to die for the conviction that the freedom of America must be saved, it will not be saved."[22] It was the closest anyone in the administration had come to saying that war was at hand. America First issued a statement accusing Stimson of being "old womanish and defeatist"[23] and saying that he should have openly asked for congressional consent to convoy and a declaration of war against Germany.

The same evening, at Madison Square Garden, Willkie told a capacity crowd at a "Freedom Rally" that isolationism was an inadequate defense. "One might as well seek to guard his own home with an iron fence while all his neighbors are sickening and dying of a contagious disease," he said. "I care not whether you call safe delivery [of arms supplies to Britain] convoying, patrolling, airplane accompaniment, or what not. . . . We want them protected at once." Arming Britain was the "last probable chance to ultimately avoid war." He denounced "self-styled practical men" like Lindbergh, who said that Britain was heading to defeat, as "looking into the small end of a telescope."[24]

On May 12, the Nazis bolstered the interventionists' view that democracy itself was in danger when the House of Commons was bombed and American newspapers were filled with pictures of Churchill standing in the rubble of "the cradle of democracy," proclaiming it would be rebuilt exactly as before.

The same day, Lindbergh visited Ford at his home in Dearborn and asked for money to mount a national campaign. Ford was "very much interested," assured Lindbergh "there was almost no limit to what he would do in opposing American intervention in the war,"[25] and ordered the Ford Motor Company's advertising chief, Lou Maxon, to design a $250,000 campaign ($4 million in 2014 terms), with a promise that this sum was just a start.

Maxon put Ford's "four best ad writers"[26] to work. Then, on May 20, Lindbergh was thrown into despair when Ford abruptly canceled the campaign without explanation. The car mogul's personal assistant "implied that Ford did not trust some of the people on the America First Committee," Lindbergh wrote. "What is it really due to? Eccentricity and advancing years? Actual suspicion of the America First Committee? The desire to completely control everything in which he invests heavily? Or is it government pressure in the form of 'defense' contracts?"[27] In fact, all three played their part, though Ford's increasing eccentricity and pressure from his son to stop allowing politics to interfere with business was the likely main reason for his about-turn. Ford may have been sympathetic to America First, but he was a businessman above all. The lucrative government contracts to make Pratt and Whitney engines and B-24 warplanes would have been enough to persuade Ford to back off from an activity that would have endangered making profits.

Further setbacks beset the isolationists. There was a flurry of talk about a negotiated peace to the European war when on May 10, Hitler's deputy, Rudolf Hess,[28] flew alone, unannounced, and apparently unbidden to Scotland to negotiate peace with Britain. Churchill, who had no intention of negotiating, kept Hess's arrival secret until the top Nazi had been diagnosed and found mentally unstable. Hitler was apoplectic at Hess's unauthorized mission and Stalin grew suspicious that Germany and Britain were about to unite against the Soviet Union. The German press soon dismissed the peace initiative as the act of "a deluded, deranged and muddled idealist, ridden with hallucinations traceable to World War [One] injuries."[29] As soon as it became clear that Hess was operating without Hitler's authority, speculation about peace talks, which had buoyed the isolationists for a few days, subsided.

For a while, Churchill was happy to allow speculation to build in America that Britain was so near defeat she might accept a negotiated peace. On May 4, feeling severely threatened by invasion, the prime minister wrote to the president, imploring him to show solidarity with the democracies by declaring war against Germany. Morgenthau and Ickes agreed: now was the time to formally enter the war. Stimson, who unlike others in the cabinet had experience of war, urged the president to prepare himself, the country, and the world for American involvement in the war. But Roosevelt claimed that public opinion was not yet overwhelmingly in favor, and that isolationist sentiment was still running too high. Shortly afterward, the president, rarely in the best of health, fell ill with intestinal flu and acute anemia.

On May 16, Tobey withdrew a motion in the Senate to reconfirm the ban on convoying after the America First committee asked him to call off the measure. As Lindbergh explained, "It would almost certainly have been defeated, and the Administration would then have claimed that its defeat was an implied authorization for convoys."[30]

Alf Landon, the Republican presidential candidate in 1936, was approached to head up America First and declined. His experience and national reputation would have proved useful to a wilting campaign. With congressional attempts to halt convoying running into the sand, America First began to consider campaigning for a national referendum on entering the war and talked about impeaching Roosevelt, which Lindbergh thought "possible though not probable."[31]

It was not long before an incident appeared to prove that America was already in a shooting war and that the convoying debate had been overtaken by events. On May 21, an American steamship, the *Robin Moor*, en route from New York to South Africa, was sunk by a German submarine, even though it was flying the Stars and Stripes. The captain, crew of twenty-nine, and eight passengers were given meager rations of ersatz bread and butter and time to board the lifeboats, but it was a particularly cruel sinking. The ship was 750 miles from the nearest port, Freetown, Sierra Leone, and it was two weeks before the survivors were rescued. In a message to Congress a month later, Roosevelt would call it a "ruthless sinking" designed to intimidate America "into a course of non-resistance to German plans for universal conquest" and evidence that Hitler wanted "to seize control of the high seas."[32]

Roosevelt ordered all German and Italian consulates closed and the freezing of German and Italian assets in the United States, leaving Wheeler to bluster, "At least we ought to await an explanation before we jump at conclusions."[33] Later, Wheeler justified the German sinking of the *Robin Moor* because 70 percent of the cargo consisted of war materiel. Roosevelt was happy for him to take such an unpopular line, knowing that the cruelty of the incident spoke for itself and served to reinforce his policy of escorting merchant vessels across the Atlantic.

News of the sinking of the *Robin Moor* had not reached Lindbergh by the time on May 23 when he addressed a noisy crowd of 22,000 in Madison Square Garden, with 14,000 more listening in the street on loudspeakers, and millions listening on the radio. It was an ill-tempered, highly charged audience. An attempt by the band to play "God

Bless America," composed by Irving Berlin,[34] was shouted down as it was deemed "an interventionist song."[35] Coughlin, the perennial socialist candidate Norman Thomas, and Joseph McWilliams, "self styled fuehrer of the Christian Mobilizers," Teddy Roosevelt's son Archie,[36] and his daughter Alice Roosevelt Longworth were present, and Wheeler was a fellow speaker. Telegrams of support came from the novelist Sinclair Lewis,[37] the film star Lillian Gish,[38] and Wood.

The event was more telling in exposing America First's deep divisions and its extremist support than in any new argument. Before the rally, Lindbergh issued a statement, in response to Friends of Democracy, that America First was not backed by "Bundists, Communists, or any other un-American support."[39] McWilliams's presence confounded that attempt to distance the organization from the radicals in its midst. On seeing McWilliams in the hall, organizers tried to have him ejected but police refused, saying it was none of their business, and the Fascist leader remained.

The *New Republic*'s house isolationist John T. Flynn suspected an interventionist conspiracy. "What he is doing here, how he got in, or whose stooge he is I do not know," said Flynn, "but I do know that the photographers for the war-making newspapers always know where to find him." Flynn said that America First wanted the support of "the 100 million Americans who are against the war," not "a handful of Bundists, Communists and Christian Fronters who are without number, without influence, without power and without respect in this or any other community."

Lindbergh and Anne were welcomed into the hall amid cries of "Our next president!" and his address was preceded by a parade weaving its way through the hall bearing the banner "Copperheads of Westchester." Lindbergh declared that America First meant that "American boys will not be sent across the ocean to die so that England or Germany or France or Spain may dominate other nations" and that "our soldiers will not have to fight everybody in the world who prefers some other system of life to ours. . . . Many of us do not think we can impose our way of life, at the point of a machine gun, on the peoples of Germany, Russia, Italy, France and Japan."

He said it was only a matter of the right leadership to make America "the most powerful country in the world." He argued that Roosevelt had made America a dictatorship and the presidential election had been a sham. "We had no more chance to vote on the issue of peace and war last November than if we had been in a totalitarian state ourselves," he said. It was "as if Hitler had run against Goering." If America entered the war, "losses are likely to run into the millions and . . . victory itself is doubtful." Lindbergh was aware that he was repeating himself. "I have already used up all the arguments against getting into the war," he complained to his diary.[40]

Speaking next, Wheeler condemned Halifax and "the royal refugees" for urging war "to save the British empire" which he described as "tottering," and he dismissed the suggestion Hitler would invade America as he would need a force two million strong.[41]

Stark had not waited to be asked by the president before he began making plans to convoy British ships. As early as mid-February, weeks before Lend-Lease became law, he ordered the commander of the newly created Atlantic Fleet to create a force to take over convoying from the Royal Navy. On March 20, Stark informed Roosevelt that it was ready to begin convoying duties. By March 24, Stimson and Knox let the president know they believed that convoying was "the only solution" to German raids on British shipping.[42] The following day, Hitler extended U-boat operations to the coast of Greenland.

In early April, Roosevelt called an all-day meeting at the White House attended by Stimson, Knox, Hopkins, and others, and asked for an atlas of the Atlantic. He ran his finger around Greenland and Iceland as if with a pencil and sketched a line down toward the coast of Brazil. "By drawing a line midway between the western-most bulge of Africa and the easternmost bulge of Brazil, we found that the median line between the two continents was at about longitude line 25," Stimson wrote in his diary.

> His plan is then that we shall patrol the high seas west of this median line, all the way down as far as we can furnish the force to do it, and that the British will swing their convoys over westward to the west side of this line, so that they will be within our area. Then by the use of patrol planes and patrol vessels we can patrol and follow the convoys and notify them of any German raiders or German submarines that we may see and give them a chance to escape.[43]

The same day, April 10, Roosevelt announced that he had signed an agreement with the Danish government in exile in Washington to include "Greenland in our sphere of cooperative hemispheric defense," and that naval patrols would now guarantee the safety of the surrounding waters. Just as he had avoided the neutrality legislation by inventing Lend-Lease, so Roosevelt moved to avoid the prohibition of convoying in the Lend-Lease Act by redefining the western hemisphere to include Greenland. His solution to the ban on convoying was literally to redraw the map.

Little could more graphically underline Britain's vulnerability by sea as the arrival into the North Sea on May 19 of the new German battleship *Bismarck*, accompanied by the heavy cruiser *Prinz Eugen*. On the morning of May 24, it encountered the British battle cruiser the *Hood* and the battleship *Prince of Wales* in the Denmark Strait. In the ensuing battle, the *Hood* was hit in the magazine, exploded, broke in two, and sank in three minutes. Of the 1,418 crew, only three survived. The *Prince of Wales* landed three shells on the *Bismarck* before it broke off the action. The *Bismarck* headed to the French port of Saint-Nazaire for minor repairs. Unharmed, the *Prinz Eugen* continued into the Atlantic in search of British vessels to sink.

Two days later, the *Bismarck* was sighted by an American naval ensign aboard a long-range RAF American-built Catalina flying boat, and was pursued and hit by torpedoes launched from Swordfish flying boats assigned to the carrier *Ark Royal*. One jammed the *Bismarck*'s steering gear, leaving the battleship only capable of sailing in circles. Then on the morning of May 27, the *King George V* and the *Rodney* appeared. In less than an hour, after sustaining a number of direct hits, the *Bismarck* was on fire. She was finished off with torpedoes from the cruiser *Dorsetshire*, capsized, and sank. Of her crew of 2,300, all but 118 perished.

The sinking of the *Bismarck* was a salutary lesson. It deterred Hitler from sending more surface vessels into the Atlantic, but the element of chance that caused damage to the *Bismarck* and made it vulnerable to attack demonstrated to Churchill and Roosevelt how slender was the naval advantage Britain enjoyed. The same day, May 27, the president informed Churchill that he would be sending 75,000 tons of supplies in American ships to shore up the British army in Egypt, including 200 tanks and 700 trucks.

In a fireside chat on the evening of the 27th, the president explained his current thinking about helping Britain and revealed some startling news. "The present rate of Nazi sinkings of merchant ships is more than three times as high as the capacity of British shipyards to replace them," he said. "It is more than twice the combined British and American output of merchant ships today. We have, accordingly, extended our patrol in North and South Atlantic waters. We are steadily adding more and more ships and planes to that patrol." In fact American forces had been protecting British convoys for some time.

He then addressed his isolationist opponents:

There is, of course, a small group of sincere, patriotic men and women whose real passion for peace has shut their eyes to the ugly realities of international banditry and to the need to resist it at all costs. I am sure they are embarrassed by the sinister support they are receiving from the enemies of democracy in our midst, the Bundists, the Fascists, and Communists, and every group devoted to bigotry and racial and religious intolerance.

It is no mere coincidence that all the arguments put forward by these enemies of democracy—all their attempts to confuse and divide our people and to destroy public confidence in our Government—all their defeatist forebodings that Britain and democracy are already beaten—all their selfish promises that we can "do business" with Hitler—all of these are but echoes of the words that have been poured out from the Axis bureaus of propaganda.[44]

The president proclaimed "an unlimited national emergency," though he did not explain what this would entail. In fact, it meant little except to encourage Americans to take the prospect of war even more seriously than before. It was, as ever, a case of a dramatic Roosevelt announcement followed by extreme caution. King George VI was impressed, writing to the president, "I have been so struck by the way you have led public opinion by allowing it to get ahead of you."[45]

Roosevelt's broadcast brought an immediate riposte from the isolationists, with Taft fuming, "He has no right to declare war whether a national emergency or not. It follows inevitably that he has no right to engage deliberately in military or naval action equivalent to war except when the country is attacked."[46]

The administration was by now paying little attention to isolationist complaints. In the months of May and June, Knox ordered the transfer of three battleships, an aircraft carrier, four cruisers, and smaller naval vessels from the Pacific to the Atlantic to bolster defense of the British convoys. On June 6, Churchill went to an airfield in southern England to witness the first Lend-Lease Flying Fortress bombers landing in Britain.

Although support for staying out of the war remained strong, and was certainly enough to ensure Roosevelt edged toward a full state of war with the utmost care, the isolationists were increasingly seen as out of touch, treacherous, unrealistic, and un-American. The following month, the war in Europe took a surprise turn, a radical shift that would completely alter the calculations of interventionists and isolationists alike.

BARBAROSSA

Hitler attacks the Soviet Union,
the isolationists struggle to remain united,
Ickes attacks Lindbergh, Roosevelt extends protection
to British shipping crossing the Atlantic.

THE DATE June 22 was notable in Hitler's diary. It was the day in 1940 he accepted the French surrender in the train carriage at Compiègne. It was the day in 1812 his hero Napoleon crossed the river Niemen on his way to conquer Russia. And it was the day in 1941 he launched his surprise attack on the Soviet Union.

Stalin did not see it coming. Although he had received repeated warnings that a German attack was imminent, including a message from Welles and a long personal letter from Churchill, the evening before the invasion, the Communist despot set off to his dacha for a relaxing weekend. "I am certain Hitler will not risk creating a second front," he said on June 11. "Hitler is not such an idiot."[1]

Stalin was woken in the early hours of Sunday, June 22, with news that a massive German force had crossed the border into the Ukraine and was heading fast for Moscow. The invasion should not have come as a surprise. As early as 1925, Hitler had written in his prison diary, *Mein Kampf*, "When we speak of new territory in Europe today we must think principally of Russia and her border vassal states."[2]

The invasion was a gamble. "I had no more difficult decision to make than the attack on Russia," Hitler said. "I had always maintained that we ought at all costs to avoid waging war on two fronts, and you may rest assured that I pondered long and anxiously over

Napoleon and his experiences in Russia. Why, then, you may ask, this war against Russia?"[3] The answer was the prospect of gaining the vast grain-growing lands of the Ukraine, the rich oil fields of the Caucasus, and the verdant land on which Hitler wished to settle his people in an expanded German homeland. "What India was for England, the territories of Russia will be for us," he said.[4]

The invasion also marked the clash between the twin tyrannies of Fascism and Communism. "This struggle is one of ideologies and racial differences and will have to be conducted with unprecedented, unmerciful and unrelenting harshness," Hitler told his high command.[5] Hitler was aware, too, that by the following year, when America had fully rearmed, Roosevelt would in all likelihood supply the Soviet Union and invade the European mainland from Britain. Which is why Hitler told Mussolini, "Whether or not America enters the war is a matter of indifference."[6] America would fight anyway.

Hitler thought that defeating the Soviet Union with a Blitzkrieg would not take long. He had been assured by his generals that Operation Barbarossa, named after the charismatic king of Germany and Holy Roman Emperor, "would last four to six weeks."[7] Churchill took a different view, telling colleagues, "I'll bet you a Monkey [£500] to a Mousetrap [£1] that the Russians are still fighting, and fighting victoriously, two years from now."[8] Roosevelt was convinced that Hitler had made an error. "Now comes this Russian diversion," he wrote. "If it is more than just that it will mean the liberation of Europe from Nazi domination."[9]

At 3 a.m. on June 22, Hitler had hurled four million men, including seventeen panzer tank divisions and thirteen motorized divisions, across a 2,000-mile border in what his biographer Alan Bullock called "the most powerful military force ever concentrated for a single operation."[10] Barbarossa completely changed the outcome of the war. Roosevelt and Churchill saw the Nazi invasion of the Soviet Union coming, even if Stalin did not, but they did not know what its consequences would be. In the event, Hitler made a fatal miscalculation. As the historian of Hitler's rise and fall, William L. Shirer, put it, "For Hitler, the die was cast, and, though he did not know it, his ultimate fate sealed, by this decision."[11]

Hitler's new direction of conquest called for a change in Allied strategy. Roosevelt was now set the tricky problem of having to help the Communist leadership of the Soviet Union, which was likely to prove a hard sell in free-enterprise America. The president maintained his silence, unfroze Soviet assets in America, but otherwise refused to be drawn on when or even whether he would help Stalin. He chose to shelter behind Churchill, whose broadcasts were popular in America and whose theatrical turns of phrase provided useful cover.

Explaining why he felt comfortable with backing Stalin, Churchill argued in a broadcast widely heard in America on June 22, "No one has been a more consistent opponent of Communism than I have for the last twenty-five years. I will unsay no word that I have spoken about it," he said, but, "Any man or state who fights on against Nazidom will have our aid. Any man or state who marches with Hitler is our foe." [12] That applied "to all representatives of that vile race of quislings who make themselves the tools and agents of the Nazi regime against their fellow-countrymen and the lands of their birth." Many Americans were left in no doubt that Churchill was referring to appeasers, Nazi sympathizers, fellow travelers, and isolationists.

On July 7, Stalin asked for $1.8 billion in aid from America. Three days later, Gallup reported that 72 percent of Americans favored a Soviet victory compared to 4 percent wanting a Hitler victory. Roosevelt agreed in principle to the Russian request and sent Hopkins to Moscow to do for Stalin what he had done for Churchill. The view of many Americans was summed up by Senator Harry S. Truman from Missouri: "If we see that Germany is winning we ought to help Russia, and if Russia is winning we ought to help Germany. . . . although I don't want to see Hitler victorious under any circumstances." [13]

The isolationists were doubly pressed by Hitler's strike eastward. They not only lost their loyal ultra-left-wing pacifist base overnight, they were left with an organization tilting noticeably rightward, a state of affairs that played into the hands of those who dismissed isolationists as Nazi dupes. Lindbergh said he was "thankful to be rid of the Communist support which we never wanted." [14]

The escalation of the war in Europe drove a sharp increase in membership of America First. It had 300,000 members at the start of 1941; by year's end, 800,000. The New York branch of America First operated out of a small office at 515 Madison Avenue with a staff of about forty, of which half were volunteers. It was led jointly by Edwin S. Webster Jr., a young New York investment banker, and John T. Flynn, a left-liberal *New Republic* journalist, but the marriage was not happy. At first, Lindbergh appeared oblivious of the disagreements, reporting that "in spite of all the difference in their viewpoints, they somehow manage to get along together."[15] Beneath the surface, however, the tensions, heightened by the Nazi assault upon the Soviet Union, were becoming untenable. The Baltimore and San Francisco branches of America First were also in disarray and witnessed acrid battles between competing factions.

At national level, however, the isolationist leaders were working more or less in concert. Hoover, Lindbergh, Wood, and the isolationists in Congress were determined to keep up pressure on the administration. Lindbergh flew between sympathetic Midwestern cities to speak. He had become a hugely popular if polarizing figure, reflected in the vast audiences his speeches attracted.

There was, however, also considerable opposition to his message. In Oklahoma City he was subject to threats of "shooting, of cutting light and telephone (radio) wires, eggs, stones, etc."[16] Lindbergh cancelled a rally in Washington DC because, he was told, "the government is in such a strong position there that the success of our meeting would be doubtful" and "we cannot afford to hold an unsuccessful meeting in the nation's capital."[17]

Lindbergh paid a call on anyone who could fund or support the isolationist view, including Hearst, though "the Hearst press has done things to me in the past which I cannot forgive," and Ford, though he avoided raising the car maker's abrupt and unexplained cancellation of a coast-to-coast America First ad campaign. Ford's factories were completing hugely profitable government contracts producing warplanes, tanks, and gun sights, yet Ford still expressed his desire to make financial contributions to America First. Lindbergh was irritated by the lack of courage of most businesspeople. "Few of them are willing to expose their own position enough to take part in opposing that which they believe is wrong," he complained.[18]

Over time, perhaps sensing a losing battle, Lindbergh began to despair of his own country. On May 4, in San Francisco, he bemoaned the fact that "a refugee who steps from the gang-planks and advocates war is acclaimed as a defender of freedom. A native born American who opposes war is called a fifth-columnist."[19] On May 9, in Minneapolis, Lindbergh prophesied that war would make America "a military nation . . . that surpasses Germany herself in totalitarian efficiency" and that "our way of life [would become] a thing of the past, that our children will be fortunate if they live long enough to see it again."

After Lindbergh denied he was advocating "anything but constitutional methods," America First issued its own dream isolationist cabinet: Farley as war secretary, the former president's son Charles P. Taft II[20] as navy secretary, the New York district attorney Thomas E. Dewey as attorney general, the mineworkers' union leader John L. Lewis as secretary of labor, and Lindbergh as secretary of the air.

Ickes, who kept "a complete indexed collection" of Lindbergh's speeches and writings, thought he was jeopardizing the president's delicate balancing act between peace and war and took delight in reminding everyone of Lindbergh's Nazi connections, calling him by the name of his Nazi medal, "Knight of the German Eagle." "In preaching defeatism and helping to bring about disunity he was doing what . . . Germany wanted done," Ickes declared. As for the Nazi medal, "He should have returned it long ago."[21]

Ickes told Roosevelt that Lindbergh was "a ruthless and conscious fascist. Motivated by hatred for you personally and for democracy in general, his speeches show an astonishing identity with those of Berlin."[22] In a speech on July 14, Ickes went to the heart of the matter. "No one has ever heard Lindbergh utter a word of horror at, or even aversion to, the bloody career that the Nazis are following, nor a word of pity for the innocent men, women and children who have been deliberately murdered by the Nazis," he said.[23] He accused Lindbergh of wanting to depose the president and put himself in the White House.

Lindbergh became so agitated by Ickes's accusations that he wrote an open letter to Roosevelt asking him to call his dog off. "Is it too much to ask that you inform your Secretary of the interior that I was decorated by the German Government while I was carrying out the request of your Ambassador?" he asked. "I have no connection with any foreign government. I have had no communication, directly or indirectly, with anyone in Germany or Italy since I was last in Europe, in the spring of 1939."[24]

Ickes was ecstatic at having scored a direct hit. "I had begun to think that no one could get under his skin enough to make him squeal," he wrote in his diary. "At last I have succeeded."[25] The president did not respond, Early telling Lindbergh that an open letter was not a piece of correspondence but a press release. Ickes turned the knife. "Why doesn't he send back the disgraceful decoration and be done with it?" he asked. "Americans remember that he had no hesitation about sending back to the President his commission in the United States Army Air Corps Reserve."[26]

Roosevelt continued steadily to redefine where the western hemisphere began and ended, on July 7 sending troops to occupy Iceland on the grounds that America could not allow "the occupation by Germany of strategic outposts in the Atlantic to be used as air or naval bases for eventual attack against the Western Hemisphere."[27] This freed British ships and troops for more urgent duties. Four days later, the president issued a secret order to "protect United States and Iceland shipping against hostile attacks by escorting, covering, and patrolling, as required by circumstances, and by destroying hostile forces which threaten such shipping" and to "escort convoys of United States and Iceland flag shipping, including the shipping of any nationality which may join such convoys between United States ports and bases and Iceland."[28] Convoying to and from Iceland and sinking German vessels was now official administration policy, and British ships were welcome to join any American convoy. British losses continued to mount, though the number of tons sunk in the North Atlantic during 1941 was less than the previous year.

Unaware of Roosevelt's secret command, the isolationists persisted in trying to embarrass Roosevelt by attempting to discover whether American patrols were in fact protecting convoys. On July 11, the Senate opened an investigation into newspaper reports "that naval units were convoying or escorting ships at sea or dropping depth charges on German naval units."[29]

Alsop and Kintner contended in the *Washington Post* that the first American act in the shooting war against Germany took place some time in May. The pair concluded, "Although the President is waiting for the Germans to shoot first, the truth is that there has been shooting already."[30] Some time in the previous month, an American destroyer was picking up sixty survivors of a British steamer sunk by a U-boat near Greenland when its sonar detection system reported a German submarine circling nearby, they wrote. Fearing attack, the commander of the destroyer dropped three depth charges.

Knox told the Senate Naval Affairs Committee, "There isn't a particle of truth in [the story]," and while he admitted depth charges had been dropped during the incident, "it is quite possible no submarine was there. The equipment echo might have been received from a whale or large fish."[31]

A detailed account of the operation of an American-led convoy was reported in the syndicated column "Washington Merry-Go-Round" by Drew Pearson and Robert S. Allen. "A group of American naval vessels has just returned from its first experience at Atlantic patrol, or convoying, whatever it is called—they helped to get about 80 British merchantmen safely most of the way to the west coast of Africa," they wrote. The pair reported the convoy was made up of three aircraft carriers, posted on three sides of the convoy, with two destroyers protecting each carrier, planes from the carriers scouting for U-boats, and three battle cruisers. Perhaps to ensure they were not accused of convoying, the American flotilla maintained a discreet distance from the British vessels.

Again Knox told the committee that the report was a "fabrication. There isn't a word of truth in it." Asked by the chairman, "We can assure the American people that there is no undeclared war, a hidden war, or a naval war as far as we are concerned?" Knox replied, "That is right." The committee concluded that it "did not consider it necessary to do more at this time" than to report to the Senate that it found no evidence of shooting or convoying.[32]

The Nazi invasion of the Soviet Union in June was uncomfortable for the Japanese, who since April 1941 had been enjoying the benefits of a nonaggression pact with Stalin and with whom they were reluctant to reignite hostilities. Roosevelt biographer Black's belief is that Hitler's "failure to secure the collaboration of the Japanese against the Soviet Union must rank as one of Hitler's most serious errors." Coming so soon after his decision to invade the Soviet Union, Hitler's flawed judgment at this time set Germany firmly on the road to defeat.

Japan was already in bad odor with America, from which it tradi-
tionally bought three-quarters of its oil, because of its decade-long
occupation of large tracts of China. In early July 1941, as a preliminary to conquering the whole of Southeast Asia, Japan had invaded
French Indochina. Roosevelt froze Japanese assets in America in
response. Soon after, America imposed a total oil embargo against
Japan. In search of new fuel supplies, the Japanese coveted the oil-
rich Dutch East Indies. In August 1941, all licenses for the export of
American petroleum products to Japan were rescinded. Scrap metal
exports to Japan were banned.

These punitive acts were pushing Japan into the war, as Roosevelt almost acknowledged when, on freezing Japanese assets, he
defended the failure to impose an oil embargo upon Japan earlier.
"Now, if we cut the oil off, they probably would have gone down to
the Dutch East Indies a year ago, and you would have had war," he
said. "Therefore, there was—you might call—a method in letting this
oil go to Japan, with the hope—and it has worked for two years—of
keeping war out of the South Pacific."[33]

As a precaution against the threat of a Japanese assault on American interests in East Asia, in July 1941 the president recalled General
Douglas MacArthur from retirement and put him in charge of the
defense of the Philippines, an American quasi-colony. MacArthur
demanded and received half of the Flying Fortress bombers coming
off the assembly line, arguing that air power alone would deter a Japanese invasion while putting the Japanese mainland within range of
American bombs.

After moving the headquarters of the Pacific Fleet to Pearl Harbor, on the island of Oahu, Hawaii, the previous year, the president
felt confident that his back was well protected from Japanese attack,
allowing him to concentrate on the defeat of Hitler in Europe. On
August 3, Roosevelt set out for the submarine base at New London,
Connecticut, to join the *Potomac* for a restorative few days' sailing up
the New England coast. From the shore, he could be seen on deck,
cigarette holder at a jaunty angle, sipping martinis. Each day a press
release confirmed that "all on board" were having a good time.

It was one of the most entertaining subterfuges of the war. A
member of Roosevelt's Secret Service detail donned the president's
trademark metal-framed spectacles, puffed smoke from his trade-

mark cigarette holder, drank his trademark martinis, and sat bolt upright in his wheelchair on deck to throw spectators with binoculars off the scent. After surreptitiously switching to the USS *Augusta* in the Menemsha Bight, Vineyard Sound, Massachusetts, Roosevelt had steamed off to confer with Churchill, the first meeting since their glancing encounter in 1918, which had left no trace at all with the former First Lord of the Admiralty but an abiding memory of having been snubbed with the former assistant secretary of the US Navy. The Atlantic summit was a strange combination of a kiss and make-up, a first date, and the long-delayed honeymoon of a well-established marriage of convenience.

Notwithstanding the glowing report of Churchill from Hopkins, the president felt he should get to know his fellow warlord better. He needed to take the measure of this by all accounts brilliant, colorful, eloquent, and amusing force of nature. Churchill, too, was looking forward to meeting his co-conspirator and savior. The rendezvous point was Placentia Bay in the southwest corner of Newfoundland, where the *Augusta* met up with the *King George V*, newly restored after its battering at the hands of the *Bismarck*.

Roosevelt had with him Welles, generals Marshall and Arnold, admirals Stark and King, and the banker and railroad heir W. Averell Harriman;[34] Churchill was accompanied by the chief of the Imperial General Staff Field Marshal Sir John Dill, the First Sea Lord, Admiral of the Fleet Sir Dudley Pound, vice air chief Sir Wilfred Freeman, and the under secretary of state in the Foreign Office, Sir Alexander Cadogan. Also in Churchill's party was Hopkins, returning from Moscow via London. The military chiefs continued where the ABC talks left off. Well out of sight of the isolationists, Roosevelt and Churchill embarked upon a council of war.

Both men were somewhat in awe of each other. Roosevelt asked Frances Perkins, who knew Churchill a little, to brief him on what to expect. Hopkins, who was tapped by the prime minister for the president's every last detail, recalled, "You'd have thought Winston was being carried up into the heavens to meet God Almighty!"

The first day, Churchill was the president's sole lunch guest aboard the *Aurora*, after which Roosevelt wrote to his cousin Margaret Suckley, "He is a tremendously vital person." That evening, Hopkins encouraged Churchill after dinner to embark on one of his rambling tours d'horizon. Without the lubrication of alcohol, which was forbidden on US Navy ships, the prime minister's performance was perhaps less commanding than usual.

He continued to promote his belief that Hitler could be defeated in a long war made up of small assaults on the periphery and massive bomb raids on industrial cities that would sap German morale and encourage insurrection. On the third day of the summit, Marshall and Hull let Churchill know that America had little interest in postponing the only way they believed Nazism could be defeated: a full-scale invasion of the European mainland.

Churchill was preoccupied with the increasing Japanese threat to the British colonies in Asia, in particular Singapore, the commercial capital of Britain's Asian empire, and urged Roosevelt to issue a demand that Japan should unconditionally withdraw from French Indo-China and that any attack upon British territories would be considered an attack on America. Roosevelt said he would consider it. Welles let it be known that the State Department believed that the devastating American economic sanctions would in any case soon lead to war with Japan.

Roosevelt was uncertain whether it was best to try to delay the inevitable conflict with Japan, the better to concentrate on the European front, or whether an early confrontation in the east would not be an easy way for America to be drawn into the war. By the summer of 1941, after the Japanese invasion of Vichy-controlled Indo-China the previous year, the embargo on the passage of Japanese ships through the Panama Canal, and the freezing of Japanese assets in the US, two-thirds of Americans were prepared to go to war with Japan. At the floating summit, Churchill, too, began to think that Japan rather than Germany might drag America into war.

The following day, Sunday, August 10, the British hosted their American partners aboard the *King George V* and Churchill led the singing in a Christian service of Anglo-Saxon hymns with a sea theme, to emphasize the cultural bonds between the two nations. The president's primary goal of the Newfoundland summit was to define the Allied war aims, and he sent some sketched suggestions for Churchill to work up into a draft.

The emerging Atlantic Charter would come to articulate the most permanently interventionist American foreign policy since

Wilson's "Fourteen Points" envisioned the League of Nations. Roosevelt wanted to replace the exclusive system of preferential trade that Britain enjoyed with its colonies and dominions and replace it with a worldwide free trade system. He also wanted to establish that the Allied victory would result in "the right of all peoples to choose the form of government under which they will live," an anticolonial aspiration which the imperialist Churchill found hard to swallow.

Further, the Charter hoped to provide a means whereby German-occupied nations would be restored to freedom, the freedom of the high seas, an international program of disarmament "pending the establishment of a wider and permanent system of general security," and, for Roosevelt's benefit, a nod to the New Deal's aims of "improved labor standards, economic advancement and social security."[35]

It was not the president's intention at this stage to promote a system of world government in the postwar world, as he thought it too politically difficult to arrange. The isolationists would be sure to oppose anything that suggested a world governing body as surely as the Irreconcilables had doomed the Treaty of Versailles. "The establishment of a wider and permanent system of general security" was therefore left vague.

Other decisions were made at Placentia Bay that, had they been made known, would also have alarmed the isolationists. Roosevelt pledged to help the Soviet Union "on a gigantic scale." He promised to increase the numbers of American ships ferrying supplies to Britain. He agreed that every transatlantic convoy would be protected by an American cruiser, or a similar capital ship such as an aircraft carrier, and five destroyers. Trained American pilots would deliver warplanes to Britain and West Africa and would stay on to train British pilots.

Fearful that the British, French, and Russians would outmaneuver America when the war ended, as they had done in 1918 to Wilson's embarrassment, Roosevelt had asked Churchill on July 15 to promise that he would make "no secret commitments to any of its Allies" without "the agreement of the United States." He had received no answer. In Placentia Bay, therefore, the prime minister was made to promise that no "secret deals" had been or would be made. Most explosive of all, Roosevelt made a remark to Churchill that, had it been reported, would have been certain to set off impeachment proceedings. "I may never declare war. I may make war," the president said. "If I were to ask Congress to declare war they might argue about it for three months."[36]

The Atlantic Charter, which was announced in a joint statement on August 14, 1941, set a sure course for the Allies, bound America and Britain together in a set of inspirational war aims, and began to hint at the new world organizations that would regulate the postwar world. The return of Wilsonian thinking in the White House was not lost on the *New York Times*, which wrote, "No mention is made in the eight-point declaration of a new League of Nations or any association like it. But in every line of the document . . . is implied the creation of a post-war organization to maintain peace, with the United States a full partner in this effort."

Roosevelt and Churchill concluded, "This is the end of isolation. It is the beginning of a new era in which the United States assumes the responsibilities which fall naturally to a great World Power."[37] Louis I. Newman, a prominent rabbi on the east side of Manhattan, described the Charter as a restatement of the principles "for which America fought under Woodrow Wilson." "It may well be that Franklin D. Roosevelt and Winston Churchill can bring to pass in reality the principles which Mr. Wilson enunciated, but could not implement," he said.[38]

As ever, having struck out in a new direction, as soon as he was on dry land Roosevelt played down the importance of Placentia Bay and the Atlantic Charter, referring to the meeting as an "interchange of views, that's all. Nothing else." Asked whether America was any closer to war as a result of the summit, he replied, "I should say, no."[39]

Support for the war in Congress remained fragile. On August 12, a measure to extend the draft sailed through the Senate but squeaked past the House by a single vote, 203 to 202. As Black notes, the vote showed "that the isolationist dragon, though consistently confounded and defeated by the President, was not dead."[40] Roosevelt decided to let Congress calm itself with a long period in which he said and did little about the war, a display of inaction that did not play well with Churchill.

The president failed to make the announcement agreed at Placentia, that if Japan continued her conquests "the United States Government would be compelled to take counter-measures, even though these might lead to war between the United States and Japan."[41] Churchill felt he had been let down over guarantees about British territories threatened by Japan and blindsided into agreeing the Charter, which had not been mentioned before the face-to-face meeting. He felt "bitterly disappointed to return, almost like Neville Chamberlain, with little more than a piece of paper."[42]

He was alarmed by the anticolonial tone of the Charter and was obliged to tell Parliament that "we had in mind, primarily, the restoration of the sovereignty, self-government and national life of the States and nations of Europe now under the Nazi yoke" which was "a quite separate problem from the progressive evolution of self-governing institutions in regions [like India and the African colonies] whose peoples owe allegiance to the British Crown."[43]

The prime minister was becoming impatient at Roosevelt's continuing failure to commit to the war. Churchill cabled Hopkins, "There has been a wave of depression through Cabinet and other informed circles here about President's many assurances about no commitments and no closer to war, etc."[44] And he wrote to his son, Randolph, "One is deeply perplexed to know how the deadlock is to be broken and the United States brought boldly and honorably into the war."[45]

DAY OF INFAMY

*Congress investigates prowar movies,
Lindbergh is accused of anti-Semitism, the neutrality
laws are amended, the Japanese mount a
surprise attack on Pearl Harbor.*

WHILE ROOSEVELT AND CHURCHILL were at sea, the isolationists opened a new front, launching a congressional investigation into "the groups agitating for war in this country." Flynn claimed to have discovered "amazing results" in research he had commissioned into the motives of Hollywood studio heads and employees that revealed "a strong undercover movement for war."[1]

On August 1, at an America First rally in St. Louis, Nye, who had headed the congressional investigation into the "merchants of death" who profited from the arms trade in World War One, railed against Hollywood for luring America into war. "Who has brought us to the verge of war?" he asked. "At least twenty pictures have been produced in the last years, all designed to drug the reason of the American people, set aflame their emotions, turn their hatred into a blaze, fill them with fear that Hitler will come over here and capture them," he said.[2]

Nye described the Hollywood studios as "the most gigantic engines of propaganda in existence to rouse war fever in America and plunge the Nation to her destruction." When he started to list the fifteen studio heads, thirteen of whom were Jewish, the America First crowd booed, "Jews!"[3] "In each of these companies," Nye continued, "there are a number of production directors, many of whom have come from Russia, Hungary, Germany and the Balkan countries. . . . The place swarms with refugees. It also swarms with British actors."[4]

That day, Champ Clark and Nye cosponsored a Senate motion calling for a "complete investigation of any propaganda disseminated by motion pictures and radio or any other activity of the motion picture industry to influence public sentiment in the direction of participation of the United States in the present European war." In response, Wheeler, chairman of the Senate Interstate Commerce Committee, set up a five-man subcommittee under D. Worth Clark, who called for three weeks of hearings starting September 9. The battle of Hollywood had begun. America First wrote to its members:

> Write to the members of the committee. Inform them of every instance of "war propaganda" observed in the motion pictures. Give the name of the picture, the producer, the theater at which it was shown, and a brief outline of the propaganda incident. . . . Urge your members also to send copies of their letters to the theater managers. When it becomes evident that it is unprofitable to book war-propaganda pictures the practice will quickly be discontinued.[5]

The movie industry's self-imposed censor, Will Hays, tried to contact the president to tell him that Hollywood was merely making "entertainment" and that there was no truth in the suggestion the studios were peddling pro-democracy propaganda. Presidential aide Lowell Mellett,[6] who was charged with trying to draw Hollywood into preparing for war, was relieved when a number of prominent movie figures said they welcomed the chance to declare their anti-Nazi beliefs before Congress and Roosevelt realized that good publicity for interventionism was likely to result.

First on the stand was Nye, who prefaced his remarks, literally, with "some of my best friends are Jews"[7] before deploring "the injection of anti-Semitism" into the war debate. He said:

> I will not consent to [the committee's investigation] being used to cover the tracks of those who have been pushing our country on the way to war with their propaganda intended to inflame the American mind with hatred for one foreign cause and magnified

respect and glorification for another foreign cause, until we shall come to feel that wars elsewhere in the world are really after all our wars.

He thought it telling that "those primarily responsible for the propaganda pictures are born abroad. They came to our land and took citizenship here entertaining violent animosities toward certain causes abroad."[8] He suggested, as had Kennedy and Lindbergh, that Jews in Hollywood were inviting trouble on themselves by making anti-Nazi films and harbored a "persecution complex." "I wish those who would be its victims would sense the possibilities and afford a conduct that would not lend itself to fanning later on," he said, before blaming "those of the Jewish faith" for raising "the anti-Semitic issue."[9]

He attributed the "growing spirit" of anti-Semitism in America "to the quite natural Jewish sympathy for and support of" intervening in the European war. There was more than a hint of menace when he came to talk of a time when Americans would go in search of scapegoats to "blame for every misery that grows out of this present world madness." "Who that goat will most likely be we have good reason to recognize from what we are hearing and seeing every day," he said.

Nye went on to accuse writers sympathetic to Britain of slipping into movies a prowar message that "is not easily eliminated" in the minds of impressionable moviegoers. He listed eight movies he considered anti-Nazi, including Charles Chaplin's *The Great Dictator* (United Artists, 1940), the British movie *Convoy* (Ealing, 1941), *I Married a Nazi* (Twentieth Century–Fox, 1940) with Joan Bennett, and Walter Pidgeon stalking Hitler with a sniper rifle in Fritz Lang's *Man Hunt* (Twentieth Century–Fox, 1941). This and a further thirteen movies cited by the committee became known as "the isolationist blacklist."[10]

Citing a 1915 Supreme Court decision, Nye contended that because movies were "a business pure and simple" they could be censored as they did not qualify as "part of the press of this country, and are not protected by the first amendment to our Constitution."[11] Senator Bennett Champ Clark of Missouri told the committee, "Not one word on the side of the argument against war is heard"[12] because "the moving picture industry is a monopoly controlled by a half dozen men dominated by hatred, who are determined in order to wreak vengeance on Adolf Hitler, a ferocious beast, to plunge this nation into war." He condemned Henry Luce's *March of Time* newsreel series explaining the war because it "poisons the minds of the American people to go to war."[13]

Nye described British movie people in Hollywood as "the British occupation." One producer in his sights was Alexander Korda,[14] who made one of the blacklisted movies, *That Hamilton Woman*, released in America in April 1941. As if to confirm the isolationists' suspicions, the story of Nelson and his mistress was screened for Churchill en route to his Atlantic rendezvous with Roosevelt and became the prime minister's favorite wartime movie. It contained a line written by Walter Reisch,[15] spoken by Laurence Olivier, that presented an inescapable contemporary allusion: "Napoleon can never be master of the world until he has smashed us up—and believe me, gentlemen, he means to be master of the world. You cannot make peace with dictators. You have to destroy them. Wipe them out!"

Willkie, whom Wheeler had started describing as "the leader of the war party," was hired for a fee of $100,000 to represent the studios at the hearings. Korda wrote a brief for Willkie on *That Hamilton Woman*, explaining that everything in the screenplay was based on fact, though the word "despot" had been exchanged for "dictator" to make it more contemporary. "We would not use 'thees' and 'thous' in a picture," he explained.[16] Korda suggested to Willkie that "the fact that the film shows a great similarity between the Napoleonic era and the present day is only natural"[17] and that an American silent picture had already been made about Hamilton, *Divine Lady* (1929), and there was even a German silent, *Lady Hamilton* (1921), with Conrad Veidt,[18] a refugee from Nazism now living in Hollywood, as Nelson.

Willkie was forthright about Hollywood's anti-Nazi bias. "The motion picture industry and its executives are opposed to the Hitler regime," which in turn represented the views of the "great overwhelming majority of the people of our country," he wrote in a submission to the committee.[19] He denied there was a conspiracy between the studios and foreign powers to denigrate Nazism. He ridiculed the committee's failure to come up with any proposals, let alone legislation, to oblige Hollywood to be evenhanded. He asked the committee to allow him to call German witnesses of Nazi oppression to show that Hollywood's portrayal of life under Hitler was accurate. The committee declined.

Willkie called upon Harry M. Warner, president of Warner Brothers, whom Nye had accused of producing more prowar propaganda movies than any other studio boss. Warner's prided itself on using contemporary themes as backgrounds for its gritty dramas and eagerly pursued the burgeoning audience for anti-Nazi movies. Warner told the committee:

> I am opposed to Nazi-ism. I abhor and detest every principle and practice of the Nazi movement. To me, Nazi-ism typifies the very opposite of the kind of life every decent man, woman, and child wants to live. I believe Nazi-ism is a world revolution whose ultimate objective is to destroy our democracy, wipe out all religion, and enslave our people—just as Germany has destroyed and enslaved Poland, Belgium, Holland and France. I am ready to give myself and all my personal resources to aid in the defeat of the Nazi menace to the American people.

"If Warner Bros. had produced no pictures concerning the Nazi movement, our public would have had good reason to criticize," he said. "Our accusers desire that we change our policy of picturing accurately world affairs and the national defense program. This Warner Bros. will never do." He said he had backed the president's foreign policy since war was declared in 1939 and that "the freedom which this country fought England to obtain, we may have to fight with England to retain. . . . The President knows the world situation and our country's problems better than any other man. I would follow his recommendation concerning a declaration of war."

Next on the stand was Darryl F. Zanuck,[20] in charge of production at Twentieth Century–Fox.

> In the time of acute national peril, I feel that it is the duty of every American to give his complete cooperation and support to our President and our Congress to do everything to defeat Hitler and preserve America. If this course of necessity leads to war, I want to follow my President along that course.

Zanuck reminded the committee that Hollywood had promoted the American way of life around the world. "They sold it so strongly that when dictators took over Italy and Germany, what did Hitler and his flunky, Mussolini, do? The first thing they did was to ban our pictures." His words were met with applause.

When it was Flynn's turn to testify, he offered a paradox: "Sometimes the worst kind of propaganda is propaganda which is particularly true." He accused the movie business of establishing a monopoly in production, distribution, and exhibition that should be broken up. Flynn, who was never the most charismatic or eloquent of speakers despite his chosen profession, believed the odds were stacked against isolationists like him. "When I am talking in a hall to two or three thousand people, there is some fellow who practically has just arrived here from Europe a few months ago who is talking to 5,000,000 over the radio." Anyone who cornered the market in movies and radio shows "has got the other side licked almost before they start." He threatened a change in the law. "There is censorship for you gentlemen to worry about," he said.[21]

From the committee bench, D. Worth Clark extended the monopoly argument beyond movies to the "small oligarchy" that owned the media. He complained, "The man who owns the radio machine can cut off from discussion those who disagree with him by the simple expedient of saying 'No.' And who is this man? . . . He is just a businessman who by virtue of his acquisitive talents has gotten possession of this little microphone."

The small group of men who owned and ran the movie business—Paramount, Loew's, RKO, Warner's, Twentieth Century-Fox, Universal, and United Artists—"have opened those 17,000 theaters to the idea of war, to the glorification of war, to the glorification of England's imperialism, to the hatred of the people of Germany and now of France, to the hatred of those in America who disagree with them." Going to the movie theater was little more than attending "daily and nightly mass meetings for war," he said, while "not one word on the side of the argument against war is heard."[22]

As time went on, the hearings turned to comedy. Nye admitted that he had not seen all the films he listed as prowar and couldn't remember much about those he had. Asked by Senator Ernest McFarland whether he had seen *Convoy*, Nye replied, "I think I did."

Pressed on why he objected to the movie, Nye said, "I am at a loss to call to mind any particular feature about it that led me to draw the conclusion which I have drawn." He had seen *Confessions of a Nazi Spy* and *I Married a Nazi*, but "for the life of me I could not tell you which was which." He admitted that "the representations of others have played a large part in the conclusions that I have drawn."[23]

Nye had seen Chaplin's *The Great Dictator* and thought it a "portrayal by a great artist, not a citizen of our country," but felt it "could not do other than build within the heart and mind of those who watched it something of a hatred, detestation of conditions and of leadership that existed abroad." Willkie asked Nye whether, if Hollywood was expected to portray both sides evenhandedly, he meant that "since Chaplin made a laughable caricature of Hitler, the industry should be forced to employ Charles Laughton to do the same on Winston Churchill?"[24]

By the time Champ Clark admitted he was "so disgusted" with Hollywood that he "very seldom attend[ed] a motion picture show" and therefore had seen none of the eight films named, the subcommittee had become a laughingstock. After three weeks of hearings, the isolationists on the committee had merely allowed a string of high-profile show people to draw attention to the merits of the anti-Nazi cause.

The interventionist group Fight for Freedom called the hearings "the most barefaced attempt at censorship and racial persecution which has ever been tried in this country."[25] The *New York Herald Tribune* was alarmed by "the note of hysteria which every day becomes more apparent."[26] The *Nation* condemned the committee's work, saying, "The American people are expected to believe, after all that has happened in the past decade, that the Nazi menace is a figment of the Jewish imagination."[27]

Everyone agreed that Willkie, with his goading and prodding of inept, ill-prepared witnesses like Nye, had earned his generous fee. The hearings were adjourned on September 26, never to be resumed.[28] The committee never issued a report.

Then came a speech by Lindbergh on September 11 in the Coliseum, Des Moines, Iowa. The circumstances were awkward from the start. A week earlier, the US Navy destroyer the *Greer* had been sunk by a German U-boat and Roosevelt's mother, Sara, died three days later, obliging the president to put off a scheduled fireside chat about the naval incident until September 11, the date of Lindbergh's address. Such was the general appetite on both sides to hear the president that the Des Moines chapter of America First decided to relay the broadcast to the hall before calling Lindbergh and the other speakers.

The president railed against Hitler's "piracy legally and morally." "It is the Nazi design to abolish the freedom of the seas, and to acquire absolute control and domination of these seas for themselves," he said. Alluding to Lindbergh and the America Firsters, the president condemned "Hitler's advance guards—not only his avowed agents but also his dupes among us." He said it was time Americans stopped being "deluded by the romantic notion that the Americas can go on living happily and peacefully in a Nazi-dominated world." There should be "no tender whisperings of appeasers that Hitler is not interested in the Western Hemisphere, no soporific lullabies that a wide ocean protects us from him." It was not an act of war to defend oneself, he declared, before announcing that "if German or Italian vessels of war enter the waters, the protection of which is necessary for American defense, they do so at their own peril."[29] Belatedly, Americans were being told that US Navy captains had in effect been put under standing orders to shoot on sight.

Lindbergh felt that having to follow the president's address "gave us about as bad a setting as we could have had for our meeting." He took to the stage amid boos and jeering, "the most unfriendly crowd of any meeting to date, by far." His troubles were magnified when the sound system worked intermittently for the first few minutes. But it was the content of his message that caused the most consternation.

"I can understand why the Jewish people wish to overthrow the Nazis," he said. "The persecution they have suffered in Germany would be sufficient to make bitter enemies of any race." But, "though I sympathize with the Jew," he said, "let me add a word of warning. No person of honesty and vision can look on their pro-war policy here today without seeing the dangers involved in such a policy, both for us—and for them."

It was a veiled threat that if American Jews persisted in encouraging the nation toward war, they would come to pay a heavy price. Lindbergh continued:

Instead of agitating for war, the Jewish groups in this country should be opposing it in every possible way, for they will be among the first to feel its consequences. . . . A few far-sighted Jewish people realize [that wartime spells an end to tolerance] and stand opposed to intervention. But the majority still do not. Their greatest danger to this country lies in their large ownership and influence in our motion pictures, our press, our radio, and our Government. . . . We cannot blame them for looking out for what they believe to be their own interests, but we also must look out for ours.[30]

Lindbergh was aware of the controversy he was courting. In an early draft of the speech he had written, "I realize that in speaking this frankly I am entering in where angels fear to tread. I realize that tomorrow morning's headlines will say 'Lindbergh attacks Jews.' The ugly cry of anti-Semitism will be eagerly joyfully pounded upon and waved about my name."[31] Although he chose to omit those words from the speech he delivered, it would not have made any difference. "It seems that almost anything can be discussed today in America except the Jewish problem," he complained to his diary.[32]

As predicted, Lindbergh was bombarded with accusations of anti-Semitism. As the historian Wayne Cole put it, "They came from Jews, but also from Protestants and Catholics. They came from interventionists, but also from noninterventionists. They came from Democrats, but also from Republicans and Communists. They came from high government leaders, but also from grassroots America."[33]

The New York Herald Tribune condemned Lindbergh for raising a subject that "all good Americans pray might be confined to the pages of the [Nazi Party daily paper] Völkischer Beobachter and the addresses of Adolf Hitler."[34] Lindbergh protested his innocence of all charges, though he confessed to his diary, "The power of our opposition is great. . . . Their ranks include the American government, the British government, the Jews, and the major portion of the press, radio, and motion picture facilities." Anne Lindbergh, who had tried to rewrite her husband's speech to soften its racial message, was "very disturbed" and was enduring a "profound feeling of grief"[35] that he had become "the symbol of anti-Semitism in this country & looked to as the leader of it."[36]

Lindbergh's remarks went too far for a number of leading isolationists. While Webster told him that the "majority" of America

First members "were in accord" with what he said, Flynn said "it was inadvisable to mention the Jewish problem,"[37] though he did not question the truth of what Lindbergh had said. Hoover told Lindbergh that the address was "a mistake."[38] Wood, under pressure from the Sears, Roebuck board for spending too much time campaigning, called a meeting in Chicago and proposed "adjourning" the America First committee until the following year's congressional elections, on the grounds that "since the President had already involved us seriously in war, the committee saw nothing gained by continuing its activities."[39] Lindbergh offered to issue a statement that the views expressed in Des Moines were his own and not those of the committee.

Lindbergh was becoming increasingly paranoid and his accusations more wild. The next month, he delivered a broadcast address from Fort Wayne, Indiana, saying he feared that that might be his last broadcast as he fully expected to be stopped from speaking in future. "Pressure," "smear campaigns," and "censorship" were being used to silence non-interventionists, he claimed, and "Congress, like the Reichstag, is not consulted."

The president was "drawing more and more dictatorial powers into his own hands," he said, and only elections could put a stop to his power grab. "But what if there are no elections next year?" he asked. "Such a condition may not be many steps ahead on the road our President is taking us."[40] He was taken to task by the *New York Times* for suggesting that "the President is planning a coup d'état." Such accusations "can only serve one purpose—to bring aid and comfort to the enemies of democracy."[41]

Lindbergh was becoming too hot for radio networks to handle. Later in October, when he spoke again at Madison Square Garden to a crowd of 20,000 inside and 30,000 out, alongside Wheeler, Flynn, John Cudahy, and others, all three major networks agreed to broadcast only part of Wheeler's speech and none of Lindbergh's. "We know of no reason why Lindbergh should have a nationwide network every time he speaks," said a CBS spokesman. "We do not intend to provide one just because tactics of hullabaloo and threats are used against us."

A former magistrate, Joseph Goldstein, threatened to arrest any speaker who made slurring remarks against Jews if the police

did not do so. And if the police did not do so, he would also prefer charges against the mayor and the police commissioner. Outside
in the street, Fight for Freedom volunteers shouted, "Read the facts
about America's Number One Nazi!" and handed out envelopes containing a pamphlet linking Lindbergh to Hitler.

Lindbergh renewed his assault upon the administration. "They
preach about preserving democracy and freedom abroad, while they
practice dictatorship and subterfuge at home," he said. "In spite
of the opposition of the American people, we have been led step by
step to war, until today we are actually engaged in undeclared naval
warfare." Wheeler said that if the Neutrality Act made it clear that
America wanted to avoid becoming entangled in war, the repeal of
the act "makes it equally clear that we seek foreign entanglements,
that we will become involved in war."[42]

The New York Times commented, "We cannot find a word or a line
in Mr. Lindbergh's speech last night that will not be cheered to the
echo by the gangsters in Berlin," and pondered why "an American
citizen, richly honored by his countrymen, loving his country and
its institutions, could make a carefully prepared speech on this subject and include in it not even a whisper of reproach for Nazi perfidy,
Nazi blasphemy, Nazi insolence and Nazi cruelty."[43]

The rush to war overwhelmed the isolationists in Congress and,
on November 7, a revision of the Neutrality Act was passed by fifty
votes to thirty-seven in the Senate, and the next week agreed by 212
to 194 in the House. The following day, America First discussed
proposing a "peace plan" to bring an end to the European war and
prevent a war with Japan, though Lindbergh was against such an
idea as "we would find ourselves in the position of guaranteeing a
peace that could not last."[44] Lindbergh proposed that America First
should stand as an independent "non-partisan" group in the congressional elections of 1942, and the group considered campaigning
for candidates who opposed American entry into the war.

At the start of November, rumors began circulating that Japan
was about to launch a major invasion of another nation, prompting Churchill to ask Roosevelt to "prevent a melancholy extension
of the war" by threatening that any further Japanese aggression
would lead to America declaring war. The president replied that
he was limited by the Constitution and could not deliver such an

ultimatum. He told Halifax that "his perpetual problem was to steer a course between the two factors represented by: (1) The wish of 70 per cent of Americans to keep out of war; (2) The wish of 70 per cent of Americans to do everything to break Hitler, even if it means war,"[45] and urged Churchill to threaten war if Japan invaded Siam (Thailand), a threat which would be "whole-heartedly supported by the United States," though he failed to mention the exact nature of that support. On December 2, Churchill told the cabinet that British policy "is not to take forward action in advance of the United States."

On December 7, Roosevelt agreed with Churchill that any attempt by Japan to invade Siam or British and Dutch possessions would be considered "a hostile act"[46] against America. Churchill told his military chief in the Middle East, Claude Auchinleck,[47] that the president's commitment was "a great relief as I had long dreaded being at war with Japan without or before the United States." The same day, Churchill sent a message to the Siamese premier. "There is a possibility of imminent Japanese invasion of your country," he wrote. "If you are attacked, defend yourself. The preservation of the full independence and sovereignty of Siam is a British interest and we shall regard an attack on you as an attack on ourselves."[48]

The same evening, Churchill was dining at Chequers with Averell Harriman and Kennedy's successor as ambassador in London, John G. Winant.[49] Listening to the BBC news, Churchill heard an early report that spoke of "an attack by Japanese on American shipping at Hawaii." As the facts became clearer, it emerged that Japanese warplanes had mounted a surprise attack lasting about ninety minutes on American warships at anchor in Pearl Harbor. Four battleships were sunk and 2,000 servicemen killed. Churchill called Roosevelt. "Mr. President," he asked, "what's this about Japan?" "It's quite true," replied the president. "They have attacked us at Pearl Harbor. We are all in the same boat now."[50]

Still Roosevelt offered conflicting signals about his true wishes. Lunching with Hopkins that day, as the news dribbled in about the attack, Roosevelt "discussed at length his efforts to keep the country out of the war and his earnest desire to complete his administration without war, but that if this action of Japan's were true it would take the matter entirely out of his hands, because the Japanese had made the decision for him."[51] It was a sure sign that the isolationists were left with nowhere to turn. War had arrived.

The sudden attack on American soil overshadowed the rest of the news. At the same time as Pearl Harbor, Japan invaded Siam and the Dutch East Indies and tried to land forces in British Malaya. On the evening of December 8, Congress voted to declare war against Japan. The Senate approved the declaration of war all but unanimously, with a single holdout: Jeannette Rankin, Republican from Montana.

As soon as the vote was in, Roosevelt cabled Churchill: "Today all of us are in the same boat with you and the people of the Empire, and it is a ship which will not and cannot be sunk."[52]

ISOLATIONISM REDUX

*The United States finally joins World War Two,
the isolationists disband, Roosevelt founds the United
Nations. After the Cold War ends, isolationism
in America starts to reappear.*

BY ATTACKING the US Navy's Pacific Fleet, the Japanese shot the isolationists' fox. All arguments about America staying out of war were made redundant. In a specially summoned meeting on November 7, Roosevelt asked his cabinet whether "the people would back us up in case we struck at Japan down there" and, Stimson recalled, they were "unanimous in feeling the country would support us."[1] The cabinet were right. There was an immediate, overwhelming patriotic response from the American people demanding that the president declare war on Japan.

Many isolationists had anticipated the course of events. One of Roosevelt's most persistent critics, Senator Gerald Nye, thought it "probable that if we got into the [European] war it would be through the back door of Japan,"[2] and there had been a frantic effort by America First on December 5 to mobilize sympathetic congressmen to speak out against action against Japan. But it was too late. The attack on Pearl Harbor on Sunday, December 7, came before the isolationists could mount a preemptive peace campaign. On the evening of the surprise assault, Roosevelt invited to the White House the stalwart isolationist Senator Hiram Johnson, ranking member of the Foreign Relations Committee, who expressed the view that "the worst part of this Japanese war" was that it would slide "very easily into the European war."[3]

Other isolationists and non-interventionists were quick to rally around the president. Old campaigner Senator Burton Wheeler declared that "the only thing to do now is to do our best to lick the hell out of them." He was joined by Senator Arthur H. Vandenberg, another stalwart opponent of intervention, who promised Roosevelt support "without reservation." "Nothing matters except VICTORY," he wrote in his diary. "The 'arguments' must be postponed."[4] Arthur Capper, a longstanding isolationist senator from Kansas, wrote to Roosevelt pledging his "fullest support and cooperation in steps which may be required to bring the war to a successful conclusion."[5] Even the president's favorite punching bag, Congressman Hamilton Fish, had the good grace to write saying that "the time for debate and controversy has passed" and asking how he could "best help promote unity, uphold your war program, serve my country."[6]

On December 8, Roosevelt addressed both houses of Congress and described the Japanese attack the previous day as "a date which will live in infamy. . . . I believe I interpret the will of the Congress and of the people when I assert that we will not only defend ourselves to the uttermost but will make very certain that this form of treachery shall never endanger us again."[7] The same day, the Senate voted unanimously in favor of war with Japan, with Vandenberg the only senator to speak. Isolationists and non-interventionists, he said, were "not deserting our beliefs, but . . . were postponing all further arguments over policy until the battle forced upon us by Japan is won." "To better swing the vast anti-war party in the country into unity,"[8] he would vote in favor.

Losing so many prominent supporters overnight, America First soon followed suit, the national headquarters in Chicago suggesting in a mass mailing on December 7 that the movement's members should "give their support to the war effort of this country until the conflict with Japan is brought to a successful conclusion. In this war the America First Committee pledges its aid to the President as commander in chief." All campaigning and leafleting was halted. The statement's allusion to Japan, like that of Vandenberg, was significant, for some of the leadership held out the possibility that America would restrict its fighting to the Pacific theater. Those who had a sneaking sympathy for Germany hoped it might be possible for

America to retaliate against the Japanese without also confronting Hitler's expansionism. Roosevelt, too, was careful not to ask Congress for a declaration of war against Germany lest he be seen as the aggressor by those Americans still reluctant to consent to joining Britain in the war against Nazism.

Pearl Harbor might not have been enough to deter continued efforts to keep America out of the European conflict by a rump of isolationists had it not been for Hitler's surprising response to the attack. He had long urged the Japanese leaders to attack British interests in the East, but had not ventured to encourage an assault upon America. Germany and Japan enjoyed an alliance that stopped short of mutual defense, so there was no public obligation for Hitler to spring to Japan's defense. It might have suited him to have the US preoccupied with a Pacific war that would distract it from helping Britain in the Atlantic. What few knew at the time, however, was that in April 1941 Hitler had made a secret pledge that "in case of a conflict between Japan and America" Germany "would promptly take part."[9] On December 11, therefore, after a blistering personal assault upon Roosevelt delivered to the Reichstag, in which he blamed the war on the president and "the Jews, in all their satanic baseness, gathered around this man,"[10] Hitler declared war against the United States. On hearing the news, Roosevelt promptly asked Congress for a declaration of war against Germany and Italy, which was approved unanimously.

The same day, in Chicago, the leaders of America First met. A minority still felt that "some method of adjourning was preferable to complete liquidation," but, led by Robert E. Wood and John T. Flynn, the majority of the ruling committee voted to dissolve the organization. In a final statement, they maintained to the end, "Our principles were right. Had they been followed, war could have been avoided. No good purpose can now be served by considering what might have been. . . . Today, though there may be many important subsidiary considerations, the primary objective is . . . victory." The conclusion could not have been more emphatic: "The America First Committee has determined immediately to cease all functions and to dissolve as soon as that can legally be done."[11]

A few dissenting isolationists still held out, but overwhelmingly, prominent members of America First not only bowed to the inevitable but volunteered to serve the war effort. Roosevelt was less than gracious in dealing with some of those who, he felt, had been so wrong for so long and, he suspected, still harbored pro-German sympathies. These included Wood, a brigadier general in World War One, who, despite his age of sixty-two, offered his services. The president wrote to army chief of staff George C. Marshall, "I do not think that General R. E. Wood should be put in uniform. He is too old and has, in the past, shown far too great approval for Nazi methods."[12] Wood was restricted to offering advice to Henry H. Arnold, chief of the Army Air Forces, as a civilian. One of the principal founders of America First, R. Douglas Stuart Jr., was treated more gently and went on to serve as a major on Eisenhower's Supreme Headquarters Allied Expeditionary Force in Britain. He saw active duty, landing in Normandy in the Allied invasion of German-occupied France shortly after D-Day.

Charles Lindbergh greeted Pearl Harbor not with the indignation shared by the vast majority of Americans but with a pointed question about whether Roosevelt had not left the Pacific Fleet vulnerable when he sent part of the navy to protect the trade route to Britain in the Atlantic. Lindbergh's response was one of reluctant patriotism. "We have brought it on our own shoulders," he told his diary, "but I can see nothing to do under these circumstances except to fight. If I had been in Congress, I certainly would have voted for a declaration of war."[13] He considered writing directly to Roosevelt, "telling him that while I had opposed him in the past and had not changed my convictions, I was ready in time of war to submerge my personal viewpoint in the general welfare and unity of the country."[14] He decided instead to approach Arnold with a view to offering his considerable expertise in flight engineering to the Army Air Corps.

As soon as it became known that Lindbergh was volunteering for service, a barrage of hostile stories appeared in the press calling him a traitor and a Nazi. A number of Americans said they would not be happy for Lindbergh to join the armed forces. One couple wrote to a newspaper, "Our son is in the service and we want no Quislings behind his back."[15] Lindbergh was the subject of similar vitriol from those in government, led by his perennial enemy, Interior secretary Harold Ickes. Lindbergh should not be allowed to serve in the armed forces, Ickes wrote to Roosevelt, because he was "a ruthless and conscious fascist, motivated by a hatred for you personally and a contempt for democracy in general." Lindbergh should be "buried in merciful oblivion."[16]

Roosevelt replied, "What you say about Lindbergh and the potential danger of the man, I agree with wholeheartedly,"[17] and passed Ickes's letter on to secretary of war Stimson and secretary of the navy Frank Knox. Roosevelt suggested to Stimson that the solution to Lindbergh's request was that "for the time being the matter can be possibly maintained 'under consideration'."[18] After meeting with Stimson, who told Lindbergh to his face that he was hampered by his "political views" and consequent "lack of aggressiveness," he said it would be inappropriate to appoint Lindbergh to a "position of command." Lindbergh abandoned all attempts to join the services.

He soon discovered he was also persona non grata in the commercial aircraft companies in receipt of federally funded arms orders. He enquired about work at Pan American, United Aircraft, and Curtiss-Wright, but each time the War Department or the White House was consulted, Lindbergh's application for work was rejected. By February 1942 he was in despair, though he appeared to remain oblivious of why his past words and actions had caused so much offense. "I have always believed in the past that every American citizen had the right and the duty to state his opinion in peace and to fight for his country in war," he told his diary. "But the Roosevelt Administration seems to think otherwise."[19]

Salvation came in the form of his old isolationist friend Henry Ford, whose assembly lines since the summer of 1941 had been busily building Consolidated B-24 Liberator bomber planes. Unlike the management of the other commercial airlines and plane manufacturers, Ford was prepared to defy Roosevelt in the belief that the administration could ill afford to withdraw contracts to build urgently needed warplanes over such a trivial issue. "It annoys him to think he has to ask anyone what he wants to do in his own factory," wrote Lindbergh. "And, as a matter of fact, it annoys me to have to ask the government's position to make a connection with a commercial company; it's too damn much like Russia!"[20] Ford put Lindbergh to work at his Willow Run plant.

Once war was engaged in earnest, there was little time for anyone in the Roosevelt administration to concern themselves with the part Lindbergh was playing, which led to him operating as a test pilot improving the Navy Marine Chance Vought F4U Corsair fighter for United Aircraft Corporation. By April 1944, he was in the South Pacific and, unknown to the military authorities, flying combat missions against the Japanese. In total, he flew in combat fifty times in Lockheed P-38s and Marine Corps Vought F4U Corsair fighters. On July 28, flying a P-38, he shot down a Japanese fighter over Elpaputih Bay, Seram island, Indonesia, in an aerial duel. In September, anxious that Lindbergh's combat role would become known back home or that he would be shot down, he was ordered back to the United States. After all his profound reservations about countering Fascism, it might be said that Lindbergh had a "good war."

Other isolationists, such as William Randolph Hearst, were less fortunate. Though he was allowed to retain editorial control of his newspapers after his forced bankruptcy in 1936, when his company was acquired by his creditors, led by Chase Manhattan bank, who put his vast collection of semiprecious antiques under the hammer, his strident newspaper columns laden with isolationist opinions had long lost their potency. Increasingly he came to be viewed as a silly old man brought low by women and his own profligacy. He told his financial adviser, John Neylan, that when it came to antiques, "I'm like a dipsomaniac. They keep sending me these catalogs and I can't resist them."[21] When a bombastic, bullying newspaper proprietor's private life becomes news, it marks the beginning of the end of his influence. Once a great power in the land, Hearst had become a laughingstock.

His friendly advice to Hitler after Kristallnacht had appeared naive and out of touch, and his hectoring of Roosevelt for daring to anticipate a war with Germany had sounded increasingly petty. When war broke out in Europe in September 1939, his view that "occidental culture and political policies and material advancement will be lost. Only cruel, destructive Asiatic tyranny will triumph,"[22] echoing Lindbergh's racial theories, had appeared insular and irrelevant. In late 1939 and early 1940, his financial state became even more parlous when his investors began to sue him for mismanaging his company. His hysterical response to Roosevelt's sale of old destroyers to Britain—"Well folks, as your columnist foretold, we are in war. . . . We all have in the neighborhood of three weeks, according to our admirals, in which to prepare boarders. . . . Mr Roosevelt has his wish at last."[23]—had appeared alarmist and plain wrong.

After Pearl Harbor, Hearst effected a perfect backward somersault which diminished his influence further. "Well, fellow Americans, we are in the war and we have got to win it," he wrote. "There may have been some differences of opinion among good Americans about getting into the war, but there is no difference about how we should come out of it. We must come out victorious."[24] Paradoxically, it was the great increase in the public's appetite for news about the war that he had tried so hard to prevent that eventually returned Hearst to financial health. By early 1945, he had regained control of his company. It had come, however, at a huge price to both Hearst's political influence and his personal health.

Pearl Harbor also brought an abrupt end to the activities of the radio priest Charles Coughlin, who had for years been playing a cat and mouse game with his Roman Catholic superiors and the federal authorities. Roosevelt had tried many times to silence Coughlin, whose anti-Semitic and isolationist Sunday broadcast sermons and his vitriolic attacks on the president through his newspaper, *Social Justice*, continued despite his being banned from the main networks. The president had offered a bargain to the Catholic hierarchy—to appoint to the Vatican an official US envoy, if not quite a full ambassador, if Coughlin were silenced—but to no avail. Roosevelt had even threatened the Catholic archbishops with an income tax audit if they did not act.[25] With America now at war, however, an investigation was launched into the funding and content of *Social Justice*, and evidence was found by the FBI and Justice Department that the paper was partly funded by a pro-German lobbyist and that the paper was urging dissent in the armed forces and publishing seditious articles that undermined the war effort. Finally, the reluctant Catholic authorities, who had been flummoxed by Coughlin's dodging and weaving, were obliged to act.

A deal was finally struck in May 1942 between US attorney general Francis Biddle and Coughlin's bishop, Edward Mooney, which agreed that the case against Coughlin and *Social Justice* would be dropped, thereby avoiding the spectacle of the Justice Department prosecuting a Catholic priest, and the Catholic Church being shown to have for decades protected America's most vocal anti-Semite. The quid pro quo was that Coughlin would be muzzled. The agreement did not entirely stop Coughlin from trying to spread his hateful creed, and not long afterward he was threatened with further prosecution when he began collecting the names and addresses of members of the armed forces to mail them antiwar literature. The deal did, however, mark the end of Coughlin's malignant national influence and he went to his grave in 1979 cursing Roosevelt, protesting his innocence, and insisting that he had at all times remained within the law and the spirit of Catholic teaching.

Like Henry Ford, Walt Disney's silence was bought off through the awarding of federal government contracts. Disney's animations were highly labor-intensive and expensive to produce, but the ease with which they could be dubbed into foreign languages raised substantial revenues around the world. The start of the European conflict in September 1939 had put an abrupt end to those foreign earnings because of the closure of German and other Nazi-occupied markets. In the summer of 1941, the federal government stepped in to make up the lost returns by sending Disney and a team of animators to South America for ten weeks to make animated shorts that would stress the importance of having the US as an ally and neighbor. The result was a pair of charming animated features, *Saludos Amigos* (1942) and *The Three Caballeros* (1944), which proved to be hits with audiences in both North and South America. War with Germany and Japan entailed even more government work being passed Disney's way, with commissions for short films to introduce new draftees into the ways of army life, such as Donald Duck in *Donald Gets Drafted* (1942), and morale-boosting comedies at the expense of Hitler, such as *Der Fuhrer's Face* (1943).

As soon as he heard about the attack on Pearl Harbor, Joe Kennedy, who had worked hard and long to keep America at arm's length from the European war, sent a cable to Roosevelt: "In this great crisis all Americans are with you. Name the Battle Post. I'm yours to command." After repeatedly ignoring the letter, Roosevelt offered him a lowly post running two shipyards in Maine. Kennedy declined. He was obliged to spend the rest of the war in forced retirement. He watched as his two elder sons volunteered for military service. Of all the isolationists to have been defeated by Roosevelt, Kennedy suffered most at the hands of a war he had tried so hard to prevent. He had once said that the inspiration for his isolationism was simply to protect his children from an early grave. As he watched the war unfold from the gilded cage of his compounds in Hyannis Port, Cape Cod, Massachusetts, and Palm Beach, Florida, he suffered a series of personal family tragedies which he had for ten years been trying so hard to avoid.

Kennedy had high ambitions for his eldest son, Joseph P. Kennedy Jr. Through young Joe he plotted a long and vicarious campaign to take the White House. It was Kennedy's plan that his eldest son should become governor of Massachusetts, then president. The first step was to win an empty House seat in Massachusetts's 11th District in the 1946 election, which, given the pull of the Kennedys and Joe Jr.'s mother's family, the Fitzgeralds, in their home state, was sure to be a shoo-in. But the war intervened. Young Joe was served with a low-numbered draft card while in his final year at Harvard, and rather than wait to see what post the War Department awarded him, in August 1942 he enlisted in the navy, won his wings as a pilot, and found his way back to Britain as a naval flier. Kennedy was proud of his firstborn taking such a prominent and dangerous role. "Wouldn't you know," he told a friend. "Naval aviation. The most dangerous thing there is."[26]

His second son, John F. Kennedy, known as Jack, suffered from severe back troubles and in September 1941 was rejected by both the army and navy on medical grounds. Undeterred, he had his father write to Captain Alan Kirk, director of naval intelligence in Washington DC, to intervene. After passing a cursory medical examination that made no attempt to discover his many ailments, John Kennedy served briefly in the office of the secretary of the navy before training to become a motor torpedo boat captain. On August 2, 1943, while patrolling for Japanese shipping at night near New Georgia in the Solomon Islands, his patrol boat, PT-109, was rammed and cut in two by a Japanese destroyer, the *Amagiri*. Joe Kennedy was immediately informed that his son was missing in action, but did not pass on the news to Rose. Four days later, it emerged that John and ten of his crew had survived the sinking and swum to shore. After an SOS message scribbled on a coconut shell was passed to a sympathetic islander, they were all rescued.

In July the following year, after two tours of duty, young Joe, who had just celebrated his twenty-ninth birthday, embarked on a most dangerous mission. He and another pilot were to fly a Consolidated PB4Y Privateer bomber, built at Henry Ford's factory at Willow Run, laden with 22,000 pounds of explosives to penetrate the deep concrete defenses of German submarine bases on the Belgian coast. The plan was to bail out over the North Sea and be picked up by British patrols, leaving the plane to be directed by remote control to its target. Just before the two men were due to jump out of the plane, it blew up. Neither body was ever found.

When Kennedy was told the news by a priest, he took to his room in his home in Hyannis Port and remained there for days, listening to classical music on a gramophone. "It has been a terrible blow to us both," he wrote to Roosevelt's secretary, Grace Tully, "particularly as he was the oldest boy and I had spent a great deal of time making what I thought were plans for his future."[27] Kennedy was devastated and for the rest of his life was never able to mention young Joe's name without weeping. Twenty-five years later, he told a reporter, "Every night of my life I say a prayer for him."[28]

A month after young Joe's death, Kennedy was struck a further blow. His daughter Kathleen, known as Kick, had abandoned her job as a reporter on Colonel McCormick's *Washington Times–Herald* to volunteer for Red Cross service in London, where she fell in love with and soon became engaged to a young aristocrat, William, Marquess of Hartington,[29] heir to the Duke of Devonshire, the scion of one of the most socially grand families in Britain and a major in the Coldstream Guards. The love affair was troubled because she was a Roman Catholic and he an Anglican. Protocol insisted that any children of the marriage be brought up as Protestants. The Kennedys, in particular the pious Rose, were wholly against the union and it was young Joe who intervened, encouraging his sister to follow her heart. Behind his wife's back, the socially ambitious Kennedy quietly encouraged the union, sending Kathleen a paternal note of support: "With your faith in God you can't make a mistake. Remember you are still and always will be tops with me."[30] Instead of the lavish wedding that was Hartington's due, the couple married quietly at Chelsea Register Office on May 6, 1944, with Nancy Astor in attendance. The groom's family sent hearty congratulations; no word came from either Joe or Rose Kennedy. The happy couple spent just five weeks together before Hartington joined the Allied invasion of France. Four months later, on September 9, 1944, he was shot dead by a German sniper outside Heppen, Belgium.

Four years later, on May 13, 1948, while flying to meet her father for a vacation on the French Riviera, Kathleen's plane crashed into the mountains of the Ardèche above the Rhône. Kennedy rushed to identify the remains of his twenty-eight-year-old daughter, who was buried next to her husband in the Cavendish family cemetery at Chatsworth, Derbyshire. Kennedy was inconsolable. He told the *Boston Globe*'s Joe Dineen, "Nothing means anything any more. There's nothing I can say."[31]

In a letter to Beaverbrook, Kennedy summed up the nature of his grief. "For a fellow who didn't want this war to touch your country or mine, I have had a rather bad dose," he wrote. "Joe dead, Billy Hartington dead, my son Jack in the Naval Hospital. I have had brought home to me very personally what I saw for all the mothers and fathers of the world."[32]

HITLER'S POOR JUDGMENT in declaring war against the United States immediately after Pearl Harbor ensured his defeat. The Axis, already starved of the raw materials and energy supplies needed to fight the war, now invited the full wrath of the world's greatest industrial power. Thanks to Roosevelt's percipience, and with no thanks to the isolationists, the non-interventionists and the rest, rearmament was already in full spate, with highly advanced plants delivering planes, tanks, ammunition, and assorted weaponry and military vehicles day and night. The logistics of winning back the Pacific islands and mounting an assault on Tokyo, and invading Europe and defeating the Germans from the west, would prove a severe test of American logistics, and there would undoubtedly be setbacks. But the outcome of the war was no longer in doubt. Just as Woodrow Wilson's intervention in World War One ensured that the Germans would lose, so Roosevelt's involvement in World War Two made the result a foregone conclusion. It was little wonder that when Churchill heard that Hitler had declared war on the United States he cabled his foreign secretary, Anthony Eden: "The accession of the United States makes amends for all, and with time and patience will give certain victory."[33]

In making arrangements for the peace, Roosevelt learned the lessons of Wilson's vain attempts to have the Versailles Treaty ratified by the Senate. There would be no treaty to ratify this time. He would insist that the Axis leaders surrender unconditionally. He took a similar view of the United Nations, his iteration of the League of Nations. It would be a fait accompli, designed and constructed by his administration without reference to Congress.

Roosevelt encouraged other key elements of a new, permanent international order, by which he ensured that the United States would bear the international responsibilities that stemmed from its position as the world's preeminent economic power. At the Bretton Woods Conference in 1944, presided over by the British economist John Maynard Keynes, he encouraged the establishment of the International Monetary Fund, to regulate the world's financial and monetary system, the World Bank, to lend money to developing nations, and an agreement named after Bretton Woods to maintain order in the trading of world currencies.

At conferences with Churchill in Casablanca, Morocco, in January 1943, and with Churchill and Stalin at Yalta, Crimea, in February 1945, the world was divided into spheres of influence. By the time of the third great Allied conference, at Potsdam, in eastern Germany, Roosevelt was dead.[34] He died of a cerebral hemorrhage in Warm Springs, Georgia, in the company of his mistress, Lucy Rutherfurd, the married name of the woman he had promised Eleanor thirty years before he would never see again. They had kept up a love affair for three decades.

When victory came, the American people appeared to take their new world role in their stride. No sooner had the Axis been defeated than a new specter arrived in the shape of the expansionist plans of the two great Communist powers, the Soviet Union and China. Under Stalin's despotic direction, the focus of what came to be known as the Cold War was the division of Germany. In June 1948, to press the western Allies to vacate the still-occupied German capital of Berlin, the Soviets besieged the city. The United States, Britain, and France responded with the Berlin Airlift, a daring display of American military and economic might that lasted until May the following year. Other proxy wars between Communism and the West broke out in June 1950 in Korea, where forces under the flag of the United Nations fought to halt a Communist takeover of the peninsula. Korea was left divided between a Communist north and a democratic south. A similar, ideologically-driven war divided Vietnam into north and south, which was to lead to the Vietnam War, perhaps the most tragic and traumatic conflict of the Cold War.

By 1953, a million US troops were deployed abroad, rising to nearly 1.1 million at the height of the Vietnam War in 1968, when civilians were once again drafted to fight a foreign war. In the two decades between the early 1970s and the early 1990s, when the Soviet Union collapsed, there were still almost half a million American troops permanently stationed abroad, after which the numbers dropped to a little over 200,000.[35]

Throughout the postwar period, America's role as the world's policeman was barely questioned at home and was rarely a prominent issue for debate, except briefly during the Vietnam War. Indeed, it became a proud element of the American character that the United States had been charged with ensuring that democracy was promoted and protected around the world. President George H. W. Bush led the American military alliance that restored Kuwait to independence after it was annexed by Saddam Hussein's Iraq. The response by George W. Bush to the terrorist attacks by the fundamental Muslim group Al-Qaeda on the American mainland in 2001, however, set off a string of events that markedly changed the argument about the US's global role. The 2001 war in Afghanistan, where Al-Qaeda bases trained terrorists to destroy Western targets, passed without much hostile domestic comment.

However, the 2003–11 war that liberated Iraq from the dictatorship of Saddam Hussein proved highly controversial. What was sold to the American people as an essential war to rid the world of a despot who had proved willing to use weapons of mass destruction was, before long, when no such weapons could be found, widely redefined as an unnecessary war of choice. US Senator Barack Obama's elec-

tion to the presidency in 2008 was in large part due to the popularity of the early stand he took against the Iraq War when an Illinois
state senator.

Alongside a largely leftist peace movement derived from the remnants of the anti-Vietnam protesters rose a new isolationist line of
reasoning that emerged from a growing libertarian movement. The
libertarians, who had infiltrated the Republican Party, resented
both the amount of treasure spent on permanent troop deployments
and police actions abroad and the notion that it was any business
of America how other nations were governed. Chief among them
was the 1988 Libertarian Party presidential candidate and persistent Republican presidential hopeful Ron Paul,[36] a US congressman
from Texas, who, like his predecessors, traced his isolationism back
to the Founding Fathers[37] and who combined fiscal rectitude and a
wariness about foreign entanglements in the same way as the Mid-
westerners who opposed both the New Deal and America entering
World War Two. "The moral and constitutional obligations of our
representatives in Washington are to protect our liberty, not cod-
dle the world, precipitating no-win wars, while bringing bankruptcy
and economic turmoil to our people," Paul wrote.[38]

As with the isolationists of the first half of the twentieth century, neo-isolationism was often passed off as non-interventionism.
Again the confusion between the two terms was often mere seman-
tics. Such views, however, elicited considerable public sympathy.
By November 2013, a narrow majority of Americans believed that
America "should mind its own business internationally and let other
countries get along the best they can on their own,"[39] the most isolationist position in the fifty years the polling organization had been
asking the question. Two months later, in early 2014, when Russian
forces occupied the Ukrainian province of Crimea, a full 56 percent
of Americans said they did not want America to become involved.[40]

Nearly eighty years after Franklin Roosevelt charmed, provoked,
prodded, and appealed to the better natures of Americans to accept
their responsibilities in the wider world, the pendulum had swung
halfway back to its prewar position, when nine out of ten wished
to stay out of war in any circumstances. So, was American involvement in the world just a passing phase? It seems unlikely. By the
twenty-first century, through travel and technology, the world had

appeared to shrink. It had become so economically interdependent that the old, fond wish that America could retreat behind its protective oceans was an impossible dream.

As Roosevelt put it when running for vice president in 1920, "We must open our eyes and see that modern civilization has become so complex and the lives of civilized men so interwoven with the lives of other men in other countries as to make it impossible to be in this world and out of it."[41]

ACKNOWLEDGMENTS

ALAS, THERE WERE FEW primary sources still alive by the time I reached this subject. One of the last standing, Robert J. Stuart, who when a student at Yale cofounded the organization that became the isolationists' principal campaigning body, America First, died shortly after the book was completed, in May 2014, aged ninety-eight. The original documents, too, have been so finely combed through that genuinely new material was scarce. I am therefore indebted to those who left firsthand accounts of their contribution to this story. And I owe a debt to the many fine editors, such as Elliott Roosevelt in the case of Franklin D. Roosevelt's personal letters, Amanda Smith for Joseph P. Kennedy's letters, William Jovanovich for Charles A. Lindbergh's wartime journals, and Jane D. Ickes for the secret diary of Harold L. Ickes, among many others, who did so much of the preliminary work for me. I would not have dared start out on this account of how Franklin Roosevelt outsmarted the isolationists while persuading his countrymen to come to the defense of democracy had I not been able to draw upon the many hundreds of books on related topics written and published on both sides of the Atlantic. I thank all the authors listed in the bibliography, and many I have omitted to mention.

I am grateful, as ever, to my literary agent, Rafe Sagalyn, for his wisdom, encouragement and good humor, and to Brendan Curry, my editor at W. W. Norton, for the elegance of his touches on the tiller. Thanks, too, to my copyeditor, Allegra Huston, for her clear thinking and meticulous attention to detail. Similarly, George Herrick, Sean Wilentz, Conrad Black, and Rockwell Stensrud read through the book and provided helpful comments. And I am particularly grateful to my eldest brother, Paul Wapshott, who lent me his extensive knowledge of military affairs and World War Two. I should stress, however, that all errors found in the text are mine. Thanks also to Fern Hurst for providing me with a welcome refuge to write.

As always, I must thank my wife, Louise Nicholson, who, along with my sons, William and Oliver, have met with patience my endless ruminations on the respective merits of isolationism and interventionism and have suffered without complaint having our home invaded by tall stacks of dusty books. But I am above all grateful to Roosevelt and those who thought like him, who worked so hard to ensure that Nazism was defeated. Had a less brilliant and persuasive leader been at the helm of the United States at this critical turning point in history, this story would have had a tragic outcome. And it would most likely have been written in German.

Nicholas Wapshott
New York City
May 2014

NOTES

Prologue: THE SPHINX

[1] The FDR sphinx was sculpted by James D. Preston, assistant administrative secretary of the National Archives and former superintendent of the Senate press gallery.

[2] Black, *Franklin Delano Roosevelt*, 29.

[3] Quoted in Black, 4.

[4] Franklin's father, James Roosevelt, had also married a close relative, Sara Delano, a sixth cousin.

[5] Black, 83.

[6] Roosevelt, *Autobiography of Eleanor Roosevelt*, 98.

[7] The tributes to Teddy Roosevelt were suitably extravagant; Vice President Thomas R. Marshall declared, "Death had to take Roosevelt sleeping, for if he had been awake, there would have been a fight." Quoted in Manners, *TR and Will*, 310.

[8] Roosevelt, *Autobiography of Eleanor Roosevelt*, 101.

[9] Ibid.

[10] Warren Gamaliel Harding (November 2, 1865–August 2, 1923), Republican newspaper publisher, senator from Ohio 1915–21, and president of the United States, 1921–23. He was the first to use the phrase "Founding Fathers."

[11] Russell, *Warren G. Harding*, 208.

[12] Roosevelt, *Letters*, 470.

[13] James Middleton Cox (March 31, 1870–July 15, 1957), Democratic governor of Ohio, representative from Ohio 1909–13, and Democratic candidate for president in the 1920 election.

[14] Roosevelt, *Letters*, 503–4.

[15] Morgan, *FDR*, 232.

[16] Barbara Leahy to Franklin Roosevelt, June 9, 1920, Roosevelt Papers.

[17] http://www.pbs.org/wgbh/americanexperience/features/transcript/fdr-tran script/.

[18] Morgan, *FDR*, 229.

[19] Theodore "Teddy" Roosevelt Jr. (September 13, 1887–July 12, 1944), eldest son of President Theodore Roosevelt and his second wife, Edith, Assistant Secre-

tary of the Navy 1921–24, governor of Puerto Rico 1929–32, governor-general of the Philippines 1932–33. He served in both world wars, latterly as a brigadier general, and was awarded the Congressional Medal of Honor.

20 Morgan, *FDR*, 230.

21 Ibid., 232.

22 http://www.bartleby.com/124/pres16.html.

23 Robert Rutherford "Colonel" McCormick (July 30, 1880–April 1, 1955), newspaper editor and publisher whose *Chicago Tribune* led his campaigns against Prohibition, the New Deal, and involvement in World War Two.

24 BBC broadcast, October 1, 1939. Available at: http://www.churchill-society -london.org.uk/RusnEnig.html.

Chapter One: LONDON CALLING

1 The first and only Irish American to represent the United States in London to this point was General Patrick A. Collins, appointed consul general by President Cleveland in 1893. He later became mayor of Boston.

2 Roosevelt, *My Parents*, 209.

3 Quoted in Casey, *Cautious Crusade*, 4.

4 Adolf Hitler (April 20, 1889–April 30, 1945), Austrian-born German leader of the Nazi Party, Chancellor of Germany 1933–45, Führer 1934–45.

5 Benito Amilcare Andrea Mussolini (July 29, 1883–April 28, 1945), leader of the Italian Fascists, head of government 1925–43. Executed without trial by Italian partisans.

6 Roosevelt to William Allen White, in Roosevelt, *Letters*, 968.

7 William Randolph Hearst (April 29, 1863–August 14, 1951), American newspaper publisher credited with inspiring Orson Welles's character John Foster Kane. Twice a Democratic representative from New York, he ran unsuccessfully for mayor of New York City in 1905 and 1909, for governor of New York in 1906, and for lieutenant governor of New York in 1910.

8 Father Charles Edward Coughlin (October 25, 1891–October 27, 1979), Roman Catholic priest at Royal Oak, Michigan's National Shrine of the Little Flower church, and inventor of hate radio who attracted a weekly radio audience of 30 million.

9 Quoted in Adler, *The Isolationist Impulse*, 255.

10 Charles Augustus Lindbergh (February 4, 1902–August 26, 1974), the first man to fly the Atlantic nonstop, in 1927. He used his fame to winfluence Americans to support his pet topics.

11 Henry Ford (July 30, 1863–April 7, 1947), founder of the Ford Motor Company, who introduced the assembly line into car-making.

12 Adler, *The Uncertain Giant*, 250.

13 Herbert Clark Hoover (August 10, 1874–October 20, 1964), Secretary of Commerce 1921–28, president of the United States 1929–33.

14 FDR's idea of a "New Deal" for America deliberately harked back to Teddy Roosevelt's election-winning platform of a strong federal government offering the people a "Square Deal."

15 Quoted in Cole, *Roosevelt and the Isolationists*, 24.

16 Wiltz, *From Isolation to War*, 8.

17 Adler, *The Uncertain Giant*, 9.

18 Creel, *The War, the World and Wilson*, 202.

19 Homer Truett Bone (January 25, 1883–March 11, 1970), Democratic senator from Washington 1933–44.

20 Quoted in Wiltz, *From Isolation to War*, 7.

21 "The Veterans of Future Wars," *Yes*, January 1962.

22 Eugene Victor Debs (November 5, 1855–October 20, 1926), American union leader and former Democrat who was the presidential candidate of the Socialist Party of America in 1900, 1904, 1908, 1912, and (from his prison cell) 1920. In 1918 he was sentenced to ten years under the 1917 Espionage Act. President Harding commuted Debs's sentence to time served and he was freed on February 12, 1921.

23 George William Norris (July 11, 1861–September 2, 1944), Republican/independent, representative from Nebraska 1903–13, senator 1913–43.

24 Adler, *The Uncertain Giant*, 132.

25 Wiltz, *From Isolation to War*, 9.

26 Gerald Prentice Nye (December 19, 1892–July 17, 1971), Republican senator from North Dakota 1925–45.

27 Quoted in Wiltz, *From Isolation to War*, 10.

28 The Senate isolationists included Frank B. Brandegee, of Connecticut (July 8, 1864–October 14, 1924), who committed suicide; Albert B. Fall, of New Mexico (November 26, 1861–November 30, 1944), Secretary of the Interior 1921–23 until found guilty of accepting bribes for which he served a year in jail; Bert M. Fernald, of Maine (April 3, 1858–August 23, 1926), governor 1909–11, senator 1916–26; Joseph I. France, of Maryland (October 11, 1873–January 26, 1939), senator 1917–23, who met Lenin in Russia and advocated closer ties with the Soviet Union; Asle J. Gronna, of North Dakota (December 10, 1858–May 4, 1922), senator 1911–20, one of just six senators to vote against America entering World War One; Philander C. Knox, of Pennsylvania, senator 1904–09, 1917–21; Robert M. La Follette Sr., of Wisconsin, senator 1906–25; Medill McCormick, of Illinois, senator 1919–25; George H. Moses, of New Hampshire, senator 1918–33; George W. Norris, of Nebraska, senator 1913–43; Miles Poindexter, of Washington, senator 1911–23; James A. Reed, of Missouri, senator 1911–29; Lawrence Sherman, of Illinois, senator 1913–21; and Charles S. Thomas, of Colorado, senator 1913–21. Reed and Thomas were Democrats, the others Republicans.

29 Speech to the Senate, August 12, 1919. Available at: http://www.speeches-usa .com/Transcripts/henry_cabot_lodge-league.html.

30 William Edgar Borah (June 29, 1865–January 19, 1940), Republican senator from Idaho 1907–40, chairman of the Senate Committee on Foreign Relations 1924–33.

31 Speech to the Senate, November 10, 1919. Available at: http://www.history central.com/documents/Borah.html.

32 Hiram Warren Johnson (September 2, 1866–August 6, 1945), Lincoln–Roosevelt League governor of California 1911–17, Progressive senator 1917–45, Theodore Roosevelt's running mate in 1912.

33 Andrew William Mellon (March 24, 1855–August 26, 1937), banker, industrialist, philanthropist, art collector, Secretary of the Treasury 1921–32.

34 Henry Clay Frick (December 19, 1849–December 2, 1919), American industrialist, financier, railroad baron, and art patron.

35 Frank Andrew Munsey (August 21, 1854–December 22, 1925), newspaper and magazine publisher and author, pioneer of pulp magazines through his use of cheap, untrimmed paper.

36 William Rockhill Nelson (March 7, 1841–April 13, 1915), influential Kansas City newspaper owner.

37 Henry Lewis Stimson (September 21, 1867–October 20, 1950), Secretary of War 1911–13 and 1940–45, governor-general of the Philippines 1927–29, Secretary of State 1929–33.

38 Quoted in Dawes, *Journal as Ambassador*, 76.

39 Wilbur and Hyde, *The Hoover Policies*, 600ff.

40 Quoted in Adler, *The Uncertain Giant*, 145.

41 Ferrell, *American Diplomacy*, 356.

42 Paul Ludwig Hans Anton von Beneckendorff und von Hindenburg (October 2, 1847–August 2, 1934), second president of Germany, 1925–34.

43 http://www.archives.gov/education/lessons/fdr-inaugural/images/address-4 .gif.

44 Sir Ronald Charles Lindsay (May 3, 1877–August 21, 1945), British ambassador to the United States 1930–39. He married in turn two great-nieces of the Union Civil War general William Tecumseh Sherman.

45 Quoted in Cole, *Roosevelt and the Isolationists*, 54.

46 http://www.archives.gov/education/lessons/fdr-inaugural/images/address-6.gif.

47 Cordell Hull (October 2, 1871–July 23, 1955), America's longest-serving Secretary of State (1933–44), described by Franklin Roosevelt as the "father of the United Nations."

48 Charles Evans Hughes Sr. (April 11, 1862–August 27, 1948), governor of New York 1907–10, Secretary of State 1921–25, and 11th Chief Justice of the United States 1930–41. He ran as the Republican presidential candidate in the 1916 election, losing narrowly to Wilson.

49 Adler, *The Uncertain Giant*, 163.

50 *Franklin D. Roosevelt and Foreign Affairs*, 3–37; quoted in Casey, *Cautious Crusade*, 3.

51 Ernest Hemingway, "Notes on the Next War: A Serious Topical Letter," *Esquire*, September 1935.

52 http://trove.nla.gov.au/ndp/del/article/11008283.

53 Ibid.

54 Adler, *The Isolationist Impulse*, 255–6.

55 Known at the time as Abyssinia.

56 General Francisco Franco Bahamonde (December 4, 1892–November 20, 1975), prime minister of Spain 1938–73, head of state and dictator 1939–75.

57 Adler, *The Isolationist Impulse*, 240.

58 Roosevelt won 27.8 million votes against Alf Landon's 16.7 million, and 531 electoral votes to Landon's eight.

59 Speech, October 31, 1936, Madison Square Garden. Available at: http://miller center.org/president/speeches/detail/3307.

60 Douglas MacArthur (January 26, 1880–April 5, 1964), superintendent of the US Military Academy, West Point, 1919–22, chief of staff of the US Army 1930–37, military advisor to the Commonwealth Government of the Philippines 1937–41, commander of US Army Forces in the Far East 1941–51. Administered the occupation of Japan 1945–51. Led United Nations forces in Korea 1950–51.

61 *Franklin D. Roosevelt and Foreign Affairs,* 1st series, 3:102–3.

62 Ibid., 3:251.

63 FDR diaries, vol 2, p876.

64 Congress extended the arms embargo to both sides in the Spanish dispute.

65 Quoted in Adler, *The Isolationist Impulse,* 264.

66 The third Neutrality Act passed overwhelmingly in the House, 376 to 16, and 63 to 6 in the Senate.

67 Adler, *The Isolationist Impulse,* 265.

68 Ibid.

69 http://millercenter.org/president/speeches/detail/3310.

70 FDR diaries, vol 1, pp 716-17.

71 Samuel Irving Rosenman (February 13, 1896–June 24, 1973), Texan lawyer, judge, FDR's favorite speechwriter. First White House counsel, 1943–46.

72 Rosenman, *Working With Roosevelt,* 167.

Chapter Two: ONE GOOD TURN

1 Kennedy, *Hostage to Fortune,* 5.

2 Ibid., 6.

3 Ibid.

4 Quoted in Beschloss, *Kennedy and Roosevelt,* 77.

5 Rose Elizabeth Fitzgerald Kennedy (July 22, 1890–January 22, 1995), wife of Joseph P. Kennedy, whose nine children included President John F. Kennedy and Senator Robert F. Kennedy.

6 Kennedy, *Hostage to Fortune,* 415.

7 Clarence John Boettiger (March 25, 1900–October 31, 1950), publisher of the *Seattle Post–Intelligencer* and second husband of FDR's daughter Anna.

8 Goodwin, *No Ordinary Time,* 211-2.

9 Kennedy, *Hostage to Fortune,* 65.

10 Robert Marion "Fighting Bob" La Follette Sr. (June 14, 1855–June 18, 1925), Republican representative from Wisconsin 1885–91, governor 1901–06, senator 1906–25, who ran in 1924 for president as the candidate of the Progressive Party he founded.

11 Alfred Emanuel "Al" Smith (December 30, 1873–October 4, 1944), governor of New York 1923–28.

12 Kennedy, *Hostage to Fortune,* 77.

13 Ibid., 65.

14 Kennedy, *Hostage to Fortune*, 66.

15 Henry Morgenthau Jr. (May 11, 1891–February 6, 1967), near neighbor of the Roosevelts in Dutchess County who, as secretary of the Treasury 1934–45, influenced all parts of the Roosevelt administration, in particular the New Deal, the execution of World War Two, and the planning of the postwar world.

16 There is considerable doubt whether Hearst actually sent such a telegram. Although it is quoted in James Creelman, *On the Great Highway: The Wanderings and Adventures of a Special Correspondent* (Boston: Lothrop, 1901), 178, several authors cast doubt on its authenticity, in particular W. Joseph Campbell, in *Getting it Wrong: Ten Greatest Misreported Stories in American Journalism* (Berkeley: University of California Press, 2010), the whole of chapter 1, and Ralph Keyes, *The Quote Verifier: Who Said What, Where, and When* (New York: Macmillan, 2006), 165. Keyes suggests that Creelman's story was, as journalists sometimes say, too good to check, and that it gained credence after Orson Welles, in his 1941 movie *Citizen Kane*, put it in the mouth of Charles Foster Kane, a character based upon Hearst; a reporter cables Kane, "Could send you prose poems about scenery but don't feel right spending your money. Stop. There is no war in Cuba," to which Kane responds, "You provide the prose poems, I'll provide the war."

17 William McKinley (January 29, 1843–September 14, 1901), Republican governor of Ohio 1892–96, president of the United States 1897–1901.

18 Neal, *Happy Days Are Here Again*, 52.

19 James Beauchamp "Champ" Clark (March 7, 1850–March 2, 1921), Democratic representative from Missouri 1893–95, 1897–1921, Speaker of the House 1911–19.

20 Winkler, *W. R. Hearst*, 280.

21 Procter, *William Randolph Hearst*, 84.

22 Quoted in Neal, *Happy Days Are Here Again*, 57.

23 Joseph Edward Davies (November 29, 1876–May 9, 1958), US ambassador to the Soviet Union 1936–38, to Luxembourg 1938–39, and to Belgium 1938–39.

24 Quoted in Neal, *Happy Days Are Here Again*, 58.

25 Hearst front-page editorial, *New York American*, December 24, 1931.

26 Neal, *Happy Days Are Here Again*, 58.

27 John Nance Garner IV (November 22, 1868–November 7, 1967), Democratic representative from Texas 1903–33, Speaker of the House 1931–33, vice president of the United States 1933–41.

28 George Rothwell Brown, quoted in Procter, *William Randolph Hearst*, 166.

29 Radio address, NBC network, January 2, 1932. See Nasaw, *The Chief*, 452.

30 Neal, *Happy Days Are Here Again*, 61.

31 Roosevelt, *My Own Story*, 79.

32 Quoted in Dallek, *Franklin D. Roosevelt and American Foreign Policy*, 19.

33 Robert Wickliffe Woolley (April 29, 1871–December 15, 1958), director of the US Mint 1915–16.

34 Neal, *Happy Days Are Here Again*, 62.

35 Ibid., 63.

36 Newton Diehl Baker Jr. (December 3, 1871–December 25, 1937), mayor of Cleveland 1912–15, Secretary of War 1916–21.

37 Arthur Bernard Krock (November 16, 1886–April 12, 1974), long-standing *New York Times* Washington correspondent.

38 Krock, "Reminiscences," 7–8.

39 Nomination address, July 2, 1932, Chicago. Available at: http://newdeal.feri .org/speeches/1932b.htm.

40 Kennedy to Hearst, October 19, 1932, in Kennedy, *Hostage to Fortune*, 100.

41 Kennedy, *Hostage to Fortune*, 66.

42 Roy Wilson Howard (January 1, 1883–November 20, 1964), editor and journalist who managed the United Press agency 1907–25 and headed the Scripps-Howard newspaper chain 1925–52.

43 Quoted in Beschloss, *Kennedy and Roosevelt*, 74.

44 Ibid., 116.

45 Hall Roosevelt to Roosevelt, May 5, 1931. Roosevelt Library.

46 Quoted in Beschloss, *Kennedy and Roosevelt*, 115.

47 Eleanor Roosevelt to Charles Tull, March 16, 1960, quoted in Warren, *Radio Priest*, 42.

48 Coughlin to FDR, September 12, 1932, file 306, Franklin D. Roosevelt Library, Hyde Park, New York.

49 Warren, *Radio Priest*, 61.

50 Quoted in Marcus, *Father Coughlin*, 64.

51 Quoted in Beschloss, *Kennedy and Roosevelt*, 117–8.

52 The speech was largely drafted by Adolf Augustus Berle Jr. (1895–1971), lawyer and member of FDR's "Brain Trust."

53 Campaign address, August 20, 1932, Columbus, Ohio. Available at: http:// newdeal.feri.org/speeches/1932e.htm.

54 Composed in 1929 by Milton Ager (music) and Jack Yellen (lyrics), first featured in the MGM movie *Chasing Rainbows* (1930).

55 Quoted in Beschloss, *Kennedy and Roosevelt*, 116.

56 William Harrison Hays Sr. (1879–1954), chairman of the Republican National Committee 1918–21, Postmaster General 1921–22, first president of the Motion Picture Producers and Distributors of America 1922–45, whose puritanical censorship regulations were nicknamed the Hays Code.

57 Kennedy, *Hostage to Fortune*, 103.

58 Louis McHenry Howe (January 14, 1871–April 18, 1936), *New York Herald* reporter who became Roosevelt's chief political adviser.

59 Raymond Charles Moley (September 27, 1886–February 18, 1975), Roosevelt speechwriter and early champion of the New Deal who coined the term "the forgotten man."

60 Beschloss, *Kennedy and Roosevelt*, 79.

61 Roosevelt, *Letters 1905–1928*, 340.

62 Whalen, *The Founding Father*, 131.

Chapter Three: NEW DEALERS

1 The suggestion that Kennedy was a bootlegger is a canard. His acquisition of medicinal alcohol permits was investigated and found to be legal.

2 William Hartman Woodin (May 27, 1868–May 3, 1934), Secretary of the Treasury March–December 1933.

3 Farley, *Jim Farley's Story*, 115.

4 Moley, *The First New Deal*, .

5 Ibid., 288.

6 *New Republic*, July 18, 1934.

7 Harold Lill Ickes (March 15, 1874–February 3, 1952), Secretary of the Interior 1933–46, co-architect of the New Deal.

8 Ickes, *The First Thousand Days*, 173.

9 Krock to Joseph Kennedy, July 1, 1935, quoted in Kennedy, *Hostage to Fortune*, 155.

10 Arthur Krock, *New York Times*, April 28, 1935.

11 Eleanor Roosevelt quoted by Drew Pearson and Robert S. Allen, *Washington Times–Herald*, September 18, 1937.

12 Quoted in Tully, *F. D. R., My Boss*, 160–1.

13 http://c0403731.cdn.cloudfiles.rackspacecloud.com/collection/papers/1930/1935_09_06_JPK_to_FDR.pdf.

14 http://c0403731.cdn.cloudfiles.rackspacecloud.com/collection/papers/1930/1935_09_20_FDR_to_JPK_t.pdf.

15 Arthur Hays Sulzberger (September 12, 1891–December 11, 1968), publisher of the *New York Times*, 1935–61.

16 *New York Times*, September 21, 1935.

17 Beschloss, *Kennedy and Roosevelt*, 118.

18 Radio address, "The Menace of the World Court," January 27, 1935, quoted in Davis, *The Fear of Conspiracy*, 249.

19 Borah to Coughlin, January 30, 1935, in William Edgar Borah papers 1905–40: Speeches, Statements, and Articles, 1908–39, Manuscript Division, Library of Congress.

20 Beschloss, *Kennedy and Roosevelt*, 118.

21 Marcus, *Father Coughlin*, 99.

22 Beschloss, *Kennedy and Roosevelt*, 119.

23 Ibid., 120.

24 Associated Press report, May 26, 1936. Available at: http://www.fultonhistory.com/Process%20small/Newspapers/Utica%20NY%20Daily%20Press/Utica%20NY%20Daily%20Press%201936.pdf/Utica%20NY%20Daily%20Press%201936%20-%202035.pdf.

25 Speech, New Bedford, MA, Associated Press report, August 6, 1936.

26 Speech, Providence, RI, Associated Press report, August 1, 1936. See *Montreal Gazette*, August 3, 1936.

27 Felix Frankfurter (November 15, 1882–February 22, 1965), Harvard lawyer, Justice of the US Supreme Court, 1939–62.

28 William Frederick Lemke (August 13, 1878–May 30, 1950), member of the quasi-socialist Nonpartisan League and two-term Republican representative from North Dakota.

29 Quoted in Warren, *Radio Priest*, 94.

30 Alfred Mossman Landon (September 9, 1887–October 12, 1987), governor of Kansas 1933–37, Republican nominee for president in 1936.

31 Vermont and Maine.

32 *New York Times*, November 6, 1936.

33 Radio address, November 7, 1936. See *Pittsburgh Press*, February 6, 1940.

34 Robert Houghwout Jackson (February 13, 1892–October 9, 1954), US Solicitor General 1938–40, Attorney General 1940–41, Justice of the Supreme Court 1941–54, chief US prosecutor at the Nuremberg Trials.

35 Jackson quoted in Black, *Franklin Delano Roosevelt*, 431.

36 Homer Stille Cummings (April 30, 1870–September 10, 1956), US Attorney General 1933–39.

37 Interview with George Creel, *Collier's*, December 1936.

38 James Clark McReynolds (February 3, 1862–August 24, 1946), Woodrow Wilson's attorney general 1913–14, Justice of the Supreme Court 1914–41, vociferous opponent of the New Deal.

39 Alsop and Catledge, *The 168 Days*, 154.

40 Henry Fountain Ashurst (September 13, 1874–May 31, 1962). Democratic senator from Arizona 1912–41.

41 Marriner Stoddard Eccles (September 9, 1890–December 18, 1977), Federal Reserve board member 1934–51, chairman 1934–48.

42 Wapshott, *Keynes Hayek*, 188.

43 Associated Press report, December 29, 1937, available at: http://news.google.com/newspapers?nid=2199&dat=19371229&id=R2ZeAAAAIBAJ&sjid=F2EN AAAAIBAJ&pg=1160,1969882.

44 No president had served a third term and those, such as Grover Cleveland and Woodrow Wilson, who had sought a third term had been defeated.

45 Harvey Klemmer (July 29, 1900–May 27, 1992), American diplomat and writer.

46 Beauchamp, *Joseph P. Kennedy Presents*, 357.

47 Roosevelt, *Letters*, 595.

48 Krock was paid $1,000 a week for five weeks, or a total of more than $80,000 in 2014 dollars, to write the book. See Kennedy, *Hostage to Fortune*, 186.

49 Roosevelt, *Letters*, 595.

50 *New York Times*, July 26, 1936.

51 *Milwaukee Sentinel*, July 21, 1960.

52 McCarthy, *The Remarkable Kennedys*, 64.

53 Kennedy, *Hostage to Fortune*, 194.

54 Frances Coralie Perkins (April 10, 1880–May 14, 1965), Secretary of Labor 1933–45, the first woman appointed to the US cabinet.

55 *Boston Herald*, August 16, 1942.

56 Roosevelt, *My Parents*, 208–9.

57 McCarthy, *The Remarkable Kennedys*, 68–9.

58 In 1957, Kennedy's wealth was estimated by *Fortune* to be $250 million, or more than $2 billion in 2014 money. He had never told Rose how much he was worth and when she read the magazine she asked him, "Why didn't you tell me we had all that money?"

59 Quoted in Kennedy, *Hostage to Fortune*, 187, August 18 1936,

60 Quoted in Maier, *The Kennedys*, 120.

61 Kennedy, *I'm For Roosevelt*, 3.

62 Stephen Tyree Early (August 27, 1889–August 11, 1951), White House press secretary under FDR 1933–45, under President Harry S. Truman 1950.

63 Roosevelt, *Letters 1928–1945*, vol. 1, 710.

64 Ibid., 689.

65 Speech, October 5, 1937, Chicago. Available at: http://millercenter.org/president/speeches/detail/3310.

66 *Boston Herald*, quoted in http://www.alba-valb.org/resources/lessons/the-spanish-civil-war-u.s.-foreign-policy-individual-conscience-between-the-world-wars/roosevelt2019s-201cquarantine-speech201d.

67 Roosevelt, *Letters 1928–1945*, vol. 1, 718.

68 The Reverend Endicott Peabody (May 30, 1857–November 17, 1944), Episcopal priest who founded the Groton School for Boys in Groton, MA, in 1884.

69 Roosevelt, *Letters 1928–1945*, vol. 1, 716–17

70 Quoted in Whalen, *The Founding Father*, 200.

71 Joseph Ignatius Breen (October 14, 1888–December 5, 1965), head of the Production Code Administration, which ensured films obeyed the censorious Hays Code, 1934–54.

72 Kennedy, *Hostage to Fortune*, 218.

73 Joseph Patrick Tumulty (May 5, 1879–April 19, 1954), private secretary to Woodrow Wilson 1911–21.

74 Kennedy, *Hostage to Fortune*, 219.

75 James Francis Byrnes (May 2, 1882–April 9, 1972), Democratic representative from South Carolina 1911–25, senator 1931–41, Justice of the Supreme Court 1941–42, Secretary of State 1945–47, governor of South Carolina 1951–55.

76 Quoted in Kennedy, *Hostage to Fortune*, 115.

77 Ibid., 119–20.

78 Dorothy Schiff (March 11, 1903–August 30, 1989), owner and publisher of the liberal *New York Post*.

79 Cook, *Eleanor Roosevelt*, 501.

80 Quoted in Kennedy, *Hostage to Fortune*, 223.

Chapter Four: CLIVEDEN AND WINDSOR CASTLE

1 Arthur Neville Chamberlain (March 18, 1869–November 9, 1940), British Conservative prime minister May 1937–May 1940.

2 (Robert) Anthony Eden, Earl of Avon (June 12, 1897–January 14, 1977), British Conservative prime minister 1955–57, Foreign Secretary three times 1935–55, including under Churchill during World War Two.

3 Joseph Kennedy, diary entry, February 18, 1938, in Kennedy, *Hostage to Fortune*, 236.

4 Kennedy to James F. Byrnes, December 23, 1937, ibid., 219.

5 Quoted in Whalen, *The Founding Father*, 215.

6 Kennedy, *Hostage to Fortune*, 239.

7 Morgenthau Diaries, December 8, 1937, Book 101, FDR Library.

8 Kennedy, *Hostage to Fortune,* 223.

9 *New York Times,* February 24, 1938.

10 Bernard Mannes Baruch (August 19, 1870–June 20, 1965), American financier who became an adviser to both Woodrow Wilson and FDR.

11 Coit, *Mr. Baruch,* 467.

12 John Fitzgerald "Jack" Kennedy (May 29, 1917–November 22, 1963), Democratic representative from Massachusetts 1946–52, senator 1952–60 beating incumbent Henry Cabot Lodge Jr., son of the isolationist Henry Cabot Lodge, who had led Senate opposition to ratification of the Treaty of Versailles. President of the United States 1960–63.

13 Quoted in Coit, *Mr. Baruch,* 467.

14 The Hossbach memorandum, available at: http://www.yale.edu/lawweb/avalon/imt/document/hossbach.htm.

15 Feiling, *The Life of Neville Chamberlain,* 325.

16 Kennedy, *Hostage to Fortune,* 239.

17 Joseph Chamberlain (July 8, 1836–July 2, 1914), former mayor of Birmingham and leading Liberal Unionist, later Conservative, MP—rare for being a self-made businessman.

18 Whalen, *The Founding Father,* 218.

19 Quoted in Beschloss, *Kennedy and Roosevelt,* 163.

20 Whalen, *The Founding Father,* 218.

21 Freda Kirchwey, "Watch Joe Kennedy," *Nation,* December 14, 1940.

22 Edward Frederick Lindley Wood (April 16, 1881–December 23, 1959), Lord Irwin 1925–34, Earl of Halifax 1934–44, Foreign Secretary 1938–40, British ambassador to the US 1940–46.

23 Ickes, *The First Thousand Days,* 406.

24 Hull, *Memoirs,* 581.

25 http://www.pbs.org/greatwar/resources/casdeath_pop.html.

26 http://hansard.millbanksystems.com/commons/1938/feb/21/personal-explanations#S5CV0332P0_19380221_HOC_250.

27 Swift, *The Kennedys Amidst the Gathering Storm,* 26.

28 Harold Joseph Laski (June 30, 1893–March 24, 1950), history professor at the London School of Economics 1926–50.

29 Harry Lloyd Hopkins (August 17, 1890–January 29, 1946), architect of the New Deal, especially the Works Progress Administration (WPA), which he directed and built into the largest employer in the nation, and of the $50 billion Lend-Lease program that sent war materiel to the Allies. FDR's chief diplomatic emissary.

30 Quoted in Whalen, *The Founding Father,* 215.

31 Kurt Alois Josef Johann Schuschnigg (December 14, 1897–November 18, 1977), chancellor of the First Austrian Republic.

32 Swift, *The Kennedys Amidst the Gathering Storm,* 28.

33 Joseph and Rose Kennedy had lunched with Churchill at his country home, Chartwell, in 1935.

34 Swift, *The Kennedys Amidst the Gathering Storm,* 29.

35 Kennedy, *Hostage to Fortune*, 242.

36 Ibid., 241.

37 Ibid., 240.

38 Ibid., 245.

39 Ibid., 227.

40 Ibid., 243.

41 Ibid., 244.

42 Waldorf Astor, Viscount Astor (May 19, 1879–September 30, 1952), American-born Conservative member of the British parliament 1910–16, owner of the *Observer* newspaper.

43 Swift, *The Kennedys Amidst the Gathering Storm*, 32.

44 Hull, *Memoirs*, 577.

45 Walter Lippmann (September 23, 1889–December 14, 1974), Pulitzer Prize-winning columnist. Thomas Justin White (1884–July 9, 1952), general manager of Hearst's newspaper chain. Burton Kendall Wheeler (February 27, 1882–January 6, 1975), Democratic senator from Montana 1923–47, ardent New Dealer who fell out with Roosevelt over packing the Supreme Court and became a stalwart isolationist. Byron Patton "Pat" Harrison (August 29, 1881–June 22, 1941), Democratic representative from Mississippi 1911–19, senator 1919–41. Key Denson Pittman (September 19, 1872–November 10, 1940), Democratic senator from Nevada 1913–40, chairman of the Committee on Foreign Relations 1933–40.

46 Kennedy, *Hostage to Fortune*, 246–7.

47 Quoted in McKenna, *Borah*, 354.

48 Kennedy, *Hostage to Fortune*, 248–9.

49 Kathleen Agnes "Kick" Kennedy (February 20, 1920–May 13, 1948), married in May 1944 William John Robert Cavendish, heir apparent to the Duke of Devonshire. Patricia Helen "Pat" Kennedy (May 6, 1924–September 17, 2006), married in 1954 film actor Peter Lawford. Robert Francis "Bobby" Kennedy (November 20, 1925–June 6, 1968), Attorney General 1961–64, Democratic senator from New York 1965–68. Jean Ann Kennedy (born February 20, 1928), eighth of Joseph P. Kennedy's nine children, US ambassador to Ireland 1993–98. Edward Moore "Ted" Kennedy (February 22, 1932–August 25, 2009), Democratic senator from Massachusetts 1962–2009. Joseph Patrick "Joe" Kennedy Jr. (July 25, 1915–August 12, 1944), eldest of Joseph P. Kennedy's nine children. Wrote his senior thesis on isolationist efforts to keep America from intervening in the Spanish Civil War. Rose Marie "Rosemary" Kennedy (September 13, 1918–January 7, 2005). Deemed psychologically troubled, she was subjected to a prefrontal lobotomy at age 23, leaving her permanently disabled. Eunice Mary Kennedy (July 10, 1921–August 11, 2009), fifth of Joseph P. Kennedy's nine children. Founder of the Special Olympics. Married Robert Sargent Shriver Jr., Democratic vice presidential candidate in 1972.

50 Kennedy, *Times to Remember*, 217.

51 Swift, *The Kennedys Amidst the Gathering Storm*, 35.

52 Henry Robinson Luce (April 3, 1898–February 28, 1967), proprietor of *Time*, *Fortune*, and *Life*, among other titles.

53 *Life*, April 11, 1938, 17.

54 Edward VIII (Edward Albert Christian George Andrew Patrick David Windsor, June 23, 1894–May 28, 1972), King of the United Kingdom January 11, 1936–December 11, 1936, Duke of Windsor 1936–72. Wallis Simpson, a.k.a. Wallis Spencer, born Bessie Wallis Warfield (June 19, 1896–April 24, 1986), American socialite, Duchess of Windsor 1936–86.

55 George VI (Albert Frederick Arthur George Windsor, December 14, 1895–February 6, 1952), became King of the United Kingdom on the abdication of his brother Edward VIII in 1936.

56 Designed in the Italianate style in 1851 by Charles Barry, architect of the Houses of Parliament, for George Sutherland-Leveson-Gower, the Duke of Sutherland.

57 Alfred Milner, Viscount Milner (March 23, 1854–May 13, 1925), High Commissioner for Southern Africa 1897–1901. Milner's "Kindergarten," charged with reuniting the divided population of South Africa after the Boer War, included Philip Kerr (later Lord Lothian), Geoffrey Dawson, Edward Wood (later Lord Halifax), William Lionel Hichens (later Lord Hichens), and Robert Brand (later Lord Brand), who was managing director of the French bank Lazard Brothers from 1904–44 and married Nancy Astor's sister. They were all regular houseguests at Cliveden.

58 Philip Henry Kerr, Marquess of Lothian (April 18, 1882–December 12, 1940), Under Secretary of State for India 1931–32, British ambassador to the United States 1939–40.

59 Rogers, *Political Quotes*, 40.

60 Sir Nevile Meyrick Henderson (June 10, 1882–December 30, 1942), British ambassador to Germany 1937–40.

61 Advice to the British Foreign Office in February 1939 on how to approach the Munich agreement. Quoted in Ikle, *Every War Must End*, 109.

62 George Geoffrey Dawson (born Robinson, changed by deed poll 1917; October 25, 1874–November 7, 1944), editor of *The Times* 1912–19, 1923–41.

63 MacDonald, *The History of the Times*, 465.

64 Francis Claud Cockburn (April 12, 1904–December 15, 1981), journalist and Communist sympathizer, grandson of the eminent Scottish judge and historian Lord Cockburn.

65 *The Week*, November 17, 1937. Quoted in Aaron L. Goldman, "Claud Cockburn, *The Week*, and the 'Cliveden Set,'"*Journalism Quarterly* 49 (Winter 1972): 724.

66 Cockburn, *Crossing the Line*, 19.

67 Ibid., 19–20.

68 http://userwww.sfsu.edu/epf/journal_archive/volume_XVI,_2007/cushner_a .pdf.

69 Harold Nicolson thought the Cliveden Set exerted a malign influence on British foreign policy. On September 19, 1938, he spoke with Anthony Eden about "how terrible has been the influence of the Cliveden set." Four days later, he wrote, "The Cliveden set and the *Times* people prevented us from taking a strong line which it could have made for peace." Nicolson, *Diaries and Letters*, 361, 366.

70 Andrew Russell "Drew" Pearson (December 13, 1897–September 1, 1969), Robert Sharon Allen (July 14, 1900–February 23, 1981), political reporters who cowrote the highly influential gossip column "Washington Merry-Go-Round."

71 Kennedy, *Hostage to Fortune*, 255.

72 Ibid., 255, n. 74.

73 Ibid., 256.

74 Konrad Ernst Eduard Henlein (May 6, 1898–May 10, 1945), German-speaking Sudeten who joined the Nazi Party and the SS when Germany occupied the Sudetenland and was appointed Reichsstatthalter of the Sudetenland by Hitler in 1939.

75 Roosevelt, *Letters 1928–1945*, vol. 2, 769.

76 Quoted in Beschloss, *Kennedy and Roosevelt*, 160.

77 Kennedy, *Times to Remember*, 221.

78 Kennedy, *Hostage to Fortune*, 252.

79 Whalen, *The Founding Father*, 205.

80 Beschloss, *Kennedy and Roosevelt*, 165.

81 Ickes, *The First Thousand Days*, 404, 415, 406–7.

82 Maier, *The Kennedys*, 132.

83 Beschloss, *Kennedy and Roosevelt*, 168.

84 Ibid.

85 Ibid.

86 Colonel Josiah Clement Wedgwood, Baron Wedgwood (March 16, 1872–July 26, 1943), Chancellor of the Duchy of Lancaster in Ramsay MacDonald's first Labour government, 1924.

87 Ickes, *The First Thousand Days*, 370.

88 Beschloss, *Kennedy and Roosevelt*, 170.

89 Beauchamp, *Joseph P. Kennedy Presents*, 357; Maier, *The Kennedys*, 132.

90 Beschloss, *Kennedy and Roosevelt*, 168–9.

91 Hugh Samuel "Iron Pants" Johnson (August 5, 1881–April 15, 1942), member of FDR's "Brain Trust" 1932–34, speechwriter, co-architect of the New Deal. Head of the National Recovery Administration (NRA) from 1933 until it was ruled unconstitutional by the Supreme Court in 1935.

92 Beschloss, *Kennedy and Roosevelt*, 169.

93 Ibid.

94 Joel Bennett Clark, known as Bennett Champ Clark (January 8, 1890–July 13, 1954), Democratic senator from Missouri 1933–45.

95 Ickes, *The First Thousand Days*, 413.

96 Collier and Horowitz, *The Kennedys*, 68.

97 Kennedy, *Hostage to Fortune*, 264.

98 Quoted in Beschloss, *Kennedy and Roosevelt*, 170.

99 Walter J. Trohan (July 4, 1903–October 30, 2003), *Chicago Tribune* bureau chief in Washington DC. The first reporter on the scene after Al Capone's St. Valentine's Day massacre of Bugs Moran's gang.

100 Beschloss, *Kennedy and Roosevelt*, 171.

101 Kennedy, *Hostage to Fortune*, 265.

102 Colonel Robert Rutherford McCormick, whose *Chicago Tribune* also published a version of the story, later confirmed Kennedy's suspicion that it was Roosevelt

himself who had authorized the leak. "The reporter has produced for me the sources of his information," he wrote to Kennedy. "You are the victim not of the reporter, but of your political associates." Ibid., 269.

103 Ibid., 266.

104 Ibid., 228.

105 Beschloss, *Kennedy and Roosevelt*, 167.

Chapter Five: LINDBERGH'S FLIGHT

1 *New York Post*, July 6, 1938.

2 *New York Times*, September 7, 1937.

3 Coit, *Mr. Baruch*, 467.

4 In a secret meeting at the Reich Chancellery on November 5, 1937, Hitler explained his racist Lebensraum policy, which entailed first expanding into Austria and Czechoslovakia, to his War Minister and chiefs of military staff. See Bullock, *Hitler*, 367–71.

5 Formerly Hempstead Plains Aerodrome, renamed in 1919 in memory of Theodore Roosevelt's son Quentin, who was killed in air combat in World War One.

6 Anne Morrow Lindbergh (née Anne Spencer Morrow, June 22, 1906–February 7, 2001), poet and author of, among many other titles, *Listen! The Wind* and *The Wave of the Future: A Confession of Faith*.

7 Quoted in Berg, *Lindbergh*, 345.

8 Sir Harold George Nicolson (November 21, 1886–May 1, 1968), English diplomat, author, diarist, and politician, Labour MP 1935–45, husband of Victoria Mary "Vita" Sackville-West (March 9, 1892–June 2, 1962), English author, poet, and gardener. Nicolson was a robust anti-Fascist and anti-Nazi who, when invited to Germany to see how it had changed, replied, "Yes, I should find all my old friends either in prison, or exiled, or murdered." Nicolson, *Diaries and Letters*, 265.

9 Nicolson, *The Harold Nicolson Diaries*, 120.

10 Hermann Wilhelm Göring (January 12, 1893–October 15, 1946), much-decorated World War One German fighter pilot who became president of the German Reichstag 1932–33, Hitler's head of the Gestapo 1933–34, Minister for Aviation 1933–35, commander-in-chief of the Luftwaffe 1935–45. Committed suicide after being sentenced to death at the Nuremberg Trials.

11 Berg, *Lindbergh*, 356.

12 Hans-Heinrich Dieckhoff (December 23, 1884–March 21, 1952), German ambassador to the United States 1937–38.

13 Mosley, *Lindbergh*, 218.

14 Erhard Milch (March 30, 1892–January 25,1972), founding director of the German national airline Deutsche Luft Hansa, who as state secretary of the German Air Ministry expanded the Luftwaffe.

15 Smith, *Berlin Alert*, 102.

16 Quoted ibid., 95.

17 Quoted in Mosley, *Lindbergh*, 217.

18 Smith, *Berlin Alert*, 101.

19 Lindbergh, *Autobiography of Values*, 146.

20 Smith, *Berlin Alert*, 104.

21 Quoted in Berg, *Lindbergh*, 361.

22 Quoted ibid.

23 Quoted ibid., 362.

24 Quoted ibid., 357.

25 Nicolson, *Diaries and Letters*, 272.

26 Quoted in Berg, *Lindbergh*, 365.

27 Nicolson, *Diaries and Letters*, 272.

28 Quoted in Berg, *Lindbergh*, 368.

29 Alexis Carrel (June 28, 1873–November 5, 1944), French surgeon and biologist, awarded the Nobel Prize in Physiology or Medicine in 1912 for pioneering vascular suturing techniques. His links to the French Foundation for the Study of Human Problems, which practiced eugenics in Vichy France, led to accusations of Nazi collaboration.

30 Quoted in Berg, *Lindbergh*, 369.

31 Mosley, *Lindbergh*, 220.

32 Quoted ibid., 206.

33 Quoted in Berg, *Lindbergh*, 362.

34 Franklin Nathaniel Daniel Buchman (June 4, 1878–August 7, 1961), founder of the Oxford Group (known as Moral Re-Armament 1938–2001).

35 Heinrich Luitpold Himmler (October 7, 1900–May 23, 1945), head of the Nazi storm troopers the Schutzstaffel (SS) 1929–45, set up and ran Hitler's extermination camps, chief of police and minister of the interior 1943–45. In April 1945, when the war was lost, he attempted to negotiate with the Allies and was fired by Hitler from all posts.

36 Mosley, *Lindbergh*, 218.

37 Charles August Lindbergh Sr. (born Carl Månsson, January 20, 1859–May 24, 1924), Republican representative from Minnesota 1907–17, opposed American entry into World War One and the 1913 Federal Reserve Act.

38 Lindbergh, *Banking, Currency, and the Money Trust*, available at: (http://patri otsoath.com/Banking%20and%20Currency%20and%20the%20Money%20 Trust%20-%20Charles%20A.%20Lindbergh.pdf.

39 William Howard Taft (September 15, 1857–March 8, 1930), President of the United States 1909–13, Chief Justice of the Supreme Court 1921–30.

40 Lindbergh, *Why Is Your Country at War?*, 20. Available at: http://www.jrbookson line.com/PDF_Books/Your_Country_At_War.pdf.

41 Ibid., 17.

42 Lindbergh, *Wartime Journals*, 3.

43 Ibid., 5.

44 Conversation with Colonel Martin F. Scanlon, assistant military attaché for air at the US Embassy in London 1936–41. Ibid., 22.

45 Ibid., 23.

46 Ibid., 11.

47 Ibid., 13.

48 Ibid., 20.

49 Nicolson, *Diaries and Letters*, 343.

50 Lindbergh, *Wartime Journals*, 28.

51 Nicolson, *Diaries and Letters*, 272.

52 Ibid., 343.

53 Lindbergh, *Wartime Journals*, 9.

54 Ibid., 25–6.

55 Thomas Walker Hobart Inskip, Viscount Caldecote (March 5, 1876–October 11, 1947), Minister for Co-ordination of Defence 1936–39.

56 Lindbergh, *Wartime Journals*, 26.

57 Mosley, *Lindbergh*, 222.

58 Lindbergh, *Wartime Journals*, 26.

59 Kennedy, *Hostage to Fortune*, 280.

60 Quoted in Beschloss, *Kennedy and Roosevelt*, 176.

61 Leslie Hore-Belisha, Baron Hore-Belisha (September 7, 1893–February 16, 1957), Secretary of State for War 1937–40.

62 Lindbergh, *Wartime Journals*, 28.

63 Benjamin Delahauf Foulois (December 9, 1879–April 25, 1967), US Army general who learned to fly the first military planes bought from the Wright Brothers and headed the development of air force strategy.

64 Foulois and Glines, *From the Wright Brothers to the Astronauts*, 236–7.

65 James Aloysius Farley (May 30, 1888–June 9, 1976), campaign manager for FDR's two gubernatorial campaigns, chairman of the Democratic National Committee 1932–40, Postmaster General 1933–40, head of Coca-Cola 1940–73.

66 Schlesinger, *The Age of Roosevelt*, 452.

67 Associated Press report, February 12, 1934. See *Southeast Missourian*, March 15, 1934.

68 *New York Times*, February 25, 1934.

69 Quoted in Browder and Smith, *Independent*, 196–7.

70 Quoted in Mosley, *Lindbergh*, 182.

Chapter Six: PEACE IN OUR TIME

1 Edvard Beneš (May 28, 1884–September 3, 1948), leader of the Czechoslovak independence movement, Minister of Foreign Affairs 1918–35, prime minister of Czechoslovakia 1921–22, president 1935–38.

2 William Christian Bullitt Jr. (January 25, 1891–February 15, 1967), US ambassador to the Soviet Union 1933–36, to France 1936–40.

3 Juan Terry Trippe (June 27, 1899–April 3, 1981), founder of Pan American World Airways.

4 Lindbergh, *Wartime Journals*, 32.

5 Ibid., 44.

6 Ibid., 35–6.

7 Herbert von Dirksen (April 2, 1882–December 19, 1955), German ambassador to Britain 1938–39.

8 Kennedy, *Hostage to Fortune*, 267.

9 Ibid., 270.

10 Lindbergh, *Wartime Journals*, 45.

11 Full text available at: http://www.presidency.ucsb.edu/ws/?pid=15525.

12 Black, *Franklin Delano Roosevelt*, 476.

13 *Documents on British Foreign Policy*, 212–3.

14 Blum, *Years of Urgency*, 518.

15 *Boston Evening American*, August 31, 1938.

16 Alfred Duff Cooper, Viscount Norwich (February 22, 1890–January 1, 1954), Secretary of State for War 1935–37, First Lord of the Admiralty 1937–38, Minister of Information 1940–41, Chancellor of the Duchy of Lancaster 1941–43, British ambassador to France 1944–48.

17 Beschloss, *Kennedy and Roosevelt*, 175.

18 Georges-Étienne Bonnet (July 22, 1889–June 18, 1973), French Foreign Minister 1938–39.

19 Bonnet, *Défense de la Paix*, 360–1.

20 Lindbergh, *Wartime Journals*, 67.

21 Remnants of the once distinguished Austro-Hungarian aristocrats, with vast estates in Bohemia and Austria.

22 Lindbergh, *Wartime Journals*, 68.

23 Ibid., 70.

24 Black, *Franklin Delano Roosevelt*, 476. Although the message was sent before Chamberlain set off for Munich, the timing of the note has been misconstrued by some historians to suggest that FDR approved of the Munich Agreement. Nothing could be further from the truth.

25 Whalen, *The Founding Father*, 218.

26 Feiling, *The Life of Neville Chamberlain*, 367.

27 This verbatim account is taken from the German interpreter Paul Schmidt's official report, quoted in Bullock, *Hitler*, 455–6.

28 Minney, *The Private Papers of Hore-Belisha*, 146.

29 Whalen, *The Founding Father*, 218.

30 Édouard Daladier (June 18, 1884–October 10, 1970), three times prime minister of France, 1933, 1934, 1938–40.

31 Churchill, *The Gathering Storm*, 251.

32 Dallek, *Franklin D. Roosevelt and American Foreign Policy*, 165.

33 Beschloss, *Kennedy and Roosevelt*, 177.

34 Kennedy, *Hostage to Fortune*, 280.

35 Ibid., 282.

36 Lindbergh, *Wartime Journals*, 72–4.

37 Ibid., 74.

38 Sir Oswald Ernald Mosley, Baronet (November 16, 1896–December 3, 1980), founder of the British Union of Fascists, Labour MP for Harrow 1918–24 and 1926–31, Chancellor of the Duchy of Lancaster in the Labour government 1929–31. Formed the New Party which merged with the British Union of Fascists (which included the Blackshirts) in 1932. Interned 1940–43, under house arrest 1943–45. Left Britain to live permanently in Ireland 1951.

39 Lindbergh, *Wartime Journals*, 75.

40 Black, *Franklin Delano Roosevelt*, 467.

41 Churchill, *The Gathering Storm*, 253.

42 Whalen, *The Founding Father*, 244.

43 Quoted in Bullock, *Hitler*, 457.

44 Davis, *Into the Storm*, 337.

45 Maurice Gustave Gamelin (September 20, 1872–April 18, 1958), general, commander of the French military in 1940 during the Battle of France.

46 Sir Horace John Wilson (August 23, 1882–May 19, 1972), Permanent Secretary of the Treasury 1939–42, head of the Home Civil Service 1939–42.

47 Chamberlain, *In Search of Peace*, 274–6.

48 Quoted in Bullock, *Hitler*, 461.

49 Hitler, *Speeches*, 508–27.

50 William Lawrence Shirer (February 23, 1904–December 28, 1993), reporter in wartime Berlin and author of a history of Nazism, *The Rise and Fall of the Third Reich* (1960).

51 Shirer, *The Rise and Fall of the Third Reich*, 398.

52 Margaret "Daisy" Lynch Suckley (December 20, 1891–June 29, 1991), distant cousin, intimate friend, and confidante of FDR. They may also have been lovers.

53 September 26, 1938, in Conrad Black collection of Roosevelt papers. Quoted in Black, *Franklin Delano Roosevelt*, 474.

54 Lindbergh, *Wartime Journals*, 76.

55 Quoted in Hamilton, *JFK*, 239.

56 Nicolson, *Diaries and Letters*, 370.

57 Ibid.

58 The deluded Lindbergh, no doubt basing his view on Kennedy's self-serving braggadocio, noted in his diary, "Kennedy has taken a large part in bringing about the conference." Lindbergh, *Wartime Journals*, 79.

59 Quoted in Ketchum, *The Borrowed Years*, 81.

60 Associated Press report, September 30 1938. Available at: http://hosted.ap.org/dynamic/files/specials/today-in-history/09/30/0930chamberlainSTY.html?SITE=TXDAM.

61 Taylor, *Munich*, 59.

Chapter Seven: KRISTALLNACHT

1 Churchill, *The Gathering Storm*, 269.

2 Quoted in Olson, *Troublesome Young Men*, 146.

3 Churchill, *The Gathering Storm*, 270–1.

4 Black, *Franklin Delano Roosevelt*, 481.

5 Kennedy, *Hostage to Fortune*, 290.

6 Lindbergh, *Wartime Journals*, 76, 78.

7 Kennedy, *Hostage to Fortune*, 293.

8 Quoted in Craig and Gilbert, *The Diplomats*, 662.

9 Gilbert, *Churchill*, 609.

10 Horatio Nelson, Viscount Nelson (September 29, 1758–October 21, 1805), admiral whose successive victories during the American War of Independence, the French Revolutionary Wars, and the Napoleonic Wars ensured his place in the British pantheon of heroes.

11 Kennedy, *Hostage to Fortune*, 294–5.

12 Quoted in Koskoff, *Joseph P. Kennedy*, 159.

13 Kennedy, *Hostage to Fortune*, 298.

14 Quoted in Hamilton, *JFK*, 247.

15 Whalen, *The Founding Father*, 249.

16 Hooker, *The Moffat Papers*, 221.

17 Kennedy, *Hostage to Fortune*, 300.

18 Ibid., 305.

19 *New York Times*, October 23, 1938.

20 Roosevelt, *Letters 1928–1945*, vol. 2, 810–1.

21 Quoted in Black, *Franklin Delano Roosevelt*, 483.

22 Radio address to the *Herald Tribune* Forum, October 26, 1938, available at: http://www.presidency.ucsb.edu/ws/?pid=15557.

23 Hamilton, *JFK*, 248.

24 Freedman, *Roosevelt and Frankfurter*, 464.

25 Ibid. Author's emphasis.

26 *New York Mirror*, November 12, 1938.

27 Jean Omer Marie Gabriel Monnet (November 9, 1888–March 16, 1979), French political economist and diplomat, Deputy Secretary General of the League of Nations 1919–23, widely regarded as the chief architect of postwar European unity, president of the European Coal and Steel Community 1952–55.

28 Lindbergh, *Wartime Journals*, 88.

29 Berthold Konrad Hermann Albert Speer (March 19, 1905–September 1, 1981), Hitler's principal architect, commissioned to remodel Berlin as a monumental capital city that matched the ambition of the Third Reich. Minister of Armaments and War Production 1942–45. Found guilty of war crimes at Nuremberg, imprisoned in Spandau 1947–66.

30 Lindbergh, *Wartime Journals*, 110.

31 Ibid., 96.

32 Quoted in Reynolds, *Lord Lothian*, 53, n. 187.

33 William Lyon Mackenzie King (December 17, 1874–July 22, 1950), longest-serving prime minister in Canadian history: 1921–26, 1926–30, 1935–48, founder of the Canadian welfare state. Roosevelt, ever playing the double game, continued to pretend to Mackenzie King on October 11, 1938, that what Europe needed above all was a "reduction of armaments." Roosevelt, *Letters 1928–1945*, vol. 2, 816.

34 George Catlett Marshall Jr. (December 31, 1880–October 16, 1959), chief of staff of the US Army, Secretary of State, Secretary of Defense 1950–51. Chief military adviser to Roosevelt and architect of the Marshall Plan, which used

American financial aid to restore Europe to economic health after World War Two. Winner of the Nobel Peace Prize 1953.

35 John Joseph "Black Jack" Pershing (September 13, 1860–July 15, 1948), US Army general who led the American Expeditionary Forces in World War One.

36 Reynolds, *From Munich to Pearl Harbor*, 46.

37 Ickes, *The Inside Struggle*, 474.

38 Reported in the *Observer*, Rockford, IL, October 6, 1938.

39 George E. Herman, "The Elusive J.F.K.," *New Republic*, June 27, 1960.

40 Kennedy, *Hostage to Fortune*, 297.

41 Roosevelt, *Letters 1928–1945*, vol. 2, 825–6.

42 Hugh Robert Wilson (January 29, 1885–December 29, 1946), career diplomat, headed the US mission to Switzerland 1927–37, Assistant Secretary of State 1937–40, ambassador to Germany March 3–November 16, 1938.

43 Lindbergh, *Wartime Journals*, 103.

44 Truman Smith, *Berlin Alert*, quoted in Mosley, *Lindbergh*, 235.

45 "France Pledges Aid to Great Britain," *Gallup Independent*, December 19, 1938.

46 Ickes, *The Inside Struggle*, 533.

47 Paul Joseph Goebbels (October 29, 1897–May 1, 1945), Nazi propaganda minister 1933–45. As Russian troops advanced on Hitler's bunker in the final days of World War Two, after ordering the deaths of his six children he and his wife committed suicide.

48 Full transcript available at: http://www.presidency.ucsb.edu/ws/?pid=15572.

49 Herbert Claiborne Pell Jr. (February 16, 1884–July 17, 1961), Democratic representative from New York, ambassador to Portugal 1937–41, to Hungary 1941–42, instigator and member of the United Nations War Crimes Commission 1943–45.

50 Roosevelt, *Letters 1928–1945*, vol. 2, 826.

51 Kennedy, *Hostage to Fortune*, 301.

52 Quoted in Beschloss, *Kennedy and Roosevelt*, 180.

53 Lindbergh, *Wartime Journals*, 116.

54 Ibid, 127.

55 Kennedy, *Hostage to Fortune*, 305.

56 Radio address, November 20, 1938, quoted in Warren, *Radio Priest*, 155–6.

57 *New York Times*, November 27, 1938, 46.

58 Helene Bertha Amalie "Leni" Riefenstahl (August 22, 1902–September 8, 2003), innovative German film documentarist who celebrated Hitler in *Triumph of the Will*, her record of the 1934 Nuremberg rally, and *Olympia*, her film of the 1936 Olympics.

59 Avery Brundage (September 28, 1887–May 8, 1975), 1912 Olympic pentathlete and decathlete, president of the US Olympic Committee 1928–53, member of the International Olympic Committee 1936–72, president of the IOC 1952–72.

60 Trimborn, *Leni Riefenstahl*, 149.

61 *Detroit News*, February 21, 1937.

62 Seventy years later, Riefenstahl rewrote history by denying that she had said, on being asked about Kristallnacht on her arrival in New York, "That is not true.

That cannot be true." In fact, she arrived five days before Kristallnacht. See Riefenstahl, *Leni Riefenstahl: Memoirs*, 236–7.

63 Ibid., 238.

64 Harold Eugene "Hal" Roach Sr. (January 14, 1892–November 2, 1992), producer of mostly silent film comedies, including the Laurel and Hardy and Little Rascals series.

65 Interview by *Tageblatt*, Hamburg, quoted in Bach, *Leni*, 179.

66 Arthur Harold Babitsky (October 8, 1907–March 4, 1992), known as Art Babbitt, chief animator at the Disney studio during its most creative period. As well as inventing the character Goofy, he contributed to key works such as *The Three Little Pigs* (1933), *Pinocchio* (1940), and *Snow White and the Seven Dwarfs* (1940).

67 Trimborn, *Leni Riefenstahl*, 150.

68 Douglas Elton Fairbanks Jr. (December 9, 1909–May 7, 2000), only son of swashbuckling silent movie star and co-founder of United Artists Douglas Fairbanks.

69 Robert Emmet Sherwood (April 4, 1896–November 4, 1955), playwright, editor, and screenwriter, whose works include *Waterloo Bridge* (play 1930, film 1940) and *The Petrified Forest* (play 1935, film 1936).

70 Harry Hines Woodring (May 31, 1890–September 9, 1967), Democratic governor of Kansas 1931–33, Assistant Secretary of War 1933–36, Secretary of War 1936–40.

71 Claude Augustus Swanson (March 31, 1862–July 7, 1939), Democratic representative from Virginia 1893–1906, governor of Virginia 1906–10, senator 1910–33, Secretary of the Navy from 1933 until his death in 1939.

72 Roosevelt, *Letters 1928–1945*, vol. 2, 843.

73 German Military Research Bureau, Specialty Group 6: Air Force and Aerial Warfare History, quoted in Mosley, *Lindbergh*, 225.

74 Ludwig August Theodor Beck (June 29, 1880–July 20, 1944). After resigning from the General Staff in 1938, he lived in retirement in Berlin. In 1944 he joined another plot to overthrow Hitler; when it failed, he attempted suicide but succeeded only in severely wounding himself, then was shot dead.

75 Churchill, *The Gathering Storm*, 258.

76 Franz Halder (June 30, 1884–April 2, 1972), Supreme High Commander of the German Army 1938–42. The full list of conspirators includes Franz Halder, Ludwig Beck, Edwin von Stuelpnagel, Erwin von Witzleben, Georg Thomas, Walter von Brockdorff-Ahlefeldt, and Wolf-Heinrich Graf von Helldorf. See Churchill, *The Gathering Storm*, 259.

77 Ibid., 259.

78 Ibid., 260.

79 Quoted in Bullock, *Hitler*, 472.

80 Erich Johann Albert Raeder (April 24, 1876–November 6, 1960), Admiral, then Grand Admiral, of the German Fleet, resigned 1943. Found guilty of war crimes at Nuremberg Trials and sentenced to life imprisonment in 1946 but released in 1955 due to failing health.

81 André Léon Blum (April 9, 1872–March 30, 1950), prime minister of France 1936–37 and March–April 1938, president and prime minister 1946–47.

82 Gilbert, *Churchill*, 608.

83 Mosley, *Lindbergh*, 226.

Chapter Eight: ON THE MARCH

1 Full text available at: http://www.let.rug.nl/usa/presidents/franklin-delano -roosevelt/state-of-the-union-1939.php.

2 Henry Harley "Hap" Arnold (June 25, 1886–January 15, 1950), chief of Army Air Corps 1938–46), general in the US Army, later general in the US Air Force, Chief of the Army Air Corps 1938–41, and Commanding General of the US Army Air Forces during World War Two.

3 Davis, *Into the Storm*, 402.

4 Black, *Franklin Delano Roosevelt*, 504.

5 Robert Rice Reynolds (June 18, 1884–February 13, 1963), Democratic senator from North Carolina 1932–45. A passionate and persistent defender of Nazi aggression. Rufus Cecil Holman (October 14, 1877–November 27, 1959), Republican senator from Oregon 1939–45.

6 This was the speech in which Hitler anticipated the Holocaust: "I will once more be a prophet. If the international Jewish financiers in and outside Europe should succeed in plunging the nations once more into a world war, then the result will not be the bolshevization of the earth, and this the victory of Jewry, but the annihilation of the Jewish race in Europe!" Available at: http://prod ucts.ilrn-support.com/wawc2c01c/content/wciv2/readings/wciv2readings hitler2.html.

7 Quoted in Black, *Franklin Delano Roosevelt*, 503.

8 James Edward Van Zandt (December 18, 1898–January 6, 1986), Republican representative from Pennsylvania 1939–43, 1947–63.

9 Andrew Jackson May (June 24, 1875–September 6, 1959), Democratic representative from Kentucky 1931–47, chairman of the House Military Affairs Committee 1939–46. In 1947 he served nine months in prison for bribery stemming from that office.

10 *New York Times*, February 1, 1939.

11 Ibid.

12 Roosevelt, *Letters 1928–1945*, vol. 2, 863.

13 John Clarence Cudahy (December 10, 1887–September 6, 1943), US ambassador to Poland 1933–37, to Ireland 1937–40, to Belgium 1939–40, and to Luxembourg January–July 1940.

14 Lincoln MacVeagh (October 1, 1890–September 9, 1974), US envoy to Greece 1933–41, ambassador to Iceland 1941–42, envoy to South Africa 1942–43, ambassador to governments in exile of Greece and Yugoslavia based in Cairo 1943–44 and in Athens 1944–47.

15 Roosevelt, *Letters 1928–1945*, vol. 2, 865.

16 George Macaulay Trevelyan (February 16, 1876–July 21, 1962), highly partisan British historian on English subjects, Master of Trinity College, Cambridge 1940–51.

17 FDR to Merriman, February 15, 1939. Merriman papers, Massachusetts Historical Society. Available at: http://www.masshist.org/database/viewer-touch

.php?item_id=1842&mode=transcript&img_step=1&tpc=&pid=3&from=/objects/2010february.php.

18 Roosevelt, *Letters 1928–1945*, vol. 2, 854.

19 Herzstein, *Roosevelt and Hitler*, 254. Hitler envisioned imposing Nazism—"a great European New Order"—on the nations he conquered.

20 The estate's name, La Guerida, given by its former owner, Rodman Wanamaker, a Philadelphia, PA, department store mogul, acquired new irony at this time as in Spanish it meant "spoils of war."

21 Quoted in Beschloss, *Kennedy and Roosevelt*, 182.

22 Quoted ibid., 183.

23 Alfred Damon Runyon (October 4, 1880–December 10, 1946), journalist and author whose stories of gangster life inspired Frank Loesser's musical *Guys and Dolls*.

24 Walter Winchell (April 7, 1897–February 20, 1972), newspaper and radio gossip reporter.

25 Quoted in Beschloss, *Kennedy and Roosevelt*, 184.

26 Thomas Gardiner Corcoran (December 29, 1900–December 6, 1981), member of FDR's "Brain Trust" and one of his closest advisers.

27 Blum, *Years of Urgency*, 37.

28 John Allsebrook Simon (Lord Simon; February 28, 1873– January 11, 1954), Liberal politician who served in a variety of top positions, including Foreign Secretary, Home Secretary, and Chancellor of the Exchequer, under five prime ministers.

29 Tansill, *Back Door to War*, 449.

30 Langer and Gleason, *Undeclared War*, 60.

31 Black, *Franklin Delano Roosevelt*, 511.

32 Elbert Duncan Thomas (June 17, 1883–February 11, 1953), Democratic senator from Utah 1933–51.

33 Roosevelt, *Letters 1928–1945*, vol. 2, 873.

34 Ibid., 859.

35 Ibid., 862.

36 Davis, *Into the Storm*, 409.

37 Herzstein, *Roosevelt and Hitler*, 317.

38 Ibid., 295.

39 Lindbergh, *Wartime Journals*, 136.

40 Ibid, 137.

41 *New York Times*, February 1, 1939.

42 Lindbergh, *Wartime Journals*, 158.

43 Ibid, 159.

44 Ibid, 160.

45 http://www.fdrlibrary.marist.edu/daybyday/event/march-1939-6/.

46 Cameron Watt, *How War Came*, 167, n. 22.

47 Henderson, *Failure of a Mission*, 223.

48 Lindbergh, *Wartime Journals*, 166.

49 Ibid, 171.

50 Quoted in Bullock, *Hitler*, 497.

51 *Straits Times*, April 1, 1939, 11.

52 Gilbert, *Churchill*, 612.

53 Bullock, *Hitler*, 500.

54 Shoor, *Young John Kennedy*, 110.

55 Craig and Gilbert, *The Diplomats*, 669.

56 Lindbergh, *Wartime Journals*, 173.

57 Berg, *Lindbergh*, 386.

58 Lindbergh, *Wartime Journals*, 247.

59 Hamilton Stuyvesant Fish (December 7, 1888–January 18, 1991), Republican representative from New York's 26th District, 1920–45. Isolationist and thorn in FDR's side.

60 Roosevelt to Caroline O'Day. Roosevelt, *Letters 1928–1945*, vol. 2, 900.

61 William Francis "Frank" Murphy (April 13, 1890–July 19, 1949), mayor of Detroit 1930–33, governor-general of the Philippines 1933–35, High Commissioner of the Philippines 1935–36, governor of Michigan 1937–39, Attorney General 1939–40, Justice of the Supreme Court 1940–49.

62 Roosevelt, *Letters 1928–1945*, vol. 2, 900.

63 It transpired he depended on Cockburn's *The Week*.

64 Leuchtenburg, *Franklin D. Roosevelt and the New Deal*, 287.

65 Reynolds, *From Munich to Pearl Harbor*, 54.

66 Herzstein, *Roosevelt and Hitler*, 225.

67 Lindbergh, *Wartime Journals*, 185.

68 Ibid., 248.

69 Ibid., 187.

Chapter Nine: A STATE OF WAR

1 Thomas Mann (June 6, 1875–August 12, 1955), German novelist and essayist, awarded the Nobel Prize for Literature 1929, whose works include *The Magic Mountain*, *Joseph and His Brothers*, and *Death in Venice*.

2 Herzstein, *Roosevelt and Hitler*, 251.

3 Reynolds, *From Munich to Pearl Harbor*, 221.

4 Speech, April 20, 1939, to organizers of the Rome Universal Exposition 1942.

5 Éamon de Valera (October 14, 1882–August 29, 1975), hero of the Irish independence movement, founder of Fianna Fáil, Taoiseach (prime minister) 1932–48, 1951–54, 1957–59, president of Ireland 1959–73.

6 Full text in *Documents on International Affairs*, 214–56. Also see: http://www.you tube.com/watch?v=iFjKihfhxME.

7 Quoted in Graubard, *Command of Office*, 218.

8 Quoted ibid.

9 Maxim Maximovich Litvinov (July 17, 1876–December 31, 1951), Soviet Foreign Minister 1930–39, ambassador to the US 1941–43.

10 Iosif Vissarionovich Stalin (December 18, 1878–March 5, 1953), General Secretary of the Central Committee of the Communist Party of the Soviet Union 1923-52.

11 Black, *Franklin Delano Roosevelt*, 522.

12 Roosevelt, *Autobiography of Eleanor Roosevelt*, 200.

13 Ibid., 206. The king's mother, the formidable Queen Mary, was every bit as controlling as Sara Roosevelt.

14 Black, *Franklin Delano Roosevelt*, 523.

15 Quoted ibid., 524.

16 Roosevelt, *Autobiography of Eleanor Roosevelt*, 200.

17 Bradford, *George VI*, 393.

18 Roosevelt, *Autobiography of Eleanor Roosevelt*, 207.

19 Kennedy, *Hostage to Fortune*, 335.

20 *Washington Sunday Star,* June 25, 1939.

21 Ickes, *The Inside Struggle*, 685.

22 Forrestal, *Diaries*, 122.

23 Kennedy, *Hostage to Fortune*, 353, n. 318.

24 Ibid., 354-5.

25 Cameron Watt, *How War Came*, 269.

26 Roosevelt, *Letters 1928–1945*, vol. 2, 920-1.

27 Hooker, *The Moffat Papers*, 256; quoted in Koskoff, *Joseph P. Kennedy*, 205.

28 Taylor, *Origins of the Second World War*, 272.

29 Quoted in McDonough, *Neville Chamberlain*, 86.

30 Quoted ibid., 87.

31 Roosevelt, *Letters 1928–1945*, vol. 2, 914-5.

32 Whalen, *The Founding Father*, 263.

33 Hull, *Memoirs*, 671-2.

34 Black, *Franklin Delano Roosevelt*, 528.

35 Rosenman, *Public Papers and Addresses of Franklin D. Roosevelt*, 455-8.

36 Macleod, *Neville Chamberlain*, 276.

37 Full text available at: http://en.wikisource.org/wiki/War_with_Germany_declared and http://www.youtube.com/watch?v=rtJ_zbz1NyY.

38 Schmidt, *Statist auf diplomatischer Bühne*.

39 Alsop and Kinter, *American White Paper*, 68.

Chapter Ten: THE BATTLE OF NEUTRALITY

1 Speer, *Inside the Third Reich*, 165.

2 War Cabinet No. 2 of 1939, 4 September 1939, Cabinet Papers, 4/95.

3 Nicolson, *Diaries and Letters*, 403.

4 Kennedy, *Hostage to Fortune*, 347.

5 Ibid., 391.

6 Ibid., 385.

7 *The Times*, London, June 28, 1939.

8 Full text available at: http://www.winstonchurchill.org/learn/speeches/speeches-of-winston-churchill/127-war-speech.

9 Quoted in Gilbert, *Churchill and America*, 174–5.

10 Full text available at: http://www.fdrlibrary.marist.edu/daybyday/event/september-1939-15/. Audio file available at: http://www.youtube.com/watch?v=hCU0P4zkyDI&feature=c4-overview-vl&list=PL3833257914F80DA9.

11 Lindbergh, *Wartime Journals*, 251.

12 Ibid., 254.

13 Antoine Marie Jean-Baptiste Roger, comte de Saint-Exupéry (June 29, 1900–July 31, 1944), French author and aviator, best known for *The Little Prince* and his flying memoir *Wind, Sand and Stars*.

14 Kennedy was aware of the correspondence, as it passed through the embassy's wire room, and read every exchange, but the failure of the president to include him in the conversation from the get-go was a further and intended snub.

15 Although John F. Kennedy enjoyed a warm, avuncular relationship with Harold Macmillan, British prime minister 1957–63, nothing approached the closeness of Roosevelt and Churchill until the "political marriage" of Ronald Reagan and Margaret Thatcher, which extended from 1975 until Reagan's death in 2004. There were, however, some disadvantages to Roosevelt and Churchill short-circuiting the traditional means of diplomacy. The British ambassador in Washington, Lord Lothian, for one, told Churchill that as he was not used as the conduit for messages between them, his own access to the president was restricted and therefore the British were deprived of a more subtle means of nudging the president in the right direction.

16 Kennedy, *Hostage to Fortune*, 411.

17 Black, *Franklin Delano Roosevelt*, 532. John Churchill, Duke of Marlborough, Prince of Mindelheim (May 26, 1650–June 16, 1722), commander-in-chief of the British army, victor of battles including Malplaquet, Ramillies, and Blenheim.

18 Churchill, *The Gathering Storm*, 355.

19 Kennedy, *Hostage to Fortune*, 392.

20 Ibid., 393.

21 Roosevelt, *Letters 1928–1945*, vol. 2, 918.

22 Jenkins, *Churchill*, 555. Roy Harris Jenkins (Lord Jenkins of Hillhead; November 11, 1920–January 5, 2003), reforming British Labour politician who was Home Secretary and Foreign Secretary, then president of the European Commission. Biographer of H. H. Asquith, Stanley Baldwin, Harry Truman, William Gladstone, Winston Churchill, and Franklin Roosevelt.

23 William Allen White (February 10, 1868–January 29, 1944), Republican supporter of the New Deal, who helped Theodore Roosevelt found the Bull Moose Party, reported on the Versailles peace talks for the Kansas *Emporia Daily and Weekly Gazette*, and strongly supported American entry into the League of Nations.

24 Members included Lindbergh's mother-in-law, Mrs. Dwight L. Morrow, Mayor LaGuardia of New York, and the publisher of *Time* and *Life*, Henry Luce.

25 Roosevelt, *Letters 1928–1945*, vol. 2, 968.

26 Alfred Mossman "Alf" Landon (September 9, 1887–October 12, 1987), Republican nominee for president in 1936.

27 William Franklin "Frank" Knox (January 1, 1874–April 28, 1944), editor and publisher of the Chicago *Daily News*, 1936 Republican vice presidential candidate, Secretary of the Navy 1940–44.

28 http://www.ibiblio.org/pha/policy/1939/1939-09-01d.html.

29 Lindbergh, *Wartime Journals*, 260.

30 Full text available at: http://www.ibiblio.org/pha/policy/1939/1939-09-14a.html.

31 Fulton Lewis Jr. (April 30, 1903–August 20, 1966), syndicated political reporter of "The Washington Sideshow" and conservative radio broadcaster.

32 Quoted in Berg, *Lindbergh*, 393.

33 Lindbergh, *Wartime Journals*, 250.

34 Black, *Franklin Delano Roosevelt*, 533.

35 Lindbergh, *Wartime Journals*, 255.

36 Ibid., 257–8.

37 Full text available at: http://www.ibiblio.org/pha/policy/1939/1939-09-15a.html.

38 Quoted in Berg, *Lindbergh*, 395.

39 Dorothy Thompson (July 9, 1893–January 30, 1961), journalist and author. In 1939, *Time* described her as the second most influential American woman after Eleanor Roosevelt. Her third husband was the author Sinclair Lewis.

40 Kennedy, *Hostage to Fortune*, 379.

41 Lindbergh, *Wartime Journals*, 282.

42 William Roy DeWitt Wallace (November 12, 1889–March 30, 1981), Republican activist and cofounder of *Reader's Digest*.

43 Wallace, *The American Axis*, 211.

44 Quoted in Berg, *Lindbergh*, 395.

45 Harry Flood Byrd Sr. (June 10, 1887–October 20, 1966), Democratic governor of Virginia 1926–30, senator 1933–65. Lindbergh met on September 26 with senators Byrd, Josiah W. Bailey (North Carolina), Walter George (Georgia), Hiram W. Johnson (California), Peter G. Gerry (Rhode Island) and Edward R. Burke (Nebraska). All except Burke were in favor of, in Lindbergh's words, "repeal of the present law with drastic substitutions which would minimize the chances of the United States becoming involved in the war." Only Burke was in favor of going to war "rather than let England and France lose." Lindbergh, *Wartime Journals*, 263.

46 Full text available at: http://www.ibiblio.org/pha/policybyrd/1939/1939-09-21 a.html.

47 Lindbergh, *Wartime Journals*, 274–5.

48 This was the first time the world heard of this terrifying means of warfare.

49 John Buchan, Baron Tweedsmuir (August 26, 1875–February 11, 1940), Scottish author of *The Thirty-Nine Steps*, historian, governor-general of Canada 1935–40.

50 Roosevelt, *Letters 1928–1945*, vol. 2, 934.

51 Ibid., 947.

52 "24 Senators Organize To Fight Neutrality Repeal," *Laredo Times*, September 22, 1939.

53 Robert Alphonso Taft (September 8, 1889–July 31, 1953), Republican senator from Ohio 1939–53.

54 Jeffrey Kraus, "Taft, Robert A.," in Robert E. Dewhirst, *Encyclopedia of the United States Congress* (New York: Facts On File, 2007).

55 Philip Fox La Follette (May 8, 1897–August 18, 1965), twice elected governor of Wisconsin, 1931–33 and 1935–39.

56 Doenecke, *Storm on the Horizon*, 60.

57 Full text available at: http://www.ibiblio.org/pha/policy/1939/1939-10-01a.html.

58 Roosevelt, *Letters 1928–1945*, vol. 2, 933.

59 Full text available at: http://www.ibiblio.org/pha/policy/1939/1939-10-13a.html.

60 Lindbergh, *Wartime Journals*, 286.

61 "Poll Shows Shift on Entering War," *New York Times*, October 20, 1939.

62 Langer and Gleason, *Undeclared War*, 233.

63 Harry S. Truman (May 8, 1884–December 26, 1972), Democratic senator from Missouri 1935–45, vice president of the United States January 20–April 12, 1945, president of the United States 1945–53.

64 Kennedy, *Hostage to Fortune*, 390.

65 Roosevelt, *Letters 1928–1945*, vol. 2, 985.

66 Ibid., 952.

67 Ibid., 953.

68 Ibid., 971.

69 Lindbergh, *Wartime Journals*, 265.

70 Ibid., 269.

71 Kennedy, *Hostage to Fortune*, 374.

72 Full text available at: http://www.ibiblio.org/pha/policy/1939/1939-10-06a.html.

73 Quoted in Bullock, *Hitler*, 557–8.

74 Ibid., 566.

75 Ibid., 569.

76 Kennedy, *Hostage to Fortune*, 380.

77 Leased to him on a peppercorn rent by Horace Dodge, heir to the American motor manufacturer. It is now a Legoland theme park.

78 Kennedy, *Hostage to Fortune*, 376.

79 Ibid., 376, n. 360.

80 Ibid., 382, n. 383.

81 Ibid., 411–12.

82 Roosevelt, *Letters 1928–1945*, vol. 2, 967.

83 John Allsebrook Simon, Viscount Simon (February 28, 1873–January 11, 1954), Foreign Secretary 1931–35, Home Secretary 1935–37, Chancellor of the Exchequer 1937–40, Lord Chancellor 1940–45.

84 Kennedy, *Hostage to Fortune*, 383.

85 Ibid., 383–4.

86 http://www.ibiblio.org/pha/policy/1939/1939-10-01a.html.

87 Kennedy, *Hostage to Fortune*, 385.

88 Ibid., 398.

89 Ibid., 386.

90 Ibid., 398.

91 Ibid., 394.

92 Ibid., 410.

93 Ibid., 391.

94 Roosevelt, *Letters 1928–1945*, vol. 2, 968.

95 Full text available at: http://www.winstonchurchill.org/learn/speeches/speeches-of-winston-churchill/98-the-war-situation-house-of-many-mansions.

96 Churchill, *War Papers: At the Admiralty*, 560.

97 Letter of December 25, 1939, Neville Chamberlain Papers, University of Birmingham, UK.

98 Roosevelt, *Letters 1928–1945*, vol. 2, 995.

Chapter Eleven: THIRD TERM FEVER

1 Full text available at: http://www.infoplease.com/t/hist/state-of-the-union/151.html#ixzz2XLxD4kfI.

2 Parmet and Hecht, *Never Again*, 13.

3 Ibid., 18.

4 James Farley, "Why I Broke with Roosevelt," *Collier's*, June 21, 1947.

5 Alfred Emanuel "Al" Smith (December 30, 1873–October 4, 1944), four-time governor of New York, Democratic US presidential candidate 1928.

6 Farley, "Why I Broke with Roosevelt."

7 George Howard Earle III (December 5, 1890–December 30, 1974), US minister to Austria 1933–34, Democratic governor of Pennsylvania 1935–39.

8 Burton Kendall Wheeler (February 27, 1882–January 6, 1975), Democratic senator from Montana 1923–47, vice presidential running mate of Robert La Follette Sr. for the Progressive Party, 1924.

9 John Llewellyn Lewis (February 12, 1880–June 11, 1969), president of the United Mine Workers of America (UMW) 1920–60, first president of the Congress of Industrial Organizations (CIO) 1938–41.

10 Farley, *Jim Farley's Story*, 224.

11 Paul Vories McNutt (July 19, 1891–March 24, 1955), Democratic governor of Indiana 1933–37, High Commissioner of the Philippines 1937–39, 1945–46, administrator of the Federal Security Agency 1939–42, chairman of the War Manpower Commission 1942–45, ambassador to the Philippines 1945–47.

12 Gugin and St. Clair, *The Governors of Indiana*, 291.

13 Jesse Holman Jones (April 5, 1874–June 1, 1956), head of Herbert Hoover's Reconstruction Finance Corporation (RFC) 1932–45, Secretary of Commerce 1940–45.

14 Stephen Grover Cleveland (March 18, 1837–June 24, 1908), president of the United States 1885–89 and 1893–97.

15 Thomas Edmund Dewey (March 24, 1902–March 16, 1971), Republican governor of New York 1943–54, Republican candidate for president 1944 and 1948

16 Farley, "Why I Broke with Roosevelt."

17 *Newsweek*, October 2, 1939, 46.

18 Farley, "Why I Broke with Roosevelt."

19 Roosevelt, *Letters 1928–1945*, vol. 2, 1012.

20 November 19, 1939. Available at: http://docs.fdrlibrary.marist.edu/php1139 .html.

21 *New York Times*, December 8, 1939, 24.

22 Kennedy, *Hostage to Fortune*, 350.

23 Ibid., 403.

24 "Washington Merry-Go-Round," November 9, 1939. Available at: http://dspace .wrlc.org/doc/bitstream/2041/18706/b03f13-1109zdisplay.pdf#search=".

25 "Washington Hums with Reaction to 'Draft F.D. for 3d Term' Boom," *Brooklyn Eagle*, January 9, 1940. Available at: http://fultonhistory.com/Newspaper %205/Brooklyn%20NY%20Daily%20Eagle/Brooklyn%20NY%20Daily%20 Eagle%201940%20Grayscale/Brooklyn%20NY%20Daily%20Eagle%201940%20 Grayscale%20-%200206.pdf.

26 Mary "Molly" Williams Dewson (February 18, 1874–October 21, 1962), feminist activist, head of the women's division of the Democratic National Committee, 1932.

27 Roosevelt, *Letters 1928–1945*, vol. 2, 999.

28 Quoted in Beschloss, *Kennedy and Roosevelt*, 200.

29 Rose's father, "Honey Fitz," and Joe Kennedy Jr., in his first adventure into politics, had joined the Farley campaign.

30 *New York Times*, February 14, 1940.

31 Neither felt they had a journalistic duty to pass on what would have been a front-page scoop to their readers. Kennedy's "lurid" and "unrestrained" assault on the president was left unreported until publication of Harold Ickes's diaries in 1954.

32 Ickes, *The Lowering Clouds*, 147.

33 Kennedy, *Hostage to Fortune*, 409.

34 Jenkins, *Churchill*, 572.

35 Berkeley Gage, quoted ibid., 573.

36 *New York Times*, March 8, 1940.

37 Full text available at: http://www.presidency.ucsb.edu/ws/index.php?pid=159 24&st=&st1=.

38 Kennedy, *Hostage to Fortune*, 412.

39 Ibid., 415.

40 Ibid., 403.

41 Herzstein, *Roosevelt and Hitler*, 313.

42 Kennedy, *Hostage to Fortune*, 412.

43 By 1940, Swedish iron ore supplies amounted to 11.5 million tons out of total German consumption of 15 million tons.

44 Lindbergh, *Wartime Journals*, 332.

45 In the Gallipoli campaign, a.k.a. the Dardanelles campaign, between April 1915 and January 1916, more than 250,000 Allied lives were lost, with a similar

number killed on the Ottoman side. It was, however, the Ottomans' greatest victory in World War One.

46 Full transcript of the second day of the Commons debate on May 8 available at: http://hansard.millbanksystems.com/commons/1940/may/08/conduct-of -the-war.

47 Kennedy, *Hostage to Fortune*, 422.

48 David Lloyd George, Lord Lloyd-George of Dwyfor (January 17, 1863–March 26, 1945), leader of the Liberal Party 1926–31, Chancellor of the Exchequer 1908–15, prime minister 1916–22.

49 Leopold Charles Maurice Stennett "Leo" Amery (November 22, 1873–September 16, 1955), First Lord of the Admiralty 1922–24, Secretary of State for the Colonies 1924–29, Secretary of State for India and Burma 1940–45.

50 Churchill, *The Gathering Storm*, 529.

Chapter Twelve: THE BATTLE OF FRANCE

1 Roosevelt, *Letters 1928–1945*, vol. 2, 1020–1.

2 Full text available at: http://www.winstonchurchill.org/learn/speeches/ speeches-of-winston-churchill/92-blood-toil-tears-and-sweat.

3 Kennedy, *Hostage to Fortune*, 425.

4 Loewenheim et al., *Roosevelt and Churchill*, 94–5.

5 Ibid., 95–6.

6 Paul Reynaud (October 15, 1878–September 21, 1966), prime minister of France March–June 1940.

7 Churchill, *Their Finest Hour*, 42.

8 Loewenheim et al., *Roosevelt and Churchill*, 97.

9 Full text available at: http://www.presidency.ucsb.edu/ws/?pid=15954.

10 Grenville Clark (November 5, 1882–January 13, 1967), Wall Street lawyer and member of the World War One veterans association the Military Training Camps Association.

11 Roosevelt, *Letters 1928–1945*, vol. 2, 1026.

12 Soames, *Speaking for Themselves*, 454.

13 Lewis Williams Douglas (July 2, 1894–March 7, 1974), Democratic representative from Arizona 1927–33, director of the Bureau of the Budget 1933–34, ambassador to the United Kingdom 1947–50. William Joseph "Wild Bill" Donovan (January 1, 1883–February 8, 1959), informal US emissary to Britain 1940–41, founding Coordinator of Information, combining US intelligence efforts.

14 Edward Raymond Burke (November 28, 1880–November 4, 1968), Democratic senator from Nebraska 1935–41. James Wolcott Wadsworth Jr. (August 12, 1877–June 21, 1952), Republican representative from New York 1935–51.

15 Albert Victor Alexander, Earl Alexander of Hillsborough (May 1, 1885–January 11, 1965), First Lord of the Admiralty 1929–31, 1940–46, Minister of Defence 1946–50.

16 Kennedy, *Hostage to Fortune*, 426.

17 Ibid., 427.

18 Ibid., 433.

19 Ibid., 435.

20 Merwin Kimball Hart (June 25, 1881–November 30, 1962), Republican pro-Franco, anti-Communist, and anti-Israel chairman of the John Birch Society and Holocaust denier, whose New York State Economic Council opposed government involvement in the economy. Accused by Harold Ickes of being a Nazi sympathizer and American Quisling.

21 Lindbergh, *Wartime Journals*, 347.

22 Ibid., 349.

23 *New York Times*, May 20, 1940.

24 Ibid.

25 Lindbergh, *Wartime Journals*, 352.

26 Ibid., 356.

27 Ibid., 357.

28 Quoted in Berg, *Lindbergh*, 399.

29 Full text available at: http://millercenter.org/president/speeches/detail/3316.

30 Edward Vernon Rickenbacker (October 8, 1890–July 23, 1973), America's most successful fighter ace in World War One, with 26 aerial victories. Head of Eastern Air Lines 1934–63.

31 Quoted in Black, *Franklin Delano Roosevelt*, 554.

32 Address to the Commons, June 4, 1940. Full text available at: http://www.winstonchurchill.org/learn/speeches/speeches-of-winston-churchill/128-we-shall-fight-on-the-beaches. Churchill would first give a speech in the House of Commons, which did not allow its proceedings to be broadcast, then repeat the speech for the BBC, to reach his home audience as well as audiences around the world.

33 Dwight David "Ike" Eisenhower (October 14, 1890–March 28, 1969), US Army 1915–53, commander of the Allied landings in North Africa 1942, supreme commander of the Allied landings in Normandy 1944, supreme commander of NATO 1951–52, president of the United States 1953–61.

34 Eisenhower, *Crusade in Europe*, 4.

35 http://docs.fdrlibrary.marist.edu/psf/box2/t12ab01.html.

36 Full text available at: http://millercenter.org/president/speeches/detail/3317.

37 Lindbergh, *Wartime Journals*, 356.

38 Ibid., 357.

39 Churchill, *Their Finest Hour*, 117.

40 Henri Philippe Benoni Omer Joseph Pétain (April 24, 1856–July 23, 1951), French general who in World War One was dubbed "the Lion of Verdun" but was later disgraced by collaborating with Germany as chief of the French state 1940–45.

41 Loewenheim et al., *Roosevelt and Churchill*, 99–100.

42 Ibid., 100.

43 Ibid., 101, n. 2.

44 Ibid., n. 3.

45 Ibid., 101–2.

46 Ibid., 102–3.

47 Ibid., 105.

48 Ibid., 106, n. 3.

49 Ibid., 106.

50 Henri Philippe Benoni Omer Joseph Pétain (April 24, 1856–July 23, 1951), French World War One marshal known as the "Lion of Verdun." Led Vichy France after the German occupation in 1940 until the liberation of France in 1944.

51 Shirer, *Berlin Diary*, 760.

Chapter Thirteen: LIFE OF THE PARTY

1 Marguerite Alice "Missy" LeHand (September 13, 1898–July 31, 1944), private secretary to FDR 1920–41.

2 "Washington Merry-Go-Round," *Palm Beach Post*, June 12, 1940. Available at: http://news.google.com/newspapers?nid=1964&dat=19400612&id=LUIjAAA AIBAJ&sjid=SbYFAAAAIBAJ&pg=2260,3992584.

3 Roosevelt, *Letters 1928–1945*, vol. 2, 1041.

4 Ibid., 1042–4.

5 Harold Rainsford Stark (November 12, 1880–August 20, 1972), Chief of US Naval Operations 1939–42.

6 Reynolds, *From Munich to Pearl Harbor*, 98.

7 Lothian to Lady Astor, June 12 1940. Astor Papers, 4/49, College of William & Mary, Williamsburg, VA. Available at: https://digitalarchive.wm.edu/handle /10288/18788.

8 Wendell Lewis Willkie (February 18, 1892–October 8, 1944), Democratic senator from Indiana, who after a spell as a Wall Street lawyer became Republican presidential candidate 1940.

9 http://www.youtube.com/watch?v=ggs58Z3J0b8&feature=youtu.be.

10 http://www.presidency.ucsb.edu/ws/?pid=75629.

11 Alsop, *I've Seen the Best of It*, 93.

12 Peters, *Five Days in Philadelphia*, 153.

13 Ickes, *The Lowering Clouds*, 92.

14 Charles Linza McNary (June 12, 1874–February 25, 1944), Republican senator from Oregon 1917–44, Senate Minority Leader 1933–44.

15 William Tecumseh Sherman (February 8, 1820–February 14, 1891), Civil War general in the Union Army whose "scorched earth" policy helped defeat the Confederacy.

16 Farley, *Jim Farley's Story*, 249–51.

17 The suite, 308/309, was the one occupied by Warren G. Harding in his epic battle to become the Republican presidential nominee in 1920.

18 Edward Joseph Kelly (May 1, 1876–October 20, 1950), mayor of Chicago 1933–47.

19 *Chicago Daily News*, July 16, 1940.

20 Quoted in Lash, *Eleanor and Franklin*, 619.

21 Roosevelt, *Letters 1928–1945*, vol. 2, 1048.

22 Ickes *The Lowering Clouds*, 244–5.

23 Ibid., 245.

24 Ibid., 249.

25 Perkins, *The Roosevelt I Knew*, 131–2.

26 Alben William Barkley (November 24, 1877–April 30, 1956), Democratic representative from Kentucky 1913–27, senator 1927–49, 1955–56, Senate Majority Leader 1937–47, Senate Minority Leader 1947–49, vice president of the United States 1949–53.

27 Full text available at: http://www.presidency.ucsb.edu/ws/?pid=15979.

28 Millard Evelyn Tydings (April 6, 1890–February 9, 1961), Democratic senator from Maryland 1927–51.

29 Farley, *Jim Farley's Story*, 254.

30 William Orville Douglas (October 16, 1898–January 19, 1980), chairman of the Securities and Exchange Commission 1937–39, longest-serving Justice of the Supreme Court, 1939–75.

31 William Brockman Bankhead (April 12, 1874–September 15, 1940), Democratic representative from Alabama 1917–33, 1933–40, House Majority Leader 1935–36, Speaker of the House 1936–40. An ardent supporter of the New Deal. Father of actress Tallulah Bankhead.

32 Samuel Taliaferro "Sam" Rayburn (January 6, 1882–November 16, 1961), Democratic representative from Texas 1913–61, Speaker of the House 1940–47, 1949–53, and 1955–61, the 17-year total making him the longest-serving House speaker in history.

33 Eurith Dickenson Rivers (December 1, 1895–June 11 1967), Democratic governor of Georgia 1937–41.

34 Farley, *Jim Farley's Story*, 302.

35 Full text as reported in *The New York Times*, July 19, 1940, available at: http://www.gwu.edu/~erpapers/teachinger/q-and-a/q22-erspeech.cfm.

36 Roosevelt, *Autobiography of Eleanor Roosevelt*, 217.

37 Farley, *Jim Farley's Story*, 302.

38 Ickes, *The Lowering Clouds*, 265.

Chapter Fourteen: THE BATTLE OF BRITAIN

1 Alfred Josef Ferdinand Jodl (May 10, 1890–October 16, 1946), chief of the operations staff of the German high command during World War Two, found guilty of war crimes at Nuremberg and hanged.

2 Shirer, *Berlin Diary*, 758.

3 Ibid., 760.

4 Shirer, *Berlin Diary*, 765.

5 Jenkins, *Churchill*, 632–3.

6 William Maxwell "Max" Aitken, Lord Beaverbrook (May 25, 1879–June 9, 1964), Conservative Unionist MP for Ashton-under-Lyne 1910–16, Minister of Information 1918, Minister of Aircraft Production 1940–41, Minister of Supply 1941–42, Minister of War Production 1942, Lord Privy Seal 1943–45.

7 Jenkins, *Churchill*, 633.

8 Shirer, *Berlin Diary*, 781.

9 Lowenheim et al., *Churchill and Roosevelt*, 107–8.

10 Berle diary, September 21 and 22, 1939, Roll 1, FDR Library.

11 Reynolds, *Lord Lothian*, 26.

12 Lothian to Churchill, August 20, 1940, Foreign Office Papers, FO 800/398.

13 Dean Gooderham Acheson (April 11, 1893–October 12, 1971), Secretary of State 1949–53, co-architect of the Marshall Plan, the Truman Doctrine, and the North Atlantic Treaty Organization.

14 Langer and Gleason, *The Challenge to Isolation*, 758–9.

15 Goodwin, *No Ordinary Time*, 147.

16 Reynolds, *From Munich to Pearl Harbor*, 98.

17 Roosevelt, *Letters 1928–1945*, vol. 2, 1084.

18 Loewenheim, et al., *Churchill and Roosevelt*, 109–10.

19 Kennedy, *Hostage to Fortune*, 461.

20 Ibid., 464.

21 Ibid., 463.

22 Roosevelt, *Letters 1928–1945*, vol. 2, 1061.

23 Shirer, *Berlin Diary*, 776.

24 Loewenheim et al., *Churchill and Roosevelt*, 111.

25 Full text available at: http://www.winstonchurchill.org/learn/speeches/speeches-of-winston-churchill/113-the-few.

26 Shirer, *Berlin Diary*, 779.

27 Ibid., 769, note.

28 Ibid., 769.

29 Ibid., 770.

30 Ibid., 774.

31 Roosevelt, *Letters 1928–1945*, vol. 2, 1085.

32 Though no further. At the first opportunity, they removed Churchill, who had acceded to the premiership without benefit of election. In 1945, his modest coalition deputy prime minister, Labour's Clement Attlee, was elected in a landslide for the Labour Party.

33 Jenkins, *Churchill*, 635.

34 Ibid., 641.

35 James Barrett Reston (November 3, 1909–December 6, 1995), Scottish-born US journalist who reported events in London 1939–40 before returning to establish the US Office of War Information in 1942.

36 *New York Times*, July 25, 1940.

37 Clement Richard Attlee, Earl Attlee (January 3, 1883–October 8, 1967), leader of the Labour Party 1935–55, Lord Privy Seal 1940–42, deputy prime minister 1942–45, prime minister 1945–51, Leader of the Opposition 1951–55.

38 *New York Times*, September 21, 1940.

39 Edward R. Murrow, born Egbert Roscoe Murrow (April 25, 1908–April 27,

1965), pioneering radio and television broadcaster whose commentary brought to an end the influence of the anti-Communist Senator Joseph McCarthy.

40 Archibald MacLeish (May 7, 1892–April 20, 1982), American poet and friend of Felix Frankfurter, Librarian of Congress 1939–44.

41 Quoted in Cull, *The British Propaganda Campaign*, 109.

42 Frank Humphrey Sinkler Jennings (August 19, 1907–September 24, 1950), pioneering, lyrical English documentary filmmaker.

43 Harry Watt (October 18, 1906–April 2, 1987), Scottish documentary filmmaker best remembered for *Night Mail* (1936), his collaboration with Basil Wright, set to a poem by W. H. Auden with music by Benjamin Britten.

44 Quentin James Reynolds (April 11, 1902–March 17, 1965), journalist on *Collier's Weekly* 1933–45, author of *London Diary* and *Courtroom*.

45 Full film available at: http://www.youtube.com/watch?v=Gno3mIrh7PM.

46 Jenkins, *Churchill*, 630.

47 The most priceless Churchill memo concerned what the British should be given to eat under rationing. "Almost all the food faddists I have ever known," he wrote to the minister of food, Frederick Woolton, "nut-eaters and the like, have died young after a long period of senile decay. The British soldier is far more likely to be right than the scientists. All he cares about is beef. . . . The way to lose the war is to try to force the British public into a diet of milk, oatmeal, potatoes, etc, washed down on gala occasions with a little lime juice." Churchill, *War Papers: The Ever-Widening War*, 514.

48 Full text available at: http://www.presidency.ucsb.edu/ws/?pid=15978.

49 Kennedy, *Hostage to Fortune*, 456.

50 Quoted in Beschloss, *Kennedy and Roosevelt*, 213.

51 Kennedy, *Hostage to Fortune*, 467.

52 Ibid., 457.

53 http://www.youtube.com/watch?v=MFeoDO1X-Kg.

54 *New York Times*, September 24, 1940.

55 Kennedy, *Hostage to Fortune*, 451.

56 Ibid., 454.

57 Ibid., 462.

58 Ibid., 455.

59 Ibid., 456.

60 Ibid., 452.

61 Ibid., 453.

62 Ibid., 459.

63 Full text available at: http://www.winstonchurchill.org/learn/speeches/speeches-of-winston-churchill/113-the-few.

64 Associated Press report, *Milwaukee Journal*, August 20, 1940.

Chapter Fifteen: FORD'S PLANS FOR PEACE

1 Henrik Shipstead (January 8, 1881–June 26, 1960), isolationist senator from Minnesota 1923–47 (Labor Party 1923–41, Republican 1941–47).

2 Lindbergh, *Wartime Journals*, 380.

3 On August 23, 1940, Lindbergh met with representatives Melvin J. Maas, James E. Van Zandt, Carl T. Curtiss, and Senator Nye, and with newspapermen sympathetic to isolationism C. B. Allen, of the *New York Herald Tribune*, and Frazier Hunt. Three days later he met with senators Clark of Missouri and Ernest Lundeen of Minnesota and Representative George H. Tinkham.

4 Melvin Joseph Maas (May 14, 1898–April 14, 1964), Republican representative from Minnesota 1927–33, 1935–45.

5 Lindbergh, *Wartime Journals*, 380.

6 Ibid., 370, 379.

7 Ibid., 378.

8 February 17, 1921. Quoted in Gardell, *Gods of the Blood*, 364, n. 61.

9 Lindbergh, *Wartime Journals*, 300.

10 Ibid., 351.

11 Ibid., 371.

12 Ibid., 377.

13 "The foundation of Brundage's political world view was the proposition that Communism was an evil before which all other evils were insignificant. A collection of lesser themes basked in the reflected glory of the major one. These included Brundage's admiration for Hitler's apparent restoration of prosperity and order to Germany, his conception that those who did not work for a living in the United States were an anarchic human tide, and a suspicious anti-Semitism which feared the dissolution of Anglo-Protestant culture in a sea of ethnic aspirations." Carolyn Marvin, *Avery Brundage and American Participation in the 1936 Olympic Games* (Annenberg School for Communication Departmental Papers, University of Pennsylvania, 1982). Available at: http://repository.upenn .edu/cgi/viewcontent.cgi?article=1073&context=asc_papers, 99.

14 Speech, "Our Relationship With Europe," August 4, 1940, Soldier Field, Chicago. Full text available at: http://www.charleslindbergh.com/americanfirst/ speech3.asp.

15 Lindbergh, *Wartime Journals*, 375.

16 Ibid., 375–6.

17 Quoted in Berg, *Lindbergh*, 412. One of many anti-Semitic remarks omitted by the editor of Lindbergh's diaries, William Jovanovich.

18 Madison, *Wendell Willkie*, 69.

19 Address accepting the Republican nomination, August 17, 1940. Full text available at: http://www.presidency.ucsb.edu/ws/?pid=75629.

20 Davis, *Into the Storm*, 611.

21 Lindbergh, *Wartime Journals*, 379.

22 Robert Douglas Stuart Jr. (born April 26, 1916). Heir to the Quaker Oats fortune and cofounder of America First.

23 John Gillis Townsend Jr. (May 31, 1871–April 10, 1964), Republican governor of Delaware 1917–21, senator 1929–41.

24 William Richards Castle Jr. (June 19, 1878–October 13, 1963), State Department chief of Western European affairs 1921, US ambassador to Japan 1930, Under Secretary of State 1931–33.

25 Lindbergh, *Wartime Journals*, 382.

26 Arthur Hendrick Vandenberg (March 22, 1884–April 18, 1951), Republican senator from Michigan 1928–51.

27 Lindbergh, *Wartime Journals*, 383.

28 Ketchum, *The Borrowed Years*, 586.

29 Kennedy, *Hostage to Fortune*, 453.

30 Roosevelt, *Letters 1928–1945*, vol. 2, 1069.

31 Kennedy, *Hostage to Fortune*, 467.

32 Ibid., 472.

33 *Washington Star,* October 7, 1940.

34 Kennedy, *Hostage to Fortune*, 475.

35 Quoted in Beschloss, *Kennedy and Roosevelt*, 213.

36 Ibid.

37 Reynolds, *From Munich to Pearl Harbor*, 99.

38 The Senate passed the Selective Service Act on August 28 by 58 votes to 21, the House by 185 to 155, with an amendment delaying the draft for 60 days while it was seen whether a more aggressive voluntary draft worked.

39 Lothian to Foreign Office, 21 September 1940, quoted in Reynolds, *Lord Lothian*, 43.

Chapter Sixteen: THE OLD CAMPAIGNER

1 Lindbergh, *War Within and Without*, 143.

2 Lindbergh, *The Wave of the Future*, 13, 36, 34.

3 Lindbergh, *War Within and Without*, 145.

4 Berg, *Lindbergh*, 406.

5 Wystan Hugh Auden (February 21, 1907–September 29, 1973), perhaps Britain's greatest poet of the twentieth century.

6 Quoted in Berg, *Lindbergh*, 406.

7 Quoted in Doenecke, *Storm on the Horizon*, 54.

8 Quoted in Mosley, *Lindbergh*, 276.

9 Lindbergh, *Wartime Journals*, 425.

10 Lindbergh *War Within and Without*, 148.

11 Ibid., 161.

12 Parmet and Hecht, *Never Again*, 251.

13 *Life*, November 4, 1940.

14 President's Personal File 1820, Roosevelt Library.

15 Sherwood, *Roosevelt and Hopkins*, 187.

16 Robert Elkington Wood (June 13, 1879–November 6, 1969), brigadier general who became an executive with Sears, Roebuck and leader of the Old Right conservatives. First president and leading donor of the Chicago America First Committee, then of the whole America First movement.

17 Lindbergh, *Wartime Journals*, 389.

18 Ibid., 394.

19 Ibid., 398.

20 Ibid., 406.

21 Full text available at: http://www.ibiblio.org/pha/policy/1940/1940-10-13a.html.

22 *Spokesman Review*, October 15, 1940.

23 *Evening Independent*, St. Petersburg, FL, October 22, 1940.

24 Address to a meeting of the Law Society of Massachusetts, October 16, 1940, Boston City Club. Full text available at: http://www.roberthjackson.org/the-man/speeches-articles/speeches/speeches-by-robert-h-jackson/democracy-under-fire/.

25 Kennedy, *Hostage to Fortune*, 475.

26 Ibid., 477.

27 Address, October 23, 1940, Convention Hall, Philadelphia. Full text available at: http://www.presidency.ucsb.edu/ws/?pid=15883.

28 *New York Times*, October 24, 1940.

29 Kennedy, *Hostage to Fortune*, 480.

30 Ibid.

31 Later LaGuardia Airport.

32 Lyndon Baines Johnson (August 27, 1908–January 22, 1973), Democratic representative from Texas 1937–49, senator 1949–61, vice president of the United States 1961–63, president 1963–69.

33 Quoted in Goodwin, *The Fitzgeralds and the Kennedys*, 611.

34 Kennedy, *Hostage to Fortune*, 481.

35 Ibid., 482.

36 Ibid., n. 593.

37 Address, October 28, 1940, Madison Square Garden, New York. Full text available at: http://www.presidency.ucsb.edu/ws/?pid=15885.

38 On May 16, 1789, John Adams wrote to Washington, "The unanimous suffrage of the elective body in your favor, is peculiarly expressive of the gratitude, confidence and affection of the citizens of America."

39 Francis Joseph Spellman (May 4, 1889–December 2, 1967), auxiliary bishop of the Archdiocese of Boston 1932–39, Archbishop of New York 1939–67. Made cardinal in 1946.

40 Cooney, *The American Pope*, 122.

41 Kennedy, *Hostage to Fortune*, 483.

42 Ibid., 484.

43 Ibid., 485.

44 Ibid., 489.

45 Ibid.

46 Ketchum, *The Borrowed Years*, 523.

47 Comparing the Roosevelt dynasty with the Kennedys, Gore Vidal wrote, "The sad story of the Kennedys bears about as much resemblance to the Roosevelts as the admittedly entertaining and cautionary television series *Dallas* does to Shakespeare's chronicle plays." *New York Review of Books*, August 13, 1981.

48 Kingman Brewster Jr. (June 17, 1919–November 8, 1988), President of Yale 1963–77, US ambassador to Britain 1977–81, Master of University College, Oxford, 1986–88.

49 Lindbergh, *Wartime Journals*, 411.

50 Full text in *Scribner's Commentator* 9, no. 3 (March 1941).

51 FDR's first inaugural address, March 4, 1933. Full text available at: http://www
   .presidency.ucsb.edu/ws/?pid=14473.

52 Sherwood, *Roosevelt and Hopkins*, 191.

53 Address, October 30, 1940, Boston Garden. Full text available at: http://www
   .presidency.ucsb.edu/ws/?pid=15887.

54 Quoted in Black, *Franklin Delano Roosevelt*, 596.

Chapter Seventeen: "Over My Dead Body"

1 Quoted in Barnes, *Willkie*, 255. Robert Sherwood quipped, "I doubt that statement. It was a virtue of Wendell Willkie's that he never knew when he was
  licked."

2 Kennedy, *Hostage to Fortune*, 491.

3 Samuel Miller Breckinridge Long (May 16, 1881–September 26, 1958), donor to
  FDR's 1932 campaign, US ambassador to Italy 1933–36, Assistant Secretary of
  State 1940–41.

4 Long, *War Diary*, 147.

5 Quoted in Freedman, *Roosevelt and Frankfurter*, 553–60.

6 Quoted in Beschloss, *Kennedy and Roosevelt*, 225.

7 *New York Times*, November 12, 1940.

8 Dineen, *The Kennedy Family*, 86.

9 Ickes, *The Lowering Clouds*, 386.

10 Freedman, *Roosevelt and Frankfurter*, 564.

11 Ibid., 553–60.

12 Quoted in Beschloss, *Kennedy and Roosevelt*, 225.

13 Quoted ibid.

14 Quoted in *New York Times*, December 7, 1940.

15 *Daily Mail*, November 30, 1940.

16 Freedman, *Roosevelt and Frankfurter*, 554.

17 Ibid.

18 Full text available at: http://www.presidency.ucsb.edu/ws/?pid=16041.

19 Roosevelt, *Letters 1928–1945*, vol. 2, 1060.

20 Full text available at: http://www.presidency.ucsb.edu/ws/?pid=16041.

21 Harry Morris Warner (December 12, 1881–July 25, 1958), one of the four Warner
   brothers who founded the eponymous Hollywood movie studio. Samuel Goldwyn, born Szmuel Gelbfisz, also known as Samuel Goldfish (July 1879–January 31, 1974), Oscar-winning producer of the movies *The Little Foxes* and *Guys
   and Dolls*. Louis Burt Mayer, born Lazar Meir (July 12, 1884–October 29, 1957),
   hugely successful Hollywood movie producer who ran Metro-Goldwyn-Mayer.

22 Edward G. Robinson (December 12, 1893–January 26, 1973), Romanian-born
   Jewish actor most famous for his sinister roles as a mobster boss in *Little Caesar*
   (1931) and *Key Largo* (1948), and as an intelligent sleuth in *Double Indemnity*

(1944) and *The Stranger* (1946). Active member of the Anti-Nazi League, Bundles for Britain, and the Committee to Defend America by Aiding the Allies.

23 Quoted in Beschloss, *Kennedy and Roosevelt*, 226.

24 The Hollywood branch of the committee was populated with prominent actors, among them Edward G. Robinson, Claude Rains, Paul Muni, John Garfield, James Cagney, Groucho Marx, and Henry Fonda.

25 Melvyn Edouard Hesselberg, known as Melvyn Douglas (April 5, 1901–August 4, 1981), actor who made his name opposite Greta Garbo in *Ninotchka* (1939). Member of the William Allen White Committee and the Anti-Nazi League.

26 Douglas, *See You at the Movies*, 114.

27 Myrna Loy (August 2, 1905–December 14, 1993), prolific actress whose career took off after she appeared as Nora Charles opposite William Powell in the *Thin Man* movies.

28 Loy, *Myrna Loy*, 161.

29 On December 12, 1941, the committee was renamed the War Activities Committee of the Motion Picture Industry.

30 Davies, *The Times We Had*, 300.

31 Quoted in Davis, *The War President*, 60.

32 Ickes, *The Lowering Clouds*, 386.

33 Beschloss suggests that the account was cleaned up by Eleanor and that Roosevelt actually said "son of a bitch." *Kennedy and Roosevelt*, 229.

34 Gore Vidal, "Eleanor," *New York Review of Books*, November 18, 1971.

35 Kennedy, *Hostage to Fortune*, 496.

36 Ibid., 497.

37 *New York Times*, December 3, 1940.

38 Bernard E. Smith (1888–May 10, 1961), financier, acquitted in 1903 of conspiracy to murder, he made a vast fortune selling stocks short during the Wall Street crash of 1929.

39 Abner Carroll Binder (February 20, 1896–1956),long-standing foreign correspondent for the Chicago *Daily News*.

40 Although the plot has been reported as fact by both Michael Beschloss (*Kennedy and Roosevelt*, 231) and Charles Higham (*American Swastika*, 33), it is hard to believe that Kennedy would risk involving himself in such treacherous skulduggery.

Chapter Eighteen: HIGH NOON

1 Quoted in Reynolds, *Lord Lothian*, 45.

2 Record of conversation, December 1940, British Cabinet Papers, CAB 65/10, WM 299 (40) 4.

3 Ickes, *The Lowering Clouds*, 367.

4 *New York Times*, November 24, 1940. Most historians have suggested that Lothian used the words, "Well, boys, Britain is broke. It's your money we want." That is most likely a canard. Not only is it totally out of character for Lothian, a former journalist who was aware of what havoc such a lively phrase might

wreak both in Washington and London, to use words more fitting for a tabloid newspaper, but the source of the quote, Sir John W. Wheeler-Bennett's biography of George VI (*King George VI: His Life and Reign*, London: St. Martin's Press, 1958, 521) is contradicted by eyewitnesses, by the absence of such words in contemporaneous newspaper reports, including New York's tabloids, and by Lothian's report to the Foreign Office. It is a good example of historians adopting the slipshod journalist's adage, "too good to check." See Reynolds, *Lord Lothian*, 48–9 and n. 169.

5 Associated Press report, December 6, 1940. See "U.S. Given Balance Sheet Showing British Finances," *Tuscaloosa News*, December 6, 1940.

6 Moser, *Twisting the Lion's Tail*, 127.

7 Reynolds, *Lord Lothian*, 54.

8 Sir Frederick Phillips (1884–1943), lifelong civil servant at the Treasury, head of the Treasury mission in Washington 1940–43.

9 Phillips had met with Morgenthau and the president for a daylong meeting on July 8, 1940, ostensibly to talk about preserving the gold standard. They spoke about Britain's fast-diminishing dollar reserves.

10 *New York Times*, December 7, 1940.

11 John Maynard Keynes, Lord Keynes (June 5, 1883–April 21, 1946), British economist whose *The General Theory* (1936) transformed the theory and practice of modern macroeconomics and provided the intellectual justification for the intervention of governments in economies.

12 Skidelsky, *Fighting for Freedom*, 97–8.

13 Blum, *Years of Urgency*, 171.

14 Kingsley Wood quoted in Colville, *The Fringes of Power*, 327.

15 Gilbert, *Churchill*, 687.

16 Roosevelt, *Letters 1928–1945*, vol. 2, 1104–5.

17 Quoted in Reynolds, *From Munich to Pearl Harbor*, 104.

18 Ziegler, *King Edward VIII*, 399.

19 Churchill, *Their Finest Hour*, 501. Although one of Churchill's most memorable and eloquent letters, it was the result of an agonizing writing and rewriting effort led by Lothian, with Halifax also contributing. It was Lothian who suggested that the letter should arrive while Roosevelt was afloat and had nothing else to do but concentrate on its contents.

20 Full text in Loewenheim et al., *Roosevelt and Churchill*, 122–6.

21 Telephone conversation, Lothian and Churchill, December 6, 1940. Reynolds, *Lord Lothian*, 47.

22 Read by Neville Butler to the American Farm Bureau Federation in Baltimore. Kerr, *The American Speeches of Lord Lothian*, xxxiv.

23 Loewenheim et al., *Roosevelt and Churchill*, 119–20.

24 Black, *Franklin Delano Roosevelt*, 605.

25 Full text available at: http://www.presidency.ucsb.edu/ws/?pid=15913.

26 Blum, *Years of Urgency*, 210–7.

27 Bennett Cohen (August 28, 1890–June 10, 1964), veteran Hollywood screenwriter, mostly of "B" westerns.

28 Parrish, *To Keep the British Isles Afloat*, 166.

29 *New York Times*, January 11, 1941.

30 Quoted in Doenecke, *In Danger Undaunted*, 17.

31 Kauffman, *America First!*, 18. Gerald Rudolph "Jerry" Ford Jr. (July 14, 1913–December 26, 2006), Republican representative from Michigan 1949–73, vice president of the US 1973–74, president 1974–77. Robert Sargent Shriver Jr. (November 9, 1915–January 18, 2011)., husband of Eunice Kennedy, first director of the Peace Corps 1961–66, US ambassador to France 1968–70.

32 *New York Times*, January 4, 1941, 1.

33 Theodore Roosevelt first used the expression "bully pulpit" in 1909 when he said, "I suppose my critics will call that preaching, but I have got such a bully pulpit!" His use of the word "bully" was not to do with imposing his views, but meaning "good," as in "Bully for you!" Lyman Abbott, "A Review of President Roosevelt's Administration," *Outlook* 91 (February 27, 1909): 430, 433-4.

34 Lindbergh, *Wartime Journals*,. 428.

35 Ibid., 429.

36 Ibid.

37 Ibid., 434.

38 Ibid., 422.

39 Ibid., 420–1.

40 Hanford "Jack" MacNider (October 2, 1889–February 18, 1968), cofounder of the American Legion, Assistant Secretary of War 1925–28, US ambassador to Canada 1930–32, failed candidate for the vice presidential slot on Willkie's 1940 ticket.

41 Roosevelt did not appoint John Gilbert Winant to succeed Kennedy until February 1941.

42 Beschloss, *Kennedy and Roosevelt*, 232.

43 Lindbergh, *Wartime Journals*, 432.

44 Callaghan, *The Lend-Lease Debate*, 235.

45 Frankfurter letters, Syracuse University Libraries, 573.

46 Full text available at: http://docs.fdrlibrary.marist.edu/122940.html. Video available at: http://www.presidency.ucsb.edu/mediaplay.php?id=15917&admin =32.

47 Cantril, *Public Opinion*, 976. Available at: http://archive.org/stream/publicopin ion19300unse/publicopinion19300unse_djvu.txt.

48 Churchill, *Their Finest Hour*, 455.

49 Colville, *The Fringes of Power*, 332.

50 *New York Times*, January 4, 1941.

Chapter Nineteen: THE BATTLE OF LEND-LEASE

1 Ernest Lundeen (August 4, 1878–August 31, 1940), Republican representative from Minnesota 1915–17, 1935–37, senator 1937–40. James J. Couzens (August 26, 1872–October 22, 1936), Republican mayor of Detroit 1919–22, senator from Michigan 1922–36. Lynn Joseph Frazier (December 21, 1874–January 11, 1947), Republican/non-partisan, governor of North Dakota 1917–21, senator

1923–41. Hiram Warren Johnson (September 2, 1866–August 6 ,1945), Progressive/Republican, governor of California 1911–17, senator 1917–45. Theodore Roosevelt's running mate in the 1912 presidential election. Arthur Capper (July 14, 1865–December 19, 1951), Republican governor of Kansas 1915–19, senator 1919–49.

2 The leadership quartet were senators Gerald P. Nye, Robert M. La Follette Jr., Bennett Champ Clark, and Arthur H. Vandenberg, who were joined, among others, by Burton K. Wheeler, David I. Walsh, Wallace H. White Jr., Henrik Shipstead, Robert A. Taft, D. Worth Clark, William Langer, and C. Wayland Brooks.

3 Other active isolationist House members included Karl E. Mundt and Dewey Short.

4 77th Congress, 1st Session, *Congressional Record* 87, part 1: 1588.

5 *Chicago Tribune,* January 12, 1941.

6 *New York Times,* January 2, 1941.

7 Beard, *Roosevelt and the Coming of the War,* 20.

8 *New York Times,* January 22, 1941.

9 Sherwood, *Roosevelt and Hopkins,* 254.

10 Lindbergh, *Wartime Journals,* 499.

11 Best, *Herbert Hoover,* 170, n. 37.

12 Ibid., 176.

13 Ibid.

14 *New York Times,* January 5, 1941.

15 Full text available at: http://www.presidency.ucsb.edu/ws/?pid=16092.

16 Lindbergh, *Wartime Journals,* 437.

17 Full text available at: http://www.presidency.ucsb.edu/ws/?pid=16092.

18 Sidney Hillman (March 23, 1887–July 10, 1946), head of the Amalgamated Clothing Workers of America and key figure in the founding of the Congress of Industrial Organizations.

19 William Signius Knudsen (March 25, 1879–April 27, 1948), executive with Ford and General Motors, recruited by Roosevelt to maximize war materiel output.

20 Roosevelt, *Public Papers and Addresses,* 645 ff.

21 Roosevelt, *Letters 1928–1945,* vol. 2, 1100.

22 Full text available at: http://www.ibiblio.org/pha/policy/1941/1941-01-08a.html.

23 *New York Times,* January 13, 1940.

24 Full text available at: http://poetry.poetryx.com/poems/6310/.

25 Full text available at: http://unix.cc.wmich.edu/~cooneys/poems/Clough.struggle.html.

26 Warren Robinson Austin (November 12, 1877–December 25, 1962), Republican senator from Vermont 1931–46, US ambassador to the United Nations 1946–53.

27 *Chicago Tribune,* January 18, 1941.

28 Lewis Deschler (March 3, 1905–July 12, 1976), first Parliamentarian of the US House of Representatives, 1927–74.

29 *New York Times,* January 11, 1941.

30 Ibid.

31 *New York Times,* January 12, 1941.

32 Speech, January 12, 1941, reprinted in 77th Congress, First Session *Congressional Record,* appendix: 178–9.

33 Full press conference transcript available at: http://www.presidency.ucsb.edu/ws/?pid=16147.

34 *New York Times,* January 18, 1941.

35 *New York Times,* January 15, 1941.

36 *New York Times,* January 14, 1941.

37 *New York Times,* January 18, 1941.

38 When asked by reporters whether he had heard McCormick's testimony, the president retorted, amid laughter, "Did he speak as an expert?" Roosevelt, *Public Papers and Addresses,* 11.

39 Whalen, *The Founding Father,* 352.

40 Kennedy, *Hostage to Fortune,* 525.

41 Ibid.

42 *New York Times,* January 17, 1941.

43 Kennedy, *Hostage to Fortune,* 526.

44 Full text available at: http://www.ibiblio.org/pha/policy/1941/1941-01-18a.html.

45 Whalen, *The Founding Father,* 354.

46 Goodwin, *No Ordinary Time,* 211.

Chapter Twenty: LINDBERGH'S BEST SHOT

1 Full text available at: http://www.presidency.ucsb.edu/ws/?pid=16022.

2 Lindbergh, *Wartime Journals,* 442.

3 77th Congress, 1st Session, *Congressional Record,* HR 1776: 371–435.

4 Berg, *Lindbergh,* 415.

5 Lindbergh, *Wartime Journals,* 452.

6 *New York Times,* January 25, 1941.

7 *New York Times,* January 26, 1941.

8 *New York Times,* January 28, 1941.

9 Full text of Lindbergh's statement to the Senate available at: http://www.ibiblio.org/pha/policy/1941/1941-02-06a.html.

10 Full text of speech before Senate Foreign Affairs Committee available at: http://www.ibiblio.org/pha/policy/1941/1941-02-06a.html.

11 *Richmond News Leader,* January 28, 1941, leading article.

12 77th Congress, 1st Session, *Congressional Record,* S 275: 211.

13 77th Congress, 1st Session, *Congressional Record,* HR 1776: 158.

14 77th Congress, 1st Session, *Congressional Record,* HR 1776: 101–2.

15 77th Congress, 1st Session, *Congressional Record,* S 275: 115–6.

16 Quoted in Black, *Franklin Delano Roosevelt,* 613.

17 77th Congress, 1st Session, *Congressional Record*, HR 1776: 582.

18 77th Congress, 1st Session, *Congressional Record*, S 275: 209.

19 Blum, *Years of Urgency*, 217-214.

20 *New York Times*, January 28, 1941.

21 Best, *Herbert Hoover, the Postpresidential Years*, 179.

22 John William McCormack (December 21, 1891–November 22, 1980), Democratic representative from Massachusetts 1928-71, Speaker of the House 1962-71.

23 77th Congress, 1st Session, *Congressional Record*, HR 1776: 592.

24 77th Congress, 1st Session, *Congressional Record*, HR 1776: 575.

25 77th Congress, 1st Session, *Congressional Record*, S 275: 1162.

26 77th Congress, 1st Session, *Congressional Record*, S 275: 1037.

27 *New York Times*, February 12, 1941.

28 Quoted in Peters, *Five Days in Philadelphia*, 192.

29 Barnard, *Wendell Willkie*, 291.

30 Quoted in Peters, *Five Days in Philadelphia*, 192.

31 *New York Times*, January 28, 1941.

32 Full, final text of the Lend-Lease Act available at: http://www.ourdocuments.gov /doc.php?flash=true&doc=71&page=transcript.

33 Full text available at: http://www.winstonchurchill.org/learn/speeches/speeches -of-winston-churchill/97-give-us-the-tools.

34 Jenkins, *Churchill*, 667.

35 Quoted in O'Toole, *Outing the Senator*, 218.

36 John Edgar Hoover (January 1, 1895–May 2, 1972), first director of the Federal Bureau of Investigation (FBI), 1935-72.

37 Jay Catherwood Hormel (September 11, 1892–August 30, 1954), known as the "Spam Man" for finding a profitable use for surplus pork shoulder.

38 Lindbergh, *Wartime Journals*, 515.

39 Sherwood, *Roosevelt and Hopkins*, 264.

40 Black, *Franklin Delano Roosevelt*, 617.

Chapter Twenty-One: JESUS CHRIST! WHAT A MAN!

1 Sherwood, *Roosevelt and Hopkins*, 200.

2 *New York Times*, January 25, 1941.

3 Birkenhead, *Halifax*, 474.

4 Churchill, *The Grand Alliance*, 26.

5 The main American planners were, for the Navy, admirals R. L. Ghormley and Richmond Kelly Turner, and captains A. G. Kirk, C. M. Cooke, and DeWitt Ramsey; for the Army, generals S. D. Embick, Sherman Miles, and L. T. Gerow, and Colonel Joseph T. McNarney. The British were admirals R. M. Bellairs and V. H. Danckwerts, General E. L. Morris, Lieutenant Colonel A. T. Cornwall-Jones, and Air Commodore J. C. Slessor. Military representatives from Canada, Australia, and New Zealand met with the British contingent but did not attend joint sessions.

6 Quoted in Davis, *The War President*, 123.

7 Quoted in Roll, *The Hopkins Touch*, 85.

8 Brendan Bracken, Lord Bracken (February 15, 1901–August 8, 1958), Minister of Information 1941–45, First Lord of the Admiralty May–July 1945. Founder of the *Financial Times*.

9 Colville, *The Fringes of Power*, 331.

10 Memo to prime minister, UK Public Record Office, PRO, PREM/4 25/3.

11 Eleanor was fond of telling the story that after spending four weeks with Churchill, Hopkins told Roosevelt, "You know, Winston is much more Left than you." Lash, *Eleanor Roosevelt*, 208.

12 Sherwood, *Roosevelt and Hopkins*, 234.

13 Churchill, *The Grand Alliance*, 23.

14 Lyttelton, *Memoirs of Lord Chandos*, 159. Sherwood doubted his account of events.

15 Sherwood, *Roosevelt and Hopkins*, 238.

16 Ibid., 236.

17 Davis, *The War President*, 124.

18 Churchill, *The Grand Alliance*, 26.

19 Goodwin, *No Ordinary Time*, 212.

20 Sherwood, *Roosevelt and Hopkins*, 243.

21 Roosevelt, *Letters 1928–1945*, vol. 2, 1115.

22 Colville, *The Fringes of Power*, 331.

23 Sherwood, *Roosevelt and Hopkins*, 243.

24 Ibid.

25 Ibid., 249.

26 Ibid., 247.

27 Ibid., 257.

28 Loewenheim et al., *Roosevelt and Churchill*, 131.

29 Full text available at: http://hansard.millbanksystems.com/commons/1941/mar/12/united-states-lease-lend-bill#S5CV0369P0_19410312_HOC_266.

30 Full text available at: http://www.presidency.ucsb.edu/ws/?pid=16089.

31 Churchill, *War Papers: The Ever-Widening War*, 182.

32 Ibid., 243.

33 Ibid., 249.

34 Ibid., 361.

35 Erwin Johannes Eugen Rommel (November 15, 1891–October 14, 1944), German field marshal known as the "Desert Fox" for his brilliant command of tank regiments in North Africa. When in charge of western defenses, he was accused of plotting against Hitler and was obliged to commit suicide.

36 Davis, *The War President*, 152.

37 Roosevelt summoned the Irish ambassador, former IRA commander Frank Aiken, and told him that America would not provide Ireland with munitions or ships unless they cooperated with Britain. The president sent a message via Aiken to the Irish people saying he supported them in their resistance to Ger-

man aggression. Aiken asked, "Can I also tell my people that you support them in their resistance to British aggression?" to which Roosevelt replied, "There's no such thing as British aggression." Lindbergh, *Wartime Journals*, 495.

Chapter Twenty-Two: WE'VE GOT OURSELVES A CONVOY

1　Halifax to Foreign Office, March 18, 1941, UK Public Record Office, PRO, A893/18/45.

2　Davis, *The War President*, 153.

3　Robert Gilbert Vansittart, Lord Vansittart (June 25, 1881–February 14, 1957), prominent opponent of appeasement, Permanent Under Secretary for Foreign Affairs 1930–38.

4　UK Public Record Office, PRO, A893/18/45.

5　Hearings before the House Committee on Foreign Affairs, 77th Congress, 1st Session, *Congressional Record*, HR 1776: 101.

6　*New York Times*, January 22, 1941.

7　Full text available at: http://www.presidency.ucsb.edu/ws/index.php?pid=1608 9&st=Nazi+forces+are+not+seeking+mere+modifications&st1=.

8　Carter Glass (January 4, 1858–May 28, 1946), Democratic representative from Virginia 1902–18, Treasury secretary 1918–20, senator 1920–46, president pro tempore of the Senate 1941–45.

9　*New York Daily News*, April 17, 1941.

10　*New York Times*, April 16, 1941.

11　*New York Times*, April 25, 1941.

12　Ibid.

13　Lindbergh, *Wartime Journals*, 475.

14　International News Agency report, April 17, 1941, *Milwaukee Sentinel*, April 18, 1941.

15　Cole, *Charles A. Lindbergh*, 148.

16　Clement Laird Vallandigham (July 29, 1820–June 17, 1871), Democratic representative from Ohio, 1858–63.

17　Partial text of press conference available at: http://www.presidency.ucsb.edu/ ws/?pid=16107.

18　Full text available at: http://www.ushistory.org/paine/crisis/c-01.htm.

19　Lindbergh, *Wartime Journals*, 480.

20　Ibid., 481.

21　*Milwaukee Sentinel*, May 4, 1941. Full text available at: http://news.google.com/ newspapers?nid=1368&dat=19410504&id=jFNQAAAAIBAJ&sjid=HA4EAAA AIBAJ&pg=3100,159973.

22　*New York Times*, May 7, 1941.

23　Ibid.

24　*New York Times*, May 8, 1941.

25　Lindbergh, *Wartime Journals*, 488, 490.

26　Ibid., 489.

27　Ibid., 492.

28 Rudolf Walter Richard Hess (April 26, 1894–August 17, 1987), Hitler's amanuensis for *Mein Kampf*. Deputy Führer 1933– 41. Found guilty at the Nuremberg
Trials and sentenced to life imprisonment. Hanged himself in Spandau prison
aged 93.

29 Quoted in Shirer, *Berlin Diary*, 838.

30 Lindbergh, *Wartime Journals*, 490.

31 Ibid., 498.

32 Full text available at: http://www.presidency.ucsb.edu/ws/?pid=16132.

33 Associated Press report, *Milwaukee Journal*, June 14, 1941.

34 Irving Berlin, born Israel Isidore Beilin (May 11, 1888–September 22, 1989),
American composer of popular songs and musical theater shows including
"Alexander's Ragtime Band" (1911), *Easter Parade* (1933), and "There's No Busi-
ness Like Show Business" (1946).

35 It was nothing of the sort. Berlin released the song in 1938 to commemorate the
twentieth anniversary of the 1918 Armistice.

36 Archibald Bulloch "Archie" Roosevelt (April 10, 1894–October 13, 1979), fifth
child of Theodore Roosevelt.

37 Husband of the pro-interventionist columnist Dorothy Thompson.

38 Lillian Diana Gish (October 14, 1893–February 27, 1993), film actress whose
career lasted from 1912 to 1987.

39 Lindbergh, *War Within and Without*, 177.

40 Lindbergh, *Wartime Journals*, 496.

41 *New York Times*, May 24, 1941.

42 Stimson and Bundy, *On Active Service*, 367.

43 Ibid., 368.

44 Full text available at: http://www.presidency.ucsb.edu/ws/?pid=16120.

45 President's Secretary's File 6, Roosevelt Library.

46 77th Congress, 1st Session, *Congressional Record* 87, part 5, Senate, (May 29, 1941).

Chapter Twenty-Three: BARBAROSSA

1 Quoted in Reynolds, *Munich to Pearl Harbor*, 134.

2 Hitler, *Mein Kampf*, 654.

3 Domarus, *Hitler: Speeches and Proclamations*, quoted in Bullock, *Hitler and Stalin*,
707.

4 Trevor-Roper, *Hitler's Table Talk*, 24.

5 Quoted in Shirer, *Berlin Diary*, xx.

6 Hitler to Mussolini, June 21, 1941, Nazi-Soviet Relations, from the files of the
German Foreign Office, 349–53. Quoted in Shirer, *Berlin Diary*, 830.

7 Diary of Franz Halder, quoted in Shirer, *Berlin Diary*, 797.

8 Quoted in Gilbert, *Churchill*, 701.

9 Roosevelt to William D. Leahy, June 26, 1941, Personal Secretary's File (Diplomatic). Roosevelt Library.

10 Bullock, *Hitler and Stalin*, 696.

11 Shirer, *Berlin Diary*, 812.

12 Full text available at: https://www.winstonchurchill.org/learn/speeches/speeches-of-winston-churchill/809-the-fourth-climacteric.

13 *New York Times,* June 24, 1941.

14 Lindbergh, *Wartime Journals,* 538.

15 Ibid., 501.

16 Ibid., 530.

17 Ibid., 536.

18 Ibid., 529.

19 Quoted in Berg, *Lindbergh,* 422.

20 Charles Phelps Taft II (September 20, 1897–June 24, 1983), son of William Howard Taft, Republican mayor of Cincinnati 1938–42, 1948–51, 1955–77.

21 Ickes, *The Lowering Clouds,* 581.

22 Quoted in Mosley, *Lindbergh,* 292.

23 Quoted in Berg, *Lindbergh,* 423.

24 Quoted in Mosley, *Lindbergh,* 295.

25 Ickes *The Lowering Clouds,* 581.

26 Quoted in Berg, *Lindbergh,* 424.

27 Full text available at: http://www.presidency.ucsb.edu/ws/?pid=16140.

28 Beard, *President Roosevelt,* 106, n. 27.

29 *New York Times,* July 30, 1941.

30 *Washington Post,* June 9, 1941.

31 *New York Times,* July 30, 1941.

32 77th Congress, 1st Session, *Congressional Record* 87, part 5, Senate (June 30, 1941): 5700.

33 Full text available at: http://www.presidency.ucsb.edu/ws/index.php?pid=16146.

34 William Averell Harriman (November 15, 1891–July 26, 1986), FDR's special envoy to Europe 1941–43, US ambassador to the Soviet Union 1943–46, ambassador to the United Kingdom 1946, Secretary of Commerce 1946–48, governor of New York 1955–58. Candidate for the Democratic presidential nomination 1952 and 1956.

35 Full text of Atlantic Charter available at: http://avalon.law.yale.edu/wwii/atlantic.asp.

36 Churchill, *The Grand Alliance,* 593.

37 *New York Times,* August 15, 1941.

38 *New York Times,* August 17, 1941.

39 Press conference, August 16, 1941. Full text available at: http://www.fdrlibrary.marist.edu/daybyday/event/august-1941-10/.

40 Black, *Franklin Delano Roosevelt,* 656.

41 Quoted in Gilbert, *Churchill,* 705.

42 Reynolds, *Munich to Pearl Harbor,* 146.

43 Full statement available at: http://hansard.millbanksystems.com/commons/1941/sep/09/war-situation.

44 Quoted in Gilbert, *Churchill,* 706.

45 Quoted ibid.

Chapter Twenty-Four: DAY OF INFAMY

1 Lindbergh, *Wartime Journals*, 524.

2 Carr, *Hollywood and Anti-Semitism*, 242.

3 Quoted in Rosenbaum, *Waking to Danger*, 169–70. They even booed Darryl F. Zanuck (September 5, 1902–December 22, 1979), a Protestant of Swiss descent from Wahoo, Nebraska.

4 Quoted in Hoopes, *When the Stars Went to War*, 69–70.

5 Carr, *Hollywood and Anti-Semitism*, 266.

6 Lowell Mellett (1886–1960), FDR's head of polling and information 1939-45. In 1942 he began producing films for Frank Capra (May 18, 1897–September 3, 1991), Italian-born director of films such as *Mr. Deeds Goes to Town* (1936), *Mr. Smith Goes to Washington* (1939) and *It's a Wonderful Life* (1946), in which humble people triumph against bureaucracy or big organizations, as well as the newsreel series *Why We Fight*.

7 Quoted in Woll, *The Hollywood Musical Goes to War*, 4.

8 http://www.digitalhistory.uh.edu/historyonline/senate_subcommittees.cfm.

9 Quoted in Carr, *Hollywood and Anti-Semitism*, 260.

10 http://www.digitalhistory.uh.edu/historyonline/senate_subcommittees.cfm.

11 Ibid.

12 Ibid.

13 Quoted in Woll, *The Hollywood Musical Goes to War*, 5.

14 Alexander Korda (September 16, 1893–January 23, 1956), Hungarian-born British film producer and director, founder of London Films and owner of British Lion Films.

15 Walter Reisch (May 23, 1903–March 28, 1983), Austrian-born director and screenwriter whose screenplays included *Ninotchka* (1939).

16 Quoted in Drazin, *Korda*, 239.

17 Quoted ibid., 240.

18 Hans Walter Conrad Veidt (January 22, 1893–April 3, 1943), a top-earning star at the German Ufa studio, he fled Germany with his Jewish wife in 1933.

19 Quoted in Woll, *The Hollywood Musical Goes to War*, 6.

20 Darryl Francis Zanuck (September 5, 1902–December 22, 1979), Hollywood screenwriter turned studio boss who headed production at Warner Brothers and Fox, which he combined with the company he founded, Twentieth Century, to form Twentieth Century–Fox.

21 Carr, *Hollywood and Anti-Semitism*, 263.

22 http://www.digitalhistory.uh.edu/historyonline/senate_subcommittees.cfm.

23 Koppes and Black, *Hollywood Goes to War*, 45.

24 Ibid., 43.

25 Carr, *Hollywood and Anti-Semitism*, 260.

26 Glancy, *When Hollywood Loved Britain*, 65.

27 Quoted in Rosenbaum, *Waking to Danger*, 170.

28 The committee did, however, prepare the ground for investigations into Communist infiltration of Hollywood led by Senator Joseph McCarthy's Senate Permanent Subcommittee on Investigations, 1953-57.

29 Full text available at: http://www.presidency.ucsb.edu/ws/index.php?pid=16012.

30 Full text available at: http://www.pbs.org/wgbh/amex/lindbergh/filmmore/reference/primary/desmoinesspeech.html.

31 Cole, *Charles A. Lindbergh*, 173.

32 Lindbergh, *Wartime Journals*, 539.

33 Cole, *Charles A. Lindbergh*, 173.

34 Quoted in Mosley, *Lindbergh*, 300.

35 Lindbergh, *War Within and Without*, 223.

36 Quoted in Berg, *Lindbergh*, 428.

37 Lindbergh, *Wartime Journals*, 541.

38 Ibid., 546.

39 Ibid., 540.

40 *New York Times*, October 4, 1941.

41 Quoted in Mosley, *Lindbergh*, 304–5.

42 *New York Times*, October 31, 1941.

43 Ibid.

44 Lindbergh, *Wartime Journals*, 557.

45 Halifax to Churchill, October 11, 1941, Doc. 4.11, Lord Halifax Papers, Churchill Archives Centre, Churchill College, Cambridge, UK.

46 Quoted in Gilbert, *Churchill*, 710.

47 Field Marshal Sir Claude John Eyre Auchinleck (June 21, 1884–March 23, 1981), Commander of British forces in the Middle East 1941–43 and India 1943–47.

48 Quoted in Gilbert, *Churchill*, 710.

49 John Gilbert Winant (February 23, 1889–November 3, 1947), three times Republican governor of New Hampshire, 1925–35, ambassador to the United Kingdom 1941–46.

50 Quoted in Gilbert, *Churchill*, 711.

51 Quoted in Jenkins, *Churchill*, 666.

52 Quoted in Gilbert, *Churchill*, 711.

Chapter Twenty-Five: ISOLATIONISM REDUX

1 Cole, *Roosevelt and the Isolationists*, 496.

2 Nye to Millard C. Dorntge, November 22, 1941, Nye Papers, Hoover Presidential Library, Palo Alto, CA.

3 Quoted in Cole, *Roosevelt and the Isolationists*, 503.

4 Vandenberg diary, December 8, 1941. Scrapbook #14, Vandenberg Papers, Bentley Historical Library, University of Michigan.

5 Capper to Roosevelt, December 9, 1941, President's Personal File 7332, FDR Papers.

6 Fish to Roosevelt, December 12, 1941, President's Personal File 4744, FDR Papers.

7 Full text available at: http://www.ibiblio.org/pha/77-1-148/77-1-148.html#joint-1.

8 Vandenberg diary, December 8, 1941, Scrapbook #14, Vandenberg Papers.

9 Paul Schmidt, notes of meeting between Hitler and the Foreign Minister of Japan, Yosuke Matsuoka, April 4, 1941. Quoted in Shirer, *Berlin Diary*, 875.

10 Full text available at: http://www.ihr.org/jhr/v08/v08p389_Hitler.html.

11 Quoted in Cole, *Roosevelt and the Isolationists*, 505.

12 Private memorandum to Marshall, December 7, 1942, H. H. Arnold Papers, Manuscript Division, Library of Congress.

13 Lindbergh, *Wartime Journals*, 561.

14 Ibid., 567.

15 Quoted in Cole, *Roosevelt and the Isolationists*, 510. Vidkun Abraham Lauritz Jonssøn Quisling (July 18, 1887–October 24, 1945) was a Norwegian Nazi who mounted a coup against the legitimate government of Norway after the German invasion of April 1940. His name immediately became a byword for a pro-Nazi traitor.

16 Ickes to Roosevelt, December 30, 1941, President's Secretary's File, Interior: Harold Ickes 1941 folder, FDR Papers.

17 Ibid.

18 Roosevelt to Stimson, January 12, 1942, President's Secretary's File, War Department: Henry L. Stimson folder, FDR Papers.

19 Lindbergh, *Wartime Journals*, 597.

20 Ibid., 608.

21 William A. Swanberg Papers, Special Collections, Columbia University.

22 Quoted in Nasaw, *The Chief*, 555.

23 Quoted ibid., 560.

24 Quoted ibid., 561.

25 Cooney, *The American Pope*, 119.

26 Quoted in Searls, *The Lost Prince*, 178.

27 Kennedy to Grace Tully, August 29, 1944, President's Personal File 207, FDR Library.

28 Edward T. Folliard, "Joe Kennedy: a tough Irishman with the Midas touch," *Washington Post*, November 19, 1969.

29 William John Robert "Billy" Cavendish, Marquess of Hartington (December 10, 1917–September 9, 1944), eldest son of the 10th Duke of Devonshire.

30 Cameron, *Rose*, 139.

31 *Boston Globe*, May 28, 1948, 3.

32 Joseph P. Kennedy to Beaverbrook, October 23, 1944. Beaverbrook Library, Houses of Parliament Library, London.

33 Quoted in Gilbert, *Churchill*, 713.

34 Churchill, too was absent as he was dismissed by the British voters at the general election of July 1945. At Potsdam, Stalin bartered over the fate of the world with Roosevelt's successor, Harry S. Truman, and the new British Labour prime minister Clement Attlee.

35 http://www.heritage.org/static/reportimages/E71571F1F72D8AA034BCF06A EE80D7A7.gif. Further details available at: http://www.heritage.org/research/ reports/2006/05/global-us-troop-deployment-1950-2005.

36 Ronald Ernest "Ron" Paul (born August 20, 1935), Republican representative

from Texas 1976–77, 1979–85, 1997–2013, Libertarian Party presidential candidate 1988, Republican presidential hopeful 2008 and 2012.

37 "I advocate the same foreign policy the Founding Fathers would." *New Hampshire Union Leader*, October 8, 2007.

38 Paul, *Freedom Under Siege*, 60.

39 http://www.people-press.org/2013/12/03/public-sees-u-s-power-declining-as-support-for-global-engagement-slips/.

40 http://www.people-press.org/2014/03/11/most-say-u-s-should-not-get-too-involved-in-ukraine-situation/.

41 Miller, *F.D.R.*, 173.

BIBLIOGRAPHY

Adler, Selig. *The Isolationist Impulse: Its Twentieth-Century Reaction.* London and New York: Abelard-Schuman, 1957.

——. *The Uncertain Giant: 1921–1941: American Foreign Policy Between the Wars.* New York: Macmillan, 1965.

Aero Digest. Chicago: Aeronautical Digest Publishing Corporation, 1936.

Alsop, Joseph. *I've Seen the Best of It.* New York: Norton, 1992.

——, and Turner Catledge. *The 168 Days.* New York: Doubleday, Doran, 1938.

——, and Robert Kintner. *American White Paper: The Story of American Diplomacy and the Second World War.* New York: Simon and Schuster, 1940.

Auchincloss, Louis. *Woodrow Wilson.* New York: Viking Penguin, 2000.

Bach, Steven. *Leni: The Life and Work of Leni Riefenstahl.* New York: Random House, 2007.

Bailey, Thomas A. *Woodrow Wilson and the Great Betrayal.* New York: Macmillan, 1945.

——. *Woodrow Wilson and the Lost Peace.* Chicago: Quadrangle, 1963.

Barnard, Ellsworth. *Wendell Willkie: Fighter for Freedom.* Amherst, MA: University of Massachusetts Press, 1966.

Barnes, Joseph. *Willkie: The Events He Was Part of, the Ideas He Fought For.* New York: Simon and Schuster, 1952.

Bartlett, Ruhl Jacob. *The League to Enforce Peace.* Chapel Hill, NC: University of North Carolina Press, 1944.

Baynes, Norman H., ed. *The Speeches of Adolf Hitler, 1922–39.* Vol. 2. Oxford: Oxford University Press, Oxford, 1942.

Beard, Charles A. *President Roosevelt and the Coming of the War, 1941: Appearances and Realities.* New Haven: Yale University Press, 1948.

Beauchamp, Cari. *Joseph P. Kennedy Presents: His Hollywood Years.* New York: Knopf, 2009.

Berg, A. Scott. *Lindbergh.* New York: G. P. Putnam's Sons, 1998.

Berle, Adolf A., Jr. *The Diary of Adolf A. Berle, 1937–1971.* Hyde Park, NY: Franklin D. Roosevelt National Archives and Records, 1978.

Bernstein, Arnie. *Swastika Nation: Fritz Kuhn and the Rise and Fall of the German-American Bund.* New York: Macmillan, 2013.

Beschloss, Michael R. *Kennedy and Roosevelt: The Uneasy Alliance.* New York: Norton, 1980.

Best, Gary Dean. *Harold Laski and American Liberalism*. Piscataway, NJ: Transaction, 2004.

———. *Herbert Hoover, 1933–1945*. Palo Alto, CA: Hoover Institution Press, 1983.

Birkenhead, Earl of. *Halifax: The Life of Lord Halifax*. Boston: Houghton Mifflin, 1966.

Black, Conrad. *Franklin Delano Roosevelt: Champion of Freedom*. New York: Public Affairs, 2003.

Blum, John Morton, ed. *From the Morgenthau Diaries*. Vol. 2, *Years of Urgency, 1938–1941*. Boston: Houghton Mifflin, 1959.

Bonnet, Georges. *Défense de la Paix de Washington au Quai D'Orsay*. Paris: Éditions du Cheval Ailé, 1946.

Bradford, Sarah. *George VI, the Reluctant King, 1895–1952*. New York: St Martin's Press, 1990.

Brands, H. W. *Woodrow Wilson*. New York: Henry Holt, 2003.

Breitman, Richard, and Allan J. Lichtman. *FDR and the Jews*. Cambridge, MA: Bellknap Press/ Harvard University Press, 2013.

Browder, Robert Paul, and Thomas Gary Smith. *Independent: A Biography of Lewis W. Douglas*. New York: Knopf, 1986.

Bullock, Alan. *Hitler: A Study in Tyranny*. Revised edition. New York: Smithmark, 1962.

———. *Hitler and Stalin: Parallel Lives*. New York: Knopf, 1992.

Calder, Robert L. *Beware the British Serpent: The Role of Writers in British Propaganda in the United States, 1939–1945*.Montreal & Kingston: McGill–Queens University Press, 2004.

Callaghan, Joseph Calvin. *The Lend-Lease Debate, December, 1940—March, 1941: The Role of Persuasion in a Momentous Public Discussion*. Vol. 1. Madison WI: University of Wisconsin—Madison, 1949.

Cameron, Gail. *Rose: A Biography of Rose Fitzgerald Kennedy*. London: Michael Joseph, 1972.

Cameron Watt, Donald. How War Came: The immediate origins of the Second World War 1938-1939. London: Heinemann, 1989.

Cantril, Albert Hadley, and Mildred Strunk, eds. *Public Opinion, 1935–1946*. Princeton: Princeton University Press, 1951.

Caro, Robert A. *Master of the Senate: The Years of Lyndon Johnson*. New York: Knopf, 2002.

Carr, Steven Alan. *Hollywood and Anti-Semitism: A Cultural History Up to World War II*. Cambridge, UK: Cambridge University Press, 2001.

Carroll, James Robert. *The Real Woodrow Wilson*. Bennington, VT: Images From the Past, 2000.

Casey, Steven. *Cautious Crusade: Franklin D. Roosevelt, American Public Opinion, and the War Against Nazi Germany*. Oxford: Oxford University Press, 2001.

Chadwin, Mark Lincoln. *The Hawks of World War II*. Chapel Hill, NC: University of North Carolina Press, 1968.

Chamberlain, Neville. *In Search of Peace: Speeches, 1937–1938*. Edited by Arthur Bryant. London: Hutchinson, 1939.

Churchill, Winston S. *The Churchill War Papers: At the Admiralty, September 1939–May 1940*. Edited by Martin Gilbert. London: Heinemann, 1993.

———. *The Churchill War Papers: The Ever-Widening War, 1941.* Edited by Martin Gilbert. New York: Norton, 2001.

———. *The Second World War: The Gathering Storm.* Boston: Houghton Mifflin, 1948.

———. *The Second World War: Their Finest Hour.* Boston: Houghton Mifflin, 1948.

———. *The Second World War: The Grand Alliance.* Boston: Houghton Mifflin, 1950.

Cockburn, Claud. *Crossing the Line.* New York: Monthly Review Press, 1960.

Cohen, Adam. *Nothing to Fear: FDR's Inner Circle and the Hundred Days That Created Modern America.* New York: Penguin, 2009.

Coit, Margaret L. *Mr. Baruch.* Cambridge, Mass.: The Riverside Press, 1957.

Cole, Wayne S. *Roosevelt and the Isolationists, 1932–45.* Lincoln, NE: University of Nebraska Press, 1983.

———. *Charles A. Lindbergh and the Battle Against American Intervention in World War II.* New York: Harcourt Brace Jovanovich, 1974

Collier, Peter, and David Horowitz. *The Kennedys: An American Drama.* Vol. 1. London: Secker and Warburg, 1984.

Colville, John. *The Fringes of Power: 10 Downing Street Diaries 1939–1955.* New York: Norton, 1985.

Cook, Blanche Wiesen. *Eleanor Roosevelt.* Vol. 2: *The Defining Years, 1933–1938.* New York: Penguin, 2000.

Cooney, John. *The American Pope: The Life And Times Of Francis Cardinal Spellman.* New York: Crown, 1984.

Craig, Gordon Alexander, and Felix Gilbert, eds. *The Diplomats: 1919–1939.* Vol. 2. Princeton: Princeton University Press, 1994.

Creel, George. *The War, the World and Wilson.* New York: Harper, 1920.

Cull, Nicholas John. *The British Propaganda Campaign Against American Neutrality in World War II.* Oxford: Oxford University Press, 1995.

Cutler, John Henry. *"Honey Fitz": Three Steps to the White House: The Life and Times of John F. (Honey Fitz) Fitzgerald.* Indianapolis: Bobbs-Merrill, 1962.

Dallek, Robert. *Franklin D. Roosevelt and American Foreign Policy, 1932–1945.* New York: Oxford University Press, 1979.

Daniels, Josephus. *The Life of Woodrow Wilson.* Illustrated. New York: Will H. Johnston, 1924.

Davies, Marion. *The Times We Had: Life with William Randolph Hearst.* Indianapolis: Bobbs-Merrill, 1975.

Davis, David Brion, ed. *The Fear of Conspiracy: Images of Un-American Subversion from the Revolution to the Present.* Ithaca, New York: Cornell University Press, 1971.

Davis, Kenneth. *FDR.* Vol. IV: *Into the Storm, 1937–1940.* New York: Random House, 1993.

———. *FDR.* Vol. V: *The War President, 1940–1943.* New York: Random House, 2000.

Dawes, Charles G. *Journal as Ambassador to Great Britain.* Whitefish, MT: Kessinger, 2006.

Day, Donald, ed. *Woodrow Wilson's Own Story.* Boston: Little, Brown, 1952.

De Kay, James Tertius. *Roosevelt's Navy: The Education of a Warrior President, 1882–1920.* New York: Open Road Media, 2012.

DeSilvio, David M. *The Influence of Domestic Politics on Foreign Policy in the Election of 1940.* Ann Arbor, MI: ProQuest, 2008.

Dewhirst, Robert E. *Encyclopedia of the United States Congress*. New York: Facts On File, 2007.

Dineen, Joseph F. *The Kennedy Family*. Boston: Little, Brown, 1959.

Documents on British Foreign Policy, 1919–1939. Vol. 2. London: Her Majesty's Stationery Office, 1946.

Documents on International Affairs, 1939–1946. Vol. 1: *March–September 1939*. London: Her Majesty's Stationery Office, 1951.

Doenecke, Justus D. *Storm on the Horizon: The Challenge to American Intervention, 1939–1941*. Lanham, MD: Rowman and Littlefield, 2000.

———. *In Danger Undaunted: The Anti-Interventionist Movement of 1940–1941 as Revealed in the Papers of the America First Committee*, Palo Alto: Hoover Institution Press, 1989.

Domarus, Max, ed. *Hitler: Speeches and Proclamations, 1932–1945*. Translated by Mary Fran Golbert. Würzburg: Richter, 1963.

Douglas, Melvyn, and Tom Arthur. *See You at the Movies: The Autobiography of Melvyn Douglas*. Lanham, MD: University Press of America, 1986.

Drazin, Charles. *Korda: Britain's Movie Mogul*. London: Sidgwick and Jackson, 2002.

Dunn, Susan. *1940: FDR, Willkie, Lindbergh, Hitler—The Election amid the Storm*. New Haven: Yale University Press, 2013.

Eisenhower, Dwight D. *Crusade in Europe*. London: Heinemann, 1948.

Farley, James A. *Jim Farley's Story: The Roosevelt Years*. New York: McGraw-Hill, 1948.

Faus, Albert Bernhardt. *The German Element in the United States with Special Reference to Its Political, Moral, Social, and Educational Influence*. Vol. 2. Boston: Houghton Mifflin, 1909.

Feiling, Keith. *The Life of Neville Chamberlain*. London: Archon, 1946.

Ferrell, Robert H. *American Diplomacy: A History*. New York: Norton, 1959.

Forrestal, James V. *The Forrestal Diaries*. New York: Viking, 1951.

Foulois, Benjamin D., and Carroll Vane Glines. *From the Wright Brothers to the Astronauts: Flight, Its First Seventy-Five Years*. New York: McGraw-Hill, 1968.

Franklin D. Roosevelt and Foreign Affairs. 1st series. Cambridge, MA: Belknap Press of Harvard University Press, 1979.

Freedman, Max, ed. *Roosevelt and Frankfurter: Their Correspondence 1928–1945*. Boston: Little, Brown, 1967.

Freud, Sigmund, and William C. Thomas Bullitt. *Woodrow Wilson: A Psychological Study*. Boston: Houghton Mifflin, 1967.

Gardell, Mattias. *Gods of the Blood: The Pagan Revival and White Separatism*. Durham, NC: Duke University Press, 2003.

George, Alexander L., and Juliette L. George. *Woodrow Wilson and Colonel House: A Personality Study*. New York: Dover, 1964.

Gilbert, Martin. *Churchill: A Life*. New York: Henry Holt, 1991.

———. *Churchill and America*. New York: Free Press, 2005.

———, and Richard Gott. *The Appeasers*. Boston: Houghton Mifflin, 1963.

Glancy, Mark. *When Hollywood Loved Britain: The Hollywood "British" Film 1939–1945*. Manchester: Manchester University Press, 1999.

Goodwin, Doris Kearns. *The Fitzgeralds and the Kennedys: An American Saga*. New York: Simon and Schuster, 1987.

———. *No Ordinary Time: Franklin and Eleanor Roosevelt: The Home Front in World War II.* New York: Simon & Schuster, 1994.

Graubard, Stephen Richards. *Command of Office: How War, Secrecy, and Deception Transformed the Presidency from Theodore Roosevelt to George W. Bush.* New York: Basic Books, 2004.

Grayson, Cary T. *Woodrow Wilson: An Intimate Memoir.* New York: Holt, Rinehart and Winston, 1960.

Gugin, Linda C., and James E. St. Clair, eds. *The Governors of Indiana.* Indianapolis: Indiana Historical Society Press, 2006.

Hagendorn, Ann. *Savage Peace: Hope and Fear in America, 1919.* New York: Simon and Schuster, 2007.

Hakim, Joy, ed. *Sourcebook and Index: Documents That Shaped the American Nation.* Vol. 11, revised third edition. Oxford: Oxford University Press, 2002.

Hamilton, Ian. *Writers in Hollywood 1915–1951.* London: Faber and Faber, 2011.

Hamilton, Nigel. *JFK: Life and Death of an American President.* Vol. 1: *Reckless Youth.* London: Century, 1992.

Harris, Robert. *Fatherland.* New York: Random House, 1992.

Hecht, Ben. *A Child of the Century.* New York: Simon and Schuster, 1954.

Henderson, Sir Nevile. *Failure of a Mission: Berlin, 1937–1939.* New York: Putnam, 1940.

Hendrick, Burton J. *The Life and Letters of Walter H. Page.* New York: Doubleday, Page, 1926.

Herzstein, Robert. *Roosevelt and Hitler: The Prelude to War.* New York: Paragon House, 1989.

Higham, Charles. *American Swastika.* New York: Doubleday, 1985.

Hitler, Adolf. *Mein Kampf.* Boston: Houghton Mifflin, 1943.

———. *The Speeches of Adolf Hitler, 1922–39.* Vol. 2. Edited by Norman H. Baynes. Oxford: Oxford University Press, 1942.

Hooker, Nancy Harvison, ed. *The Moffat Papers: Selections from the Diplomatic Journals of Jay Pierrepont Moffat, 1919–1943.* Cambridge, MA: Harvard University Press, 1956.

Hoopes, Roy. *When the Stars Went to War.* New York: Random House, 1994.

Hoover, Herbert. *The Ordeal of Woodrow Wilson.* New York: McGraw Hill, 1958.

Horne, Charles F., ed. *Source Records of the Great War: 1917.* San Diego: Stuart-Copley Press, 1923.

Horne, John. *A Companion to World War I.* London: John Wiley and Sons, 2012.

Hull, Cordell. *The Memoirs of Cordell Hull.* New York: Macmillan, 1948.

Ickes, Harold. *The Secret Diary of Harold L. Ickes: The First Thousand Days 1933–1936.* New York: Simon and Schuster, 1954.

———. *The Secret Diary of Harold L. Ickes: The Inside Struggle 1936–1939.* New York: Simon and Schuster, 1954.

———. *The Secret Diary of Harold L. Ickes: The Lowering Clouds 1939–1941.* New York: Simon and Schuster, 1954.

Ikle, Fred Charles. *Every War Must End.* New York: Columbia University Press, 2005.

Jackson, Henry Ezekiel, ed. The League of Nations: a document prepared to stimulate discussion and promote organized public opinion. New York: Prentice-Hall, 1919.

Jamieson, Kathleen Hall. *Eloquence in an Electronic Age: The Transformation of Political Speechmaking.* Oxford: Oxford University Press, 1988.

Jenkins, Roy. *Churchill.* London: Macmillan, 2001.

Johnson, Walter. *The Battle Against Isolation.* New York: Da Capo, 1973.

Josephson, Matthew. *The President Makers: The Culture of Politics and Leadership in an Age of Enlightenment 1896–1919.* New York: Harcourt, Brace, 1940.

Katznelson, Ira. *Fear Itself: The New Deal and the Origins of Our Time.* New York: Liveright, 2013.

Kennedy, Joseph P. *Hostage to Fortune: The Letters of Joseph P. Kennedy.* Edited by Amanda Smith. New York: Viking, 2001.

——. *I'm For Roosevelt.* New York: Reynal and Hitchcock, 1936.

Kennedy, Rose Fitzgerald. *Times to Remember.* New York: Doubleday, 1974.

Kerr, Philip, Lord Lothian. *The American Speeches of Lord Lothian: July 1939 to December 1940.* Oxford: Oxford University Press, 1941.

Kessler, Ronald. *The Sins of the Father: Joseph P. Kennedy and the Dynasty He Founded.* New York: Warner Books, 1996.

Ketchum, Richard M. *The Borrowed Years, 1938–41: America and the Way to War.* New York: Random House, 1989.

Keynes, John Maynard. *The Economic Consequences of the Peace.* New York: Harcourt, Brace and Howe, 1920.

Kissinger, Henry A. *Diplomacy.* New York: Simon and Schuster, 1994.

Koppes, Clayton R., and Gregory D. Black. *Hollywood Goes to War: Patriotism, Movies and the Second World War from Ninotchka to Mrs. Miniver.* New York: Tauris Parke, 1988.

Koskoff, David E. *Joseph P. Kennedy: A Life and Times.* New Jersey: Prentice Hall, 1974.

Krock, Arthur. "Reminiscences." Oral History Research Office, Columbia University, 1950.

Langer, William L., and Everett S. Gleason. *The Challenge to Isolation: The World Crisis of 1937–1940 and American Foreign Policy.* New York: Harper and Row, 1952.

——. *Undeclared War: 1939–1940.* New York: Harper and Row, 1952.

Lash, Joseph P. *Eleanor and Franklin.* New York: Norton, 1971.

——. *Eleanor Roosevelt: A Friend's Memoir.* New York: Doubleday, 1964.

Lawrence, William. *Henry Cabot Lodge: A Biographical Sketch.* Boston: Houghton Mifflin, 1925.

Leuchtenburg, William E. *Franklin D. Roosevelt and the New Deal, 1932–1940.* New York: Harper and Row, 1963.

Lewis, Terrance. *Prisms of British Appeasement: Revisionist Reputations of John Simon, Samuel Hoare, Anthony Eden, Lord Halifax, Alfred Duff Cooper.* Eastbourne: Sussex Academic Press, 2011.

Lindbergh, Anne Morrow. *War Within and Without: Diaries and Letters of Anne Morrow Lindbergh, 1939–1944.* New York: Harcourt Brace Jovanovich, 1980.

——. *The Wave of the Future: A Confession of Faith.* New York: Harcourt, Brace, 1940.

Lindbergh, Charles A., Jr. *Autobiography of Values.* Boston: Mariner Books, 1992.

——. *The Wartime Diaries of Charles A. Lindbergh.* New York: Harcourt Brace Jovanovich, 1970.

Lindbergh, Charles A., Sr. *Banking, Currency, and the Money Trust.* Washington DC: National Capital Press, 1913.

——. *Why Is Your Country at War and What Happens to You After the War, and Related Subjects?* Washington DC: National Capital Press, 1917.

Link, Arthur S. *Woodrow Wilson: A Profile.* New York: Hill and Wang, 1968.

Lodge, Henry Cabot. *The Senate and the League of Nations.* New York: Charles Scribner's Sons, 1925.

Loewenheim, Francis L., Harold D. Langley, and Manfred Jonas, eds. *Roosevelt and Churchill: Their Secret Wartime Correspondence.* New York: Saturday Review Press, 1975.

Long, Breckinridge. *The War Diary of Breckinridge Long: Selections from the Years 1939–1944.* Edited by Fred L. Israel. Lincoln, NE: University of Nebraska Press, 1966.

Loy, Myrna, and James Kotsilibas-Davis. *Myrna Loy: Being and Becoming.* New York: Knopf, 1987.

Lyttelton, Oliver. *Memoirs of Lord Chandos.* London: Bodley Head, 1962.

MacDonald, Iverach. *The History of the Times, Part II: Struggles in War and Peace, 1939–1966.* London: Times Books, 1966.

Macleod, Iain. *Neville Chamberlain.* London: F. Muller, 1961.

Madison, James H. *Wendell Willkie: Hoosier Internationalist* Bloomington, IN: Indiana University Press, 1992.

Maier, Thomas. *The Kennedys: America's Emerald Kings: A Five-Generation History of the Ultimate Irish-Catholic Family* New York: Basic Books, 2004.

Manners, William. *TR and Will: A Friendship that Split the Republican Party.* New York: Harcourt, Brace, 1969.

Marcus, Sheldon. *Father Coughlin: The Tumultuous Life of the Priest of the Little Flower.* New York: Little, Brown, 1973.

Matloff, Maurice, and Edwin M. Snell. *Strategic Planning for Coalition Warfare.* Washington DC: US Army Center of Military History, 1990.

Maynard, William Barksdale. *Woodrow Wilson: Princeton to the Presidency.* New Haven: Yale University Press, 2008.

McCarthy, Joe. *The Remarkable Kennedys.* New York: Dial Press, 1960.

McDonough, Frank. *Neville Chamberlain, Appeasement, and the British Road to War.* Manchester: Manchester University Press, 1998.

McKenna, Marion G. *Borah.* Ann Arbor, MI: Michigan University Press, 1961.

Miller, Nathan. *F.D.R.: An Intimate History.* New York: Doubleday, 1983.

Minney, R. J. *The Private Papers of Hore-Belisha.* New York: Doubleday, 1961.

Moley, Raymond. *After Seven Years.* New York: Harper and Brothers, 1939.

——. *The First New Deal.* New York: Harcourt, 1966.

Morgan, Ted. *FDR: A Biography.* New York: Simon and Schuster, 1985.

Moser, John E. *Twisting the Lion's Tail: American Anglophobia Between the World Wars.* New York: New York University Press, 1999.

Mosley, Leonard. *Lindbergh: A Biography.* New York: Doubleday, 1976.

Nasaw, David. *The Chief: The Life of William Randolph Hearst*. Boston: Houghton Mifflin, 2000.

Neal, Steven. *Happy Days Are Here Again: The 1932 Democratic Convention, the Emergence of FDR—and How America Was Changed Forever*. New York: Morrow, 2004.

Nicolson, Harold. *Diaries and Letters: 1930–1939*. Edited by Nigel Nicolson. London: Collins, 1968.

——. *The Harold Nicolson Diaries, 1907–1963*. Edited by Nigel Nicolson. London: Weidenfeld and Nicolson, 2004.

Olsen, Lynne. *Troublesome Young Men*. New York: Farrar, Straus and Giroux, 2007.

O'Toole, David. *Outing the Senator: Sex, Spies, and Videotape*. Worcester, MA: James Street, 2005.

Parmet, Herbert S., and Marie B. Hecht. *Never Again: A President Runs for a Third Term*. New York: Macmillan, 1968.

Parrish, Thomas. *To Keep the British Isles Afloat*. New York: HarperCollins, 2009.

Paul, Ron. *Freedom Under Siege*. Auburn, AL: Ludwig von Mises Institute, 2007.

Perkins, Frances. *The Roosevelt I Knew*. New York: Viking, 1946.

Perry, Barbara A. *Rose Kennedy: The Life and Times of a Political Matriarch*. New York: Norton, 2013.

Peters, Charles. *Five Days in Philadelphia: 1940, Wendell Wilkie, and the Political Convention That Freed FDR to Win World War II*. New York: Public Affairs, 2006.

Phillips, William. *Ventures in Diplomacy*. Boston: Beacon Press, 1952.

Procter, Ben. *William Randolph Hearst: The Later Years, 1911–1951*. New York: Oxford University Press, 2007.

Renehan, Edward J., Jr. *The Lion's Pride: Theodore Roosevelt and His Family in Peace and War*. New York: Oxford University Press, 1998.

Reynolds, David. *From Munich to Pearl Harbor: Roosevelt's America and the Origins of the Second World War*. Washington DC: Ivan R. Dee, 2001.

——. *Lord Lothian and Anglo-American Relations, 1939–1940. Transactions of the American Philosophical Society Held at Philadelphia for Promoting Useful Knowledge* 73, part 2. Philadelphia: American Philosophical Society, 1983.

Riefenstahl, Leni. *Leni Riefenstahl: Memoirs*. New York: St. Martin's Press, 1992.

Robb Ellis, Edward. *Echoes of Distant Thunder: Life in the United States, 1914–1918*. New York: Kodansha International, 1996.

Roberts, Andrew. *Hitler and Churchill: Secrets of Leadership*. London: Orion, 2003.

——. *The Holy Fox: The Life of Lord Halifax*. London: Weidenfeld and Nicolson, 1991.

——. *Masters and Commanders: How Four Titans Won the War in the West, 1941–1945*. New York: Harper, 2009.

——. *The Storm of War: A New History of the Second World War*. New York: Harper, 2011.

Rogers, Michael. *Political Quotes*. London: David and Charles, 1982.

Roll, David. *The Hopkins Touch: Harry Hopkins and the Forging of the Alliance to Defeat Hitler*. Oxford: Oxford University Press, 2013.

Roosevelt, Eleanor. *The Autobiography of Eleanor Roosevelt*. New York: Harper and Brothers, 1961.

Roosevelt, Franklin. *F.D.R.: His Personal Letters: 1905–1928*. Edited by Elliott Roosevelt. New York: Duell, Sloan and Pearce, 1948.

—— *F.D.R.: His Personal Letters: 1928–1945*. Edited by Elliott Roosevelt. Two volumes. New York: Duell, Sloan and Pearce, 1950.

——. *My Own Story: From Private and Public Papers*. Edited by Donald Day. New York: Little, Brown, 1951.

——. *Public Papers and Addresses of Franklin D. Roosevelt*. 1940 volume. New York: Macmillan, 1941.

Roosevelt Papers. Franklin D. Roosevelt Library, Hyde Park, New York.

Roosevelt, James. *My Parents: A Differing View*. Chicago: Playboy Press, 1976.

Rose, Norman. *The Cliveden Set: Portrait of an Exclusive Fraternity*. London: Pimlico, 2001.

Rosen, Robert N. *Saving the Jews: Franklin D. Roosevelt and the Holocaust*. New York: Basic Books, 2007.

Rosenbaum, Robert A. *Waking to Danger: Americans and Nazi Germany, 1933–1941*. Santa Barbara, CA: ABC–CLIO, 2010.

Rosenman, Samuel Irving. *Working With Roosevelt*. New York: Da Capo Press, 1972.

——, ed. *Public Papers and Addresses of Franklin D. Roosevelt*. 13 vols. New York: Harper and Brothers, 1938–50.

Ross, Ishbel. *Power with Grace: The Life of Mrs. Woodrow Wilson*. New York: Putnam, 1975.

Roth, Philip. *The Plot Against America*. Boston: Houghton Mifflin, 2004.

Russell, Thomas Herbert. *The Illustrious Life and Work of Warren G. Harding: Twenty-Ninth President of the United States: From Farm to White House*. Chicago: Thomas H. Russell, 1923.

Schlesinger, Arthur M. *The Age of Roosevelt*. Vol. 2: *The Coming of the New Deal, 1933–1935*. Boston: Houghton Mifflin, 1958.

Schmidt, Paul Otto. *Statist auf diplomatischer Bühne*. Bonn: Athenäum, 1949.

Searls, Hank. *The Lost Prince*. New York: New American Library, 1969.

Sherwood, Robert E. *Roosevelt and Hopkins: An Intimate History*. New York: Grosset and Dunlap, 1948.

Shirer, William L. *Berlin Diary: The Journal of a Foreign Correspondent, 1934–1941*. New York: Knopf, 1941.

——. *The Rise and Fall of the Third Reich*. New York: Simon and Schuster, 1960.

Shoor, Gene. *Young John Kennedy*. New York: Harcourt, Brace and World, 1963.

Sirevåg, Torbjörn. *The Eclipse of the New Deal and the Fall of Vice-President Wallace, 1944*. New York: Garland Publishing, 1986.

Skidelsky, Robert. *John Maynard Keynes*. Vol. 3: *Fighting for Freedom, 1937–1946*. New York: Viking, 2001.

Smith, Amanda, ed. *Hostage to Fortune: The Letters of Joseph P. Kennedy*. New York: Viking, 2001.

Smith, Gene. *When the Cheering Stopped*. New York: Bantam, 1965.

Smith, Truman. *Berlin Alert: The Memoirs and Reports of Truman Smith*. Stanford, CA: Hoover Institution Press, 1984.

Soames, Mary, ed. *Speaking for Themselves: The Personal Letters of Winston and Clementine Churchill*. London: Black Swan, 1999.

Sontag, Raymond James, and James Stuart Beddie. *Nazi–Soviet Relations 1939–1941: Documents from the Archives of the German Foreign Office*. Washington DC: US Department of State, 1948.

Speer, Albert. *Inside the Third Reich*. London: Macmillan, 1970.

Stimson, Henry L., and McGeorge Bundy. *On Active Service in Peace and War*. New York: Harper Brothers, 1948.

Swift, Will. *The Kennedys Amidst the Gathering Storm*. New York: HarperCollins, 2008.

Tansill, Charles Callan. *Back Door to War: Roosevelt Foreign Policy, 1933–1941*. Chicago: Regnery, 1952.

Tardieu, André. *The Truth about the Treaty*. Indianapolis: Bobbs-Merrill, 1921.

Taylor, A. J. P. *Origins of the Second World War*. New York: Simon and Schuster, 1961.

Taylor, Telford. *Munich: The Price of Peace*. New York: Doubleday, 1979.

Trevor-Roper, H. R., ed. *Hitler's Table Talk: His Private Conversations 1941–1944*. Translated by Norman Cameron and R. H. Stevens. New York: Enigma Books, 2000.

Tribble, Edwin. *A President in Love*. Boston: Houghton Mifflin, 1981.

Trimborn, Jürgen. *Leni Riefenstahl: A Life*. New York: Macmillan, 2008.

Tully, Grace. *F. D. R., My Boss*. New York: Charles Scribner's Sons, 1949.

Tumulty, Joseph P. *Woodrow Wilson as I Know Him*. New York: Doubleday, Page, 1921.

Underhill, Robert. *The Rise and Fall of Franklin Delano Roosevelt*. New York: Algora, 2012.

US Department of State. *Foreign Relations of the United States Diplomatic Papers*. Vol. 2: *1938*. Washington DC: US Government Printing Office, 1938.

Wallace, Max. *The American Axis: Henry Ford, Charles Lindbergh, and the Rise of the Third Reich*. New York: St. Martin's Press, 2003.

Wapshott, Nicholas. *Keynes Hayek: The Clash That Defined Modern Economics*. New York: Norton, 2011.

Warren, Donald. *Radio Priest: Charles Coughlin, the Father of Hate Radio*. New York: Free Press, 1996.

Welky, David. *The Moguls and the Dictators: Hollywood and the Coming of World War II*. Baltimore: Johns Hopkins University Press, 2008.

Whalen, Richard J. *The Founding Father: The Story of Joseph P. Kennedy*. New York: New American Library, 1964.

Wheeler-Bennett, John W. *King George VI: His Life and Reign*. London: St. Martin's Press, 1958.

Whiticker, Alan J. *Speeches that Shaped the Modern World*. London: New Holland Publishers, 2007.

Widenor, William C. *Henry Cabot Lodge and the Search for an American Foreign Policy*. Berkeley: University of California Press, 1980.

Wilbur, R. L., and A. M. Hyde. *The Hoover Policies*. New York: Scribner, 1937.

Wilson, Edith Bolling. *My Memoir*. New York: Bobbs-Merrill, 1939.

Wilson, Woodrow. *The Addresses of Woodrow Wilson*. Washington DC: US Government Printing Office, 1919.

———. *The Papers of Woodrow Wilson.* Edited by Arthur S. Link. Vols. 1-69. Princeton, NJ: Princeton University Press, 1989.

———. *President Wilson's State Papers and Addresses.* New York: George H. Doran, 1917.

Wiltz, John E. *From Isolation to War, 1931–1941.* New York: Thomas Y. Crowell, 1968.

Winkler, John Kennedy. *W. R. Hearst: An American Phenomenon.* New York: Simon and Schuster, 1928.

Wolff, Wendy, ed. *The Senate, 1789–1989.* Vol. 3: *Classic speeches, 1830–1993.* Washington DC: US Government Printing Office, 1994.

Woll, Allen L. *The Hollywood Musical Goes to War.* Chicago: Nelson-Hall, 1983.

Ziegler, Philip. *King Edward VIII: A Biography.* New York: Knopf, 1991.

INDEX

Page numbers beginning with 355 refer to notes.